OXFORD READINGS IN FEMINISM

FEMINISM AND HISTORY OF PHILOSOPHY

PUBLISHED IN THIS SERIES:

Feminism and Renaissance Studies
edited by Lorna Hutson

Feminism and Science
edited by Evelyn Fox Keller and Helen E. Longino

Feminism, the Public and the Private
edited by Joan B. Landes

Feminism and Politics
edited by Anne Phillips

Feminism and History
edited by Joan Wallach Scott

Feminism and Cultural Studies
edited by Morag Shiach

Feminism and Pornography
edited by Drucilla Cornell

Feminism and the Body
edited by Londa Schiebinger

OXFORD READINGS IN FEMINISM

Feminism and History of Philosophy

Edited by

Genevieve Lloyd

UNIVERSITY PRESS

OXFORD
UNIVERSITY PRESS

Great Clarendon Street, Oxford OX2 6DP

Oxford University Press is a department of the University of Oxford.
It furthers the University's objective of excellence in research, scholarship,
and education by publishing worldwide in

Oxford New York

Athens Auckland Bangkok Bogotá Buenos Aires Cape Town
Chennai Dar es Salaam Delhi Florence Hong Kong Istanbul Karachi
Kolkata Kuala Lumpur Madrid Melbourne Mexico City Mumbai Nairobi
Paris São Paulo Shanghai Singapore Taipei Tokyo Toronto Warsaw

with associated companies in Berlin Ibadan

Oxford is a registered trade mark of Oxford University Press
in the UK and in certain other countries

Published in the United States
by Oxford University Press Inc., New York

First published 2002

British Library Cataloguing in Publication Data
Data available

Library of Congress Cataloging in Publication Data
(Data applied for)

ISBN 0–19–924374–3

1 3 5 7 9 10 8 6 4 2

Typeset in Minion
by RefineCatch Limited, Bungay, Suffolk
Printed in Great Britain by
T. J. International Ltd., Padstow, Cornwall

Contents

Notes on Contributors

SYLVIANE AGACINSKI has taught at the École des Hautes Études en Science Sociale (EHESS), Paris. She is author of *Aparte: Conceptions and Deaths of Soren Kierkegaard* (trs. 1997), *Critique de l'égocentrisme* (1996), and *Politique des Sexes* (1998). She has also published on the philosophy of architecture.

ANNETTE BAIER is retired from teaching at the University of Pittsburgh. Her current writing is on trust and its relation to the traditional moral virtues. She is also at work on a biography of her husband Kurt Baier.

SEYLA BENHABIB holds the Eugene Meyer Chair in Political Science and Philosophy at Yale University, and has also been Professor of Government at Harvard University, Senior Research Fellow at the Center for European Studies, and Chair of the Committee on Degrees in Social Studies. Her books include *Critique, Norm and Utopia: A Study of the Foundations of Critical Theory* (1986); *Situating the Self: Gender, Community and Postmodernism in Contemporary Ethics* (1992); and *The Reluctant Modernism of Hannah Arendt* (1996). Her new book on multiculturalism, originally published in German, will appear with Princeton University Press as *Democratic Equality and Cultural Diversity. Political Membership in the Global Era* (2000).

SUSAN BORDO holds the Otis A. Singletary Chair in the Humanities at the University of Kentucky. She is the author of many books and articles, including *Unbearable Weight: Feminism, Western Culture and the Body* which was a *New York Times* 'Notable Book' and nominated for a Pulitzer Prize, and *The Male Body: A New Look at Men in Public and in Private.*

PENELOPE DEUTSCHER is currently Senior Lecturer in Philosophy at the Australian National University. She is the author of *Yielding Gender: Feminism, Deconstruction and the History of Philosophy* and co-edited with Kelly Oliver a collection of essays: *Enigmas: Essays on Sarah Kofman.* She recently guest edited the special issue of *Hypatia* (15/4): 'Contemporary French Women Philosophers'.

BARBARA HERMAN is Griffin Professor of Philosophy at the University of California, Los Angeles. Her publications include *The Practice of Moral Judgement* (1993) and *Morality as Rationality: A Study of Kant's Ethics* (1990).

MARCIA L. HOMIAK is Professor of Philosophy at Occidental College in Los Angeles, California. Her research interests are in classical ethics, the history of ethics, and moral psychology. A recent paper on feminist issues is 'On the Malleability of Character', in *On Feminist Ethics and Politics*, ed. Claudia Card.

LUCE IRIGARAY is Director of Research at the Centre National de la Recherche Scientifique in Paris, and has been influential within the feminist movement in France and Italy, and also in English-speaking countries, for several decades. She is author of many articles and books, including *The Speculum of the Other Woman* (trs. 1985), *This Sex which Is Not One* (trs. 1985), and *An Ethics of Sexual Difference* (trs. 1993).

SUSAN JAMES is Professor of Philosophy at Birkbeck College London. Her recent publications include *Visible Women*, edited with Stephanie Palmer, and an edition of the *Political Writings of Margaret Cavendish.*

SARAH KOFMAN was a philosopher of psychoanalysis and feminist theory and taught philosophy at the University of Paris. Her books on history of philosophy include *Nietzsche et la métaphore*, *Le Respect des femmes (Kant et Rousseau)*, and *Nietzsche et la scène philosophique*, as well as *Socrate(s)*. She died in 1994.

GENEVIEVE LLOYD is Emeritus Professor in Philosophy at the University of New South Wales in Sydney. She is the author of *The Man of Reason: 'Male' and 'Female' in Western Philosophy*; *Being in Time: Selves and Narrators in Philosophy and Literature*; *Part of Nature: Self-Knowledge in Spinoza's Ethics*; *Spinoza and the Ethics*; and *Collective Imaginings: Spinoza, Past and Present* (with Moira Gatens).

MARTHA NUSSBAUM is Ernst Freund Distinguished Service Professor at the University of Chicago, with appointments in philosophy, law, divinity, and gender studies. Her most recent books are *Sex and Social Justice* and *Women and Human Development: The Capabilities Approach.* A book on the emotions, *Upheavals of Thought: The Intelligence of Emotions*, is due out in 2001.

AMÉLIE OKSENBERG RORTY is Professor of the History of Ideas at Brandeis University. She has published numerous articles on the philosophy of mind and the history of conceptions of the emotions; she has also edited anthologies on self-deception, the philosophy of education, and, more recently, *The Many Faces of Evil.*

LISA SHAPIRO is Assistant Professor at Simon Fraser University. Her teaching and research focus is on early modern philosophy and feminism, with particular interests in early modern theories of the passions and seventeenth-century women philosophers. She is working on a book titled *Descartes through the 'Passions of the Soul'*.

Introduction

Genevieve Lloyd

PHILOSOPHY AND ITS PAST

Philosophy has an uneasy—and largely unexamined—relationship with its past, which often surfaces in uncertainties about the place of history of philosophy in the philosophy curriculum: is it to be construed in its own right as philosophical thinking, or as mere historical background to the real thing? Pedagogically, in English-speaking universities, the issue is often resolved by treating the history of philosophy as a repository of mistaken philosophical positions which can provide appropriate stimulation for the development of real philosophical skills—the techniques of analysis and argumentation developed in more central parts of the curriculum. There is, however, a growing interest in the historiography of philosophy, which has put more firmly on the philosophical agenda methodological issues posed by the reading of past philosophical texts.[1] Feminist philosophy has played an important part in this development.

Feminist history of philosophy has often been understood in terms of resistance to a denigration of women or of 'the feminine', grounded in the misogyny of past philosophers. Ironically, this stance in some ways mirrors the conception of history of philosophy as a repository of mistaken positions, unacceptable from the standpoint of a more enlightened present. The selection and arrangement of this volume aims to offer a different picture of feminist history of philosophy—as an emerging set of self-reflective reading strategies which are contributing to the transformation of history of philosophy as a scholarly activity.

The orientation of the volume towards methodological issues and strategies has inevitably meant that many important contributions to the development of feminist history of philosophy are not included here. Methodological reflection and the refining of reading strategies, not surprisingly, came later than the pioneering attempts to make visible the ways in which the history of philosophy neglected or disparaged female lives. Some of the earliest feminist critiques defended female capacities and intellectual character without seriously challenging the norms in relation to which women had been found wanting. Others attempted to extricate and affirm an excluded 'feminine'. Despite those contrasts, which often reflected debates within feminist theory about difference and sameness, there was a common orientation in early feminist history of philosophy. It presented the history of philosophy as a succession of male-centred ideals, towards which feminism took up a negative, defensive posture. In more recent history of philosophy inspired by feminism a different mood has emerged—a more positive, though still strongly critical engagement with texts of the past in ways that illuminate issues of the present.

What makes an approach to history of philosophy 'feminist'? Readers will notice some themes which recur throughout this collection: dissatisfaction with the 'maleness' of reason and the denigration of supposedly feminine non-rational traits; the negative effects of dichotomous oppositions—between minds and bodies, between reason and emotion; the revaluation of traditional philosophical emphases on the individual rather than the collective, on autonomy rather than collaboration, on 'justice' rather than 'care'. But the selection and arrangement of the volume aims to highlight, not any defining subject matter, but rather an overlapping array of techniques for bringing out often neglected aspects of philosophical texts. It is easy to recognize feminist philosophers' preoccupations with the relations between intellect, emotion, and imagination in the subject matter of feminist history of philosophy. It can be harder to see that much of their work involves also innovative attention to the interplay of intellect, emotion, and imagination in the philosophical texts themselves; and that feminist ideals of the unity of the mind are not merely talked about but enacted in new interpretative strategies.

Anomalies in the experience of reading past philosophical texts as contemporary women have motivated much of the methodological reflection included in this volume. Some of the essays are explicitly concerned with feminist issues; but even those which are most explicitly feminist in subject matter illustrate reading strategies which can be readily applied to other issues. Other essays are not explicitly 'feminist', although their authors may have published other works which can be so described. The contributions by Sarah Kofman, Martha Nussbaum, Amélie Rorty, and Sylviane Agacinski are not specifically concerned with feminist issues. But the volume as a whole shows a convergence on an ideal which Annette Baier has described as 'thinking with the whole mind'. The reading strategies illustrated here enact unities of intellect, imagination, and emotion even where the reclaiming of those unities from past philosophical dichotomies is not part of their subject matter.

The effort to better understand the processes through which the history of western philosophy has excluded or denigrated women has brought with it a wider rethinking of the practices of history of philosophy, which goes beyond any explicitly feminist agenda. But that fluidity in what is to count as 'feminist' philosophy can be seen as a strength of the approaches to history of philosophy illustrated here.[2] Reading strategies which may originally have been motivated by feminism are passing into broader attempts to treat the intelligent reading of history of philosophy as a conceptual resource for rethinking our present.

READING TEXTS: PHILOSOPHY AND LITERATURE

Many of the essays in this collection offer textual readings which address the literary and rhetorical dimensions of philosophical writing—the philosophical upshot of imagery and metaphor, the subtleties of the positioning of the speaker, the exploitation of narrative devices. Attention to the operations of imagination has proved an effective way of engaging with significant but frequently neglected aspects of the texts. Here the work of Michèle Le Dœuff has been particularly important.

In the preface to her book *The Philosophical Imaginary*, Le Dœuff describes her strategies for bringing out strands of 'the imaginary' operating in philosophical texts, where they are not supposed to belong. Although philosophical discourse has defined itself through a break with myth and fable, she says, the texts which are supposed to embody this freedom from the 'domain of the image' confront us with 'statues that breathe the scent of roses, comedies, tragedies, architects, foundations, dwellings, doors and windows, sand, navigators, various musical instruments, islands, clocks, horses, donkeys and even a lion, representatives of every craft and trade, scenes of sea and storm, forests and trees: in short a whole pictorial world sufficient to decorate even the driest "history of Philosophy" '.

Le Dœuff's work illustrates the conjunction of two concerns which have been central in feminist critique: the engagement with literary aspects of philosophical writing and the concern with points of tension within a text. The use a philosopher makes of imagery can open up connections with a text's surrounding cultural context. But it also operates, as she shows, as part of the philosophical enterprise itself. There is not just 'an *imaginary* in philosophy' but 'a properly philosophical imaginary', the exploration of which has the potential to transform the study of philosophical texts.

What does all this have to do with feminism? It is not coincidental that such reading strategies should be associated with reflection on the ambiguous presence of women in philosophy.[3] The role of imagery of the feminine in philosophical texts is not unrelated to the fact that the philosophical tradition was dominated by men. But to understand why the attention to imagery—even where it is not imagery particularly about women—has been so important in feminist history of philosophy, we need to see how the operations of imagination have interacted with the affective dimensions of philosophical writing. Le Dœuff's concern with imagery and metaphor goes beyond exposing the operations of male fantasy. Her work alerts us to a frequently unnoticed level of emotion which can be brought to the surface by careful attention to the affective resonances of imagery.

Sensitivity to the interplay between affect and imagination—in works which are nonetheless supposed to epitomize the exercise of pure intellect—has been central in feminist history of philosophy. It has often yielded challenges to the partiality of philosophical pretensions to universality. Here the concerns of feminists have converged with deconstructive reading strategies associated with the work of Jacques Derrida. Le Dœuff's attention to the operations of imagery and affect in philosophical writing challenges the ideal of philosophical thought as enacting a distinctive transparency of thought to itself—an idealized transparency which, ironically, brings its own masking illusions about the thought processes involved. Le Dœuff's strategies have attempted to demonstrate this presence of such an 'unthought element' in philosophy. But the upshot of such 'unmasking' strategies does not have to be negative. In a brief discussion of history of philosophy in her book *Hipparchia's Choice*—which I address in the essay 'Le Dœuff and History of Philosophy'—she reflects on the positive implications for philosophical writing of this concern with reconnecting philosophical texts with their 'outside'.[4]

The exercise of unmasking 'the unthought', Le Dœuff observes, confronts us with choices with regard to how we are to think of the relations between philosophy and history of philosophy. We can think of ourselves as better able to understand the text than its author, who cannot see his own mystification. Or we can think of the philosophical work as itself best placed for its own understanding, so that the aim of history of philosophy becomes the poignant odyssey of a return to the understanding which the author might have had of his own thought. Le Dœuff goes on to offer a third, preferred way of thinking of the activity of history of philosophy—an approach which is particularly relevant to appreciating some of the reading strategies illustrated in this volume. On this preferred approach the 'history' in history of philosophy becomes not so much a search for origins as a continued shared dynamic of work in which each element—the history and the philosophy—leads to and from the other. History of philosophy becomes an effort to 'shift thought from one state to another'. The borders between philosophy and history of philosophy thus shift, along with those between philosophy and what is not philosophy. Such a reorientation throws up rich possibilities for feminist approaches to history of philosophy and for understanding their unstable borders with other forms of intellectual enquiry. It becomes possible to do history of philosophy as a way of engaging with the present.

THE FIGURE OF THE PHILOSOPHER

Taking seriously the literary dimensions of philosophical writing can help us to recapture continuities between ancient and modern philosophy which have been largely left behind in the aspirations of contemporary philosophy. Here, as often in the history of philosophy, some of the most important insights of contemporary feminist philosophy may be better seen as not so much a break with the past as an enriched understanding of the full resources of that past. One of the most striking instances of the ways in which a clearer understanding of the relations between the philosophical and the literary can help us reclaim the past is in the development of feminist critique of prevailing ideas and ideals of reason.

The history of philosophy is not just a succession of positions and arguments. It is the history also of the idealized figure of the philosopher as the epitome of the supremacy of reason. Feminist critique of the 'maleness' of past philosophy has often been seen as a radical break with a misogynist past. It may be better seen as itself participating in an old history of the fashioning and refashioning of ideals of intellectual character. But to see this we must first make visible the operations of imagination and affect in philosophical writing which modern philosophy has often eradicated from its version of its past.

The figure of the philosopher is itself a construction of the imagination which goes back at least to Plato's dramatic realizations of the figure of Socrates. As the title of Sarah Kofman's book—*Socrates: Fictions of a Philosopher*—suggests, Plato in constructing the figure of Socrates was engaging in an exercise which was no less literary than philosophical. To read Plato adequately we must engage with both aspects of the texts, often in ways that resist any sharp separation between the two. Plato's Socrates is a fiction—not in the sense that he is an illusion but in that he is fashioned as a construction of the imagination. The 'real Socrates', as Kofman stresses, is inherently elusive; he is never there in person.

Kofman's discussion of Plato's Socrates, in the extract included here, focuses on *The Symposium*, Plato's dialogue on the nature of love. *The Symposium*, she suggests, is the text which, more than any other, reveals the way Plato 'fictionalizes' Socrates. Kofman presents its dramatic structure as enacting its content. The definitions of love are bound up with its unfolding dramatic presentation. Plato carefully constructs the figure of the philosopher as eliciting the emotion of love, with all its ironies and ambivalences. In the book from which this chapter is taken, Kofman goes on to consider a range of later refashionings of the figure of Plato's Socrates—by Hegel, by Nietzsche, by Kierkegaard. Her discussion highlights the subtle internal structure of nested narratives in which the figure of the philosopher emerges from the interplay of carefully constructed representations. The narrative structure in turn makes possible an emphasis on relationships: we are shown the interactions between Socrates and his listeners; the influence he exerts on them, and his responses to their presence; the fantasies his presence elicits in them, and his responses to those fantasies. We are thus brought to see not only the enunciation of a series of philosophical definitions but the interactions within which philosophical ideas are formed and communicated.

Not all philosophical texts are so strikingly illustrative of the play of 'fictions' in philosophical writing; but Kofman's reading of *The Symposium* is indicative of an approach to the activity of history of philosophy which we will see repeatedly enacted throughout this collection. Several authors confront us with the history of philosophy as a succession of makings and remakings of fictions in which intellect, imagination and emotion come together. The growing awareness of such interplays between different aspects of mind—all occurring in what has been traditionally supposed to be the supreme activity of pure reason—has been one of the central insights of feminist critiques of the history of philosophy. It is a striking instance of the convergence of methodology and subject matter. Readings which bring imagination, intellect and emotion together have uncovered hitherto unsuspected possibilities in the texts themselves.

Early feminist critiques of the western philosophical tradition attempted to articulate the unease women felt with the privileging of reason over supposedly inferior thought styles associated with imagination and emotion. Those early concerns have yielded increasingly self-reflective reading strategies in which intellect, imagination, and emotion come together to challenge the fiction of the philosopher as supremely rational man. In the process the successive figures of individual philosophers evoked by dissatisfied feminists have become less monochrome. The maturing of feminist history of philosophy has yielded less severe portraits of past philosophers, refreshingly different from their familiar personae—even, at times, allies in modern feminist causes. Indeed the true targets of feminist critics often emerge as the inadequate textual readings of blinkered contemporary male philosophers, rather than the past philosophers themselves.

MEN OF REASON

Feminists have often criticized male ideals of intellectual character embedded in the history of western philosophy.[5] Several of the essays included here illustrate the refining of the content of that alleged 'maleness'. Marcia Homiak, in 'Feminism and Aristotle's Rational Ideal', discusses Aristotle's notorious privileging of traits associated with reason and men over supposedly lesser traits associated with women and non-rational emotion. This essay also raises some important general issues about the position of feminists engaged in serious scholarly study of philosophers who have been regarded as sources of ideals antithetical to feminism. Values associated with the philosophical canon have, as a matter of historical fact, been used to denigrate women. But does it follow, Homiak asks, that those values are themselves suspect or that they cannot be now reclaimed to accommodate previously excluded groups? Aristotle's rational ideal can be appropriately criticized for its exclusion and downgrading of women. But the ideal, she argues, can be restated in ways that not only make it more acceptable than the original to a modern political consciousness but also strengthen the very ideals in the name of which the original has been rejected. Homiak offers a reading of Aristotle's ideal of reason which incorporates rather than repudiates the power and importance of non-rational emotion, and which lends new strength and resilience to the values of 'care and concern' which some feminists have opposed to it. Here feminist critique yields not a final rejection of the Aristotelian ideal but its reconstruction as an ideal worthy of emulation by both women and men.

It is important to see that more is going on here than a defence of the original ideal against feminist critics. The ideal itself undergoes transformation when it is rethought in a new context. The original ideal is coloured by Aristotle's notorious belief that women are incapable of realizing the full capacities of human nature. By thinking the original ideal through in a contemporary context, suffused with attitudes to women very different from Aristotle's own, Homiak has transformed the original while taking care nonetheless to ensure that it remains genuinely Aristotelian. The exercise is a delicate one which demands both detailed knowledge of the original texts and insight into the bases of contemporary feminist hostility to them. Homiak extends the resources of the texts, acknowledging their actual limitations but drawing on scholarly insight into their argumentative structure, in order to put them to work in ways that were not available to Aristotle.

On Homiak's analysis, the Aristotelian ideal of reason is guided and constrained by the non-rational side of the soul. She argues that, although Aristotle organizes his version of the best human life around the pleasures of rational activity, this does not commit him to a model in which emotion is suppressed or even subordinated. In the process of thus rehabilitating Aristotle, Homiak offers an enriched articulation of contemporary affirmations of the importance of the non-rational. Both the Aristotelian philosophy and contemporary feminist affirmations of 'care and concern' are deepened by being brought together. Homiak shows how contemporary 'feminine' ideals can be strengthened by being articulated through the intellectual resources of the philosophical tradition; and how, when thus formulated, they can be clearly seen to be inclusive ideals, important to both women and men. Rather than rejecting the Aristotelian ideal as irretrievably 'male', she develops it as a source of insight into the unhealthy kinds of dependence that can prevent contemporary women from fully realizing their rational abilities.

The 'maleness' of philosophy is multi-layered. Homiak's essay shows how, by separating the layers out and seeing how they affect one another, we can gain both fresh perspectives on past texts and a clearer conceptualization of contemporary feminist ideals. Her essay throws up also another interpretative issue, which we will see recurring throughout this collection: does the 'maleness' of reason reside in the texts themselves or in the limitations of later male commentators? Have later men of reason overlooked ways in which Aristotle's text itself recognizes the power of the non-rational? Homiak's challenge here is at least as much to the gender-blindness of modern commentary as it is to the limitations of the Aristotle text.

Aristotle's views on women have made him an obvious target for feminist critics. But it was the seventeenth-century philosopher René Descartes who became the epitome of the alleged maleness of philosophical ideals of reason. The case of Descartes is instructive in understanding the momentum of feminist dissatisfaction with the history of philosophy. For Descartes himself did not endorse the exclusion of women from the practice of his famous 'method' for obtaining certainty, or from his related programme for control of the passions through the training of the will. What made the Cartesian philosophy suspect for feminists was its association with the doctrine of dualism—the rigid separation of minds and bodies as utterly distinct kinds of being. The dichotomy came to be seen as reinforcing the denigration of women, in association with body, in opposition to an ideal of reason associated with 'male' transcendence.

This feminist version of Descartes was in some respects a partial representation, highlighting the dualism of the first two Meditations, rather than the contrasted emphasis on mind–body union in the Sixth Meditation and in *The Passions of the Soul.* The Descartes who became the target of feminist criticism was the notorious doubter of all things bodily—the Descartes for whom nothing is certain except his own existence as a thinking thing. This Descartes was also associated—rightly or wrongly—with the denigration of the passions, and with the affirmation of the dominance of intellect over imagination and the senses. There is a second 'Descartes' whose importance for feminism has taken rather longer to be recognized—the Descartes who returns, at the end of the Meditations, to a confident affirmation of his existence as an assured union of mind and body. For this Descartes the relation of mind and body is so close that he thinks of himself in the end not as two separate entities but as one 'intermingling': he is so closely bound up with body that he constitutes with it but one thing. The closeness of this union gives a different emphasis to the notorious Cartesian privileging of reason over passions and to the role of emotions in the good life, articulated especially in *The Passions of the Soul.*

It is not surprising that it should be the first 'Descartes' that initially dominated feminist discussion. Descartes's account of mind–body union lies beyond a chasm crossed in the text only with the assistance of an argument for the existence of a non-deceiving God whose validity is problematic for modern readers. But even his contemporaries had difficulty in reconciling his dualism with the union of mind and body. The power of the method of doubt enacted in the early parts of the Meditations is such that, once persuaded of the separability of mind and body, we then find it difficult to grasp them as unified. It was a dilemma pointed out by Descartes's friend and correspondent Princess Elisabeth of Bohemia, and restated, less politely, by Benedict de Spinoza:[6] if mind and body are indeed as radically distinct as Descartes claims, how can we put them together again into a plausible union, or even think of them as able to interact causally?

There was, however, also another reason for contemporary feminist preoccupation with the Descartes of mind–body dualism. It emerges in Susan Bordo's contribution, taken from her book *The Flight to Objectivity*. The dualist Descartes speaks to us in a voice we find familiar from our own cultural formation as rationally autonomous individual minds. The self of the first two Meditations is a dramatically exaggerated version of a familiar form of self-consciousness which causes disquiet to feminists: the contemporary ideal of a mind separated out from body, set over against Nature—autonomous rather than interconnected, intellectual rather than passionate. Take away the reassuring ultimate certainties which the role of God provided for seventeenth-century thinkers, and the Cartesian self speaks to us poignantly of our own cultural predicaments of isolation and fragmentation.

Lisa Shapiro's essay, in contrast, emphasizes the Descartes of mind–body union—the Descartes who takes passions seriously and is sceptical about the ideals associated with pure intellect. But there is, again, more at stake in this essay than the rehabilitation of a maligned man of reason. Shapiro comes to a more congenial version of Cartesian dualism by reading the texts in the light of insights offered by his correspondent Elisabeth. She draws on Elisabeth's adaptation of Descartes's views to offer a way of thinking of mind–body relations which opens up a middle space between materialism and dualism. Mind's dependence on body becomes more complex than is suggested in familiar readings of Cartesian mind–body interaction: the body makes a mind what it is, so that sexual difference becomes important to the understanding of differences between minds. Shapiro argues that Elisabeth's reflections on her bodily experience as a woman have prompted her to think through a more general philosophical position which tempers Cartesian dualism.

Rather than repudiating Descartes's philosophy as denigratory of the feminine, Shapiro extends it by approaching his view of the mind through bodily experience. Here again a rational ideal becomes more congenial to women by being thought through in the light of female experience. But Shapiro's transformation of Descartes has an interesting twist: the transformation of Cartesian dualism comes out of an attentive reading of the views of a seventeenth-century female thinker. I will comment in a later section on Shapiro's discussion of the connections between issues of philosophical genres and the ambiguous position of actual women in seventeenth-century philosophy.

The relations between reason and emotion have been important also in feminist critique of eighteenth-century philosophy. The figure of Descartes the dualist came to dominate feminist critique of seventeenth-century rationalism. It is the figure of Kant, the advocate of abstract, universal ethical principles, that has dominated feminist dissatisfaction with eighteenth-century versions of reason. But here again what begins as rejection develops into reconstruction and appropriation into contemporary debates. Feminist critique of Kant has converged with current discussions of the bearing of sexual difference on moral theory—with debate about the viability of a distinctive 'ethics of care' as opposed to an 'ethics of justice'. Much of the thinking in this area draws on the work of the psychologist Carol Gilligan on gender differences in moral reasoning, and especially on her resistance to Kantian assumptions embedded in Lawrence Kohlberg's theories of moral development.[7]

Just as recent feminist critiques of Descartes have offered more nuanced textual readings, reconstructing his philosophy in ways that make him more congenial to women, Kant too has been undergoing feminist rehabilitation. Barbara Herman's essay 'Agency, Attachment, and Difference' re-examines a cluster of Kantian themes associated with the ideal of impartiality. Feminist critics of Kantian moral theory have pointed to important issues which have been ignored by Kantian theorists. They have criticized Kantian theory for devaluing the affective life constituted by feeling, intimacy, connection. But Herman argues that, rather than justifying rejection of Kantian theory, these inadequacies can become the starting point for the development of resources internal to the texts. 'As we discover (or uncover) things a theory as formulated did not know about or attend to, we have occasion to further elaborate or develop the theory in the light of what we now know.' When we try to respond to feminist criticism from within the texts, the resources of Kantian ethics can be extended and developed. What then becomes important is not so much either to reject or defend a theory but to find out what happens when it is put under strain, seeing what it can and cannot absorb.

Feminist criticism here becomes a starting point for a deeper engagement with the text. The failure of a theory, Herman insists, can only instruct if we are scrupulous in finding the source of the fault. 'The fact that a theory, as traditionally understood, omits something should be the beginning, not the end of inquiry.' By working through in detail exactly where the theory comes under strain we become clearer not only about the internal workings of the texts but also about the nature of the alleged lack. Much of the supposed conflict between impartial ethics and the concerns of partiality, Herman argues, is caused by misunderstanding of the requirements of both.

As with Homiak's treatment of the Aristotelian rational ideal, what is at stake here is not just a desire to defend Kant against unfair criticism. What emerges from Herman's careful working through of the central maxims of Kantian ethics—from a perspective informed by the demands of 'the affective life'—is a very different way of thinking of the relations between reason and affect from that with which Kant has often been associated. But the exercise also clarifies and deepens contemporary understanding of affectivity. The core of Kantian moral theory comes to be seen as the concern with a 'deliberative field', which includes interests and attachments as well as grounds of obligation, principles of prudent rationality, and general conceptions of the Good. Becoming a mature moral agent involves the integration and transformation of ends in relation to one another and to the context of an individual's practical situation in the pursuit of a good life.

Rather than repudiating Kant in the name of a feminist ideal of the self as 'situated', Herman thus tries to construct a version of that ideal from within the Kantian theory itself. The dismissal of affect in favour of reason, and of fully embodied, socially connected persons in favour of pure reasoners, gives way to a reconstruction of situated agency which can accommodate the recognition of difference. The upshot is a version of rational detachment which is no longer at odds with the demands of attachment, but which remains nonetheless distinctively Kantian. The philosophy has been rethought in a new context—put under pressure by the demand for recognition of values which, as feminists have rightly complained, were not taken seriously by earlier Kantian theorists. In place of a choice between Kant and feminist ideals, we are offered a development of the resources of Kantian theory, inspired by feminism. Kantian ethics is then seen not as a static theory, rigidly fixed in a posture of rejection of affective attachment, but as a resource for conceptualizing how attachment and desire might be incorporated into the structure of moral development.

Herman has relocated Kant's philosophy into a new context. Feminist critique here draws on the energies of Kantian moral theory to think, in a challenging way, about the concerns of the present. With all such reconstructions of the history of philosophy there is, of course, room for robust disagreement about the limits of particular theories as resources for conceptualizing contemporary challenges. It is in this connection interesting to read the Herman essay in conjunction with Annette Baier's reconstruction of David Hume as a 'women's moral theorist'.

Like Herman, Baier takes up the challenge of reconsidering eighteenth-century moral theory from the standpoint of Carol Gilligan's resistance to Kohlberg's account of moral maturity. Kohlberg's version of moral development is conceptualized in terms of a Kantian capacity for operating with abstract, universal principles. Baier suggests that since the original Kantian moral theories were framed partly in response to Hume, it is natural, after Gilligan's work, to ask whether Hume might be more of a women's moral theorist than is Kant. She finds points of connection with Gilligan's version of women's conception of morality in Hume's emphasis on sympathy rather than law-discerning reason as the fundamental moral capacity; in his recognition of the variability of communities; in his playing up of the role of feeling in moral judgement; in his treatment of the fluidity of ego boundaries in interpersonal relations; in his stress on cooperation rather than autonomy. Hume, on her analysis, 'turns out to be uncannily womanly in his moral wisdom'. Like Gilligan's female subjects

Hume takes moral problems in concrete historical settings. In contrast to the Kohlbergian equation of moral maturity with the capacity to abstract from concrete detail and emotional complexity in order to focus on general principles, he 'endorses the emotional response to a fully realised situation as moral reflection at its best, not as one of its underdeveloped stages, and he mocks those rationalists who think that abstract universal rules will ever show why, say, killing a parent is wrong for human beings but not for oak trees'.

The points of connection are striking. But here again, the mapping of Hume's theories onto contemporary feminist moral theory is not just an exercise in defence of an allegedly misunderstood male philosopher. By imaginatively moving between Hume and contemporary feminist concerns, between past and present, we get an enriched conceptual frame for understanding what is at stake in contemporary debate. The rerouting of the Gilligan–Kohlberg controversy through the differences between Hume and Kant opens up space for the accommodation of human differences in reworked versions of old philosophies.

THE HISTORY OF EMOTION: CHANGING STRUCTURES OF LOVE AND DESIRE

Feminist attempts to break down oppositions between reason and emotion have been accompanied by interest in the philosophical understanding of emotion in its own right, and in better understanding the structure of specific emotions. Here once more the maturing of feminist approaches to history of philosophy has been characterized by an increasing trend towards positive reappropriation rather than repudiation of the past. The discussions of emotion included in this collection emphasize neglected aspects of the philosophical texts, attempting to reclaim strands in the history of philosophy which may have been downplayed by excessively rationalist tendencies in modern commentary. The introductory chapter of Susan James's book *Passion and Action: The Emotions in Seventeenth-century Philosophy* gives an illuminating overview of this shift in approach. The interest in emotion which has been prominent in contemporary feminist reactions against 'male' preoccupation with reason has in fact, James argues, been itself an important element in the history of western philosophy, though one that is neglected in the versions of that tradition presented by much contemporary history of philosophy. In focusing on the theory of emotion, she suggests, contemporary feminist philosophy can fruitfully be seen as rediscovering and reworking strands in the history of philosophy whose neglect perhaps reflects a male-centred agenda in contemporary philosophy, rather than a constant feature of the tradition itself.

James's book recasts the scholarly study of seventeenth-century philosophy, putting back into the picture the missing contours of the study of emotions which was so important to the philosophers themselves. Seventeenth-century treatments of the passions—often seen as a triumphalist affirmation of the superiority of reason—are in fact framed by an interest in the understanding of the emotions and their positive role in the good life. In this respect especially, seventeenth-century philosophy has important continuities with the Aristotelian tradition and with Hellenistic philosophy. James's study puts seventeenth-century treatments of emotion back into this history of cartographies of the passions—maps of affective possibilities which have often coloured in unsuspected ways our contemporary understanding and experience of emotion.

Seeing early modern philosophical treatments of emotion as in this way a bridge to a rich past, rather than as a radically new beginning, can act as a healthy corrective to feminist tendencies to think of seventeenth-century rationalist philosophies as primarily responsible for the notorious polarizations between reason and emotion which have operated to the disadvantage of women. In the chapter included here, James explicitly addresses issues of balance in feminist versions of Cartesian dualism. Past philosophers have often orchestrated, in her phrase, 'choruses of condemnation' through which they artfully construct supposedly radical breaks with earlier thinkers. Contemporary feminist choruses too can blind us to continuities which can be utilized in remedying inadequacies in our understanding of emotion. By rediscovering and reworking neglected continuities which bind early modern philosophy to its ancient sources, feminist philosophers can both enrich their understanding of contemporary dilemmas and regain practical orientations of philosophy which have disappeared in contemporary professional philosophy.

The 'therapeutic' understanding of emotion which was developed by Stoic and Epicurean philosophers out of Plato and Aristotle is a striking case of this convergence of contemporary feminism with some ancient philosophical concerns. Martha Nussbaum's fascinating discussion of Epicurean sources, in her essay 'Therapeutic Arguments and the Structures of Desire', centres on the distinctive features of the relations between belief and emotion in Hellenistic philosophy. Nussbaum's discussion starts from a startling passage in which Epicurus speaks of the enjoyment of 'boys and women and fish and the other things that a luxurious table presents'. The juxtapositions here—which are for us amusing in their strangeness—confront us with the ways in which our own experience of desire may be structured by unexamined and changeable assumptions and distinctions. Nussbaum draws on this striking example to illustrate how Hellenistic views of the relations between belief and desire can illuminate our own contemporary concern with the distinction between what is 'natural' and what is 'socially constructed'.

Hellenistic philosophers saw the critical scrutiny of philosophy as able to change not only beliefs about emotions but the very experience of them. In this essay, and elsewhere in her work on ancient philosophy, Nussbaum explores the ways in which that commitment to the ideal of philosophy as 'practical therapy' can be of continued relevance, teaching us to distance ourselves from the social constructions that shape our thinking. The 'therapeutic arguments' of the early philosophers can point us towards applications of the history of philosophy which can have transformative effects also on modern lives.

Several of the essays included in this collection reflect on the structure of one emotion in particular—love. We have seen how Kofman's reading of *The Symposium* highlights the ways in which the content of the dialogue—the definition of love—is enacted in its dramatic form. Luce Irigaray's reading of *The Symposium* explicitly addresses gendered aspects of Socrates' definitions. Here again the literary dimensions of the dialogue are presented as bearing on its philosophical content. What are we to make, for example, of the fact that Plato presents Socrates' own definition of love as mediated through the voice of his female mentor, Diotima? On Irigaray's reading the complexities of narrative structure bear in yet more complex ways on eclipsed issues of sexual difference. For Diotima's voice is itself mediated through Plato's narration of Socrates' narrative, leaving us room to question whether Plato's Socrates has indeed got Diotima's views right.

Irigaray draws us towards an alternative feminine articulation of the nature of love which Diotima might have made had she had the opportunity to speak in her own voice. The implicit dialogue between the Diotima speech narrated in the text and what might have been

Diotima's own version resonates, not surprisingly, with Irigaray's own philosophical reflections on love. Her reconstruction of Diotima's version of love evokes conceptual movement rather than fixity, emphasizing resistance to static dichotomies and the dynamic generation of meaning out of instability. But the Diotima of the Platonic dialogue, Irigaray complains, is unable to maintain this 'method' consistently. Diotima leads love into a 'schism between mortal and immortal'. Her dynamic metaphors of generation are undermined by her focus on the product of love—on the determinate offspring in which desire is realized, rather than on its ever unstable movement; on the resolution of opposites rather than on movement and becoming. The tension between mortality and immortality, which brings something of the divine into human desire, is undermined by a hierarchical privileging of spiritual over physical procreation. Socrates's Diotima falls away from her own dynamic method into the rigidity of Plato's, with its firm distinctions, its ascent from inferior to higher forms of love.

The reading strategies here are subtle and complex. Clearly Irigaray's reading of the Diotima speech is imbued with her own philosophical critique of Platonic method—an exercise in which she ironically enlists the figure of the real Diotima lurking behind the distorting misrepresentations of Plato's Socrates. Her reading constantly calls attention to layers of ingenious dramatic construction internal to the text—reading Plato against himself. True to the spirit of her insistence on instability, Irigaray leaves us with a twist at the end, speculating that there might be yet another reading which could present Diotima as having a better idea of what she was really about. We are left with an invitation to engage in our own rereadings of the text. Imagination is less restrained in this unconventional reading than in most of the essays. Irigaray's reading strategies are not uncontroversial. But their playfulness should not be mistaken for a lack of scholarly engagement. There are real insights here into tensions in Plato's text and more generally into the operations of common philosophical metaphors drawn from procreation.

Wise reflection on the dynamics and vicissitudes of love is not part of the common understanding of seventeenth-century rationalism; and Spinoza is commonly regarded as the supreme rationalist philosopher. But Amélie Rorty in 'Spinoza on the Pathos of Idolatrous Love and the Hilarity of True Love' presents him as a philosopher who 'wrote not only truthfully but wisely about love, about its travails and dangers, about its connections with knowledge and power, about individuality and the disappearance of particularity, rather than universality, and on interconnections between subjects rather than on self-contained individual subjects—on the breaking down of borders between selves'. Rorty's essay is not explicitly concerned with issues of feminism. But, as with Baier's reading of Hume, her Spinoza emerges as a philosopher much more congenial to women than we might have expected. Spinoza is commonly perceived as concerned with universals rather than particularity, with intellect rather than emotion, with abstract reasoning rather than the exercise of imagination. While paying due attention to parts of the *Ethics* where Spinoza does affirm the supremacy of reason, Rorty presents Spinoza as 'first and last, a particularist'.

One of the most interesting things to notice about the interpretative strategies in this rich essay is the convergence of the style of reading it enacts with the philosophical content it brings to the surface. Rorty insists that we must understand Spinoza's philosophy—as, indeed, for Spinoza we must understand all else—from the particularity of our own perspectives. So, to understand his treatment of love, she has us start with 'a particular story' of the development of a love relationship, of the processes through which it is hindered, its unfolding into ambivalence and frustration, its disintegration. The essay charts a Spinozist transformation of such a passive 'idolatrous' love into a healthier state of active affect.

This essay is also instructive in its careful positioning of interpretative comment in relation to textual exegesis. The voice of Spinoza is inserted directly into the unfolding story of love through a series of quotations in parenthesis. It is an effective way of dealing with one of the stylistic challenges in writing history of philosophy: how to provide the necessary quotations or paraphrases without interrupting the argumentative flow of the commentary—the problem of the orchestration of voices. Rorty introduces Spinoza's voice into her love story without a tedious succession of indirect quotation devices. This Spinoza does not 'say', 'observe', 'insist', or 'concede'; his direct voice is there in immediate contact with the unfolding story. He is there as a shrewd observer, as it were, on the unfolding narrative—a different but not competing or distracting voice from that of the narrator.

In reading this essay we are drawn into an exercise in precisely the kinds of engaged affect and reflective imagination which Spinoza's philosophy recommends. The narrative, interspersed with the voice of Spinoza, yields an imaginative realization of an ideal of intellectual character inspired by Spinoza's philosophy. We may have different stories to tell of love's unfolding; and we may wish to challenge either the interpretation of Spinoza or what emerges of Spinoza's own treatment of love . But to do so we need to insert ourselves into a comparable exercise involving intellect, imagination, and affect. We need, that is, to enact Rorty's version of the Spinozist ideal. Such self-reflection will inevitably lead us away from contemplation of the self as a supposedly self-contained intellectual substance to a world of interrelated systems of affect, constantly transformed through reflection—into the world of Rorty's Spinoza.

Rorty's essay invites us to imagine reflectively the emotion of love in the company of Spinoza. Imagination and emotion come together with intellect in following the intricacies of some of the most difficult and powerful sections of Spinoza's *Ethics*. In that way this essay can be seen as enacting an ideal of reading with the whole mind which is continuous with the readings of Hume's philosophy offered by Annette Baier. Sylviane Agacinski's 'We Are Not Sublime: Love and Sacrifice, Abraham and Ourselves' engages in a comparable exercise in bringing together the resources of story-telling and philosophically informed reflection. This essay explores the structure of religious love, its 'absolute risks', its conflicts with individual attachments, through a reading of Kierkegaard's retellings of the biblical story of Abraham and Isaac in *Fear and Trembling*. Here the conceptual resources of history of philosophy are brought to bear on the transformations of love in contemporary consciousness. The essay focuses on the tensions between the desire for religious transcendence and the demands of attachment, especially in parental love.

Here again it is instructive to attend to the methodological devices displayed in the essay. Kierkegaard's reflections on the biblical story are already mediated through a fictional narrator. Agacinski's reading exploits the literary resources of the text to insert her own critical voice into Kierkegaard's reflections on what is at stake in the absolute faith of Abraham. But the unobtrusive positioning of that voice allows her to range with ease over related themes which link Kierkegaard's text to others—to Kant's and Hegel's treatments of concepts of the sublime. Agacinski's commentary extends from the text under discussion to more general reflection on the affective resonances of philosophical ideas of the infinite, tracing the emotional links between Kant's internalization of moral laws and the sense of the sublime; and the Hegelian mutations between religious and aesthetic sublimity.

In this essay the nestings of critically reflective tellings and re-tellings of stories bring a concrete experiential dimension to philosophical formulations of the relations between finitude and infinitude.

Ideas about the relations between philosophy and religion, reason and faith, time and eternity come together with reflection on the lived experience of human love, its anticipatory griefs, its trust, and its risks. Once more it is striking that an essay which is not explicitly concerned with feminist issues nonetheless resonates strongly with themes that have been central in feminist theory. Agacinski's reading of Kierkegaard unfolds the lived oppositions between the drive to transcendence and the pull of particular attachments. Her account of the experience of 'unappeasable responsibility' at stake in 'the decision to exist as a singularity in time' also evokes feminist concerns with the opposition between universality and particularity.

Agacinski inserts her own voice boldly into Kierkegaard's narrative: 'I like to think that Abraham might not have gone through with the sacrifice anyway, but that he did not know it.' Such play with variations in the story may seem to introduce a distorting subjectivity, at odds with scholarly respect for the text. But it can also be seen as taking up an implicit invitation and challenge which the text itself issues—the challenge to do our own reflecting on what is at stake, for love, in Abraham's absolute faith. 'If there is such a thing as love, can it refuse to take this absolute risk? Could there be a love which is not sublime?' Under the pressure of reflection from the standpoint of the present, the ideal of absolute love reveals its own hazards and limitations. 'To say that Abraham is sublime is to say that he has become a stranger to us. We tremble before the man of faith just as he trembled before his God. Abraham encounters the mystery of God, but we only encounter the mystery of Abraham.'

The shifting references of 'we' are interesting to watch here, and more generally in reading history of philosophy. Agacinski uses them effectively to form and break alliances with her readers and with the philosophers she discusses. By engaging seriously with the internal literary resources of the text itself, reflectively retelling stories and drawing us into that exercise, she is able to deal creatively with the relations between exegesis and criticism, textual analysis and appropriation. Her essay has taken up Kierkegaard's implicit invitation to his readers to engage in collective story-telling; and we are drawn with her into the circle, shaping and refining in the process our own emotional experience.

WOMEN IN/AND PHILOSOPHY

A perceived absence or, at best, ambiguous presence of women in the practices of philosophy underlies in various ways the readings which contemporary female philosophers have offered of its history. How does the past absence of women bear on the 'maleness' of history of philosophy? The effort to make visible the excluded speaking position of the feminine has been central to the work of Luce Irigaray. But the issue also surfaces in discussions of the formation of the canon of philosophy, of the significance of sexual difference for genres of philosophical writing, and of the content of the feminine as metaphor or symbol.[8]

Lisa Shapiro's subtle treatment of the figure of Descartes that emerges from his correspondence with Elisabeth offers a fresh perspective on the bearing of sexual difference on philosophical genres as well as on the complex issues of the relative absence of women from the philosophical canon. Why is it that Elisabeth, despite the subtlety of her critique of Descartes, and the development of her own significantly different version of mind–body union, has not been treated as a philosopher in her own right? At a superficial level the answer may seem obvious: Elisabeth left no systematic presentation of her own views. But the correspondence, Shapiro argues, can be seen as a genuine philosophical practice—reflecting the personal context of a friendship—rather than as just a pedagogic exercise.

The continuities between early modern philosophy and the 'practical' concerns of ancient philosophy emerge more clearly in these letters than they do if we look only to Descartes's more systematic works. The point here is not to exalt Elisabeth to a position of equal stature. If we are to understand Elisabeth, Shapiro acknowledges, we must first understand Descartes. But by taking Elisabeth seriously as a philosopher in her own right we can gain insights into Descartes which we might miss if we think of her philosophical thoughts as mere footnotes to Descartes. By taking seriously the genre in which she writes we can see more clearly that she offers an incisive and rigorous questioning of a kind which transforms Descartes's position, rather than simply providing him with an opportunity to clarify it.

Shapiro addresses the ways in which issues of genre, considered in relation to the social position of the writer, can interact with philosophical content. Seyla Benhabib in her essay 'Hegel, Women and Irony' also addresses the interplay between textual analysis and the social history of female exclusion and emancipation. Benhabib's discussion focuses on sections of the Hegel texts which have been most offensive to feminists, showing how the internal limitations of the text with regard to issues of sexual difference can be better understood in relation to an understanding of actual historical options. The juxtaposition, she suggests, can yield an empowering 'doubled vision'. In the case of Hegel, it reveals the tensions between his rejection of political patriarchy and his antagonism towards early efforts towards female emancipation—an antagonism which is reinforced by the complex conceptual structures in which Hegel assigns male and female to different stages of the unfolding of Spirit. Benhabib's 'doubled vision' allows us to see not only tensions internal to the text but also tensions between the ideal articulated there and the history of women which, ironically, the Hegelian dialectic was supposed to leave behind.

The movement of concepts and of philosophical systems is a recurring preoccupation in these essays. Some highlight the points of transition between philosophies, and the possibilities of moving thought on into a new future, showing how the history of philosophy can be seen as a study and enactment of conceptual shifts and transformations, rather than as just a succession of positions and refutations. Here study of the symbolic content of 'woman' in philosophical texts has proved crucial. For it has not only brought history of philosophy to bear on the processes of contemporary reconceptualizing of ideas of sexual difference; it has also provided points of access to the understanding of changes in core philosophical concepts.

In her essay on Rousseau and Nietzsche, Penelope Deutscher shows how the continuities and the shifts in operations with 'woman' as symbol illuminate the changing concepts of truth and nature—how Nietzsche's interventions in Rousseau's symbolic structures move thought on, not only in relation to 'the truth of woman' but in relation to the concept of truth itself. The use of 'woman' as symbol connects the texts of different authors, as well as connecting the texts to their changing cultural contexts. Drawing on the work of Jacques Derrida and Sarah Kofman, Deutscher explores the 'joins' between the Rousseau and Nietzsche texts, showing how for Nietzsche the figure of 'Rousseau' also enters the play of symbols with regard to both sexual difference and truth. Nietzsche's denunciations of Rousseau and of feminism converge in his repudiation of reactivity, *ressentiment*, idealism, and egalitarianism.

Here again the study of the operations of woman as symbol in philosophy comes together with the study of the changing structures of emotion. Rousseau's 'respect' for woman emerges as a 'voluntary self-abasement, a stunting of forces, a desire for contented ignorance'. Not only the content of sexual difference but the dynamics of sexual antagonism changes. Two very different structures of affect emerge. In contrast to the Rousseauian fear of contamination, Nietzsche offers an ideal of woman as 'a dangerous opponent who resists rather than abets man's version of her, and must in fact do so if the kind of sexual antagonism which might sharpen the wits and forces of each is to be subsumed'. Nietzsche's often-derided misogyny emerges as a more subtle structure, more readily adapted to respect for difference than its Rousseauian counterpart.

Reading strategies overlap in many of the essays included in this volume; and the strengths and the limitations of the strategies are still unfolding. They do not represent competing methods so much as complementary approaches, which can yield different outcomes but are not necessarily in conflict. The organization of the volume is accordingly not thematic but, as far as possible, chronological, by the dates of the philosopher discussed.

Inevitably, the volume offers an incomplete coverage of the history of philosophy and of the rich variety of interpretative work that has been inspired by feminism. The further reading list at the end of the volume may point readers to some of the fine pieces that have not been included. My hope is that the selection will give readers an understanding of the rich resources which the history of philosophy offers for rethinking issues of contemporary importance, and encourage them to develop their own preferred strategies for reading philosophical texts with the 'wholeness of mind' of which both female and male readers have been for too long dispossessed.

Notes

1. For useful background reading on methodological issues arising from the practice of history of philosophy see Richard Rorty, J. B. Schneewind, and Quentin Skinner (eds.), *Philosophy in History* (Cambridge: Cambridge University Press, 1984), 49–76, and Peter H. Hare (ed.), *Doing Philosophy Historically* (Buffalo, NY: Prometheus, 1988).
2. For a fuller development of these remarks on the changing identity of 'feminist philosophy' see Genevieve Lloyd, 'Feminism in History of Philosophy', in Miranda Fricker and Jennifer Hornsby, (eds.), *The Cambridge Companion to Feminism in Philosophy* (Cambridge: Cambridge University Press, 2000), 245–63.

3. See Le Dœuff;'s essay 'Women and Philosophy', *Radical Philosophy*, 17 (1977), also published as the chapter 'Long Hair, Short Ideas' in her book *The Philosophical Imaginary*, trans. Colin Gordon (London: Athlone Press, 1989).
4. *Hipparchia's Choice: Concerning Women, Philosophy, etc.*, trans. Trista Selous (Oxford: Blackwell, 1991), 166–70.
5. For an early overview of the successive alignments between maleness and ideals of reason throughout the history of western philosophy, see Genevieve Lloyd, *The Man of Reason: 'Male' and 'Female' in Western Philosophy*, 2nd edn. (London: Routledge, 1993).
6. Spinoza ridicules Descartes's treatment of the relations between mind and body in the preface to part V of the *Ethics*.
7. See Carol Gilligan, *In a Different Voice* (Cambridge, Mass.: Harvard University Press, 1982).
8. In my essay, 'Maleness, Metaphor, and the "Crisis of Reason"', in Louise M. Anthony and Charlotte Witt (eds), *A Mind of One's Own: Feminist Essays on Reason and Objectivity* (Boulder: Westview Press, 1993), I offer an overview of ways of approaching the symbolic content of 'women' in philosophy. But there is much work yet to be done in articulating exactly how the symbolic exclusions of 'women' are related to the literal exclusions of women in the history of philosophy.

Part I. **Reading Texts**

Le Dœuff and History of Philosophy

Genevieve Lloyd *

In some brief sections in the 'Third Notebook' of *Hipparchia's Choice* Michèle Le Dœuff distinguishes three ways of thinking of the relations between philosophy and history of philosophy. We can, she says, think of the philosophers themselves as knowing absolutely what they are saying, as having an absolute transparency to themselves: There is no 'unthought' to be explored in elucidating what they have said. It is a way of thinking of philosophy, she continues, that belongs with the idea of philosophy as 'self- founding' and thus 'a founding discourse.' The aim of history of philosophy is then, say, 'to understand Plato's thought as well or almost as well as Plato did and, naturally, to explain it to the dear students who need a bit of a hand,' correcting along the way the errors of earlier interpreters or those the beginner cannot fail to make.[1] It is a familiar way of engaging in history of philosophy: The commentator positions herself at the speaking position of the author, stripping away the misinterpretations that have preceded her, to offer a clear articulation of what the author really said.

Le Dœuff identifies a second way of thinking of the relations of philosophy and history of philosophy. According to this, there is 'an immense unthought element' in philosophy. The task of 'history of philosophy' is then the discipline of 'reconnecting texts to the outside.' Implicit in this second approach is the idea that 'the exegete understands a work better than its author, since the former knows not only the work, but also its outside and what links it to its outside. This focus on the 'unthought' of philosophy evokes some of Derrida's writings—especially perhaps 'White Mythology.' And it also evokes some of Le Dœuff's own earlier work in *The Philosophical Imaginary.*

* Genevieve Lloyd, 'Le Dœuff and History of Philosophy', from Max Deutscher (ed.), *Michèle Le Dœuff: Operative Philosophy and Imaginary Practice* (New York: Humanity Books, 2000), 33–44.

Explaining her methodology in the preface, Le Dœuff refers to a guiding hypothesis which can be expressed in either a 'minimalist' or a 'maximilist' form. On the weaker version, the interpretation of imagery in philosophical texts goes together with a search for points of tension in a work: The imagery is seen as inseparable from the difficulties, the 'sensitive points' of an intellectual venture. On the stronger version, the interpretation of the philosopher's imagery involves a deeper tension—approaching a contradiction—in the workings of the text. One shows how the imagery works both for and against the system that deploys it, sustaining something the system needs but cannot justify—a meaning incompatible with the system's possibilities.

In *Hipparchia's Choice* Le Dœuff sketches an approach that lies beyond this uncovering of tensions. Her third and preferred option is to think of both philosophy and the history of philosophy as 'work' and thus as 'a dynamic, which can lead to and from each other.' Philosophy thus construed, she continues, is 'neither a monument nor an effect which is blind to its origins and thus in relation to itself, but an effort to shift thinking from one state to another.[2] Neither author nor reader is in a superior position here. There will be, as she puts it, 'something upstream' of a text, for 'thought began before any philosophy.' And there will also be something 'downstream, . . . [f]or its work can be continued.' The continuation, she concludes, may take the form of that discipline called 'history of philosophy.'

These brief remarks are suggestive but elusive. I think they are important—both for understanding Le Dœuff's work and for reflecting on the historiography of philosophy. Le Dœuff wants to stress that the history of philosophy should be thought of as itself a philosophical activity. The boundaries between philosophy and its history are consciously blurred here. Philosophy is then seen as having neither 'completion' nor 'begining'. It is understood rather as 'impulse' and movement'[3] Le Dœuff's second approach involved a shift of perspective from past to present; the commentator's critique exposes tensions, revealed through the operations of imagery, that lie beyond the author's own grasp. Or at any rate, the imagery is not central to the author's own conception of what is going on in the text. It is from the standpoint of the present that we see tensions that the author could not, between the explicit philosophical content and the imagery through which it is expressed—tensions which reveal the 'shameful face of philosophy.'

Le Dœuff's third option—history of philosophy as an active 'communication' of a philosopher's thought—involves a more radical shift to the present. We do not simply judge past meanings from a standpoint of perceptions available from the present; we appropriate insights drawn from the text to our own concerns. This approach is more novel and more controversial. What constraints are there—or ought there to be—on such creative exercises of imagination? Is it a legitimate way of doing history of philosophy? Should it be thought of as belonging to another genre? Le Dœuff has consciously blurred the boundaries between the activities involved in philosophy and in history of philosophy. But what justifies her describing this 'movement' of thought as history of philosophy?

There are some similarities between what Le Dœuff talks of as 'continuation' and the activity described in Deleuze and Guattari's account of concept creation in *What Is Philosophy?* Le Dœuff herself, in introducing her third option, talks of the interaction of philosophy and history of philosophy in Deleuze's work, attributing this to the resonance in his thought of the Bergsonian replacement of 'philosophy as monumental system' with philosophy as 'thinking-on-the-move:'[4] There is a striking comparison between these pages from *Hipparchia's Choice* and *What Is Philosophy?* Deleuze and Guattari say this about 'concepts' in relation to the history of philosophy:

> If one can still be a Platonist, Cartesian, or Kantian today, it is because one is justified in thinking that their concepts can be reactivated in our problems and inspire those concepts that need to be created. What is the best way to follow the great philosophers? Is it to repeat what they said or *to do what they did*, that is, create concepts for problems that necessarily change?[5]

Even when filled out with resonating quotes from *What is Philosophy?* Le Dœuff's observations on philosophy and history of philosophy are elusive. In the spirit of Le Dœuff's own preferred approach to interpretation and commentary, I am not going to treat her writing as if she had taken a 'firm stance as "textual father."'[6] Rather, I shall explore implications of this way of thinking about history of philosophy, and place it in a broader context of recent thought on the role of imagination in philosophy. But to grasp what is distinctive and important in Le Dœuff's third approach we need first to examine her discussion, in the preface to *The Philosophical Imaginary*, of the importance of imagery in philosophy.

In that earlier work Le Dœuff's concern is specifically with imagery in philosophical texts—'the strands of the imaginary operating in places where, in principle, they are supposed not to belong.' Philosophy is supposed to have defined itself through a break with 'myth, fable, the poetic, the domain of the image.' But what we find in actual texts is

> statues that breathe the scent of roses, comedies, tragedies, architects, foundations, dwellings, doors and windows, sand, navigators, various musical instruments, islands, clocks, horses, donkeys and even a lion, representatives of every craft and trade, scenes of sea and storm, forests and trees: in short, a whole pictorial world sufficient to decorate even the dryest 'History of Philosophy.'[7]

To take philosophical imagery seriously, she points out, is to open out philosophical texts to their cultural context in ways that are often dismissed as irrelevant to philosophical meaning; but this is not to set aside examination of the intellectual content of a work in favor of a sociological study of it. Philosophers' imagery expresses problems posed by the theoretical enterprise itself.

For Le Dœuff, attending to imagery can thus be a serious philosophical engagement with the history of philosophy. It is no less admissible into the historiography of philosophy than attention to the histories of philosophical concepts, procedures or systems. But the emphasis falls differently here from what we have seen in *Hipparchia's Choice.* The presence of imagery is an 'inner scandal', to which one strategic response is to project the 'shameful side' of philosophy on to an 'Other'[8]—an 'inner scandal.' To investigate imagery is to engage in an unmasking operation—the uncovering of a 'complex, negating relationship' between the writing subject and his text. It is to bring into the open something 'important and troubling which cannot be acknowledged, yet is keenly cherished.' 'As far as I am concerned' she says, 'taking an interest in images and enquiring into this sort of evasion are one and the same activity.'[9] We can elucidate Le Dœuff's talk of 'evasion' here by drawing on the treatment of metaphor in philosophical texts in Derrida's 'White Mythology.' What is 'shameful' is not the mere presence of imagery or metaphor but the fact that the philosopher is not always, as he thinks, in control of the metaphors he uses. The delusion to be exposed is not that philosophical writings are free of imagery or metaphor—a presence that must have been often obvious to the author. Rather, the delusion consists in thinking that the philosopher can use metaphor as a vehicle of communication while keeping philosophical thought free of its intrusion—that he can be, in Aristotle's famous phrase, a 'master of metaphor.' The 'shameful' side of philosophy is the presence of an imagery that escapes the 'mastery' of clear and distinct thought—imagery that binds the text to an 'outside' against which it had meant to define itself.

There are continuities between Le Dœuff's concern with philosophers' imagery in *The Philosophical Imaginary*, and what she says about history of philosophy, in *Hipparchia's Choice.* Despite the language of 'uncovering evasions,' the upshot of her descriptions of the operations of imagery was not always a negative judgement. To 'unmask' is not always to 'shame.' But in the later approach she sketches in *Hipparchia's Choice* there is a more collaborative positioning of the commentator in relation to the author. Certainly, like the earlier attention to imagery, the reading of history of philosophy envisaged in *Hipparchia's Choice* opens philosophy out to concerns not circumscribed by what authors think they are about. But the 'outside' of philosophy that intrudes on the text now goes beyond the author's cultural context—beyond the intrusive images at play in the text. The text is opened out not just to its own cultural context but to the independent concerns of the contemporary reader herself.

There is no real inconsistency here. The imagery in a text can still be seen as a point of access to those dimensions of the text that escape the author's attempt to set bounds to it. But the emphasis has shifted from the objective of 'unmasking.' The contemporary reader of philosophical texts becomes not the superior judge of the author's pretensions, but rather a constructive, though tough-minded, appropriator. The difference is one of tone and spirit. The task is collaborative rather than antagonistic: not so much to confront the author with what has been repressed or evaded, but rather to rethink in a new context what the author said. The change allows us to see Le Dœuff's work in the context of other recent developments that emphasize the creativity of the philosophical imagination.[10] History of philosophy as an activity now takes its place in the critique of what has come to be called 'social imaginaries.' The concern becomes not so much the unmasking of revealing images as the critique of the dominant organizing images—the guiding fictions—of a culture, as they are manifested in philosophical texts. This opens up the possibility of a genuinely philosophical involvement in social critique through a reflection on the products of collective social imagination. It is precisely the complicity between imagination and philosophy, which Le Dœuff had earlier presented as being 'shameful' to philosophy, that now allows us to articulate a genuinely philosophical role for it.

Le Dœuff's methodology of history of philosophy can be clarified by relating it to a distinction central to contemporary debate on 'social imaginaries': the distinction, emphasized by Paul Ricoeur, between the imagination as 'passive' and 'merely reproductive,' rather than 'active' and 'creative.'[11] In unmasking the 'shameful face' of philosophy Le Dœuff emphasized the passive, 'reproductive' imagination frowned upon in the Western philosophical tradition. Imagination is downgraded precisely because it is passive—the retaining of traces from sensory perception. The senses are judged inadequate as sources of knowledge. The imagination simply shares in this, and philosophy's aspirations to pure intellect demand that it transcend this 'shameful' reliance on imagery.

But this is not the only kind of imagination that operates in philosophy. Even those philosophers who have condemned the passivity of imagination have consciously used imagery and metaphors in the articulation of conceptual points. And they have consciously engaged in the creation of 'fictions' to make sense of the natural and the social world. In Jean-Jacques Rousseau's famous fiction of the 'state of nature' in the *Essay on the Origins of Inequality*, he says that to try to describe the 'natural' man in order to distinguish between what is original and what is artificial in human nature is 'to form a true idea of a state which no longer exists, perhaps never did exist, and probably never will exist, and of which it is, nevertheless, necessary to have true ideas in order to form a proper judgment of our present state.'[12] We must, in effect, construct a fiction in order to get at the truth.

In his earlier famous talk of origins, the *Essay on the Origins of Language*, Rousseau argues that access to truth comes out of metaphor, and only arises after it. The figurative precedes literal language. He acknowledges this as counterintuitive. How could an expression be figurative before it has a proper meaning, when the figural consists only in a transference of meaning? Rousseau replies with an example. On meeting other human beings a savage will initially be frightened. Because of his fear, he sees the others as bigger and stronger than himself. He calls them 'giants.' But gradually he comes to recognize that these so-called giants are neither bigger nor stronger than he. So he invents another name, common to them and him, such as 'man,' and leaves 'giant' to the fictitious object that impressed him during his illusion. So the figurative is born before the literal, when 'our gaze is held in passionate fascination.'[13]

The illusory image presented by the passions is the first to appear; it is only later that the language corresponding to it comes to be seen by the 'enlightened spirit' as metaphorical. So metaphor has primacy over literal language. Through fictions we move to truth, but the progression is of a different kind from that involved in 'the state of nature.' In the *Essay on the Origins of Language*, we arrive at truth by leaving fiction behind, by moving beyond the exercise of imagination to the rational grasp of truth. But in the later fiction of a 'state of nature,' fiction is seen not as something to be left behind, but as the only mode of access to truth in the present. And only fiction is adequate for acquiring and expressing those deep truths about human nature and what kinds of life are best which concern Rousseau in this work.

In 'The Rhetoric of Blindness,' Paul de Man offers a reading of Derrida's reading of these passages from Rousseau. De Man highlights how Rousseau destabilizes the distinction between the literal and the figurative, and the status of fiction in philosophical writing. The detail of these nested readings in which de Man turns back on Derrida his own reading of Rousseau need not concern us, but they emphasize something we have seen already in *Hipparchia's Choice:* the interweaving of text and reading and of both with cultural context. It is Derrida's attention to these interrelations that prompts de Man to present him as having raised the complexities of reading to 'the dignity of a philosophical question.'[14]

Derrida and de Man both emphasize in Rousseau's use of 'fictions' the tensions between competing 'stories' and the ultimate impossibility of disentangling the figural from the literal, the 'fictions' from the 'facts'. In the *Essay on the Origins of Language*,[15] the literal truth collapses back into the metaphorical from which it is supposed to have emerged. Although at one level Rousseau gives primacy to the figurative in the origins of language, at another level, the primacy belongs to the opposite side of the distinction. The figurative gives way to the superior force of the literal. Metaphor is left behind when the mind grasps truth. But its access to that truth is mediated through metaphor.

Rather than presenting a literal succession of past events, these texts tell stories of origins as a way of communicating truths about the present. They use narrative as a literary device for illuminating the real object of concern—the 'present.' On de Man's analysis, the texts themselves display a transposition from the literal to the figural levels of discourse. Chronology is the structural correlative of the necessarily figural nature of literary language. The chronological fiction that the 'first' language had to be poetic means that there can be no literary statements. So the 'discursive assertions' of the text account for their rhetorical mode. What is said about the nature of language makes it appropriate that the texts should be written in the form of a fictionally diachronic narrative or an allegory. The allegorical mode is grounded in the description of all language as figural and in the diachronic structure of the reflection that reveals this insight. In accordance with its own language, the text can only tell this story as a fiction, knowing full well that the fiction will be taken for fact and the fact for fiction—'. . . such is the necessarily ambivalent nature of literary language.'[16] The fictional mode mirrors the thesis of the work—the primacy of the figural over the literal—and itself in turn renders ambivalent the status of that thesis. The only literal statement that says what it means to say, de Man suggests, is the assertion that there can be no literal statement. But this literal statement destabilizes itself. The primacy of the figural undermines its own literal enunciation. Truth and fiction cross over. It is through fictions that we grasp the truth about language.

In some ways Rousseau's texts are a special case—hybrids, as de Man points out, in which philosophical content interacts with an overt resort to fiction. And it is no accident that Derridean deconstruction typically deals with texts that are part expository, part fiction—Plato's *Phaedrus* is another example.[17] But the consideration of Rousseau's hybrids raises broader questions about the status of fictions in other philosophical texts, including some whose authors were officially much more 'rationalist' in spirit than Rousseau. Despite the daunting geometrical form of Spinoza's *Ethics*, for example, it is a work rich in the exercise of imagination. For Spinoza the imagination can be a source of illusion, as when we mistake our imaginings for understanding. The 'multitude' thus mistake the power of God for a supposedly free divine will. But there are nonetheless conscious 'feignings' described in the *Ethics* which are clearly philosophical, although they fall short of the adequacy of ideas of reason. He tells us that it is a useful fiction to think of the mind's eternity as something it acquires. Yet, strictly, this cannot be so; the status of an eternal mode of thought cannot coherently be said to be acquired. We treat the mind as able to become eternal, 'as if it were now beginning to be, and were now beginning to understand things under a species of eternity.'[18] For Spinoza, God's intellectual joy is also a fiction. Strictly speaking, God is incapable of joy, since this involves a transition to a greater state of activity or perfection. Having no transitions to greater or lesser activity or perfection, God does not have emotions. He is not affected by joy any more than by sadness. It is as a fiction that we say that he loves himself with an infinite intellectual love.

Likewise our own intellectual love of God can be treated as joy, only through a kind of feigning. This feigning is equally harmless, provided we know what we are doing. The intellectual love of God is eternal—it is the relationship between God as substance and his modes, of which the human mind is one. What is fictional is the idea that this love is something that has come about in our own individual lives. The mind's intellectual love of God is the same as that by which he loves himself.[19] Or it would be if God were really, as we feign, capable of love. Insofar as God loves himself he loves us, and consequently God's love of us and the mind's intellectual love of God are one and the same. Our salvation consists in this 'constant and eternal love of God' or, it comes to the same thing, God's love of us. According to Spinoza, such fictions of the wise mind are different in character from the 'fictions of the multitude,' who imagine the mind's eternity to be merely a kind of continued existence after death. But both kinds of fiction spring from the operations of the imagination, and it is not clear that philosophical thought, here, can be extricated from the fictions through which it is articulated. So here, imagination allows us to glimpse truths of a kind that seem to elude reason operating alone.

It is this kind of relation between a philosopher's fictions and truth that fascinated Rousseau, and the questions are still with us: What goes on when philosophers construct fictions, tell stories, use metaphors or imagery? What is involved in telling competing stories or offering competing fictions? Is it possible to tell, once and for all, a true story? Does a story, once told, evoke the possibility of another that will cancel it out? Can we stop telling stories and describe how things are, or is access to truth, about the social world at least, gained through fictions that exist in an unstable relation to truth? Le Dœuff's work does not resolve all the questions, but it opens up, afresh, the issue of how philosophical content relates to literary aspects of philosophical writing. By thinking through the contrasts between 'passive' and 'active' imagination, we can fill out Le Dœuff's distinction between history of philosophy that would *unmask* the operations of imagery in texts and one that would *collaborate* with them in appropriating them to the concerns of the present. Le Dœuff's work can help explain the otherwise mystifying fact that highly sophisticated thinkers can both inveigh against the imagination and yet, in the very same texts, engage in complex exercises of imagination. Notoriously, Plato condemns the poets, yet relies on images and metaphors himself. In the *Meditations*, Descartes instructs his readers to spurn images in favor of the clear and distinct ideas of intellect. Yet the *Meditations* are themselves full of evocative, philosophically effective, and surely self-conscious metaphors and images: metaphors of motion that draw the reader into 'thinking-on-the-move' in the phrase Le Dœuff borrows from Deleuze's summing up of Bergson.[20]

The distinction between active and passive, productive and reproductive aspects of imagination helps clarify what is at stake in a critique of the philosophical imagination. Philosophers *have* passively, unconsciously, assimilated imagery from their surrounding culture. But often they have also engaged in astonishingly creative, conscious exercises of philosophical imagination. Thus, in watching the interaction between the conscious and the unconscious—between the active and the passive aspects of the philosophical imaginary—we can best rethink a philosopher's thought in a new setting. A great deal is carried by images from the 'outside,' even where they occur in the exercises of 'active' imagination. For example, past philosophers used the male–female distinction, consciously and creatively, to express ideals of reason. In consequence, features of the male–female distinction *as it operated in their cultural context* became part and parcel of understanding what it is to be rational. Those assumptions about relations between the sexes were thus an 'unthought' element in the philosophical imaginary that can now be unmasked. But such a critique need not leave us in a posture of negativity towards the philosophical tradition. The relations between passive and active, unconscious and highly reflective operations of imagination in a text can provide us with 'points of tension' that allow us to explore a positive 'continuation' of philosophy as the creation of concepts in response to a changing social world. Perhaps we can best 'continue' the creative tasks of philosophy not by transcending the philosophical imaginary and its fictions, but by a better insight into how they work and by learning to use them more effectively in the critique of culture. The resort to imagery, metaphor, and fictions—to the resources of intelligent imagination—may then be seen not as the 'shameful' face of philosophy, but as its very core.

Le Dœuff's work helps open up a space in which to articulate how as philosophers we can engage not with Spinoza's inferior 'multitude,' but with ourselves as participants in the contingent social practices and operations of symbols that make us what we are. We shall then not only unmask inadequate and misleading imagery, but also replace it with more constructive 'fictions' of active philosophical imagination.

We may lose our fear of the giants when we come to see them as human. But, with Rousseau, to see human beings truly we may need the fictions of the imagination no less than the critical power of reason.

Notes

1. Michèle Le Dœuff, *Hipparchia's Choice: An Essay Concerning Women, Philosophy, Etc.*, trans. T. Selous (Oxford: Blackwell, 1991), pp. 166–67.
2. Ibid., p. 168.
3. Ibid.
4. Ibid.
5. Gilles Deleuze and Felix Guattari, *What Is Philosophy?* trans. Hugh Tomlinson and Graham Burchell (New York: Columbia University Press, 1994).
6. Le Dœuff, *Hipparchia's Choice*, p. 166.
7. Michèle Le Dœuff, *The Philosophical Imaginary*, trans. Colin Gordon (London: Athlone Press, 1989), p. 1.
8. Ibid., p. 6.
9. Ibid., pp. 8–9.
10. I am here thinking especially of the work of Castoriades, Paul Ricoeur, and others in John Rundell and Gillian Robinson, eds., *Rethinking Imagination: Culture and Creativity* (London: Routledge, 1994).
11. See especially Paul Ricoeur's 'Imagination in Discourse and in Action,' in *Rethinking Imagination.*
12. Jean-Jacques Rousseau and Johann Gottfried Herder, *On the Origin of Language: Two Essays by Jean-Jacques Rousseau and Johann Gottfried Herder*, trans. John Moran and Alexander Gode (New York: Frederick Ungar, 1973), p. 39.
13. Jean-Jacques Rousseau, *The Social Contract and Discourses*, trans. G. D. H. Cole (London: Dent, 1966), p. 13.
14. Paul de Man, *Blindness and Insight: Essays in the Rhetoric of Contemporary Criticism* (New York: Oxford University Press, 1978), p. 110.
15. Rousseau and Herder, *On the Origin of Language.*
16. de Man, *Blindness and Insight*, p. 136.
17. Ibid., p. 111.
18. Baruch Du Spinoza, *The Collected Works of Spinoza*, ed. and trans. Edwin Curley (Princeton: Princeton University Press, 1985), part 5, prop. 31.
19. Ibid., prop. 36.
20. Le Dœuff, *Hipparchia's Choice*, p. 168.

Part II. Rereading Ancient Philosophers: Ideals of Reason

2 Socrates and his Twins (The Socrates[es] of Plato's *Symposium*)

Sarah Kofman*

1. 'BUT WHERE IS THE MAN?'[1]

Among all of Plato's Socratic dialogues, why should the *Symposium* warrant special attention? Is it because this dialogue may have handed down a more faithful portrait than any other? Might it be possible, in this dialogue in particular, to distinguish between the master's part and the disciple's? A whole tradition seems in fact to agree that this is the case. Alongside the *Phaedo* and the *Apology*, key dialogues for readers interested in the philosopher's final moments (we shall return to these in connection with Kierkegaard), this tradition views the *Symposium* as a crucial 'document' for anyone interested in Socrates' life. Alcibiades' portrait of him in particular—a portrait produced under the influence of alcohol—seems to have been taken at face value. Does not Alcibiades himself demand such a reading? *In vino veritas.*

The situation, however, is actually much more complicated than this. Countering the traditional view, I shall argue that Alcibiades' portrait is no more faithful than the usually neglected one offered by Aristodemus at the beginning of the dialogue. To take Alcibiades' portrait literally is to ignore the entire staging of the *Symposium*, to neglect Plato's own textual indications that the dialogue is more deeply rooted in fiction than in reality. Unlike practitioners of the traditional approach, I single out this text precisely because to me it seems to reveal, more than any other, the way Plato 'fictionalized' Socrates. Where Kierkegaard—who sees the *Symposium* as a product of dual

* Sarah Kofman, 'Socrates and his Twins (The Socrates(es) of Plato's *Symposium*)', from her *Socrates: Fictions of a Philosopher*, trans. Catherine Porter (London: Athlone Press, 1998; Ithaca, NY: Cornell University Press, 1998), 11–31; originally published in French as *Socrate(s)* (Paris: Galilée, 1989). Reprinted by permission of the publisher.

authorship—attempts to spot traces of what truly belongs to Socrates, I attempt instead to find traces showing the hand of Plato, the distinguished director and stage manager.

Let me begin with a Jewish-American joke as related by Freud: Two self-made men have had their portraits painted. Very proud of the likenesses, they put the paintings on display side by side, at an evening party, along with other marvels. Instead of admiring the portraits, however, one art critic exclaims: 'But where's the Saviour?'[2]

It may seem odd to begin with this story when we are dealing with tragedy. But Socrates cannot be confined to a single category. If he is a tragic hero, he is no less a comic figure, even for Hegel, who shows that the sublime and the grotesque are two sides of the same coin, and that the appearance of Aristophanes and his comedy in Athens was as necessary as the appearance of Socrates and his tragic destiny. Nietzsche begins by comparing Socrates to the venerable masters of Greek philosophy and ends up turning this figure—who never ceases to haunt and trouble him—into a veritable monster, a hybrid creature, more Jew than Greek, a caricature buffoon who looks more like a satyr than a figure of tragedy. In any event, Xenophon, whose Socrates is fond of laughter, dancing, and word-play, seems to assure us that the person who attended a performance of *The Clouds* so that the Athenian audience could judge for itself how well Aristophanes had captured his likeness would have savored Freud's anecdote, since by asking the disconcerting question 'Where's the Saviour?' the story brings to light the true nature of the two self-made men, a pair of scoundrels who can be likened to the thieves hung on either side of Christ.

For Socrates, whose name indicates his status as master-Saviour, could have identified with that other Saviour. Did he not save Alcibiades at the battle of Potidaea, and Xenophon, 'another of his favourites', during a different campaign?[3] The entire philosophical tradition (apart from Kierkegaard, although he too sees Socrates as a 'doctor', a necessary remedy against the Sophists) has set him up as a saviour figure. For Hegel, Socrates stands in opposition to his Athenian contemporaries: their minds, remaining in a state of internal division and conflict, continue to believe in the old gods and in external oracles, whereas Socrates appeals to the voice of his demon, to an inner oracle (for this he was justifiably sentenced to death), as the only source of value, virtue, and knowledge, the sole principle of healing and redemption.

For Nietzsche (the Nietzsche who wrote *The Twilight of the Idols*), the grotesque buffoon Socrates, despite his ugliness—which for a Greek was paradoxical—and his plebeian crudeness, managed to 'seduce' the most, well-bred Athenians because they saw him as a saviour, a healer: they found a necessary 'life raft' in the remedy he proposed for their unhealthy instincts (unhealthy in the sense that they developed anarchically, excessively and disproportionately, each one for itself in bulimic pursuit of its own goals, because they had become unable to subordinate themselves to a single point of view). Socrates fascinated them because he represented in his own person—as a figure whose frightful, monstrous ugliness symbolized the anarchic power of impulses—an antidote to the malady. Against the tyranny of competing instincts he offered a stronger counter-tyrant: reason in a hypertrophical form, reason carried to absurd extremes. And the Athenians had no choice; in their life-threatening distress, this was their last resort: 'One must . . . counter the dark appetites with a permanent daylight—the daylight of reason. One must be clever, clear, bright at any price; any concession to the instincts, to the unconscious, leads *downward*'.[4]

From this standpoint, Socrates holds the fascination of a Saviour, a Saviour from decadence, one who is himself decadent, unhealthy, and degenerate. The remedy he offers—rationality at all costs—is a symptom of decadence, worse than the sickness itself, 'by no means a return to "virtue", to "health", to "happiness".'[5] That is why the Athenians were right to condemn him. By agreeing to drink the hemlock, by willing his own death, Socrates acknowledged ironically that he was a charlatan, that death alone is a true healer: he himself had been only a patient whose duty it was, at the moment of death, to sacrifice a cock to Asclepius.

By bringing 'light' to the Athenians, did Socrates give them the gift of life, or death? Was he a good doctor or a bad one, in the end? The philosophical tradition has established him as a saviour figure, like a fetish to be simultaneously attacked—since it legitimizes his condemnation—and venerated—since the same tradition holds him to be 'divine'. This tradition seems to be both unable and unwilling to choose between the two approaches.

Can we hang the saviour figure, in its undecidability, like a third painting in the empty space between the two others painted respectively by Xenophon and Plato, the first overly realistic and the second overly idealistic? Can we see a third painting that would show up the other two as counterfeit and unmask their creators as scoundrels? Be this as it may, this third portrait, like the one in Freud's story, exists nowhere except in the minds of its inventors: Socrates-as-Saviour is yet another fiction. Just as the philosopher's soul flies about freely, leaving only his corpse behind in the city, according to the *Theaetetus*, so only simulacra of Socrates remain. He is never present in person: only the interest on the debt owed this founding saviour and 'father' has been paid. And to speak of him as 'father' is already to fall under the sway of the Platonic phantasmagoria.

2. GOOD AND BAD TWINS

Thus it would be naive to suppose that somewhere there is one 'authentic' portrait of Socrates that we can use as a yardstick for evaluating all others. Plato's *Symposium*, which seems to offer a faithful rendering of statements actually made by Socrates, may in fact be the most 'mimetic' of all the Platonic dialogues. Many passages in the text indicate that we are dealing with a fiction here, even if it is a fictionalized version of actual discourse.

Two portraits of Socrates frame the *Symposium*, one painted by Aristodemus, the good thief, the best of the *deme*, the other by Alcibiades, the bad thief. Between the two, the figure of Diotima-Socrates-Plato hangs a third mythical portrait, that of the demon Eros, son of Poverty (Penia) and Resource (Poros),[6] an atopic figure of the intermediary. This third portrait, even if it too is fictitious, uses the blank space left between the others to sketch in Socrates' erotic and demonic identity (Socrates resists both a logic of identity and a speculative logic); it discredits the other two portraits and discredits in advance all the readings offered by his philosophical posterity that seek to make sense of Socrates, that attempt to reconcile his paradoxical atopicity and his 'contradictions' in a dialectical synthesis.

The two 'thieves' who offer us portraits of Socrates in the *Symposium*, each in his own way, may be viewed on more than one account as Socrates' *doubles*, as his good and bad twins.

Each is *attached* to Socrates like a *shadow*, following him step by step. Their love remains attached to a single body, or at least to a single soul; they are unable to rise to the higher dialectical level of generalization, let alone to the level of exclusive love for the essence of the beautiful. They remain 'fixated' on Socrates. When Alcibiades tries to get away from him, he finds Socrates reappearing 'uncannily' at every turn. When Aristodemus arrives alone at Agathon's house, everyone is astonished to see him without Socrates: 'But how is it that you do not bring us Socrates? . . . Very good of you to come, . . . but where is the man?' (174e). Moreover, Aristodemus is as surprised as everyone else, since Socrates had been walking alongside him—the 'two go along together', he said—right before Socrates went off on his own, sending his shadow ahead as a forerunner to Agathon's house, a shadow as disconcerted and disquieted at having lost its sun as a German Romantic hero is distressed, conversely, to lose his shadow or reflection. However, Socrates for his part feels no distress, since detaching himself from shadows is what he is trying to do at that very moment in order to 'recollect' his soul, to remember it, whereas he runs the risk of forgetting it if he goes on to Agathon's banquet. When he detaches Aristodemus and sends him on ahead, the act symbolizes the spiritual detachment that Socrates is trying to achieve, the goal of which is to incite the twin to pull away, to cut the umbilical cord, for the greater good of both disciple and master. That same master, for fear of being imprisoned by his attachments, chooses to refuse the crown he had been offered for saving Alcibiades; no doubt he recalls the equivalence between crowns and bondage that Aeschylus had established in his *Prometheus.*[7] (And Alcibiades clearly has not forgotten the equivalence either: taking a braided wreath he had earlier offered Agathon, he places it on Socrates' 'magnificent head'.)

It is because they are indeed Socrates's doubles that Aristodemus and Alcibiades both show up at the banquet *uninvited.* In this they resemble Penia (Poverty), a double for the human soul who slips in like a phantom at the gods' banquet of nectar and ambrosia on Aphrodite's birthday: there, owing to her own cunning and Poros's (Resource's) drunkenness she gives birth to Eros (Love), who offers men a means (*mechane*) to acquire a substitute for immortality, since Zeus has definitively excluded them from the feasts of the gods.[8] In Greek, the word *skia,* meaning 'shadow', 'phantom', 'simulacrum', may also mean 'to come uninvited to a banquet'. It is always the most powerful individual who neglects or refuses to invite a weaker one; the latter then takes revenge by coming to haunt the feast like an evil twin. (In a different tradition, Dostoevski's *The Double* similarly links the problematics of doubles to the absence of an invitation to a feast. Golyadkin turns up as a 'double' for the first time when his benefactor, his substitute 'father', refuses him entry to his home on the occasion of a party.[9]) Aristodemus goes to Agathon's house at Socrates' invitation, backed by Socrates' ironic reference to a proverb according to which respectable people may turn up of their own accord at parties given by their own kind ('What if they go of their own accord,/The good men to our Goodman's board?' [174b]). This proverb is then immediately contradicted by a reference to Homer, who reports that Menelaus, a warrior lacking in courage, showed up uninvited at a meal given by Agamemnon. Aristodemus, nicknamed 'the little one', also gives the lie to the proverb, for he hastens to compare himself to Menelaus in all humility.

But when he sent his shadow on ahead, Socrates may have been thinking of yet another proverb: 'People often need someone smaller than themselves'. Philip the buffoon, the parasite who also attends the banquet uninvited (as we know from Xenophon), must have been acquainted with that saying; if he arrives 'prepared, in all varieties—to dine on some other person's [food]' (*Symposium*, I, II), and if he finds it more amusing to come without an invitation than with one, it is because this clownish parasite knows that he is more necessary to the people involved than is the feast itself, because he contributes laughter, a supplement that gives the feast its full flavor. Similarly, without the indigent Penia, Eros would never have been born: in her extreme aporia, Penia weaves the plot that gets her pregnant by Poros, that overflowing repository of resources ensnared in the bonds of sleep.[10] Without little Aristodemus, without Aristodemus as his shadow and 'good' twin, Socrates, the Socrates of the *Symposium*, the master and model whom Aristodemus follows step by step, would never have been born or immortalized. Everything begins and ends with a double. Aristodemus precedes Socrates to Agathon's feast and will follow him out 'in the usual manner' (223d). His presence and his absences, the fact that he falls asleep and the fact that he forgets things, account for the unique features of the banquet narrative, its tenor and its duration.

After Alcibiades' eulogy, the ongoing dialogue between Socrates, Agathon, and Aristophanes about the relation between comedy and tragedy cannot be reported, for Aristodemus has fallen asleep: in a contingent way, his sleeping signifies the end of the *Symposium*. Furthermore, because he is Socrates' shadow, he guarantees the accuracy of the narrative: a simple man, in love with Socrates, he *follows* Socrates everywhere, in all senses of the term. Aristodemus identifies with his model, imitates him in his dress, goes barefoot as Socrates does. His identification is presumed to lend the narrative as much authenticity as if it had been related by Socrates himself; moreover, according to Apollodorus, Socrates would have confirmed the validity of his double's testimony, for the double's version, presumed purely repetitive, is deemed preferable to that of Philip's son

Phoenix. As for Apollodorus, who transmits Aristodemus's narrative, his account purports to be above suspicion as well: he too is one of Socrates' admirers, a recent convert to Socratic philosophy. Head over heels in love, he *drinks in* the loved one's words: whether he has heard Socrates' discourse directly or *indirectly*, its effect on him, as on everyone else, is overwhelming. Alcibiades highlights the influence Socrates exercises from a distance; it makes him more powerfully seductive than Pericles, the greatest of the orators, or the best flute player, for Socratic discourse, even distanced from its source, like the most remote link in the magnetic chain of the *Ion*, loses none of its effectiveness or charm. Apollodorus, who like Aristodemus follows close upon Socrates' heels, can thus serve as a warning. Assiduous in keeping Socrates company, putting all the zeal of a new convert into learning what the master has said or done each day (172d), Apollodorus seems more capable than anyone else of reporting Aristodemus's narrative faithfully.

However, what qualifies Aristodemus and Apollodorus as faithful narrators disqualifies them as philosophers, for they are more in love with Socrates, whom they idolize, than they are with *Sophia*; their ability to remember outstrips their gift for recollection. Thinking they are imitating Socrates, each one goes too far. Aristodemus always shows up barefoot, whereas Socrates is willing to put on slippers for a banquet. Apollodorus's conversion, his 'reversal of values', is hardly 'philosophical': it consists in an exaggerated repudiation of everything he valued previously. He devalues without reservation everything that can be perceived by the senses; this is something Socrates does not do. Aristodemus scorns all men for their ignorance; he excepts only Socrates, whom he views as knowledgeable and happy. But Aristodemus has forgotten that Socrates scorns no one, that if he knows anything at all it is that he knows nothing; like the 'son' of Poros and Penia, Socrates rejects all simple oppositions and is no more ignorant than he is wise. Glaucon, chatting with Apollodorus, sees this plainly. He teases Apollodorus about his extravagant temperament, which verges on melancholy: by overestimating the object of his affections (of which he sees only the poretic aspect), by pouring out all his 'narcissistic libido' onto his idol, Apollodorus is actually merely indulging in self-deprecation, and making himself miserable. After 'shedding' his ego in favor of Socrates, after rejecting all his old friends, he is no more than a shadow of his old self, and of Socrates. He is fit only to play his assigned role, faithfully repeating the speech that Aristodemus had already recounted to Phoenix.

As a narrative of a narrative of a narrative, since Plato is after all the one who writes it down, the *Symposium* is a paragon of indirect discourse, a form that is thoroughly discredited in the *Republic* and that stands in stark contrast to Socrates' own pronouncements at the beginning of the *Symposium*. Socrates in effect condemns Agathon (and thus also Aristodemus and Apollodorus), for they imagine that to philosophize is to pour knowledge from a full vessel into an empty one by simple contact. This approach is an intoxicating one for the disciple, who is simply required to remember, to repeat with the greatest fidelity (which amounts to infidelity), the inebriating words of the master, instead of giving himself over to recollection or 'conning', to what Diotima calls a 'fresh' memory' (208a).

Does the disciples' fervor at least ensure that, in the mimetic genre of dialogue, untruthful par excellence, such a narrative is the least untruthful one possible? Plato, who would like to convince the reader that such is the case, nevertheless emphasizes that there is no identification without distancing, no repetition without difference, no memory without deformation, selection, and approximation: 'Now the entire speech in each case was beyond Aristodemus's recollection, and so too the whole of what he told me is beyond mine: but those parts which, on account also of the speakers, I deemed most memorable, I will tell you successively as they were delivered' (178a). Far from being an asset, the disciple's fervor may simply compound the inevitable deficiencies of memory with lapses caused by his fanaticism, which threatens to rob his narrative of its objectivity. Instead of sketching a faithful portrait of the master, the disciple merely elaborates an imagined figure of Socrates, a master figure presented as an exemplary model for all to follow; in the same way, according to the suggestion in the Phaedrus myth, every human soul must follow the chariot of the god with which it seeks to be identified.

The portrait of Socrates drawn by the good twin is thus as suspect as the portrait fantasized by the bad one. We have access to the latter, moreover, only through the narrative of good twins who report 'somewhat as follows' (173e), if we are to believe Plato himself. And it is ultimately Plato alone who creates, *poetically*, these two fictional portraits of Socrates—a fitting revenge against the master who had succeeded in 'corrupting' him, who had required him to burn his poems before he could become a disciple.

Might not the 'recollection' scene at the beginning of the *Symposium* be read, in this case, as a dismissive gesture in which Socrates not only attempts to exercise what is perceptible to the senses before going on to Agathon's banquet, but also, as if in anticipation, places the reader ironically on guard against all the simulacra of his person that will be forged, in the *Symposium*, by the stage manager, his 'best disciple', Plato?

3. ATOPIA

The foregoing is one possible reading of the celebrated Socratic 'immobility' that has perhaps elicited more astonishment than any of his other characteristics and has perhaps contributed the most to making Socrates a demoniacal figure even more than a demonic, atopic one. According to this view he is an odd, disconcerting creature who is never where he is believed to be; his behaviour is always unexpected; he occupies a position outside genres and categories; he is an eminently paradoxical, outsized, monstrous, excessive and exceptional figure who is therefore exempt from competition and rivalry. Socrates' unexpected and unusual choice of footwear for Agathon's party astonishes Aristodemus, who is used to seeing him barefoot (and who seems mistakenly to associate him here with Penia, or ascetics). The master's bizarre behaviour is disconcerting for his disciple, who seems unaware that Socrates is master of his own body as well as of opposing possibilities; he has not pledged himself either to sobriety or to self-mortification, and he is not committed to limiting his pleasures, for he has an astonishing capacity to retain his full strength, consciousness and lucidity in the midst of bodily excesses.[11] Alcibiades recalls his tolerance for wine, for example: Socrates is able to drink more than anyone else without getting drunk, for the balanced measure of goodness that governs his behaviour is not of the quantitative order. This exceptional mastery explains how he can walk barefoot on ice in winter and allow himself to wear sandals on occasion: while his object is not simply to obey conventions and customs (he does not hesitate to show up right in the middle of a meal), he does not set out to scandalize. His choice of dress is ironic: he takes pains with his appearance because he is going to a handsome young man's house, because as a true 'hunter of young men,' he makes a 'feminine'[12] effort to seduce his host, the better to attract his soul.

Dressing up also means putting on the other's costume, mimetically, in order to win him over more easily; and it is a way for Socrates to prepare to play the unaccustomed role he has been assigned, that of delivering a eulogy which, in keeping with the rhetorical genre, ought to be more concerned with beauty than with truth. Praise for Eros has been put on the agenda by Phaedrus, who initiates the contest; it has been prescribed by the prescription-man, the doctor Eryximachus, and placed under the auspices of the god Dionysus. Now because philosophy and its dialectical order have not been invited to the contest or to the banquet, Socrates is obliged to undergo a sort of ritual to exorcise 'bad influences' before he sets foot in Agathon's theater: he suddenly stops moving, stops noticing anything that is happening outside his own soul, as if he were succumbing to the violent effects of a sudden illness. Hegel, among others, introduces this analogy,[13] comparing Socrates' abrupt immobilization to a state of catalepsy, ecstasy, or even magnetic somnambulism (we shall return to this analogy, which is dependent on the overall Hegelian reading of Socrates that reinscribes him within speculative dialectics).

Alcibiades recalls that Socrates is never free from his chronic illness, not even in wartime; indeed, in wartime an even longer period of recollection is required. In one such instance Socrates remains motionless not just for a few hours, as he does in Agathon's vestibule, but all night long. He remains standing, erect, like a rigid phallus, offering himself up as a spectacle to the amazed and fascinated warriors who bring their mattresses and rugs outdoors the better to lie in wait, to look on surreptitiously (220c). Socrates himself hears nothing; he remains deaf to all harsh assaults on the senses, assaults emblematized by Agathon's violence, for Agathon will not hear of letting Socrates spend the night outdoors: he sends slaves for him, despite Aristodemus's warnings. Aristodemus advises Agathon to leave Socrates in peace, knowing full well that, whatever happens, he will not move for any reason, for his attention is fully engaged in strengthening his resistance to sense perceptions, in mesmerizing himself, in turning his body into a corpse so that his soul can free itself. Agathon's violence turns out to be as ineffectual as that of the Athenian state when it confines Socrates to prison: it does not keep him from thinking, does not prevent his soul from evading its bodily envelope. The only prison Socrates fears is pleasure, which binds the soul to the body and which alone can constitute an obstacle to recollection.[14] Socrates' instinctual forces must be monstrous, Nietzsche says,[15] for him to need such highly plastic exercises to be able to remember his own soul and to obey the Apollonian imperative, the essentially inhibitory voice of his demon! Stupefaction, cadaverization, petrification, paralysis, catalepsy, catatonia: these are all in effect analogies for describing the difficult immobilization brought about by the period of reflection during which the soul, ceasing to wander, dies to the body and its madness.

But, paradoxically, it is precisely when the soul is closest to itself that Socrates' behaviour is most astonishing, fascinating, and strangely disturbing. Like an uncanny double, he seems to appear and disappear at will, immobilizing himself, mesmerizing himself and others through some magic trick, like a sorcerer with more power to charm than the finest flute player or the most eloquent orator. He is more powerful than Gorgias and his rhetoric, more powerful than Agathon, who hurls his Gorgon-like speeches at his listeners to frighten them and to hide the vacuity of his own thought. Socrates' seductive sorcery, on the contrary, makes him appear to be immobilizing himself in order to seek some divine wonder within, as if he possessed some tremendous secret, some knowledge he would prefer to conceal from everyone: the presumed knowledge of a presumed master, which, despite Socrates' profession of ignorance, the others persist in attempting to extract from him through a variety of strategies. Agathon thinks he can incorporate the master's science magically, through mere contact and influence, as if all Socrates had to do were to sit down beside him and wait for knowledge to be poured into him, as if from a full cup into an empty one. But Socrates rejects that image, as in the *Meno* he rejects the image of the torpedo fish, He shows that contact with him does not convey learning: on the contrary, it strips the interlocutor of whatever learning he had thought he possessed up to that point.[16] Socrates cannot pour out anything at all, for, being a man, he is himself sterile; unlike the gods, who possess true knowledge, he possesses 'merely the knowledge of dreams,' a simulacrum of knowledge. His disciples' desire, which is oneiric in nature and inspired by Socrates' seductiveness (his only source of mastery) transforms that simulacrum of knowledge into divine knowledge, a hidden adornment or *agalma* that he might bequeath them through 'magnetic transfer'.

But Socrates contrasts the magical influence of poets capable of subjugating crowds—more than thirty thousand Greeks were subjugated by Agathon—with the clarity of the Good, the condition that makes knowledge as recollection possible. To the Sun-God, the only god, Socrates addresses his morning prayer after he has remained standing all night so as to recollect not some idea, like a dove—that is Alcibiades' version—but his soul's infinite power to think. At the risk of being taken for a madman, a magician, a master:

Immersed in some problem at dawn, he stood in the same spot considering (σκοπων) it; and when he found it a tough one, he would not give it up but stood there trying (Ζητων). The time drew on to midday, and the men began to notice him, and said to one another in wonder (θαυμάζοντες): 'Socrates has been standing there (ἐστήκει) in a study (φροντιζώντι) ever since dawn!' The end of it was that in the evening some of the Ionians after they had supped—this time it was summer—brought out their mattresses and rugs and took their sleep in the cool; thus they waited to see if he would go on standing all night too. He stood till dawn came and the sun rose; then walked away, after offering a prayer to the Sun. (*Symposium*, 220c–d).

Fascinated by the power that Socrates, like Eros, exercises over them (all the protagonists of the *Symposium* wonder more about the *power* of love and its effects than about its essence), the Greeks congeal the philosopher for all eternity as a shamanic figure,[17] the figure of a master *in spite of himself.* Interpreting his profession of ignorance as a pure pose, his disavowal of mastery as a strategy of mastery, they attempt to take possession of a phallus as fantasmatic as that of the woman (the mother) whose clothes, the best fetishes of all, create the impression that she conceals an enigma, a veiled secret. Socrates, who identifies with his mother Phaenarete, with the sterility of her midwife's role, is metamorphosed fetishistically not so much into a paternal figure as into an omnipotent phallic mother from whom no one can steal the phallus, and for good reason.

Alcibiades learns this lesson the hard way. Although he places Socrates above everyone else, Alcibiades in his presumptuousness wants to make an exchange *between equals*; he seeks to swap his own beauty for the other's knowledge. Socrates does not go along with this fool's bargain; for, even if he were to possess the coveted object of exchange (this is Alcibiades' first illusion, for Socrates, full of resources, like Eros, nevertheless never holds onto anything; he dwells no more in euporia than in aporia), there can be no equivalence, no common measure (here is Alcibiades' second illusion) between the two objects of exchange, any more than there can be equivalence between the idea and its simulacrum. From these attempts at seduction, Alcibiades gains only by learning (if we may translate Plato into Lacanian language) that the law of desire is castration.[18] The hunter gets caught in his own trap; when the seducer's efforts are frustrated, the one he desires as a lover becomes the eternal loved one, a plebeian in relation to whom he himself, a well-bred nobleman, suffers a humiliation not unlike that of being enslaved to a master.

This may account for the necessary ambivalence—to say the least—of Alcibiades' feelings as revealed in his portrait of Socrates.

4. ALCIBIADES' SATYRIC DRAMA

As in all stories about doubles, the evil twin Alcibiades (like the idea of the beautiful) makes a sudden (ἐξαιφνης) appearance, announced by a commotion outdoors that introduces static into the discussion; earlier, Aristophanes' hiccups had disrupted the orderly progression of eulogies in a similar way. With Alcibiades' unexpected entrance, the outside intrudes violently upon the inside, with a disproportionate intoxication of the senses, in the form of the returning flute players. These voices external to the logos had been dismissed at the start of the *Symposium* (although in various forms they had in fact already surreptitiously snuck back into all the eulogies except the one pronounced by Socrates). Alcibiades comes in propped up by the musicians: their support is comical but crucial to someone who lacks the assistance of the paternal *logos* that has been abandoned in favor of the Athenian *demos* and projected onto the outside in the form of a persecuting double from which he tries vainly to escape. Alcibiades is hunted down and trapped by this double, waylaid by him always precisely where he least expects it—for example, at Agathon's banquet, where he is lurking in the dark, near the man with whom Alcibiades himself is in love and upon whom he is about to confer a garland when he catches sight of Socrates. 'Save us, what a surprise! Socrates here! So it was to lie in wait for me again that you were sitting there—your old trick of turning up on a sudden where least I expected you!' (213b). Alcibiades is surprised, jealous of the double and rival who is seeking to take his place next to Agathon, attempting to separate him from Agathon along with all the other handsome youths Socrates would like to keep for himself—or so Alcibiades believes. For his part, Socrates interprets Alcibiades' 'eulogy' as an attempt to enlighten Agathon about the risks involved in becoming Socrates' lover, so Alcibiades can keep Agathon for himself as a friend and have Socrates as his own exclusive lover. Alcibiades suspects Socrates of the same maneuver: Socrates seems to be trying to make him jealous, pretending to forget him in favor of Agathon (he does the same thing elsewhere in favor of Protagoras[19]) in order to make Alcibiades his lover and slave, fraudulently and crudely compelling Alcibiades to love him instead of being loved by him. Socrates always pretends to play the role of lover in order to be the loved one and in order to subject the other to his own desire. For the Greeks, this is an intolerable situation (as the eulogies of Phaedrus and Pausanias also attest[20]); subjection to another's desire is the true aporetic trap, a dead end from which, after his failed attempt to seize the unseizable, Alcibiades cannot escape:

'In what I thought was my sole means of catching him he had eluded me. So I was at a loss (ἠπόρουν), and wandered about in the most abject thraldom to this man that ever was known' (219e).

The position of lover-in-subjection is intolerable, for it convinces the lover of his own inferiority and even of his infirmity; he dreads the ridicule, shame and dishonor this position confers. Just as the other guests at the banquet had produced 'beautiful and magnificent descriptions' of Love's qualities, Alcibiades puts Socrates' performances on display, performances that show him as an incomparable being, unrivaled, superior to everyone else in all respects. This is excessive praise, a counterpart to the excessiveness of Alcibiades' own desire, which identifies Socrates' virtue with the extraordinary power (he always succeeds in doing and in having others do things that no one else can accomplish) that humiliates them all (220c), and especially Alcibiades himself: '[Socrates] has set his heart on having the better of me in every way' (222e). His 'amorous' failure affects him because he runs the risk of damaging his glorious reputation as an invincible seducer and thus damaging the high opinion he has of himself (in this respect he is the opposite of Apollodorus), of his own good looks and his wealth, both spurned by Socrates: 'for I was enormously proud of my youthful charms' (217a). '[Socrates] despises [beauty] more than any of you can believe; nor does wealth attract him, nor any sort of honor that is the envied prize of the crowd. All of these possessions he counts as nothing worth' (216d). Alcibiades felt 'affronted' (219e). In seeking to seduce Socrates, Alcibiades is not betraying a desire to 'see' or to have his 'tail' but rather his phallus,[21] precisely the thing that confers on him all his power, his *Agalma*, the marvel that Socrates is thought—because he has disavowed it—to possess, his knowledge, which Alcibiades would like to incorporate as his own in order to reverse the situation of mastery. And to that end, Alcibiades is ready to strike any bargain; he is prepared to sell his own good looks—which he believes are invincible—to the devil.[22]

But what Alcibiades finds even less tolerable than the loss of his social *timè* (honor) is the permanent sense of shame aroused in him by Socrates and Socrates alone: 'And there is one experience I have in presence of this man alone, such as nobody would expect in me,—to be made to feel ashamed by anyone; he alone can make me feel it' (216b). 'I was ashamed' (217d). Alcibiades' sense of shame is intolerable to his fragile narcissism because it brings to light his divided inner state. If Alcibiades flees Socrates as vigorously as he desires him, if he stops up his ears as if he were trying to avoid the Sirens, it is because Socrates forces him to pay attention to himself[23] rather than to the affairs of Athens; it is because Socrates would like to 'reconcile' him with the part of himself projected onto the outside that continues to haunt him in the form of Socrates, like an invincible, omnipotent phantom. Socrates is a double who pursues Alcibiades because he is more tenacious, more in love with Alcibiades than Alcibiades is 'himself', and stronger than 'he': this is the secret of Socrates' invincible superiority. For it is impossible to detach yourself from someone who is permanently attached to your soul (unlike all those who, loving only your body, will abandon it as soon as the prime of life has passed).

So long as Alcibiades seeks to improve himself, he is sure to meet Socrates, and he is not fooled by his own threat to do away with Socrates: he knows perfectly well that in death Socrates would haunt him more than ever. He understands that, as in all twin stories, killing the double would be tantamount to pronouncing his own death sentence, would kill the best part of himself, the part that still resists the Athenian *demos.* With the death of Socrates, Alcibiades would lose the eye that can look into his own soul, the mirror that alone allows him to recognize his true kinship, the divinity of his soul:[24] in other words, he would lose the 'ideal self' with which Socrates seeks in vain to reconcile him. 'No reconcilement for you and me', says Alcibiades (213d); if he flees Socrates, it is because the latter unsettles his sense of identity, the narcissistic unity which he has sought to protect by projecting outside of himself the part of himself that separates him from himself. Even though he cannot get along without the ideal other who defends him against annihilation, he cannot help feeling overcome, ridiculed, betrayed by the one whom he does not succeed either in seducing or abandoning.

Of Socrates, the divine part of his own soul who is the only invited guest at the banquet of immortality as he is at Agathon's feast, Alcibiades can thus only sketch in an ambivalent portrait, one whose ambivalence is betrayed by a cleavage into a series of opposing terms (inside and outside, appearance and reality, knowledge and ignorance, and so on) that bear negative or positive connotations as the case may be. Despite these reversing images, Alcibiades' portrait of Socrates still depends upon a logic of identity, and thus it differs from the portrait of Eros, which eludes such logic. And yet the philosophic tradition, seduced by Alcibiades' eulogy, seems to have taken his affirmations at face value and to have credited his portrait as accurate—probably because it corresponds, at best, to a tenacious, hysterical fantasy that holds Socrates to be a master seducer.

Alcibiades claims to be praising Socrates truthfully, even though a eulogy by definition focuses on beauty rather than truth. Like Socrates, whom he parodies, and unlike the other guests, Alcibiades thus offers a derisive echo of his double's words. But how could a eulogy, especially one delivered in a state of drunkenness, be truthful? To be sure, for Plato, wine is not a bad thing in itself, since it has the nature—and the ambiguity—of a *pharmakon*; consumed in moderation, it is capable of softening souls and making them susceptible, as children are, to the truths embedded in fables.[25] However, Alcibiades seems to have gone beyond the bounds of temperance, since he is drunk, and sufficiently outside his normal state to claim to be telling the truth in a eulogy. In fact, the wine he has drunk simply puts Alcibiades into a state of mind that allows him to ignore social conventions and thus to speak without shame or embarrassment about his attempts at seduction and their failure, so as to tell the 'truth'—not the truth about Socrates, but the truth of desire—and, anticipating Lacan, to formulate the law of desire: to love is to want to be loved; there is no human desire without castration, without desire for the Other's desire. The wine emboldens Alcibiades to describe love in its full violence (and in so doing he refutes the effeminate discourse in which Agathon depicted Eros, in his own image, as a tender and delicate god). It is in this sense alone that Alcibiades is right to say '*in vino veritas*'.[26]

Alcibiades' claim to be telling the truth might still be justified by the argument that drunken discourse, veering off in all directions, is more appropriate to the Socratic atopia than straightforward, reasonable, rational discourse. Is this not the lesson that Alcibiades is seeking to put across, as he multiplies images in his attempt to capture Socrates? In the Platonic optic in which images are ontologically discredited, Alcibiades' claim is paradoxical at the very least. His recourse to images seems in fact to stem from some psychological necessity rather than from an epistemological requirement: his images allow him to 'compare' the incomparable, to abolish Socrates' exceptional singularity, to reduce the extraordinary to a common standard that allows him to enter into a relation of mimetic rivalry and try to strike a bargain based on a supposed equivalence with the rival, and perhaps, finally, to take the rival's place. And yet the images proffered all tend to show that Socrates *cannot be equaled*, that he cannot be compared to ordinary mortals, that a god alone may be his rival. But Alcibiades does not compare him to a god: this singular being whose very abnormality denies him a place in the human world (the Athenian democracy, unable to tolerate exceptional beings, condemns him to death—which is one form of ostracism) instead resembles one of those hybrid creatures who are closer to animality than to divinity. This comparison does not signify that Alcibiades has grasped Socrates' demonic nature; rather, it reflects his desire to heap ridicule on this peerless being who is admirable in all respects, like a father or an elder brother; it reflects his desire to punish Socrates for his infidelity by making him look ridiculous, creating an image worthy of Aristophanes (who had already profaned Love in recounting his own myth). Viewed in this light, Alcibiades' eulogy begins to resemble a counter-trial in which he accuses Socrates of not having sufficiently corrupted young people and of having been incorruptible himself, of having resisted Alcibiades' own beauty, his wealth, his cunning and his violence. Before the tribunal of the Athenians present at the banquet, in his inebriated state,[27] he does not hesitate to denounce Socrates, to exhibit for all to see what that atopic being conceals; he does not hesitate to crack open the outer shell before their eyes so as to uncover behind the grotesque exterior a sublime inner aspect against which Alcibiades seeks to defend himself by laughter and buffoonery, turning Socrates not into a tragic hero, as Hegel will, but into a character suited to a satyric drama.

The first image Alcibiades proposes is that of a silenus, an image that echoes and responds to Socrates' own image for the Athenian people in *Alcibiades* (131b): 'For my chiefest fear is of your being blighted by becoming a lover of the people, since many a good Athenian has come to that ere now. For fair of face is "the people of great-hearted Erechtheus", but you should get a view of it stripped: so take the precaution that I recommend. . . . You must wait till you have learnt, in order that you may be armed with an antidote' (132a–b). Conversely, the image of the silenus as applied to Socrates uncovers, beneath his monstrous ugliness and repulsive exterior, a secret beauty, a divine marvel. Alcibiades does not seem to have invented this comparison. In Xenophon's *Banquet*, the same comparison is attributed to Critobulus, who declares that Socrates is the ugliest of all the silenuses that appear in satyric dramas. And it is Socrates himself who unmasks the beauty behind his ugliness, for this pseudo-ugliness is 'functional' and actually to his advantage: thus his eyes see not only straight ahead but also to the side, for they are positioned on the sides of his head like those of the crayfish—which by this criterion would be the most beautiful animal there is. Socrates' flat nose is the most beautiful of all, for it allows his nostrils to receive scents from all sides. And his mouth, which according to Critobulus is more hideous than a donkey's, can also be viewed as purposeful, and thus as beautiful, for if it were to bite, it would make off with the largest portions; as for his thick lips, they present no obstacle to the tenderness of his kisses. In any event, if Socrates resembles silenuses, these after all are children of goddesses, the Naiads, and this fact is irrefutable proof of their beauty and his.

Socrates' ugliness—fascinating and enigmatic for the Greeks, for whom *Agathos* is always also *Kalos*—is also what triggers Alcibiades' comparison with the flat-nosed, thick-lipped, bull-eyed silenus that Socrates could have seen as a statuette in his father's workshop; identifying himself with this representation, Socrates seeks to reject the identification and to avenge himself, as it were, by an act of auto-generation, an exceptional exercise in plastic art, turning himself into a statue in order to recollect his own soul, the wonder concealed under his silenus-like exterior.[28] The most important aspect of the silenus image—and Alcibiades' ambivalence leads him to go farther than Critobulus does on this point—is in fact less the ugliness itself than the contrast between external ugliness and inner beauty, between a rough-hewn lubricious exterior whose Dionysian character is attested by the statuette's customary Pan-pipes, and the marvelous hidden Apollonian inner reality, the divine Agalma. Socrates' beauty no longer lies in his ugliness, as it does for Xenophon (for Alcibiades such ambivalence is intolerable); rather, it is dissociated from that ugliness, located behind it, as an effect of cleavage: it is an extraordinary pure beauty contrasted with pure ugliness, with a pure deceptive appearance, a beauty construed as an additional ruse devised by Socrates the better to entrap and fascinate, the equivalent in a way to the torpedo fish with which Meno compares it.

The torpedo fish 'appears as a flabby body, quite without vigour but, Oppian tells us, "its flanks conceal a cunning trick, a *dólos*, its strength in weakness". Its *dólos* consists of the sudden electric shock which its harmless appearance masks and which takes its adversary by surprise, leaving it at the torpedo fish's mercy'[29] paralyzing and overcoming its prey.[30] By means of this living trap, a veritable apotrope that prevents access to his 'insides', Socrates conceals the source of his power and superiority, his knowledge, so as to keep it for himself, proclaiming aloud, too loudly to be credible, that his ignorance is general and that he knows nothing: a pure ruse, according to Alcibiades, comparable to the roughness of his seemingly foolish discourse. Anyone who can see through his defenses and perceive Socrates himself, anyone who can unmask the beauty beneath the ugliness, the knowledge beneath his self-proclaimed ignorance and the seriousness beneath his irony, anyone who does not fear to crack open this silenus cannot fail to be amazed and overwhelmed by the prodigious internal richness of the 'phallic mother' spewing forth figurines, who subdues you once and for all:

He is utterly stupid and ignorant, as he affects (σχῆμα). Is this not like a Silenus? Exactly. It is an outward casing (ἐξώθεν) he wears, similarly to the sculptured Silenus. But if you opened his inside (ἔνδοθεν), you cannot imagine how full he is, good companions, of sobriety . . . [He] spends his life in chaffing and making game of his fellow-men. Whether anyone else has caught him in a serious moment and opened him, and seen the images inside, I know not; but I saw them one day, and thought them so divine and golden, so perfectly fair and wondrous, that I simply had to do as Socrates bade me. (216d–217a).

His talk most of all resembles the Silenuses that are made to open. If you chose to listen to Socrates' discourses you would feel them at first to be quite ridiculous; on the outside they are clothed with such absurd words and phrases—all, of course, the hide of a mocking satyr. His talk is of pack-asses, smiths, cobblers, and tanners, and he seems always to be using the same terms for the same things; so that anyone inexpert and thoughtless might laugh his speeches to scorn. But when these are opened, and you obtain a fresh view of them by getting inside, first of all you will discover that they are the only speeches which have any sense in them; and secondly, that none are so divine, so rich in images of virtue, so largely—nay, so completely—proper for the study of such as would attain both grace and worth. (221e–222a).

By cracking the mother's womb open again without embarrassment before the tribunal of banquet guests, by exhibiting the divinity concealed beneath its ugliness (that of its genital organs?), the fecundity beneath its self-proclaimed sterility, just as Aristophanes, in a pastiche of Empedocles, had revealed the powers of Eros, Alcibiades reveals Socrates' *dynamis* (power), which he unmasks the better to denounce him: for, compared now not to a silenus-figure but to the mythological Silenus himself,[31] Socrates only gives up his secrets when he is required, compelled, to do so.

Alcibiades does not hesitate to tell how he himself tried to seduce Socrates on several occasions in order to drag his *dynamis* out of him, but he was not as lucky as King Midas, for Socrates managed to resist all his ploys, stood up to all the trials he imposed: the trial of solitude (for, as someone for whom *aidos* (self-mastery) is the only value,

Socrates ought to be more susceptible, more 'takable' in private than in public, since it is less shameful for a Greek to laugh or cry at home than in the theater; see *The Republic*, X), the trial of nudity in the gymnasium, the trial of treacherous violence and even rape. Socrates gave up nothing, revealed nothing at all, and by that very token he succeeded in subjugating Alcibiades for all time. Unmasking him before the Athenians is thus not a way of betraying his secret, to which Alcibiades has no more access than anyone else; it is rather a way of warning the Athenians against the perverse duplicity that endows Socrates with mastery over all: 'I assure you, not one of you knows him; well, I shall reveal him, now that I have begun' (216d).

Just as behind a woman's veil there is always another veil, according to Nietzsche, if you take off a silenus's mask you will find another mask, that of the satyr *Marsyas*. Whereas the first image implies the whole system of oppositions upon which metaphysics will come to depend, the second, above and beyond the cleavages it operates, attempts to reconcile those oppositions.

The image of Marsyas is a mythical representation of a dual being, no longer an equivocal, ambiguous man *or* god but man *and* animal in ambivalent fashion; in the coherence of its form this image creates the illusion of a possible reunion of opposites, a reconciliation, over and beyond the anguish of fragmentation, of Alcibiades with himself, of the animal portion with the divine or human portion, projected onto the outside. This image, which is reassuring for Alcibiades, seems to work against Socrates. Just as the other protagonists of the *Symposium* were convinced, wrongly, that Eros was an admirable god, the silenus image could lead to the conclusion that Socrates' divinity is 'real'. The image of the satyr turns him into a buffoon, a lubricious figure, a familiar character in satyric dramas. Satyrs were represented with goat or horse features from the waist down; their upper body was that of a man. They had long, wide tails and perpetually erect male members of superhuman proportions; they belonged to Dionysus's following. While this view of Socrates deems him comparable to satyrs in every respect, he bears a special resemblance to the satyr Marsyas, the inventor of the double-piped flute. According to another tradition, Marsyas merely appropriated the flute that Athena had invented, and was castrated by Apollo as punishment. Challenged to produce music on his lyre comparable to Marsyas's flute music, Apollo invites Marsyas to play his instrument backwards, the way he himself plays his lyre. Defeated by Apollo, Marsyas is flayed by him.

Socrates, for his part, is not castrated (contrary to Lacan's contention); he is invincible, more powerful than Marsyas. It is his disproportionate, excessive, monstrous power that allows him to be compared not so much to Apollo, whom he invokes (this gesture would be a manifestation of the dissimulation and irony practiced by Socrates and unmasked by Alcibiades here), but more to Dionysus and his band of flute-girls. For Alcibiades, only Socrates' duplicity accounts for his dismissal of the flute-girls at the beginning of the *Symposium* (the flute being a polyphonic instrument par excellence, Plato banishes it from the ideal education he describes in *The Republic* in favor of the lyre, because the flute leaves all those who hear it 'beside themselves'). And if the comparison between Socrates and a female flute-player[32] may seem surprising and even insolent, it is only because Socrates misleads us by working his magic without exhibiting a flute or any other phallic instrument: he works his charms more surely with the help of mere words than the best flute player, the greatest orator;[33] an orator may impose himself by his presence, but he does not really possess you. Socrates succeeds even when he is absent. He operates at a distance; far from being degraded, his words as reported by even the most mediocre speaker (little Aristodemus?) retain their seductive effects, their magico-magnetic power. His words may be said to be all the more powerful in his absence (and even when he is present he is always already absent, dead).

The enthusiasm Socrates provokes is analogous, but superior, to the enthusiasm produced by the corybants in their transports; his words have an unsoothable sting, more powerful than a serpent's.[34] Everyone bears witness to the power of Socrates' words, for their impact is universal: men, women, adolescents, all succumb to possession and subjugation: 'For when I hear him I am worse than any wild fanatic; I find my heart leaping and my tears gushing forth at the sound of his speech, and I see great numbers of other people having the same experience' (215e). Socrates is a true man of the theater; it is he, not Agathon, who deserved to be crowned by the thirty thousand assembled Greeks. Alcibiades carries out this hierarchical displacement by symbolically transferring a garland with which he has crowned Agathon to Socrates' head. Since the essence of beauty and the transports to which it gives rise are more powerful than perceptible beauty and its effects, Socrates himself surpasses Agathon decisively in seductiveness. His is a formidable seductiveness, for, through the disturbance it generates, it leads to a general overturning of values, to a conversion of the *thumos* (spirit), which is henceforth indignant over its subjection to the perceptible. If you think you have escaped this dangerous Marsyas, this siren, by plugging your ears, think again; you will depend on him more than ever. For if Socrates' voice can charm to such an extent, it is because it belongs neither to an exceptional individual nor to an elder brother or father nor to a silenus, satyr, serpent, or siren—these mythological monsters remain overly reassuring—but to the logos itself. It is Alcibiades' own voice, the one from which he turned away to subject himself to the other, flattering voice of the Athenian *demos*, one that covers him with honor *and* with shame because it distances him from concern with himself and his true kinship. Because Alciabiades fails to hear his own voice in that of Socrates—the voice of the philosophical Eros, which ought to direct him toward exclusive commerce with his own soul—he remains necessarily fixed at a lower degree of the dialectics of love, attached and subjected to the person of Socrates alone.

The end of the eulogy abandons the apparently deprecatory mythological images. Just as the other protagonists had showered fulsome praise on the god of love by enumerating his virtues and his good deeds, Alcibiades exhibits those of 'his' god whom he can call, after the reassuring mythological detour, an extraordinary *man*, one who resists all comparisons as he stands up to all trials, including fatigue, cold, and sleep; he is superior to all by virtue of his temperance, his courage, his indifference to honors, his mastery—even in the most perilous situations, he always knows what to do at the crucial moment; this man from whom Alcibiades seeks to save himself has saved his, Alciabiades', life at his own risk. The greatest of all orators, musicians, strategists, and so on, he has no peer among men of the past or the present; he is worthy of unreserved admiration. At the end of the eulogy, as if his drunkenness has subsided and he has remembered that the rhetorical genre he is using requires not truth but an accumulation of the virtues of the object being praised, Alcibiades abandons all ambivalence and 'deifies' Socrates, as someone to whom no image—no human, all too human image—and no mythological figure could do justice. As Socrates' own rough discourse is an envelope concealing profound wisdom, so the crude images of silenuses and satyrs are cloaks that cover over the portrait of Socrates the perfect, peerless man; they are comical only for the masses, for imbeciles and ignoramuses. Anyone who is capable of seeing through the satyric hide of Alcibiades' discourse, capable of discerning his admiration and his love, will no longer wish to mock Socrates or condemn him to death. Only one complaint against Socrates will remain: he claims to be everyone's lover the better to make himself the loved one and master of all. But in the final analysis this accusation is perhaps a ruse on Alcibiades' part, an attempt to frighten Agathon into breaking off with Socrates and thus to have Socrates all to himself.

As a simple either/or alternative, the initial question raised—'Is Alcibiades' eulogy aimed at buffoonery or truth?'—is moot, for it does not take into account either Alcibiades' ambivalence or his irony (or Plato's), nor does it take into account the end of the *Symposium*, with its suggestion that the capacity for contraries belongs to Plato, that he may be at once a comic and a tragic author, and thus also the author of this two-faced satyric drama that Alcibiades has just performed and that Plato has staged. For in the succession of eulogies pronounced by the various protagonists—each one in conformity with his own Muse—it is Plato who has succeeded in demonstrating unsurpassable mastery in the most diverse genres;[35] Plato is the sole stage manager of the *Symposium*. It is he who, concealed under the features of Aristodemus, Apollodorus, and Alcibiades, has created the fictional figure of Socrates as a figure of mastery. If he has hidden himself behind his privileged spokesperson, if he has transferred his own thoughts to that figure, it is because he knows perfectly well that there is no mastery without disavowal of mastery. By making it impossible for all time to sort out what belongs to him and what belongs to his master, Plato takes away with one hand what he gives with the other, and makes the debt unpayable.

In any event, Plato produces a veritable omnipotent *deus ex machina*, relying on the fiction of a sudden commotion, a new hubbub from outside that signals the double's disappearance just as a similar disturbance had signaled his arrival, to conclude the *Symposium* and *arrest* the portrayal of Socrates.

Notes

1. *Symposium*, in *Plato*, vol. III, trans. W. R. M. Lamb (London: William Heinemann Ltd., 1961), 174e. Subsequent references will be supplied in the text.
2. See *Jokes and Their Relation to the Unconscious, The Standard Edition of the Complete Psychological Works of Sigmund Freud*, trans. James Strachey (London: The Hogarth Press, 1953–66), vol. 8, p. 74, and the third lecture in *Five Lectures on Psycho-Analysis, Standard Edition*, vol. 11, pp. 30–31. For a reading of this *Witz*, see Sarah Kofman, *Pourquoi rit-on*? (Paris: Galilée, 1986), pp. 82–92.
3. See Georg Wilhelm Friedrich Hegel, *Lectures on the History of Philosophy. I. Greek Philosophy to Plato*, trans. E. S. Haldane (Lincoln: University of Nebraska Press, 1995), p. 391.

4. *The Twilight of the Idols*, 'The Problem of Socrates', in *The Portable Nietzsche*, trans. Walter Kaufmann (New York: Viking Penguin, 1982 [1954]), §10, p. 478.
5. Ibid., §11, p. 479.
6. On this portrait of Eros, see Sarah Kofman, 'Beyond Aporia', trans. David Macey, in Andrew Benjamin, ed., *Post-Structuralist Classics* (London: Routledge, 1988), pp. 7–44.
7. Ibid. This text explores the way the figure of Socrates communicates with that of Prometheus, the first philosopher.
8. A legend holds that in the beginning gods and men lived and feasted together, until one day Prometheus was charged with dividing up what belonged to each group and tried to fool the gods to the benefit of men. Zeus then took over the distribution: mortal men were to have the cooked flesh of dead animals, while the gods would have nectar and ambrosia. Mortals like Penia were not to be invited to the banquet of the gods. Prometheus's crime was that he attempted to trick the gods into letting mortals participate in their feasts and into giving them immortality.
9. See Claude This, 'Au-delà du double: la bète', in Marie-José Baudinet and Christian Schatter, eds., *Du visage* (Lille: Presses Universitaires de Lille, 1982), pp. 91–101.
10. In 'Beyond Aporia', I argued that it is the indigent Penia who holds the *poros* and that what she *does* contradicts what is attributed to her in *speech*. The myth projects the structure of the human soul and its desire onto three distinct characters: Penia (Poverty), Poros (Resource), and Eros (Love), all of whom make simultaneous demands. *Penia*, the soul's double, contains Poros within herself, and she is always already pregnant with Eros.
11. See Hegel, *Lectures*, I, pp. 394–95.
12. See Xenophon, *Memorabilia*, trans. Amy L. Bonnette (Ithaca, NY: Cornell University Press, 1996), Book III, Chapter 11, 4–18, and also, on this point, the introduction to the present volume.
13. See Hegel, *Lectures*, pp. 391, 422–25.
14. See *Phaedo*, in *Plato*, vol. I, trans. Harold North Fowler (London: William Heinemann Ltd., 1971), pp. 405–579.
15. See *The Twilight of the Idols*, 'The Problem of Socrates'.
16. 'So now, for my part, I have no idea what virtue is, whilst you, though perhaps you may have known before you came in touch with me, are now as good as ignorant of it also' (*Meno*, in *Plato*, vol. II, trans. W. R. M. Lamb [London: William Heinemann Ltd., 1962], 80d).
17. See Eric Robertson Dodds, *The Greeks and the Irrational* (Berkeley: University of California Press, 1951). Shamans believe in a separable soul that can be withdrawn even from a living body if appropriate techniques are used. This soul is older than the body and will outlive it (pp. 146–47).

    The shamanistic 'retreat' might provide the model for a deliberate *askesis*, a conscious training of the psychic powers through abstinence and through spiritual exercises; . . . tales of vanishing and reappearing shamans might encourage the belief in an indestructible magical or daemonic self . . . The shaman's trance, his deliberate detachment of the occult self from the body, has become [in Plato] that practice of mental withdrawal and concentration which purifies the rational soul—a practice for which Plato in fact claims the authority of a traditional *logos.* The occult knowledge which the shaman acquires in trance has become a vision of metaphysical truth; his 'recollection' of past earthly lives has become a 'recollection' of bodiless Forms which is made the basis of a new epistemology; while on the mythical level his 'long sleep' and 'underworld journey' provides a direct model for the experiences of Er. (Pp. 149–50, 210)

It is thus clear that Dodds, like Socrates' disciples, thinks that Socrates was in the habit of looking within himself to find 'truth', 'bodiless Forms' (Dodds erroneously borrows this terminology from Aristotle to speak about Plato or Socrates).

18. See Jacques Lacan, 'Du "Trieb" de Freud et du désir du psychanalyste', in *Ecrits* (Paris: Seuil, 1966), pp. 851–54.
19. See *Protagoras,* in *Plato,* vol. II, trans. W. R. B. Lamb (London: William Heinemann Ltd., 1974), 309b–c, where Socrates neglects Alcibiades in favor of the handsomer Protagoras.
20. Phaedrus goes so far as to say that the gods themselves are more admiring and generous toward the beloved than toward the lover (*Symposium,* 180b).
21. Lacan, although we owe him the distinction between penis and phallus, wrote the following: 'It is because he has not seen Socrates' prick . . . that Alcibiades the seducer exalts in him the [*Agalma*], the marvel that he would like Socrates to cede to him in avowing his desire' ('Subversion of the Subject and Dialectic of Desire in the Freudian Unconscious', in *Ecrits: A Selection,* trans. Alan Sheridan [New York: Norton, 1977], p. 322).
22. 'Thinking myself free at any time by gratifying his desires to hear all that our Socrates knew' (217a).
23. 'For he brings home to me that I cannot disown the duty of doing what he bids me, but that as soon as I turn from his company I fall victim to the favours of the crowd. So I take a runaway's leave of him and flee away; when I see him again I think of those former admissions, and am ashamed' (216c).
24. In connection with this entire issue, see *Alcibiades* I and II in *Plato,* vol. XII, trans. W. R. M. Lamb (Cambridge, MA: William Heinemann Ltd., 1986).
25. See Plato, *Laws,* vol. I, trans. R. G. Bury (London: William Heinemann Ltd., 1952 [1926]), I, 637e–639a, pp. 45–49.
26. Freud also shows in *Jokes* how wine lifts inhibitions and, by putting people in a 'good mood', facilitates the return of the repressed.
27. Alcibiades' Dionysian drunkenness may recall the way the Greeks associated court trials with tragedy, thus with the emergence of Dionysus, that is, of drunken ecstasy or the persuasive power of living discourse. See Walter Benjamin, *The Origin of German Tragic Drama* (London: NLB, 1977), p. 116.
28. Although he refers to Xenophon when he speaks of Socrates' ugliness, Hegel remains dependent on Alcibiades' portrait and on the now-classic opposition between 'outside' and 'inside'. In Socrates' case, 'his appearance indicated naturally low and hateful qualities, which, as indeed he says, he himself subdued. He lived amongst his fellow-citizens, and stands before us as one of those great plastic natures consistent through and through . . . resembling a perfect classical work of art which has brought itself to this height of perfection' (*Lectures,* I, p. 393]. For Nietzsche, Socrates' external ugliness, on the

contrary, is the expression of an internal 'ugliness', that is a symptom of the most violent impulses: 'Ugliness, in itself an objection, is among the Greeks almost a refutation. Was Socrates a Greek at all? Ugliness is often enough the expression of a development that has been crossed, *thwarted* by crossing . . . The typical criminal is ugly: *monstrum in fronte, monstrum in animo.* But the criminal is a decadent. Was Socrates a typical criminal? . . . A foreigner who knew about faces once passed through Athens and told Socrates to his face that he was a *monstrum*—that he harbored in himself all the bad vices and appetites. And Socrates merely answered: "You know me, sir!"' (*The Twilight of the Idols*, 'The Problem of Socrates', section 3, pp. 474–75). We shall come back to the problems raised by these texts.

29. Marcel Détienne and Jean-Pierre Vernant, *Cunning Intelligence in Greek Culture and Society*, trans. Janet Lloyd (Atlantic Highlands, NJ: Humanities Press, 1978 [1974]), p. 46.
30. Let us recall that Socrates rejects this comparison, which depends on a confusion between a blocking aporia, that of the Sophist, and a mobilizing aporia, that of the philosopher. Socrates compares himself rather to a gadfly or goad that provokes and arouses. See 'Beyond Aporia'.
31. According to Pierre Grimal's *Dictionary of Classical Mythology* (trans. A. R. Maxwell-Hyslop [Oxford: Blackwell, 1986]), Silenus, which is the generic name of satyrs who have grown old, is also the name of a character that was supposed to have reared Dionysus. One version of his story claims that he was born of drops of Uranos's blood when the latter was mutilated by Cronos. That Silenus possessed great wisdom, which he consented to reveal only under duress. This is how he was said to have been captured by King Midas, to whom he addressed wise words. Midas got the better of him one day when he found Silenus asleep after too many libations.
32. This is how Alcibiades might interpret the dream Socrates had in which Apollo exhorts him to make music (see *Phaedo*). See also Nietzsche, who dreams, in *The Birth of Tragedy*, of Socrates as an artist, a musician.
33. In the *Protagoras*, Socrates compares the voices of orators to those of flute-girls, extraneous voices: 'But when the party consists of thorough gentlemen who have had a proper education, you will see neither flute-girls nor dancing-girls nor harp-girls, but only the company contenting themselves with their own conversation, and none of these fooleries and frolics' (347d). See also the *Menexenus*:

    [Orators] praise in such splendid fashion, that . . . they bewitch our souls. . . . I myself, Menexenus, when thus praised by them feel mightily ennobled, and every time I listen fascinated I am exalted and imagine myself to have become all at once taller and nobler and more handsome . . . Owing to the persuasive eloquence of the speaker . . . this majestic feeling remains with me for over three days: so persistently does the speech and voice of the orator ring in my ears that it is scarcely on the fourth or fifth day that I recover myself and remember that I really am here on earth, whereas till then I almost imagined myself to be living in the Islands of the Blessed,—so expert are our orators. (*Plato*, vol. VII, trans. R. G. Bury [William Heinemann Ltd., 1961], 234c–235c).

34. Love's bite is often represented by the sting of a serpent or scorpion. The

image occurs in Xenophon's *Memorabilia*, where Socrates recommends that the love of young people be avoided, because of that sting: 'Don't you know that this creature called "fair and young" is more dangerous than the scorpion, seeing that it need not even come in contact, like the insect, but at any distance can inject a maddening poison into anyone who only looks at it?' (I, 3, [13]) The mix of styles is also what characterizes Plato for Nietzsche, the first of the great hybrids: 'The essence of the Platonic art, dialogue, is an absence of form and an absence of style produced by the mix of all possible forms and styles . . . He hovers between all genres, between prose and poetry, narrative, lyricism, drama, since he has broken the strict ancient law of unity of form, style, and language' ('Socrate et la tragédie', in *Ecrits posthumes, 1870–1873* [Paris: Gallimard, 1977], p. 41).

35. Friedrich Nietzsche, *Beyond Good and Evil*, trans. Walter Kaufmann (New York: Vintage Books, 1966), §190, p. 103.

3 Sorcerer Love: A Reading of Plato, *Symposium*, 'Diotima's Speech'

Luce Irigaray*

In the *Symposium*, the dialogue on love, when Socrates finishes speaking, he gives the floor to a woman: Diotima. She does not take part in these exchanges or in this meal among men. She is not there. She herself does not speak. Socrates reports or recounts her words. He praises her for her wisdom and her power and declares that she is his initiator or teacher when it comes to love, but she is not invited to teach or to eat. Unless she didn't want to accept an invitation? But Socrates says nothing about that. And Diotima is not the only example of a woman whose wisdom, especially about love, is reported in her absence by a man.

Diotima's teaching will be very dialectical, but different from what we usually call dialectical. In effect, it doesn't use opposition to make the first term pass into the second in order to achieve a synthesis of the two, as Hegel does. From the outset, she establishes an *intermediary* that will never be abandoned as a means or a path. Her method, then, is not a propaedeutic of the *destruction* or the *destructuration* of two terms in order to establish a synthesis that is neither one nor the other. She presents, uncovers, unveils the insistence of a third term that is already there and that permits progression: from poverty to wealth, from ignorance to wisdom, from mortality to immortality. Which, for her, always comes to a greater perfection of and in love.

But, contrary to the usual methods of dialectic, one should not have to give up love in order to become wise or learned. It is love that leads to knowledge, whether in art or more metaphysical learning. It is love that both leads the way and is the path. A mediator par excellence.

* Luce Irigaray, 'Sorcerer Love: A Reading of Plato, *Symposium*, "Diotima's Speech"', from her *An Ethics of Sexual Difference*, trans Carolyn Burke and Gillian C. Gill (Ithaca, NY: Cornell University Press, 1993) copyright © 1993 by Cornell University Press; originally published in French as *Éthique de la différence sexuelle* (Paris: Éditions de Minuit, 1984). Reprinted by permission of the publisher.

This mediating role is indicated as part of the theme, but it is also perpetually at issue, on stage, in the exposition of the theme.

Thus, Diotima immediately refutes the claim that love, Eros, is a great God[1] and that it is the love of beautiful things. At the risk of offending the practice of respect for the Gods, she also asserts that Eros is neither beautiful nor good. This leads her interlocutor to suppose immediately that Eros is ugly and bad, as he is incapable of grasping the existence or the in-stance of that which stands *between*, that which makes possible the passage between ignorance and knowledge. If we did not, at each moment, have something to learn from the encounter with reality, between reality and already established knowledge, we would not perfect ourselves in wisdom. And not to become wiser means to become more ignorant.

Therefore, between knowledge and reality, there is an intermediary that allows for the encounter and the transmutation or transvaluation between the two. Diotima's dialectic is in at least *four terms*: the here, the two poles of the encounter, and the beyond—but a beyond that never abolishes the here. And so on, indefinitely. The mediator is never abolished in an infallible knowledge. Everything is always in movement, in a state of becoming. And the mediator of all this is, among other things, or exemplarily, *love*. Never fulfilled, always becoming.

And, in response to Socrates' protestation that love is a great God, that *everyone says so or thinks so*, she *laughs*. Her retort is not at all angry, the effect of hesitating between contradictory positions; it is laughter based on other grounds. While laughing, then, she asks Socrates what he means by *everyone*. Just as she ceaselessly dismantles the assurance or *closure* of opposing terms, she undoes all *sets* of units reduced to sameness in order to constitute a whole. '"*You mean, by all who do not know?" said she, "or by all who know as well?" "Absolutely all." At that she laughed.*' (Plato, *Symposium* 202; p. 252).[2] Once the tension between opposites has subsided in this way, she shows, or demonstrates, that 'everyone' does not exist, nor does love's position as *always* a great God. Does she teach nothing that is already defined? A method of becoming wise, learned, more perfected in love and in art. Thus she ceaselessly examines Socrates on his positions but without positing authoritative, already constituted truths. Instead, she teaches the renunciation of already established truths. And each time Socrates thinks he can take something as certain, she undoes his certainty. His own, but also all kinds of certainty that are already set in language. All entities, substantives, adverbs, sentences are patiently, and joyously, called into question.

For love, or Eros, the demonstration is not so difficult to establish. For if Eros possessed all that he desired, he would desire no more. He must be lacking in order to desire still. But if he had no share in the beautiful and the good things, he could no longer desire them. He is therefore an *intermediary* in a very specific way. Does he lose his status as a God for this reason? Not necessarily. He is neither mortal nor immortal. He is between the one and the other, in a state that can be qualified as daimonic: love is a *daimon*.[3] His function is to transmit to the gods what comes from men and to men what comes from the gods. Like all that is daimonic, love is complementary to gods and to men in such a way as to put everything in touch with itself. A being of middle nature is needed so that men and gods can enter into relations, into conversation, while awake or asleep. This need is expressed in divination, in the priestly knowledge of things related to sacrifices, initiations, incantations, preaching in general, and magic.

Daimons serving as mediators between men and gods are numerous and very diverse. Eros is one of them. And his parentage is exceptional: he is the child of *Plenty* (who is the son of *Invention*) and of *Poverty*, and he was conceived on the day when the birth of Aphrodite was celebrated. So, Diotima tells Socrates, Eros is always poor and '*rough, unkempt, unshod, and homeless, ever couching on the ground uncovered, sleeping beneath the open sky by doors and in the streets, because he has the nature of his mother. . . . But again, in keeping with his father, he has designs upon the beautiful and good, for he is bold, headlong, and intense, a mighty hunter, always weaving some device or other, eager in invention and resourceful, searching after wisdom all through life, terrible as a magician, sorcerer, and sophist.*

'*As for ignorance and knowledge, here again he is midway between them. The case stands thus. No god seeks after wisdom, or wishes to grow wise (for he already is so), any more than anybody else seeks after wisdom if he has it. Nor, again, do ignorant folk seek after wisdom or long to grow wise; for here is just the trouble about ignorance, that what is neither beautiful and good, nor yet intelligent, to itself seems good enough. Accordingly, the man who does not think himself in need has no desire for what he does not think himself in need of.*'

Socrates protests: '*The seekers after knowledge, Diotima! If they are not the wise, nor yet the ignorant, who are they, then?*'

'*The point,*' said she, '*is obvious even to a child, that they are persons intermediate between these two, and that Eros is among them; for wisdom falls within the class of the most beautiful, while Eros is an eros for the beautiful. And hence it follows necessarily that Eros is a seeker after wisdom [a philosopher], and being a philosopher, is midway between wise and ignorant.*' (203–4; pp. 253–54).

Love is thus an intermediary *between* pairs of opposites: poverty/plenty, ignorance/wisdom, ugliness/beauty, dirtiness/cleanliness, death/life, and so on. And this would be inscribed in his nature given his genealogy and the date of his conception. And love is a philosopher and a philosophy. Philosophy is not a formal learning, fixed and rigid, abstracted from all feeling. It is a quest for love, love of beauty, love of wisdom, which is one of the most beautiful things. Like love, the philosopher would be someone poor, dirty, rather down-and-out, always unhoused, sleeping beneath the stars, but very curious, skilled in ruses and tricks of all kinds, constantly reflecting, a sorcerer, a sophist, sometimes exuberant, sometimes close to death. This is nothing like the way we usually represent the philosopher: a learned person who is well dressed, has good manners, knows everything, and pedantically instructs us in the corpus of things already coded. The philosopher is nothing like that. He is a sort of barefoot waif who goes out under the stars seeking an encounter with reality, the embrace, the knowledge or perhaps a shared birth [*connaissance, co-naissance*], of whatever benevolence, beauty, or wisdom might be found there. He inherits this endless quest from his mother. He is a philosopher through his mother and skilled in art through his father. But his passion for love, for beauty, for wisdom comes to him from his mother, and from the date that he was conceived. Desired and wanted, moreover, by his mother.

How does it happen that love and the philosopher are generally represented otherwise? Because they are imagined as *beloveds* and not as *lovers*. As a beloved, Love, both like and unlike the philosopher, is imagined to be of unparalleled beauty, delicate, perfect, and happy. Yet the lover is of an entirely different nature. He goes toward what is kind, beautiful, perfect, and so on. He doesn't possess it. He is poor, unhappy, always in search of. . . . But what does he seek or love? That beautiful things become his—this is Socrates' reply. But what happens to him if these things become his? To this question interjected by Diotima, Socrates cannot respond. Substituting 'good' for 'beautiful,' she repeats the question. '*That the good may be his,*' repeats Socrates. '*And what happens to the man when the good things become his?*' '*On this,*' said Socrates, '*I am more than ready with an answer: that he will be happy*' (204–5; pp. 254–55). And happiness seems to put an ultimate term to this dialogical volleying between Diotima and Socrates.

❦

How should we name that which is fitting to lovers? 'By what manner of pursuit and in what activity does the eagerness and straining for the object get the name of Eros? And what may this action really be?' asks Socrates. And Diotima answers: '*This action is engendering in beauty, with relation both to body and to soul*' (206; p. 256). But Socrates understands nothing of such a clear revelation. He understands nothing about fecundity of body and soul. '*The union of a man and woman is, in fact, a generation; this is a thing divine; in a living creature that is mortal, it is an element of immortality, this fecundity and generation*' (206; p. 256). This statement of Diotima's never seems to have been heard. Moreover, she herself goes on to accentuate the procreative aspect of love. But first she emphasizes the character of *divine generation in any union between man and woman*, the presence of immortality in the living mortal. All love is seen as creation and potentially divine, a path between the condition of the mortal and that of the immortal. Love is fecund prior to any procreation. And its fecundity is *mediumlike*, *daimonic*, the guarantee for all, male and female, of the immortal becoming of the living. But there cannot be procreation of a divine nature where harmony is lacking. And the divine cannot be in harmony with the ugly, only with the beautiful. So, according to Diotima, love between man and woman is beautiful, harmonious, divine. It must be so for procreation to take place. It is not procreation that is beautiful and that constitutes the objective of love. Love's aim is to realize the immortal in the mortal between lovers. And the energy pouring forth to produce the child results from joy at the approach of a beautiful object. Whereas an unattractive object results in a withdrawal, a hoarding of fecundity, the painfully borne weight of the desire to procreate. Procreation and generation in beauty—this is the aim of love. Because in this way the eternity and the imperishability of a mortal being are made manifest.

Fecundity of love between lovers—the regeneration of one by the other, the passage to immortality in and through each other—this seems to become the condition of procreation and not a cause in its own right. Of course, Diotima says to Socrates that the creation of beauty, of a work of art (by oneself this time?) does not suffice, that it is necessary to create a child together, that this wisdom is inscribed in the animal world itself. She continues to laugh at his going to look for his truths beyond the most obvious everyday reality, at his not seeing or even perceiving this reality. At the way in which his dialectical or dialogical method already forgets the most elementary truths. At the way his discourse on love neglects to look at, to be informed, about the amorous state. Or to inquire about its cause.

Diotima speaks of *cause* in an astonishing way. One could expect that her method would not enter into the chain of causalities, a chain that skips over or often forgets about the intermediary as a generative middle term. Causality doesn't usually play a part in her progression. She borrows it from the animal world and evokes or invokes it on the subject of procreation. Instead of leaving the child to germinate or ripen in the milieu of love and fecundity between man and woman, she seeks a cause for love in the animal world: *procreation*. Diotima's method miscarries here. From this point on, she leads love into a split between mortality and immortality, and love loses its daimonic character. Is this the foundational act of meta-physics? There will be lovers in body, lovers in soul. But the perpetual passage from mortal to immortal that lovers confer on each other is blurred. Love has lost its divinity, its mediumistic, alchemical qualities between couples of opposites. Since love is no longer the intermediary, the child plays this role. Occupying the space of love, the child can no longer be a lover and is put in the place of love's incessant movement. It is beloved, no doubt. But how can one be loved without being a lover? And isn't love trapped there *in the beloved*, contrary to what Diotima wanted in the first place? A beloved who is an *end* is substituted for love between men and women. A beloved who is a *will*, even a *duty*, and a *means* of attaining immortality, which the lovers can neither attain nor aspire to between themselves. This is the failure of love, for the child as well. If the pair of lovers cannot safeguard the place for love as a third term between them, they can neither remain lovers nor give birth to lovers. Something becomes frozen in space-time, with the loss of a vital intermediary and of an accessible transcendental that remains alive. A sort of teleological triangle is put into place instead of a perpetual journey, a perpetual transvaluation, a permanent becoming. For this, love was the vehicle. But, if procreation becomes its goal, it risks losing its internal motivation, its 'inner' fecundity, its slow and constant generation, regeneration. This error in method, in the originality of Diotima's method, is corrected soon afterward only to be confirmed later. Of course, once again, *she is not there. Socrates relates her words.* Perhaps he distorts them unwittingly or unknowingly.

The following paragraph, moreover, goes against what was just asserted. It tells how a permanent renewal takes place in us. How there is in us an unending loss of what is old or already dead, both at the most physical level—hair, bones, blood, our whole body—and in our spiritual aspect—our character, our opinions, our desires, joys and pains, our fears. None of these elements is ever the same as what it was for us, in that some come into existence while others perish. And the same is true for knowledge that is acquired and forgotten—thus in constant renewal. It is in this fashion '*in which everything mortal is preserved, not in being always perfectly identical, as is divinity, but in that the disappearing and decaying object leaves behind it another new one such as it was. By this arrangement, Socrates,*' said she, '*the mortal partakes of immortality, both in body and all else; the immortal does so in another way. So do not marvel if everything by nature prizes its own offspring; it is for the sake of immortality that every being has this urgency and love*' (208; p. 258). Here, Diotima returns to her type of argumentation, including her mockery of those who suspend the present in order to search 'for endless time, imperishable glory' (208; p. 259). She speaks—and notably through her style, which *entwines with* what she says without *tying the knot*—of becoming in time, of the permanent generation-regeneration that takes place here and now in everyone, male and female, as far as corporeal and spiritual realities are concerned. Without going so far as to say that the one is the fruition of the other. Rather, that at each moment, we are a 'regrowth' of ourselves, in perpetual increase. No more searching for immortality through the child. But in ourselves, ceaselessly. Diotima returns to a progression that admits love as it had been defined before she evoked procreation: as an intermediate terrain, a mediator, a space-time of permanent *passage* between mortal and immortal.

Then, returning to an example of the quest for immortality through fame, she resituates the object (of) love outside of the subject: in renown, immortal glory, and so on. No more of constantly becoming immortal in ourselves but instead a race toward something that would confer immortality. Similarly and differently as for the procreation of a child, the stake of love is placed outside the self. In the beloved and not in the lover? The lovers mentioned, Alcestis, Admetus, Achilles, Codrus, were cited only so that we would always remember them. It was with the goal of immortal fame that they loved until death. Immortality is the object of their love. Not love itself. '*Well then,*'

Diotima said, '*when men's fecundity is of the body, they turn rather to the women, and the fashion of their love is this: through begetting children to provide themselves with immortality, renown and happiness, as they imagine, securing them for all time to come.*

'*But when fecundity is of the soul—for indeed there are those persons who are fecund in their souls even more than in their bodies, fecund in what is the function of the soul to conceive and also to bring forth—what is this proper offspring? It is wisdom, along with every other spiritual value*' (208–9; p. 259). What seemed to me to be original in Diotima's method has disappeared once again. This intermediary milieu of love, which is irreducible, is resplit between a 'subject' (an inadequate word in Plato) and a 'beloved reality.' Falling in love no longer constitutes a becoming of the lover himself, of love in the lover (male or female), or between the lovers, but is now the teleological quest for what is deemed a higher reality and often situated in a transcendence inaccessible to our mortal condition. Immortality has already been put off until death and does not figure as one of our constant tasks as mortals, a transmutation that is endlessly incumbent upon us here, now—its possibility having been inscribed in the body, which is capable of becoming divine. Beauty of body and of soul are hierarchized, and the love of women becomes the lot of those who, incapable of being creators in soul, are fecund of body and expect the immortality of their name to be perpetuated through their offspring.

'*By far the greatest and most beautiful form of wisdom,*' said she, '*is that which has to do with regulating states and households, and has the name, no doubt, of "temperance" and "justice".*' (209; p. 259).

To fall in love, to become divine, or immortal, is no longer left to the intermediary current but qualified, hierarchized. And in the worst case, love dies as a result. In the universe of determinations, there will be goals, competitions, and loving duties, the beloved or love being the goal. The lovers disappear. Our subsequent tradition has even taught us that it is forbidden or futile to be lovers unless there is procreation, whereas Diotima had begun by affirming that the most divine act is 'the union of man and woman, a divine affair.' What she asserted at that moment accorded with what she said about the function of love as an intermediary that remains an intermediary, a daimon. It seems that during the course of her speech, she diminishes somewhat this daimonic, mediumistic function of love, such that it is no longer really a daimon, but an intention, a reduction to the intention, to the teleology of human will, already subjected to a kind of thought with fixed objectives, not an immanent efflorescence of the divine of and in the flesh. Love was meant to be an irreducible mediator, at once physical and spiritual, between the lovers, and not already codified duty, will, desire. Love that is still invoked as a daimon in a method aiming toward the beautiful and the good often disappears from discourse, reappearing only in art, 'painting,' in the form(s) of cupids that excite eroticism, and, perhaps, in the form of angels. Is love itself split between *eros* and *agape*? Yet, for lovers to love each other, between them there must be Love.

There remains what was said about love, the philosopher. But why wouldn't philosopher-Love be a lover of the other? A lover only of the Other? Or of an inaccessible transcendent. In any case, such would already be the ideal whenever daimonic love is suppressed. Love becomes political wisdom, the wisdom of order in the city, not the intermediary state that inhabits lovers and transports them from the condition of mortals to that of immortals. Love becomes a kind of *raison d'état*. It founds a family, takes care of children, and of all those children who are the citizens. The more its objective is distanced from individual becoming, the more valuable it is. Its stake gets lost in the immortal good and beautiful seen as collective goods. The family is preferable to the generating of lovers, between lovers. Adopted children are preferable to others. It is in this way, moreover, that it comes to pass that *love between men is superior to love between man and woman.* Carnal procreation is subordinated to the engendering of beautiful and good things. Immortal things. This, surprisingly enough, is the view of Diotima. At least as translated through the words of Socrates.

The beings most gifted in wisdom go directly to this end. Most begin by going toward physical beauty and '*must love one single object [physical form of beauty], and thereof must engender fair discourses*' (210; p. 260). If the instruction is properly done, this must be so. But whoever becomes attached to one body must learn that beauty resides in many. After having pursued beauty in one perceptible form, he must learn that the same beauty resides in all bodies; he will '*abate his violent love of one, disdaining this and deeming it a trifle, and will become a lover of all fair objects*' (210; p. 261). From the attraction to a single beautiful body, he passes then to many; and from there to the beauty residing in souls. Thus he learns that beauty is not housed only in the body and that someone of an unattractive bodily appearance can be beautiful and kind; that to be just is to know how to take care of him and to engender beautiful discourse for him. Thus love passes imperceptibly into love of works. The passion for beautiful bodies is transmuted into the discovery of the beauty found in knowledge. That which liberates from the attachment to a single master opens to the immense ocean of the beautiful and leads to the birth of numerous and sublime discourses, as well as thoughts inspired by a boundless love of wisdom. Until the point when the force and the development that he will have found there allow him to perceive *one single* knowledge (210; p. 261). This marvelous beauty is perceptible, perhaps, by whoever has been led along the path just described, by whoever has passed step-by-step through the different stages. He will then have the vision of a beauty '*which is eternal, not growing up or perishing, increasing or decreasing*' and which is moreover *absolutely* beautiful, '*not beautiful in one point and ugly in another, nor sometimes beautiful and sometimes not; not beautiful in one relation and ugly in another, nor beautiful in this place and ugly in that, as if beautiful to some, to others ugly; again, this beauty will not be revealed to him in the semblance of a face, or hands, or any other element of the body, nor in any form of speech or knowledge, nor yet as if it appertained to any other being, a creature, for example, upon earth, or in the sky, or elsewhere; no, it will be seen as beauty in and for itself, consistent with itself in uniformity forever, whereas all other beauties share it in such fashion that, while they are ever born and perish, that eternal beauty, never waxing, never waning, never is impaired.*' (211; pp. 261–62).

To attain this sublime beauty, one must begin with the love of young men. Starting with their natural beauty, one must, step-by-step, ascend to supernatural beauty: from beautiful bodies pass to beautiful occupations, then to beautiful sciences, until one reaches that sublime science which is supernatural beauty alone, which allows the isolated knowledge of the essence of beauty (211; p. 262). This contemplation is what gives the meaning and savor of life: '*It will not appear to you to be according to the measure of gold and raiment, or of lovely boys and striplings.*' (211; p. 262). And what can he who has perceived '*beauty in its own single nature*' ever look at again? Having contemplated '*the beautiful with that by which it can be seen*' (212; p. 262), beyond all simulacra, he is united with it and *truly* virtuous; since he attained 'authentic reality,' he becomes dear to the divine and is made immortal.

This person would have then attained what I shall call a *sensible transcendental*, the material texture of beauty. He would have 'seen' the very spatiality of the visible, the real which precedes all reality, all forms, all truth of particular sensations or constructed idealities. He would have contemplated the 'nature' of the divine? This support of the fabrication of the transcendent in its different modes, all of which, according to Diotima, come under the same propaedeutic: *love of beauty.* Neither the good nor the true nor justice nor government of the city would occur without beauty. And its best ally is love. Love therefore deserves veneration. And Diotima asks that her words be considered as a celebration and praise of Love.

In the second part of her discourse, she treated Love itself as a means. She doubled its intermediary function and subjected it to a *telos.* Her method seems less powerful here than at the beginning of her remarks, when she held love to be the mediator of a state of becoming with no objective other than becoming. Perhaps Diotima is still saying the same thing. But in the second part, her method runs the risk of being reduced to the metaphysics that is getting set up. Unless what she proposes to contemplate, beauty itself, is seen as that which confounds the opposition between immanence and transcendence. As an always already sensible horizon on the basis of which everything would appear. But one would have to go back over everything to discover it in its enchantment.

Notes

1. (Capitalization of words in the English translation follows the usage in the original French text.—Tr.)
2. Page references following the quotations from Plato are to Lane Cooper's translation of the *Symposium* in his *Phaedrus, Ion, Gorgias, and Symposium, with passages from the Republic and Laws* (London: Oxford University Press, 1938).
3. (*Démon* is translated here as 'daimon,' from the Greek for a tutelary divinity, a spirit.—Tr.)

Feminism and Aristotle's Rational Ideal

Marcia L. Homiak*

Several years ago, as part of a meeting of the Society for Women in Philosophy, I was asked, along with two other feminist philosophers working on canonical male figures in the history of philosophy, to participate in a panel entitled 'What's a Nice Girl like Me Doing in a Place like This?' The title reflected the organizers' view that there was something politically suspect about feminists working on established male figures—and something particularly suspect in this case, where the three philosophers in question (Aristotle, Hobbes, and Kant) were well-known for their benighted views on women.[1] How could we reconcile our commitment to feminism with a scholarly life devoted to the study of philosophers who explicitly describe women as inferior to men, as unfit for the best life available to human beings, as incapable of being full moral agents?[2]

In addition to these long-acknowledged problems regarding women, there have recently come to be other difficulties associated with working on Aristotle, Hobbes, and Kant. With the growing interest in revising and reorganizing the 'canon' of the humanities, so as to include works by and about not only women, but also non-Western and nonwhite peoples, devoting one's scholarly life to the study of Aristotle, Hobbes, and Kant seems to be an even more egregious departure from progressive values and ways of life. For the use and teaching of canonical works, which are predominantly white and male, has encouraged an ignorant and prejudiced view of works, writers, and subject matters outside the canon. Moreover, many of the values associated with canonical works have, historically, been used to

* Marcia L. Homiak, 'Feminism and Aristotle's Rational Ideal', from Louise Antony and Charlotte Witt (eds.), *A Mind of One's Own: Feminist Essays on Reason and Objectivity* (Boulder, Colo.: Westview Press, 1994), 1–17. Reprinted by permission of Westview Press, a member of Perseus Books, LLC.

denigrate and oppress women, nonwhite men, and the uneducated in general.[3] Thus teaching the works of the traditional canon has encouraged not only ignorance and elitism but also sexism and racism.

I have said that the values associated with the traditional canon have historically been used to denigrate women, nonwhite men, and the uneducated. One might think this historical fact renders these values themselves suspect. They may be thought skewed and incomplete or, worse yet, inherently Western, Eurocentric, or masculine. I want to explore one value in particular that is associated with most of Western philosophy and with much of the traditional humanistic canon. I am referring to the value of reason and to the value of exercising one's rational faculties. Aristotle, Kant, and Hobbes each recommend, as the best life available to human beings, a rational life, though each has a different view about what this life requires and includes. I shall discuss only Aristotle's views on these matters, and I shall argue that his picture of the rational life is neither inherently masculine nor inherently exploitative. Instead, I shall claim, his ideal is worthy of emulation by both women and men.

Ethical systems that promote rationality as an ideal have recently come under considerable criticism from feminist scholars. Much of this criticism has been influenced by Carol Gilligan's work comparing girls' and boys' ways of reasoning about ethical questions.[4] In her work *In a Different Voice*, for example, Gilligan suggests that males and females have, in general, different orientations or perspectives toward moral values and moral strategies. Women tend to adopt a 'care' perspective, in which what matters to them is the preservation of relationships and connection with others; men tend to adopt a 'justice' perspective, in which what matters is acting on impartial and universalizable principles. Since relationships are matters of intimacy and personal feeling, the care perspective is associated with a focus on emotion, especially on the altruistic emotions. Since impartial and universalizable principles are a result of reasoned reflection about what to do, where such reflection is carried out without the distractions of emotion and without a prejudiced concern for one's own interests or the interests of specific others, the justice perspective is associated with rationality and with the value of one's status as a rational being capable of such reflection.[5]

Thus the basis of the feminist criticism of rational ideals is that such ideals, in their application to moral questions, ignore the role of emotion and of the nonuniversalizable particularity of human life.[6] But these domains, of emotion and of specific and particular relationships, are the domains historically associated with women. Hence, the rational ideal suggests that the concerns most typical of women's lives are irrelevant to the best human life and to reasoning about what to do. Lawrence Blum has described the type of philosopher whom Gilligan's work has been used to attack, the type Blum calls the 'moral rationalist': 'It is the male qualities whose highest expression he naturally takes as his model. In the same way it is natural for him to ignore or underplay the female qualities as they are found in his society—sympathy, compassion, emotional responsiveness. . . . The moral rationalist philosopher thus both reflects the sexual value hierarchy of his society and indirectly gives it a philosophic grounding and legitimation.'[7] Not only are the concerns of women irrelevant to the rational ideal but they also may be thought to be incompatible with it. If that is so, then the rational ideal suggests that women are not capable of living moral lives.

In effect, the rational ideal suggests that the best human life and a moral life is available only to those who engage in the kind of rational reflection necessary to determine properly how to live. We have seen how such an ideal tends to exclude women's concerns from the moral life, or women themselves from the moral life, if women are thought incapable of the necessary rational reflection. As I have mentioned, the rational ideal can also be taken to exclude other persons whose lives tend not to be associated with the rational. In Aristotle's view, for example, menial laborers are not fit to be citizens of the best state, since Aristotle believes that menial labor is a deterrent to engaging in the rational activity characteristic of human beings. More broadly, the rational ideal can be taken to exclude persons who have been associated with the body and bodily functions rather than with rational activity, however rational activity is to be understood. Oppressive stereotypes of 'inferior' peoples have tended to include images of their lives as determined by what is animal or bodily. This is a way in which the rational ideal can support prejudiced views of nonwhites and uneducated people.

But the fact that the rational ideal has been, or can be, used to exclude particular groups from that ideal does not show that the rational ideal is defective. Even assuming one could establish that particular groups actually possessed the characteristics on which their exclusion was based—for example, that they were more 'physical' or more 'compassionate'[8]—one would have to show that their having these characteristics is incompatible with the rational ideal. And even if it could be shown that having these characteristics is incompatible with living according to the rational ideal, *that* would not be sufficient to show that the rational ideal is suspect or even that it is incomplete. The problem might lie, instead, with the way these 'non-rational' characteristics are being understood. It is possible that, upon examining them carefully, they may not be found worthy of emulation. The rational ideal may emerge as a more attractive model after all.

I want to examine Aristotle's picture of the rational ideal, and to explore its worthiness to serve as a model for a good human life, by looking at three groups that fail, in Aristotle's opinion, to embody the rational ideal. These groups are menial laborers, slaves, and women of varying political status. Once we see how these people fail to embody the rational ideal, we can understand more clearly what we are committed to in living according to that ideal. Then we will be in a better position to determine whether Aristotle's rational ideal is incompatible with the traits of character typically associated with women (for example, with being more caring, more compassionate, more altruistic) and whether it is incompatible with a more 'physical' or 'bodily' life.

I shall argue that his ideal is not incompatible with being altruistic or with performing physical labor. But, I shall claim, if altruistic traits of character and physical work are not themselves to become oppressive, they must include precisely the activities Aristotle describes as rational. I shall treat the compatibility between the rational ideal and physical work relatively briefly, since the main focus of my concern is the relationship between caring for another and being rational, as Aristotle understands it. On the view I shall propose, being caring and compassionate must be expressed within a life lived according to the rational ideal, or else these traits become destructive and unhealthy. To explicate destructive care, I use examples of contemporary women's lives, since they are often structured so as to preclude women from exercising the rational activities Aristotle most valued. Thus some of Aristotle's reservations about women's lives are sustained, though not, of course, for the reasons he offered. If my interpretation of the rational ideal is correct, and the activities Aristotle considers rational are critical components of a nonoppressive life, then we have good reason to embrace his ideal rather than to reject it.

PSYCHOLOGICAL FREEDOM IN ARISTOTLE'S IDEAL STATE

Aristotle recognizes different sociopolitical classes or categories of women and men. These classes are ordered along a spectrum that reflects the different degrees to which individuals have realized the capacities and traits characteristic of human beings, where these capacities and traits are understood to be rational. To the extent that one fails fully to realize these capacities and traits, one fails to be fully human. At the extreme end of this socio-political spectrum, some individuals—namely (natural) slaves—aren't really human beings at all and hence are not women and men, properly speaking.[9] Because they lack crucial rational characteristics, Aristotle thinks they can justifiably be treated differently from other individuals who more completely realize human capacities and traits. There is, in effect, a hierarchical ordering of different human natures, according to which those who completely realize their human nature rule all those who do not or cannot.

In Aristotle's ideal state there are three broad categories of men: citizens; free persons who are not citizens, including artisans, tradesmen, and day laborers[10] (for the sake of convenience, I shall refer to these persons simply as menial or manual laborers); and persons who are neither free nor citizens (slaves). Male citizens spend the major portion of their adult lives in democratic decision-making (after serving in the military when young and before becoming priests when too old). (*Politics* [hereafter *Pol.*] 1329a2–34). They are members of the assembly, members of juries, city officials of various kinds, and so on. They take turns ruling and being ruled (*Pol.* 1332b26–27; 1295b14–27). Ruling is the activity that distinguishes these men from other groups of men in the political community. The suggestion is that through participatory democracy with other citizens like themselves, they alone fully realize their characteristic human rational capacities and traits. These rational powers, associated with the rational part of the soul (*Nicomachean Ethics* [hereafter *EN*] 1139a12), consist of deciding, choosing, discriminating, judging, planning, and so forth (*EN* 1170b10 ff.).[11]

Menial laborers should not, according to Aristotle, be citizens in the best state, presumably because menial labor, in Aristotle's view, impedes the full exercise of one's rational powers (cf. *Pol.* 1277b2–6; 1278a20–21). How is this so? (i) One answer might be that menial labor involves much routine and monotonous work, in which little use is made of choosing, judging, deciding, and discriminating. There is little room for the personal style and self-expression that characterize more interesting and challenging activity. But obviously this need not always be the case. Though the sculptor Pheidias counts as a menial laborer, his work involves highly sophisticated decision-making and discrimination. If his doing manual labor impedes the full expression of his rational powers, it must do so in some other way. (ii) We must consider not only the work Pheidias does but also the conditions under which he does it. Like other menial laborers, Pheidias's decision-making powers are constrained by his need to survive. He must travel to the cities where his skills are needed, and the building projects he oversees must fit the constraints imposed by city officials or private citizens. The exercise of his rational powers is limited by, and therefore dependent upon, other people's decisions and desires. In this way he does not have complete control over his own decisions and actions.

This lack of control is evidenced in at least two ways. First, the fact that Pheidias's decisions and actions are constrained by his need to earn a living may require him to compromise his moral principles. He may be 'compelled' by his superiors (cf. *EN* 1110a25) to act in ways he would not ordinarily choose. His actions are then a combination of the voluntary and the involuntary (*EN* 1110a11–19). Second, even if Pheidias is not required to take 'mixed' actions (*EN* 1110a11), the fact that his decisions and actions are constrained by the desires of others means that he cannot fully express his conception of what is worth sculpting, how it is to be done, and so on. He cannot design and direct the project according to his own ideas of what is interesting and important. He must accommodate his creations to the values of others.[12]

In Aristotle's view, then, the citizen and the menial laborer (in contrast to the citizen and the slave) have the same psychological capacities. What distinguishes them are the circumstances under which they choose and decide. The menial laborer does work that often does not require much decision-making. More important, however, is the fact that the laborer's concern for economic survival constrains his decision-making, in that he does not have complete control over what work he is to do and how it is to be accomplished. On the other hand, a natural slave, in Aristotle's view lacks the very capacity for deliberation and decision (*Pol.* 1260a12). So, presumably, if he were not a slave, he would not be able to control his own life even to the extent that a menial laborer can. A slave acts wholly in the interests of another person; this is why he is not free (*Pol.* 1278b32–37). To the extent that a manual laborer lacks control over his life and must act in accordance with what others desire and require of him, his life is slavish (*Rhetoric* 1367a32–33).

Indeed, to the extent that any person's life is not the product of his own decisions and desires and is overly or improperly dependent on the desires, decisions, and opinions of other people, Aristotle deems that person's life slavish. In the *Nicomachean Ethics*, for example, Aristotle is able to say of various nonvirtuous male citizens in nonideal states that their lives are slavish. Of course, it is difficult to be precise about what constitutes 'too much' or the 'wrong kind' of dependence on others' decisions and desires. Surely every person who is not self-sufficient is dependent on others' actions and decisions. But many forms of dependence that arise from the absence of self-sufficiency are innocuous in that they do not undermine one's status as a rational being. I may not be able to fulfill my desire for hazelnut ice cream if there is no one to make it available to me; however, because I do not produce it myself and must rely on others to do so does not render me unable to make the sorts of decisions that serve to realize my specific rational abilities or the rational abilities I share with other rational beings. What Aristotle wants to avoid, and which he thinks only the virtuous person successfully avoids, is the kind of dependence on others that impedes, rather than encourages and extends, the full realization of one's rational abilities.

Let me illustrate with some examples from the *Nicomachean Ethics.* Aristotle tells us that the inirascible person is slavish in that he is willing to accept insults to himself and to overlook insults to his family and associates (*EN* 1126a7–8). He does not have enough self-esteem to allow himself to get angry at others' ill treatment of himself, his family, and his friends. He lacks confidence in his own judgments and perceptions and will have a tendency to accept the judgments and perceptions of others as correct. Hence, he is apt to allow others to make decisions for him. Flatterers are another example of servile persons (1125a2). They want to improve their position by gaining the favor of more privileged people (*EN* 1127a7–9). To do this, they must accept the correctness of the privileged person's desires and decisions, and thus they must accept a situation in which many of their decisions are, in effect, made for them by others. Flatterers and inirascible people are in a psychological situation analogous to that of skilled menial laborers like Pheidias.

Aristotle describes intemperate people as slavish too, but not because others make decisions for them. Indeed, intemperates may control their lives in just the ways that inirascible people and flatterers do not. They may make their own decisions, and they may be able to implement their decisions without having to accommodate others' preferences and interests. But they misuse their rational powers and undermine their development in that the activities they enjoy make too little use of these powers. Intemperate people enjoy physical sensations rather than the discriminating and choosing that surrounds tasting and touching (*EN* 1118a32–b1). Their psychological situation is like that of menial laborers whose work is routine and monotonous. There is so little decision-making going on that even natural slaves, who lack the powers of deliberation and decision, can experience the intemperate person's enjoyments (*EN* 1177a7).

In contrast to these various slavish types is the male citizen of Aristotle's ideal state. He is different even from a Pheidias who has full control over the specific sculptural projects he is engaged in. On Aristotle's view, not even such a Pheidias would have fully realized his powers of choosing and deciding. The male citizens of Aristotle's ideal state fully realize their characteristic human powers in the political activity of democratic decision-making. They realize their human powers fully in these circumstances because the deliberations involved in democratic decision-making are comprehensive and overarching. Here the exercise of the human powers is not restricted to specific decisions about what statues to sculpt, what materials to use, and so on. Rather, these are higher-level decisions about what is best for the community itself. So they would include decisions about other, more specific activities (cf. *EN* 1094a27). The exercise of the human powers is *generalized* and extended to cover virtually every aspect of human life, including, for example, questions of war and peace, finance, legislation, public works, cultural projects, and sexual matters.[13]

As far as men are concerned, then, we can determine a ranking from the complete human being who is able to actualize his powers fully because he is a politically active citizen of the ideal state, to a slave who cannot actualize the characteristic human powers because he is without them to begin with. In between are various types of incomplete, slavish persons, ranging from wealthy aristocrats (in nonideal states) to manual laborers.

What about the women who are the wives or companions of these different men, the wives of free citizens in the ideal state, the wives of free citizens in nonideal states, the wives of manual laborers, and the female companions of slaves? (I do not discuss unmarried daughters, since, for our purposes, their situations will not differ markedly from those of married women and married female slaves.)

Although Plato seems to have had moderately progressive views about some women (namely, those he thought capable of ruling the state),[14] Aristotle's views on women's nature are, without exception, objectionable. Aristotle claims that free women cannot be fully actualized human beings, no matter what their political status, since they are, like slaves, naturally defective. Although free women do not lack the capacity for deliberation and decision, as slaves do, their capacity for deliberation, Aristotle says, is not 'authoritative' (*Pol.* 1260a13). Women are contrasted with (presumably male, free) children, whose deliberative capacities are merely 'incomplete' (*ateles, Pol.* 1260a14). The deliberative capacity in women, then, we may assume, is permanently stunted. Unlike free, male children, no amount of education and practice in decision-making, and no change in their economic or social circumstances, will enable women to deliberate properly about what is best. They may give too much weight to what is pleasant or to what appears to be good. In effect, a woman may give over the rule of her soul to its non-rational part and thereby endanger the proper functioning of the household (cf. 1254b4 ff).[15] Hence, decisions about what is best must be made for her by men. A free woman's life will always, then, be slavish, since her life is not controlled by her own decisions.

Because natural slaves lack one of the features characteristic of human beings, they cannot, strictly speaking, be human beings, and hence they cannot be women or men—that is, they cannot be adult members of the human species. (I say they cannot 'strictly speaking' be human beings, because it seems clear that Aristotle cannot actually deny that slaves are human beings. This is suggested, for example, by *EN* 1161a34 ff., where Aristotle admits that there can be friendship and justice between masters and slaves 'to the extent that a slave is a human being.'[16]) But despite this species difference between free persons and slaves, it is hard to see the extent to which the life of any free woman is relevantly different, in regard to her departure from the ideal of fully realized human being, from that of a slave (male or female). Although a free woman presumably can deliberate about how best to carry out the decisions of her husband, or father, her actions are ultimately determined by the decisions of free men, as are those of slaves. Perhaps this is why Aristotle does not bother to discuss female slaves in any detail. As far as their legal status is concerned, it is the same as that of male slaves. As far as their psychological status is concerned, it seems no different, relative to the ideal, from that of free women.

IS ARISTOTLE'S IDEAL EXPLOITATIVE OR MASCULINE?

I have sketched a view of psychological freedom in Aristotle, according to which a complete human being is one who fully realizes his characteristically human powers (the powers of judging, choosing, deciding, planning, discriminating, and so on) in the political activity of democratic decision-making. Democratic decision-making is characterized by a political structure that is egalitarian (each citizen participates equally in decision-making) and comprehensive (each citizen participates equally in the same, broad type of decision-making). Citizens participate in decisions about matters that fundamentally affect the course of their lives. These higher-level decisions influence the lower-level decisions individuals make about the specific life-plans they pursue (cf. *EN* 1094a27).

Two questions arise about the life Aristotle admires and recommends. First, does the realization of this ideal life *require* that some segments of the political community exploit the labor of other segments so that they (the exploiters) have time for the decision-making involved in ruling? And, second, is this ideal life inherently masculine? If we answer either question affirmatively, we have good reason to reject Aristotle's recommendations. I think there is a fairly straightforward response to the first question. I shall indicate that briefly here.[17] Most of my attention will be directed to the second question.

Aristotle believes that the realization of the life he admires does require that rulers exploit menial laborers, since he believes that the conditions under which menial labor is performed will involve the laborer in relations of dependence that prevent the full actualization of the rational powers. Hence, rulers cannot be menial laborers. As I have suggested, Aristotle is not crazy to believe this. But it is important to distinguish between a menial life (a life whose main activity is menial labor performed under conditions of dependence) and a life that may involve menial labor but is not restricted to it. Aristotle may be correct to think that a life restricted to menial labor (where such labor can be monotonous, routine, exhausting, and carried out for the sake of an end external to it—housework is a good modern example) will demand little use of the human rational powers and will impede the development of the type of character one needs to exhibit the moral virtues. But surely he would not be correct to think that engaging in some menial labor, as part of a life that is devoted to the full expression of the rational powers, will have a devastating effect upon character. Indeed, as he notes at *Pol.* 1333a9–11: 'Actions do not differ as honorable or dishonorable in themselves so much as in the end and intention of them.'[18] Just as citizens take turns ruling and being ruled, then, they could take their turns at menial labor, while preserving for themselves the type of life that Aristotle considers fully human. Thus, as far as I can tell, the best kind of life, from Aristotle's point of view, does not require, even given his views about the dangers of menial labor, that some persons take up lives of menial labor to provide the necessities for others who live political lives.[19]

I have considered whether the ideal described by Aristotle is necessarily exploitative. I have argued that if citizens determine how the menial labor is to be carried out, they will not involve themselves in the dehumanizing relations of dependence Aristotle found so objectionable. And if the menial labor is distributed among the citizens in ways so as not to absorb much of any one citizen's time, then there is no reason to think that the possible monotomy of some menial labor will impede the continuing exercise of the human rational powers.

One point should perhaps be emphasized. Aristotle's citizens enjoy the complete exercise of the human rational powers that participation in ruling provides. Therefore they want to avoid both the slavishness of a menial life and the slavishness of a Pheidian life. For, as we have seen, Pheidias's life, though involving sophisticated and subtle uses of the human powers, remains seriously limited and incomplete. Just as Aristotle is not crazy to think that a life of routine menial labor is incompatible with his rational ideal, so too he is not crazy to think that a 'physical' life of the Pheidian type is also defective and incomplete. But this does not commit Aristotle to the view that physical activity itself is dehumanizing. There is nothing to prevent Aristotle's democratic decision-makers from being artisans and trades-people, as well as farmers and warriors.

I now consider the second issue I raised above—that is, the issue of whether Aristotle's ideal is masculine, and, if so, whether this is reason to reject it. I take it that the ideal is considered masculine because the life considered most worth living is the life in which the characteristic human powers, considered as rational powers, are fully realized. Since, as I suggested at the outset, reason and rational deliberation have, in the history of Western thought, been associated primarily with men, and since the non-rational (which includes passions, emotions, and feelings, all of which are thought to have some relation to the body) have been associated with women, to recommend a way of life that praises and prizes reason over all else is implicitly at least to denigrate what has traditionally been associated with women. And, historically, to accept a view that prizes and praises reason above all else provides room not only for sexist views but also for racist views—views that denigrate other peoples because they have traditionally been thought more bodily or more physical than white males. Indeed, we have seen this tendency to be true of Aristotle, whose view of slaves and women as less than fully rational enables him to justify their low status in the political community.

I want to consider whether Aristotle's view of the rational, in particular, requires a devaluation of the non-rational side of the human being. This might be true if his view were a simple one, in which reason 'rules' in some straightforward way over the passions, emotions, and feelings. But his view is not simple. I shall suggest, instead, that in Aristotle's virtuous person, the proper development of the non-rational side of the person can be seen to constrain and limit the operations of the rational side. In effect, it is as if to say that the rational part of the virtuous person's soul cannot work properly unless it is properly guided by the non-rational part.

Both Plato and Aristotle insist that the non-rational part of the soul (which includes appetites, feelings, emotions, and passions) must be educated—in the case of Plato, before one can begin to think sufficiently abstractly ultimately to see the Form of the Good, and, in the case of Aristotle, before one can learn how to deliberate properly about the contents of the best life (before, that is, one can acquire practical wisdom). For Aristotle, many of the individual virtues involve feeling or responding in the appropriate way. For example, it is a vice to take too much pleasure in eating, drinking, and sexual activity; it is also a vice to take insufficient pleasure in these activities. It is a vice to get too angry, or angry at the wrong times, or angry toward the wrong persons, and so on. But it is also a vice not to get angry or to exhibit anger at all, or not to do so when the situation is appropriate for anger. It is a vice to feel too much fear or not enough, or to feel it on the wrong occasions or toward the wrong persons. Reason, by itself, cannot create these feelings; nor can reason, by itself, destroy them. If reason could create or destroy feelings, then Aristotle would not be faced with the problem of *akrasia* (*EN* VII.1–3). Thus the first things to note about Aristotle's rational ideal are that it does not involve the suppression of feeling and emotion and passion and that if reason does rule over passion, its rule does not consist either in producing or in destroying passion. Nor does it consist simply in offering some general directives to the non-rational side of the soul, since there are no rules or rational guidelines for determining how much of an emotion or feeling is appropriate in different situations (*EN* 1109b21–24).

More important, however, is the psychological basis for all the different virtues. I have argued elsewhere[20] that they can be viewed as expressions of what Aristotle calls true self-love. The virtuous person is characterized by a love of what is most himself—that is, by a love of the exercise of the human rational powers, where these are the powers of judging, choosing, deciding, and discriminating that I have listed before (*EN* 1168b34–1169a3; cf. 1168a7–9 and 1170b10 ff.). In enjoying the exercise of his rational powers, the true self-lover enjoys rational activity in general rather than a particular kind of rational activity. His life is therefore broadly based; it is not devoted to the pursuit of specialized goals or to the completion of specialized projects. The true self-lover enjoys the intricacies and subtleties of different intellectual endeavors and also the intricacies and subtleties of endeavors not considered intellectual: he enjoys playing, or watching, a good game of baseball or tennis; he delights in telling a story others will appreciate or in finding just the right gift for a special occasion; he enjoys pleasing and benefiting his friends.

In loving what is characteristic of himself, the virtuous person enjoys who he is and what he can do. His self-love is thus a kind of self-esteem and self-confidence. But as my examples of self-expression have indicated, true self-love is to be distinguished from the self-love that we associate with selfishness and that we normally condemn (*EN* IX.8). Given that the virtuous person enjoys rational activity in a general way, he is able to take pleasure both from the exercise of his own rational powers and from others' exercise of these powers.

The self-love Aristotle admires becomes even more generalized and more stable when a person exercises the human rational powers in political activity where decision-making is shared and evenly distributed. Self-love is more generalized because its source, the exercise of the human rational powers, is now extended to cover comprehensive, higher-level decisions, as well as decisions about activities specific to one's own life. And because the decision-making has been extended in this way, it is flexible and less vulnerable to changes in circumstance and fortune than a more specialized exercise of rational activity would be. Democratic decision-makers can adjust to changes in circumstance and can redirect the use of their abilities to meet these changes. Hence the more stable and continuous their self-esteem will be. But for someone whose decision-making powers have been focused on a particular activity, self-esteem is tied to the success of that particular activity. Hence, this person's self-esteem is precarious and easily upset. This person is like Aristotle's professional soldiers who, though (improperly) confident from past success, turn and run when circumstances are against them (*EN* 1116b15–17).

The enjoyment that a person takes in who he is and in what he does, though its source and basis is the exercise of the rational powers, is not itself an instance of such exercise. Although enjoyment may be produced by rational deliberation, the pleasure taken in rational deliberation, like the enjoyment we take in any other activity, is non-rational. This affects the extent to which my enjoyment can be altered by rational deliberation, even if rational deliberation is what I enjoy and even if that deliberation produces *rational desires* for what I enjoy. When, for example, I want to play tennis because I enjoy it, I desire to play because I find it pleasant, not because I believe playing tennis is good for my health. In this sense, my desire to play tennis is non-rational. I might also want to play tennis because I think it is good for my health, and I might have reached this conclusion on the basis of deliberation about what conduces to my good overall. The desire to play tennis that arises from such deliberation is therefore rational, and it can be altered by further such deliberation. If I cease to believe that playing tennis is good for my health, I will cease to *want* to play tennis for that reason. My newly acquired beliefs produce a rational aversion to tennis. But no such deliberations will undermine my general non-rational desire to play tennis. If I somehow come to believe (correctly) that I no longer enjoy playing tennis, my having that belief is an indication that I have already stopped liking tennis. In this case, my beliefs do not produce my non-rational aversion. It comes about in some other way. The same holds for my non-rational enjoyment of rational activity itself, which, on Aristotle's view, accounts for my having self-love.

On the assumption, then, that Aristotle's virtues require self-love and that they can be understood as different ways in which self-love is expressed, being virtuous is importantly a matter of having one's non-rational desires properly structured. Without the appropriate background of non-rational desire, the agent will not perceive correctly the nature of situations calling for practical decision and action and will thus respond in ways that Aristotle describes as non-virtuous rather than virtuous. Aristotle's notoriously vague remarks at *EN* 1144a34–36 are consistent with the idea that the structure of one's non-rational desires crucially affects one's ability to perceive practical situations correctly: '[The highest end and the best good] is apparent only to the good person; for vice perverts us and produces false views about the origins of actions.'

There is a second aspect to the role of the non-rational desires in Aristotle's conception of virtue. The enjoyment taken in the expression of the human powers in cooperative democratic activity not only produces a stable self-confidence; it also produces stable feelings of friendship between the parties involved in the decision-making. Feelings of friendship arise from the fact that the democratic activity is self-expressive, that it is beneficial to the parties engaged in it, and that it is itself enjoyable (*Rhet.* 1381a30 and *EN* 1168a7–9). Friendship includes a care and concern that friends have for each other for each other's own sake (*EN* 1155b31), a tendency to rejoice and take pleasure in each other's good fortune, and a tendency to help when friends need assistance (*EN* IX.4). Feelings of friendship are maintained over time by continuing the activities that originally produced them or the comparable activities that have come to sustain them. Like enjoyment itself, friendly feelings are not produced by beliefs about what is best or about what contributes to my overall good. They thus belong to the non-rational part of the soul.

In the case of democratic decision-making, the relevant feelings of friendship are particularly stable. A combination of factors explains why this is so. First, the feelings of friendship are produced by a form of self-expression that is especially enduring in that it is overarching and generalized. They are not the product of the expression of some contingent features of the self that might disappear in a change of circumstance or fortune. Hence, the friendship is not 'coincidental' and easily dissolved (*EN* 1156a14–21). Second, the democratic decision-makers share their most basic values and goals in that they are committed to engaging in cooperative activities that promote and sustain the development and exercise of the human powers (cf. *Pol.* 1280a31–34). Thus each decision-maker can view the deliberations of the others as expressions of his thinking and reasoning self (*EN* 1168b34–1169a3). Deliberators identify with each other's decisions and actions, so that each deliberator's actions become the expression of the others' rational activity. This form of self-expression, now even more generalized, is especially enduring. Citizens in the ideal state are thus tied together by feelings of friendship that are long lasting and strong.

The care, concern, and sympathetic attachment that partly constitute these ties of friendship encourage a healthy dependence among citizens. Citizens are not uninvolved with each other or contemptuous of each other in the way several of Aristotle's vicious types are (*EN* IV.3). Nor are they overly concerned with others' opinions—that is, concerned in a way that would upset their self-esteem if they were to face criticisms or obstacles. Their concern for each other does not produce a self-destructive dependence; their autonomy does not preclude enduring ties of association. Along with the self-love of virtuous citizens, these ties of friendship will influence what citizens perceive to be central to the type of life they want to maintain. They will not act to jeopardize the activities and relationships they value and enjoy.

In summary, citizens' understanding of what is best to do, their rational deliberations about how to live and act, take place within the limits imposed by educated passions and feelings. They take place within the limits imposed by a stable selfesteem that derives from an enjoyment in rational activity and within the limits imposed by strong ties of friendship that involve care and concern for other citizens for their own sakes. If this is a rational ideal, it is one in which the proper operation of reason is guided and constrained by feeling and emotion, that is, by the nonrational side of the soul.

FEMINISM AND REASON

I have argued that Aristotle offers a picture of a rational ideal that does not exclude the emotions, passions, and feelings. In particular, the proper operation of reason is limited and constrained by the specific feelings constitutive of true self-love and civic friendship. In describing this ideal, I have not discussed the nature of the actual deliberations virtuous persons will make in specific practical contexts. But it is reasonable to suppose that virtuous persons will recognize the importance of producing and sustaining true self-love and stable ties of civic friendship that are based on enduring features of the self. When citizens come to decide how best to govern their city, these values, one would think, would be paramount in their deliberations. Specific decisions would be made with a commitment to, and appreciation of, the critical role these values play in the lives of every citizen. This does not mean that all civic decisions will be made from an 'impartial' perspective, where that is taken to imply that a consideration of the specific circumstances of particular individuals is inappropriate. Nor does it mean that deliberating from such a perspective is never appropriate.

I now want to discuss in more detail the nature of the care and concern I have attributed to Aristotle's virtuous citizens. For it is 'care and concern' that have come to be associated with feminist ethics and women's moral experience, where such care includes an interest in preserving relationships and commitments to others. In feminist ethics, an interest in applying impartial rules or comprehensive principles becomes secondary.

Assuming it is true that women's moral experiences focus more on questions of care and on preserving relationships and commitments, ought we to accept these experiences as a general model for our behavior toward others or as a more specific model of our moral behavior? What type of care and concern is appropriate? Is care and concern always to be preferred over more emotionally detached ways of relating to others?[21]

The care and concern that constitutes a virtuous citizen's friendship with other citizens resembles in important ways the care that Aristotle's 'complete friends' have for each other. Complete friends, according to Aristotle, are virtuous, know each other well, and spend much of their time together in shared activities (*EN* IX.10). As a result, it is not possible to have many complete friends, whereas political (or citizen) friendship holds among many. Yet, even though citizen friendship and complete friendship have different characteristics, it is not hard to see a resemblance between them in regard to the care that the friends extend toward each other. For though citizen friends may not know each other to the extent that complete friends do, and though they might not spend much time together, they know each other well enough to know that they share the major aims and values that guide the decisions and practices of their community. Citizen friends perceive each other as Aristotle's complete friends do, that is, as 'another oneself' (*EN* 1166a32), meaning that they value and enjoy about each other what they value and enjoy about themselves. They take pleasure, for example, in the exercise of each other's rational powers as they do in their own. In this way they are like each other and take enjoyment in the exercise of the powers they share. Each is, then, a self-lover who takes pleasure in the self-love of the other, since the exercise of self-love in one is like the exercise of self-love in the other. Their ties of friendly feeling are firm and strong and long lasting because they are grounded in the pleasure they take in who the other is as a realized human being.

The care and concern they have for each other comes from the affection that arises from their sharing in each other's rational activity. That is, they share overarching and higher-level interests and goals, and they each participate in the activities associated with these higher-level interests. This does not mean that they share each specific interest and desire.[22] The contents of their individual life-plans might be surprisingly divergent. But each has an individual plan that realizes the human powers in a specific way, and this fact is a source of enjoyment for them. So each takes an interest in the other's interests, rejoices in the other's successes, grieves with the other's losses, and so on.

None lives through the lives of the others or acquires a basis for self-esteem and self-confidence through the activities of the others. Each is independent in the sense that each enjoys the activities in her individual life-plan as well as the higher-level activities her plan shares with the plans of her friends. None is dependent on the praise and admiration of specific individuals for the maintenance of self-love, so each can endure the loss of particular friendships. Aristotle's citizens are likely to be involved in a number of relationships, since their shared general commitments and goals give them a basis for association and affection. Their emotional eggs are not all in one basket, and hence their sense of their own value and importance is not undermined by the loss of specific relationships.

The care they extend to others, then, in times of difficulty and need, is not likely to involve a sacrifice of what they take to be valuable for the sake of someone else. Care does not take the form of altruistic action, where this is thought to require self-denial or a willingness to meet another's needs without consideration for one's own. Thus, among Aristotle's citizens, one would not find relations of unhealthy dependence in which some gain a sense of their own worth only through the assistance they give to others.[23]

But in our contemporary, non-Aristotelian socioeconomic circumstances, women who live with men are often in precisely this position of unhealthy dependence in regard to them. Given the still prevailing ideology, which does not consider it deplorable that most employed women have low-paying, dead-end jobs and even that some women choose to remain unemployed, women tend to find themselves in positions of low self-esteem. Even if they are employed, they are usually economically dependent on men.[24] This dependence undermines the realization of their decision-making powers in various ways. Important family decisions, for example, are often left up to the men on whom women depend. Even women's decision-making authority over matters connected with child care and household maintenance is upset by the extent to which the market has successfully penetrated the household. Many household decisions are now made for women by men through commercials in which men promote one product or another. Women are thought to be good (that is, easily manipulated) consumers, and most commercials are directed toward women, because women often lack the self-esteem necessary to make their own decisions about how to provide the proper physical environment for their families.[25]

These problems apply to the emotional environment as well. In the context of unequal economic power, whatever care and compassion is extended to family members is likely to be distorted and unhealthy. Since family relationships are often the only means through which women obtain a sense of their own worth, preserving these relationships may take place at the cost of encouraging psychologically harmful ways of treating family members. Care within the context of unequal power relations can generate more harm than good.

In such circumstances, where the preservation of a relationship may take priority over the content of the relationship, kindness and emotional supportiveness may be offered when other emotional responses might be more appropriate. Women in these circumstances, for example, may tend not to show anger, at least toward those family members with power and control over decision-making. Women may get angry at children, since this anger does not threaten the relationships that sustain women's sense of self-worth. But women in subordinate circumstances who have little self-confidence will be much less likely to feel that they are in a position to judge adult male family members. But a belief that another has acted wrongly or improperly is part of what provokes anger; therefore, to feel angry, one must have at least enough self-esteem to be able to judge another's actions as improper.[26] But judging another in this way is difficult for persons who have survived their oppressive circumstances by encouraging calm relations with those who have power over them. A lack of confidence in their own assessments will make them tend to accept the judgments and perceptions of others as correct, just as Aristotle's inirascible persons do. Kindness in such circumstances would seem only to sustain inequality, to obscure recognition of what is best, and to undermine further the decision-making powers of the person who shows kindness.[27] In these ways, care within the context of unequal power relations can harm both the person who gives it and the person to whom it is given.

These examples suggest that altruistic actions can be damaging when undertaken in circumstances in which the altruistic person lacks self-esteem. By showing kindness and compassion when other responses might be more appropriate, the kind person can act to sustain oppressive and unhealthy ways of relating to others. Through kindness, the kind person can make the acquisition of self-esteem even more difficult. Kindness seems least likely to damage oneself or another, however, when it is offered from a position of healthy independence. But healthy independence is precisely the psychological condition of Aristotle's virtuous person, who has true self-love. Because such a person has the appropriate confidence in who he is, he need not live through the achievements of another. This kind of dependent relationship will not be of interest to him, and he will not feel the need to act in ways to develop and sustain such a relationship. If kindness can be thought of as a concern for another's good for that person's own sake and as a willingness to act to contribute to that good, then Aristotle's virtuous person will act kindly, because this is the attitude he has toward fellow citizens. Yet Aristotle's virtuous citizen knows that another's good is not equivalent simply to what another wants. He knows that another's good includes the performance of activities that will nurture and sustain the other's self-love. So Aristotle's virtuous citizen recognizes that showing concern for another's good for the other's own sake may take all sorts of forms, only some of which will look like mere behavioral niceness.

I have been suggesting that if compassion and a concern for relationships constitutes some kind of model or ideal, it is not a simple one according to which we simply act to preserve the relationship or act to help another achieve what he might want. If compassion and concern are directed toward another's good for that person's sake, then for them to be proper objects of an ideal, they must operate against the background of some sound recognition of what another's good consists in. If not, compassion and concern can serve to promote oppressive or destructive relationships. Moreover, if the compassionate person is an ideal, she must be someone whose concern for another is ungrudging and noninstrumental. Aristotle's virtuous person is most likely to offer that kind of concern, since she is secure enough in who she is not to begrudge others' successes and not to rejoice spitefully in others' losses.

Aristotle's ideal has been considered masculine because it deems the best life to be that which fully realizes the rational powers characteristic of human beings. I have argued that Aristotle's emphasis on rational powers should not deter anyone, particularly feminists, from embracing his model. Although Aristotle organizes the best life around the pleasures of rational activity, this does not commit him to a model in which the non-rational is suppressed or even subordinated. As I have argued, the realization of the virtuous person's rational powers is constrained by properly educated non-rational feelings and emotions. Moreover, Aristotle offers a way to explain how reason and emotion (and passion and feeling) can operate together to produce psychologically strong and healthy individuals—individuals who take pleasure from their own lives and from the lives of others, who are caring and concerned but not in ways that are destructive of their own self-esteem, who are independent while retaining strong and enduring ties of friendship and relationship. He offers us a view of compassion and care that is positive and constructive, not oppressive and debilitating.

There are various ways in which reason can be offered as an ideal. I think Aristotle's model of how to organize one's life around the pleasures of rational activity is worthy of emulation by both men and women.[28]

Notes

1. The title also suggests that the organizers thought it appropriate, even in this special context, to refer to the three of us as 'girls.' I leave aside the problems associated with the use of this term in relation to adult women.
2. For Aristotle's views on women, see *Generation of Animals* 728a17 ff., 732a1 ff., 775a15; *Nicomachean Ethics* [hereafter *EN*] 1162a19–27; *Politics* [hereafter *Pol.*] 1259b28–1260a24, 1277b20. For Kant, see *Observations on the Feeling of the Beautiful and Sublime*, sec. 3. For Hobbes, see *Leviathan*, chs. 19–20.
3. For a useful discussion of these issues, see Elizabeth V. Spelman, *Inessential Woman: Problems of Exclusion in Feminist Thought* (Boston: Beacon Press, 1988), esp. ch. 5.
4. See Carol Gilligan, *In a Different Voice: Psychological Theory and Women's Development* (Cambridge, Mass.: Harvard University Press, 1982). In her more recent writings, Gilligan has softened her position, to claim that though women can have the 'justice' perspective as well as the 'care' perspective, men are more likely to have only the 'justice' perspective. See 'Adolescent Development Reconsidered,' in *Mapping the Moral Domain*, ed. C. Gilligan, J. V. Ward, and J. McLean Taylor (Cambridge, Mass.: Harvard University Press, 1988). For the influence of Gilligan's work on moral theory, see Lawrence Blum, 'Gilligan and Kohlberg: Implications for Moral Theory,' *Ethics* 98, 3

(1988): 472–491; and Eva Feder Kittay and Diana T. Meyers, eds., *Women and Moral Theory* (Totowa, N.J.: Rowman and Littlefield, 1987). For a different approach to these issues, see Owen Flanagan and Kathryn Jackson, 'Justice, Care, and Gender: The Kohlberg–Gilligan Debate Revisited,' *Ethics* 97, 3, (1987): 622–637.

5. See, for example, John Rawls's account of the principles of justice as chosen in special circumstances of rational deliberation in *A Theory of Justice* (Cambridge, Mass.: Harvard University Press, 1971).
6. For a discussion of the role of 'particularity' in the moral life, see Lawrence Blum, 'Moral Perception and Particularity,' forthcoming in *Ethics* 101 (1991): 701–725, and the works cited therein.
7. Lawrence Blum, 'Kant's and Hegel's Moral Rationalism: A Feminist Perspective,' *Canadian Journal of Philosophy* 12 (1982): 296–297.
8. Claudia Card questions whether it is appropriate to associate care and compassion more with women than with men, and offers some helpful criticisms of the care perspective in 'Women's Voices and Ethical Ideals: Must We Mean What We Say?' *Ethics* 99, 1 (1988): 125–135. See also Catherine G. Greeno and Eleanor E. Maccoby, 'How Different Is the "Different Voice"?' and Carol Gilligan's reply in *Signs* 11, 2 (1986): 310–316.
9. For considerations in favor of the view that even natural slaves are men and women for Aristotle, see W.W. Fortenbaugh, 'Aristotle on Slaves and Women,' in *Articles on Aristotle*, vol. 2, ed. Jonathan Barnes, Malcolm Schofield, and Richard Sorabji (London: Duckworth, 1977), p. 136.
10. For an enumeration of the various different types of non-citizens in Aristotle's ideal state and for a discussion of their legal status, see David Keyt, 'Distributive Justice in Aristotle's *Ethics* and *Politics*,' *Topoi* 4 (1985): 23–45.
11. What to make of Aristotle's views in *EN* X.7–8 and how to integrate them into the rest of the *EN* and *Pol.* are not matters I shall discuss here. I shall be concerned only with Aristotle's broadly based view of human good, which includes the goods of social, political, and family life (*EN* 1097b8–11), as well as various intellectual goods.
12. It should be clear that Aristotle's implied and stated reservations about manual labor are not dissimilar from some of Marx's criticisms of wage labor under capitalism, in particular, from Marx's view that such labor alienates the worker from the activity of production and from his species-being. See *The Economic and Philosophic Manuscripts of 1844*, in vol. 3 of Karl Marx and Friedrich Engels, *Collected Works* (New York: International Publishers, 1971–1978), pp. 274–277, and *Communist Manifesto*, vol. 6 of *Collected Works*, passim.
13. I discuss the nature of these higher-level decisions in more detail in 'Politics as Soul-Making: Aristotle on Becoming Good,' *Philosophia* 20, 1–2 (July 1990): 167–193.
14. For a helpful discussion of Plato's views on women, see Julia Annas, 'Plato's *Republic* and Feminism,' *Philosophy* 51 (1976): 307–321; and her *Introduction to Plato's Republic* (Oxford: Clarendon Press, 1981), pp. 181–185.
15. Fortenbaugh draws a similar conclusion in 'Aristotle on Women and Slaves,' p. 138.

16. I use the translation by Terence Irwin of Aristotle's *Nicomachean Ethics* (Indianapolis: Hackett Publishing, 1985).
17. I follow, in broad outline, the more detailed argument for the same conclusion offered by Terence Irwin in *Aristotle's First Principles* (Oxford: Clarendon Press, 1988), pp. 411–416.
18. As translated by B. Jowett in the Revised Oxford Translation, vol. 2, ed. Jonathan Barnes (Princeton, N.J.: Princeton University Press, 1984).
19. It is not clear that one could provide the same type of argument for Plato. This is in part, I think, because the content of the good life is less well articulated in Plato than in Aristotle and also because, however we are to understand the content of the good life, it does not include democratic decision-making as a good in itself. For the philosopher-rulers, ruling is a burden they would prefer to be without, since they would prefer to be without the responsibilities and activities that take them away from a continual contemplation and love of the Forms. They accept the burdens of ruling only because there is no other way to replicate the beauty they see in the Forms. Although it is best for the state as a whole that they rule, their interest in ruling is purely instrumental. And since menial labor is often monotonous and routine, requiring little use of the rational powers, it would be inefficient for rulers to take it up. It is therefore better left to others.
20. In 'Virtue and Self-Love in Aristotle's Ethics,' *Canadian Journal of Philosophy* 11, 4 (December 1981): 633–651, and in 'The Pleasure of Virtue in Aristotle's Moral Theory,' *Pacific Philosophical Quarterly* 66, 1–2 (January–April 1985): 93–110.
21. See Card, 'Women's Voices and Ethical Ideals'; Greeno and Maccoby, 'How Different Is the "Different Voice"?'
22. For a related discussion, see Sharon Bishop, 'Love and Dependency,' in *Philosophy and Women*, ed. S. Bishop and M. Weinzweig (Belmont, Calif.: Wadsworth, 1979), pp. 147–154.
23. Cf. Nancy Chodorow's description of healthy dependence in 'Family Structure and Feminine Personality,' in *Woman, Culture, and Society*, ed. Michelle Rosaldo and Louise Lamphere (Stanford, Calif.: Stanford University Press, 1974), pp. 43–66, esp. pp. 60–63; and in *The Reproduction of Mothering: Psychoanalysis and the Sociology of Gender* (Berkeley: University of California Press, 1978), pp. 211 ff.
24. For current wage differentials between full-time working women and men, see U.S. Department of Labor, *Employment and Earnings: July 1987* (Washington, D.C.: Government Printing Office, 1987).
25. See Margaret Benston, 'The Political Economy of Women's Liberation,' in *Feminist Frameworks*, 2d ed., ed. Alison Jaggar and Paula Rothenberg (New York: McGraw-Hill, 1984), pp. 239–247, esp. pp. 244–245.
26. For further discussion of anger in the context of unequal power relations, see Elizabeth V. Spelman, 'Anger and Insubordination,' in *Women, Knowledge, and Reality*, ed. Ann Garry and Marilyn Pearsall (Boston: Unwin Hyman, 1989), pp. 263–273; and Friedrich Nietzsche, *On the Genealogy of Morals*, tr. Walter Kaufman and R. J. Hollingdale (New York: Vintage, 1967), passim.
27. For more discussion of these and related points, see L. Blum et al., 'Altruism

and Women's Oppression,' in Bishop and Weinzweig, eds., *Philosophy and Women*, pp. 190–200; and John Stuart Mill, *On the Subjection of Women* (Cambridge: MIT Press, 1970), ch. 2.

28. I am grateful to David Copp, Jean Hampton, Janet Levin, and the editors of this volume for helpful comments on earlier versions of this paper.

5 Therapeutic Arguments and Structures of Desire

Martha Nussbaum*

We all know that society influences our thinking and our behavior in many ways. But we frequently imagine that we also inhabit a pre-societal realm of 'nature,' and that our desires and emotions derive from that realm. This way of thinking was very much encouraged by romanticism, but it has older roots; it was alive, indeed, in the ancient Greek world. Greeks liked to talk about erotic passion as something that grows in us 'by nature,' and to refer to the compulsions of nature in explication of their sexual conduct.[1] The contrast between nature and convention, in the Greek world very much as in our own, was used to mark certain things as unchangeable and off-limits, other things as more superficial and potentially more mutable.[2]

On the other hand, in the ancient Greek world as in our own, there were also challenges to the naturalizing of emotion and desire. Philosophical arguments, some very powerful, began to question the idea that either emotions such as anger and fear or bodily desires such as sexual desires and the desire for food were simply innate and biological, unshaped by cultural forces. The paper reprinted here is an attempt to begin mining the ancient arguments for what they might yield for our contemporary debates. As such, it is part of a larger and more detailed historical inquiry,[3] and also of a more detailed philosophical inquiry in which I sort out my own position on the issues raised in the historical texts.[4] Here, then, I shall only make a few observations about distinctions that I think need to be observed and questions that need to be asked.

First, it is important to distinguish explananda of different types, and, in particular, to distinguish appetites from emotions. I believe

* Martha Nussbaum, 'Therapeutic Arguments and Structures of Desire', from Julie K. Ward (ed.), *Feminism and Ancient Philosophy* (New York and London: Routledge, 1996), 195–216. Original version in *Differences*, 2/1 (Pembroke Center for Teaching and Research on Women, Brown University). Reprinted by permission of the author and the publisher.

that these are logically distinct categories, although interrelated in complicated ways. The ancient Greek Stoics seem to me to have done better with these distinctions than the Epicureans, on whom I focus in this paper. Sexual desire probably involves both appetite and emotion, and one way of looking at Lucretius' proposal is that it attempts to separate the two components, preserving the first and eliminating the second.

Second, we should observe that positions that have been advanced in the area of 'social construction' differ over two questions: (1) What is the origin of emotions and desires? (2) Is an emotion such as fear, or anger, or sexual desire, a single thing, or are there many different forms of human emotion and desire in different times and places, exhibiting no fixed 'essence'? The answers to the two questions are connected in many complex ways. A person who holds that e.g., fear is genetic in origin is likely to be an 'essentialist' on the second question, reasoning that human biology remains relatively stable across place and time; and yet she may readily concede that behavior expressing fear will in many ways be shaped by culture. The person who holds that basic emotion categories are socially shaped is likely to recognize a diversity of forms of emotional organization with no single 'essence'—although, as my paper argues, this may also not be so, since there might turn out to be some reason why human societies all organize things in a very similar way. Getting clear about these two questions and their interrelations is a very important part of making progress on the issue.

Third, we should insist that there are several different levels on which claims of biological or social origin may be made. To focus on sexual love, my central topic in the article, at least five different areas of our life with respect to love call forth these competing forms of explanation.

(1) Custom and norms regarding the proper expression of sexual love—what acts one chooses, what partners are acceptable.
(2) Norms regarding the nature and morality of sexual conduct and emotion themselves—whether, for example, they are understood as intrinsically sinful and morally problematic.
(3) Norms regarding what is desirable in a sexual partner: body shape, features, dress, and so forth.
(4) The basic sexual categories into which erotic agents are divided, categories such as 'the heterosexual,' 'the homosexual.'
(5) The membership of particular individuals in one category rather than another.

Notice that even a hard-core biological determinist is likely to accept a large role for social construction in (1), and possibly in (2) and (3). More controversial will be (4) and (5), where the claim of social construction bites deeper. On the whole, the Hellenistic philosophers are social constructionists with respect to (4). They hold, that is, that our basic emotion categories, categories such as fear, anger, love—and also many subcategories of agent within that—are social artifacts, and may be undone by philosophical teaching. Stoics may even hold this position about gender itself; at any rate, it is clear that they treated gender as a morally irrelevant attribute on par with national origin, and as one that would be minimized in the ideal city, by a scheme of unisex clothing, and by the continual teaching that our real identity is that of rational personhood, which is, it would seem, not gendered.[5] Hellenistic philosophers have little to say about (5), since they have little interest in child development. Presumably they would need to invoke some combination of social and parental conditioning to explain the emotional repertory that the individual comes to have.

Fourth, we must carefully distinguish between the naturalness of a phenomenon, in the sense of its biological or innate origin, and its goodness. The fact that something is 'natural' has often been invoked to show that it is good. But of course it shows no such thing, without further premises about the providential design about nature. Many things, such as diseases, are 'natural' and bad; many things are man-made and good. The Greek *nomos–phusis* debate was already well aware of this, but some of our modern arguments have not always taken the point.

Finally, we should carefully distinguish between the question of social construction and the question of mutability. The fact that a phenomenon is biological in origin does not mean we are stuck with it forever. Diseases can sometimes be cured. The fact that a phenomenon is social in origin does not mean we can change it at will or easily. Seneca is aware that eradicating anger in a society, or even in an individual, will require a lifetime of patient continual effort, and that even such effort may prove unsuccessful, given the recalcitrance of habit. On the other hand, recognizing the nature of the phenomenon with which we are dealing does show us how we might alter it if we should want to alter it. So, as the Hellenistic philosophers thought, good philosophical argument on this point can be an agent of human freedom.

—*Martha Nussbaum, August 1995*

I begin with a passage from the ancient Greek Philosopher Epicurus (fourth-third century B.C.E.), who, in his *Letter to Menoeceus*, asked how human beings can be released from certain social and psychological constraints so that they can lead more fruitful human lives. This passage always occasions gasps and embarrassed giggles when I read it to undergraduate audiences; and it is from those giggles that I want to begin this inquiry. The passage goes as follows:

> The truly pleasant life is not produced by an unbroken succession of drinking bouts and revels; not by the enjoyment of boys and women and fish and the other things that a luxurious table presents. It is produced by sober reasoning that seeks out the causes of all pursuit and avoidance and drives out the beliefs that are responsible for our greatest disturbances. (*Letter to Menoeceus* 132)

That is a rather literal translation of the original Greek. I note that the most common translation by a very respectable scholar removes its peculiarities as follows:

> It is not an unbroken succession of drinking bouts and revelry, not sexual love, not the enjoyment of the fish and other delicacies of a luxurious table . . . (R.D. Hicks)[6]

This is an important passage for anyone who is interested in studying the relationship between sexual desire and socially taught beliefs. It is important for two reasons. First, because it gives striking and characteristic evidence of some ancient Greek conceptions of desire and its objects that are strikingly different from our contemporary conceptions and cast light on the status of ours by their difference. Second, because it is part of the argument for a powerful philosophical theory concerning the social origins of desire. This theory holds that many forms of human desire and emotion are grounded in and partly constituted by beliefs that are learned in society—beliefs that might be criticized and even altered, if rational people decide that they are false, silly, or in other ways inimical to human flourishing. The two interests we might have in the passage are closely connected, as it turns out. For the information about historical difference that it reveals offers us strong reasons to accept the philosophical thesis it presents: desire is, at least in part, a social construct.

I

I shall deal with the historical point first. And I shall deal with it rather briefly, since there has recently been a good deal of excellent work along these lines, some examples of which appear elsewhere.[7] But since the articles here focus on particular areas of sexual life in the ancient world, it is still worthwhile providing a general overview of the state of the question.

For years, then, indeed for centuries, the discourse of the ancient world concerning sexual desire was treated by scholars, insofar as they treated it at all, as something at once impenetrably alien and disgustingly familiar. Around the borders of the great silence that surrounded the subject of ancient Greek homosexuality, one heard embarrassed whisperings that revealed two beliefs on the part of the whisperers: first, that it was highly peculiar, almost inconceivable, and surely incomprehensible that this otherwise sensible and even admirable people should accept with equanimity and even praise forms of conduct that Englishmen found thoroughly disgusting; second, that what was being praised in works of Plato and accepted laughingly in comedies of Aristophanes was in fact the very same 'thing' that Englishmen were accustomed to forbid and find disgusting. This was why, in fact, it was thought so very bizarre that the otherwise rational Greeks did not conceal and condemn it. The result of this complex attitude—in a civilization that memorized the arguments of the *Phaedrus* even while putting homosexuals to death by hanging—was denial and embarrassed silence: the silence that is sternly enjoined at the moment in the film of E. M. Forester's *Maurice* when the eager young students are told that they may skip over certain passages in the *Phaedrus* in which they take a lively interest; the silence that is proudly proclaimed in the major scholarly edition of the works of *Catullus* by C. J. Fordyce, published in 1961 by the Oxford University Press, at the beginning of which we are told that 'A few poems which for good reason are rarely read have been omitted.' (When one examines the editor's principle of selection one discovers that poems of a 'heterosexual' and scatological nature are unproblematically included.)

The silence was officially broken in 1978, with the publication of Sir Kenneth Dover's important and first-rate book, *Greek Homosexuality*[8] But Dover, while determined to confront the subject with both tolerance and meticulous scholarship, took over in certain ways a major assumption from previous generations of non-scholarship: namely that there is such a thing as 'Greek Homosexuality'—that is, that the phenomenon lived and described by the Greeks was sufficiently similar to modern-day homosexuality that it made sense to write a continuous history of this 'thing,' homosexuality, and to talk about the ways in which Greek attitudes to 'it' differed from our own. Dover was so determined to bring to light what had been pushed behind the courtliness that it never sufficiently occurred to him to ask whether what had been denied and pushed behind was in fact the same 'thing' at all as what was there to be brought to light by historical inquiry—whether, indeed, there was any one 'thing' at all corresponding to our conception of homosexuality. Dover is a marvelous scholar; his methodological care, his mastery of evidence from many different areas, and his general intellectual acumen make his book an extremely important one, and one from which the reader can learn an enormous amount about cultural differences as well as about putative continuities. Its specific conclusions are by no means invalidated by the philosophic assumptions that I am questioning. Nonetheless, questions of a fundamental kind remained to be asked, and the unity of the phenomena had to be called into question.

More recent scholarship has asked these necessary questions—inspired by the suggestive work of Foucault in *The History of Sexuality*, but by now pressing beyond Foucault's work in historical detail and precision. The essays in this issue give some examples of ways in which younger scholars have been arguing that the ancient discourse about and also the experience of sexual desire and its objects were very different from our own. I can, therefore, simply summarize the general direction of these findings very briefly.[9]

In order to do this, it will be useful to return to our Epicurus passage.

> The truly pleasant life is not produced by an unbroken succession of drinking bouts and revels; not by the enjoyment of boys and women and fish and the other things that a luxurious table presents.

What is it that makes modern undergraduates uneasy and amused here? What is it that makes our respectable translator feel that he has to translate it oddly, in order to make sense of it? It is not only the presence of males alongside females as objects of desire for the male recipient of Epicurus' letter, and the evident absence of any question as to the naturalness or unnaturalness of such enjoyment. That is certainly one thing that is striking about the passage; and it is one of the things that Hicks' translation, with its vague expression 'sexual love,' obscures. But it is surely not the only, or even the primary odd thing. What is odd and amusing above all is the grouping of boys and women together with fish and other delicacies of 'the luxurious table'—as if the problem of sexual appetite was just one part of a general problem of bodily appetite and its management. Epicurus' oddly constructed sentence begins with something that we tend to think of as profound, intimate, defining of our selfhood, and morally problematic in a special way, and ends up with the superficial area of gastronomic choice, as if there were no difference of level or moral intensity between the two spheres. If we attempt to reconstruct what produced a sentence like this, a sentence that was supposed to speak vigorously to the experience of Epicurean pupils from many different backgrounds and social classes, we are led to attribute to Epicurus a general conception of appetitive enjoying that includes eating and drinking along with sexual activity, and does not make a very strong distinction between the two spheres.

The two striking features of this passage—its indifference about the gender of the object of desire and its treatment of sexual desire as just one part of a more general moral problem of appetitive self-control—are in fact characteristic not only of Epicurus' thought elsewhere, but also of a great deal of the discourse about desire in the ancient world. The recent scholarship to which I have alluded has convincingly argued that there was for the ancient Greeks no salient distinction corresponding to our own distinction between heterosexuality and homosexuality: no distinction, that is, of persons into two profoundly different kinds on the basis of the gender of the object they most deeply or most characteristically desire.[10] Nor is there, indeed, anything precisely corresponding to our modern concept of a 'sexuality'—a deep and relatively stable inner orientation towards objects of a certain gender. There are morally salient distinctions in the sexual sphere, certainly, but they lie elsewhere: distinctions between activity and passivity, between controlling and being controlled, and also between being self-controlling and being un-self-controlled. But the moral assessment of persons with respect to their 'sexuality' that is so ubiquitous in the modern world would have seemed to the ancient Greeks peculiar, arbitrary, and unmotivated.

David Halperin has proposed a parallel that will help us to have a vivid sense of this (Halperin, 1990b, 26–27). Imagine, he says, how we would react to a society that divided people into two distinct classes on the basis of their taste, or distaste, for a particular food. To stay close to Epicurus, let us take fish as our example, and let us imagine people divided into the ichthuphages and the non-ichthuphages. Let us, furthermore, imagine these preferences explained by the positing of an 'edility'—a deep inner orientation towards foods of a certain sort that is a fundamental determinant of one's entire identity. Let us suppose that the members of the society in question believe that the ichthuphages are somehow problematic, 'unnatural,' 'queer,' while the others are normal, 'straight,' 'all right.' Let us, finally, imagine that they believe you cannot really know who a person is, deep down, without knowing that. This example seems to show us two things about ourselves. First, it shows us that distinctions that we take to be fundamental, inevitable, and 'natural' might, from some other perfectly reasonable point of view, seem just as factitious, arbitrary, and peculiar as these food distinctions, which we ourselves would readily brand as superstitious and odd. Second, it gives us a way of beginning to imagine how social distinctions that are non-necessary and in some cases arbitrary can, nonetheless, form not only conceptions of desire but the very experience of desire, at a rather deep level. For, to take our fish example, wouldn't the member of the society in question have an experience of eating and food choice that is rather different from our own? Wouldn't the social beliefs, learned from youth and deeply internalized, totally transform the simple pleasure of biting into a grilled salmon, and cause many joyful acts to be hedged round with secrecy, guilt, and anger on the part of some agents, by embarrassment, silence, and worse on the part of others? Asking these questions helps us to begin to ask how, and to what extent, our own experience of sexual desire is informed by our own distinctions, distinctions that a study of ancient Greece shows to be non-necessary, non-natural, and perhaps not even terribly reasonable, obvious, or sensible.

These are complicated historical issues. Much more qualification and distinction-making is required if we are to understand fully how far and in what ways ancient Greek views really are different from our own. As I have said, I shall not attempt to present here the more detailed investigation that would be required. But now I want to use these historical observations to approach my second theme, the central issue of this paper. I have said that the Epicurus passage is part of a powerful argument for a philosophical conception of emotion and desire, a conception that holds that these elements of human life are to a great extent formed by socially learned beliefs, beliefs that can be altered if the participants decide that they are false, confused, or in some other way inimical to human flourishing. It is the primary purpose of this paper to investigate this conception as it was developed by ancient Greek philosophers, especially of the Hellenistic period, to ask about its implications for the analysis of sexual desire, and to see what light it may shed on contemporary debates about the 'social construction of sexuality.'[11]

II

Frequently we speak as if the emotions and desires are timeless ahistorical entities, springing up as parts of an animal level of human nature that is untouched by history and culture. Anger, fear, sexual desire, and many relatives of these are taken in this way to be parts of 'human nature,' parts that have nothing to do with what we have learned to believe as the result of the way in which we have been brought up. This picture of emotion and desire was dominant in Western intellectual circles for a long time, largely on account of the influence of British empiricism and related psychologies. And although it is now under heavy attack from many sides—from philosophy, from anthropology, from psychoanalysis, and even from cognitive psychology[12]—it retains a surprising degree of influence in people's thought and talk about themselves.

Epicurus, and with him almost all major philosophers of the ancient Greek world, had a different view about the emotions. This view is that emotions such as fear, grief, anger, pity, and love rest on, and are in part made up out of, beliefs about the way things are in the world, beliefs in which the value-laden distinctions taught in society are prominent. Take, for example, anger. Anger, as Aristotle, Epicureans, and Stoics all argue, is not a mere animal reaction; it involves an attitude towards an object that is based upon certain beliefs. It requires, that is, the belief that one has been wronged, and wronged in a more than trivial way, by the person at whom the anger is directed. If we were to alter those beliefs—either by showing that the alleged wrong did not take place, or that it was really not important, or that it was not in fact caused by the person in question, we would expect the person's anger at that other person to go away. Even if some residual irritated feeling remains, it does not seem appropriate to call it anger unless it has that complex cognitive structure. Obviously, if this general point is correct, then people's experiences of anger will vary, not only in accordance with their view of the facts as to what has happened to them, but also, and more importantly, with their view about what things are damages and what damages have importance. As the Stoics were fond of pointing out, if we could get people to believe that nothing that could even in principle be damaged by another person is of any importance at all, we would have done away with anger completely.[13]

Much the same appears to be true of other major emotions. Fear, it is argued, requires the belief that there are important damages that one may suffer in the future, in a way that one is powerless to prevent.[14] Once again, one can imagine altering those beliefs. In a particular case, one might become convinced that the impending damage is not at all likely to occur, or that if it does occur it will not be a bad thing. Or one might become convinced that a whole class of possible future events usually thought to be damages are not really such. Or finally—as the Stoics urge—one might become convinced that the only truly important things are one's own thoughts and inner activities of willing. And then, if one believes as well that these inner activities are always fully under one's own control—as, again, the Stoics teach—then there will be no room at all for fear. Indeed, one can see that the changes in belief that remove fear would remove grief and pity as well. For a loss that one fears, looking to the future, is an object of grief when it has taken place. And pity is the other-directed relative of these emotions: for it requires the belief that the suffering of another person is of serious magnitude, and also that the damage or loss is not that person's fault. (For if one thought that it was the person's fault, one would blame and reprove, rather than pity.)[15]

In short, the major emotions seem to this entire philosophical tradition to rest upon a complex family of rather controversial evaluative beliefs, beliefs that can be assessed as either rational or irrational (with respect to the manner of their formation, the evidence on which they rest), and also as either true or false (with respect to their content). They can be examined and criticized by rational arguments, and in many cases they can be altered, if agents decide that the relevant beliefs are false. At this point, the various philosophers part company. For Aristotle holds, on the whole, that these emotions are frequently well-founded, and thus have a valuable role to play in the life of a good person. There are, to be sure, many instances of ill-founded anger and fear, many things (for example, money and reputation) that people care about more than they should and whose loss they therefore fear or resent more than they should. But, he holds, human life does contain possibilities for undeserved reversals of fortune, reversals that are truly serious and that provide good reasons for fear, grief, anger, pity—or, if the changes are good ones, for sudden delight and intense gratitude and passionate love.[16] His Hellenistic successors, the Epicureans and Stoics, deny this. Because they hold that the most important things in human life are always within the agent's own control, they also hold that emotions such as fear, grief, pity, and anger are always groundless, involving a belief in the great importance of that which lies beyond one's own control, and are to be extirpated completely from human life. Their radical ethical position—which requires them to deny the outstanding importance of such highly valued goods as the love of children and spouse, affiliation and activity within a political community, even the opportunity to perform virtuous actions—grounds an equally radical position concerning the emotions.

Emotions, then, are social artifacts, formations in the soul that result from the implantation of belief by society. But what can be implanted can also be examined and assessed. This job, these philosophers argue, is the task of philosophy. And notice that the critical scrutiny of philosophy, successfully performed, will change not only people's beliefs about the emotions. It will change the emotional experience itself. The truly convinced Aristotelian will not experience anger over slights to reputation or losses of wealth. The convinced Epicurean or Stoic will experience no fear at all, and will live in a calm and undisturbed condition. Epicureans defined philosophy as 'the art that secures the happy life by means of reasonings and arguments.'[17] Reasoning does not simply produce intellectual conviction; it changes the life of desire.

This position seems to me to be a powerful one, grounded in an extremely impressive analysis of the emotions in their relation to belief. Nor are the philosophers at all naive when it comes to describing the means by which emotion-grounding beliefs can be altered by philosophical 'therapy.' The emotion-grounding beliefs have been presented to the pupil almost from birth; they are bound to be deeply lodged in the soul, and difficult to dislodge. A one-shot argument might produce superficial assent; but that is very far, these philosophers know, from real, thoroughgoing inner conviction. 'He does not really grant what he professes,' says the Roman Epicurean Lucretius of a person who professes various rational convictions while fearing death in his heart (III. 876). And he characterizes the depth and the frequently subconscious nature of the fear-grounding beliefs by calling them 'silent voices' that speak to the pupil despite her official protestations, and 'hidden goads beneath the heart' that motivate her behaviour 'without conscious awareness' (III. 55–58, III. 873–78, cf. 1053–75). This means that philosophy, if it is to have the power to change such beliefs, will need to be something much more comprehensive than an avocation or a subject of study. It must suffuse the whole of life, constructing (whether in the existing culture or in an alternative community apart from it) an alternative mode of life, in which the frequent repetition of philosophical arguments and a continual practice of self-scrutiny fill up the pupil's daily life, transforming all other activities. Epicureans were asked to live outside of the city, and Epicurus wrote to a prospective pupil: 'Happy youth—take sail, and flee from all culture.' And it seems that the Epicurean teacher asked pupils to divulge thoughts and feelings, in order to receive intense philosophical criticism.[18] The Stoic Seneca reports that at the close of every day he reviews the day's activities critically, in an extended process of self-examination and 'confessions,' while his wife, 'long since familiar with this custom of mine,' waits patiently for him to come to bed (*On Anger* III.36). And the practice of self-scrutiny is central to all of Stoic therapy. In this way, these radical social critics expect that the philosophical arguments can, as Epicurus puts it, 'become powerful' (*Letter to Herodotus* 83), in the soul and life of the pupil, transforming not simply intellectual adherence, but the experience of desire and emotion itself.

So far, I have focused on very general evaluative beliefs that are likely to be shared, in some form, by many, if not all, societies. I have not focused on the ways in which different societies construct the emotion-grounding beliefs differently, and I have not asked to what extent the ancient Greek philosophers recognize the possibility of such cultural differences. The answer here is, I think, a complex one. On the one hand, these thinkers about emotion do appear to believe that, where the major, highly general categories of emotion are concerned, all the societies with which they are concerned teach, in some form, the emotion-grounding beliefs. Death is feared in Greece and in Rome; everywhere in the known world people care about people and things in such a way as to make room for grief, for anger, for passionate joy and desire. On the other hand, when we examine the highly specific enumerations of concrete varieties of these passions, and the proposals for concrete instances of therapeutic treatment we find, I believe, a good deal of interest in cultural specificity. Lucretius assumes that Epicurus is right to suppose that everywhere there are fears and angers that need philosophical therapy. But he devotes a good deal of attention to the specifically Roman forms of these emotions in constructing his therapeutic argument for a Roman interlocutor: to the connection of the fear of death with subservience to priests, to the conventional understanding of aggressiveness and anger as linked with admirable military behavior. Not only the occasions on which these passions manifest themselves but also the peculiar shape and tonality of the experience of passions, the connections these have with other experiences, are seen to have a cultural component. (We shall shortly see this in greater detail when we discuss his account of erotic desire.) Attention to the culture's own categories shapes the lists and definitions of emotions given in the various schools.[19] Thus instead of simply translating all the terms of the Greek lists, the Roman theorists tend, instead, to look at the shape of their own experience. This cultural specificity is an essential part of therapeutic argument since, they argue, therapy is only as effective as is its grasp of the concrete experience of the pupil, including not only the pupil's theoretical beliefs, but also her fantasies, her images, even her dreams. Thus in reality, while holding that most human societies (indeed, all societies short of perfected philosophical societies, real or imagined) contain the major members of this family of diseases, the philosophers believe that, like good doctors, they ought to understand the symptoms that prevail locally and not simply do medicine from the textbook. Emotions are not simply general cultural constructs; they are complex syndromes that vary in subtle ways from place to place, and each culture constructs them somewhat differently, in keeping with its traditions of evaluation.

III

Is sexual desire like this? In the ancient world there were two schools of thought on this issue. One, represented by the Plato of the *Republic* and *Phaedo*, held that sexual desire is simply a bodily urge, like hunger and thirst. It is to be classified with these and other bodily appetites, rather than with emotions such as fear, pity, grief, and anger, which are understood to have a complex cognitive structure. The appetites are seen as pushes, forces that in their very nature reach out for a certain characteristic type of object; they do not contain in themselves any conception of a good object, or any beliefs about what is important or fine. For this reason, they are thought to be impervious to rational therapy; if they are to be managed, it will have to be through some form of suppression. Good argument about the reasons for fear can actually remove fear; but argument about the worthlessness of food does nothing to alter the bodily feeling of hunger—and sexual desire is taken to be like this as well.

The other picture also has its origins in Plato—but in the more complex account of erotic desire that Plato gives in the *Phaedrus.* According to this picture, desire still has an animal component; but the complex experience of erotic desire involves all parts of the soul together—including reason. Desire itself conceives of its object as beautiful or valuable, has various beliefs about the object, and is responsive to changes in belief. In this picture, one's experience of sexual desire is in large part a function of one's thoughts and aims, of the ways one has been brought up to see the world, the distinctions one has learned to make.[20]

This picture of sexual desire and erotic love is further developed in Epicurean teaching—above all, in a brilliant section of Lucretius' *De Rerum Natura.* The purpose of this section of Lucretius's argument is to show to what extent and in what ways the experience of erotic love is shaped by social learning, to develop a critique of these social teachings, and to propose both a therapeutic treatment for those enmeshed in bad forms of love and a glimpse of a good or healthy form that will survive the therapeutic treatment. I have analyzed these arguments at length elsewhere:[21] I shall try to provide, rather briefly, an overview of the primary points, as they bear on our overall argument.

Lucretius links his account of desire to a general account of perception. For it is essential to show the variety of ways in which experience and learning can influence the inner life, if one is really going to get a good understanding of sexual experience and its cultural formation. In this general account, he argues that perceptual experience can mislead, unless perceptions are scrutinized and criticized by mind (IV.755 ff., 818–22). One way in which such deformation can occur is through the mutual influence of desire and perception. Desire is aroused by perception: but perception is also shaped by desire, since people see things in a way that is heavily influenced by their expectations and wishes, attending only to what corresponds to those wishes and often ignoring other parts of what is present (779 ff.). The mind, furthermore, has a tendency to extrapolate rapidly from its perceptions, building up a whole picture on the basis of a few signs, instead of attending closely to all the evidence that is actually before it (816–17). Clearly, wishes, habits and expectations will all influence the way in which the mind does this. So, too, he now argues, will our physiological state: for states of need and dissatisfaction lead us to focus on objects that might seem to promise an end to the dissatisfaction (858 ff.).

Lucretius now turns to influence of habit. In waking life, and even in sleep, our habitual pursuits influence what we see (what we attend to, what we construct). Forms of habitual activity—one's professional daily life, the books one regularly reads—contain characteristic structures of pleasure and attention that influence thought even at the unconscious level. Thus, in their dreams, lawyers see themselves pleading cases, generals fighting battles. Lucretius remarks that in his dreams he does philosophy: 'I do this, and investigate the nature of things at all times and having found it I write it up in my ancestral language' (962 ff.). Since we observe similar phenomena in animals (who dream of hunting, etc.), we can conclude that this is a natural and not a god-sent process (986 ff.).

These observations, taken together, prepare us to understand how complex the experience of erotic love and its associated perception actually is, and how deeply shaped, in many different ways, by social features that work not just on consciousness, but even on the unconscious life of each of us. Stories, poems, myths, habits, expectations—all these lead us to see the person before us in a certain way, a way that may not be either correct or healthy. And Lucretius' remarks about the power of his poetry to shape thought reminds the reader that the verbal constructions of love with which any reader of love poetry is constantly assailed must have a corresponding power. Reading love poems and hearing love stories produce images and patterns of attention.

Lucretius now turns officially to the topic of erotic love. As we might by now expect, he argues that love, as most people experience it, is bad because it is based on false beliefs. But his account of the false beliefs, and the mechanism of their social transmission, is extremely complex. In his remarkable account of sexual intercourse, one of the most violent and arresting passages in all of Latin poetry, he assails both (conventional) love's beliefs about its aim and its conception of its object, describing the bad consequences of pursuing that aim and having that object.

The person in love—and his constant references to the clichés of love poetry show that he is speaking of a construction of love learned through the culture, and especially through literature—aims, above all, at union or fusion with the object of desire. (Throughout the passage, and in related passages in other books, this aim is contrasted with another aim that is available, and frequently pursued in nature: the aim of mutual pleasure.) But the aim of fusion is both internally incoherent and impossible. Incoherent because (speaking always from the point of view of the male interlocutor and pupil), the natural bodily function culminates in ejaculation into, whereas the wish of love is for taking in from. Nature's structure is at odds with love's design. Impossible, because the person never can be taken in. Even if little bits of flesh could be rubbed off, he says (cf. 1103, 1110)—or, one might add, if one's gender or sexual practices are such that one does take in something physiologically from one's partner—still, the aim of love remains unfulfilled. The aim will be satisfied only by complete possession and incorporation of the other person: and the person is far more than little surface pieces of matter. Lucretius concludes that lovers must necessarily remain frustrated, feeding themselves on perceptions, and on these alone (1095–96). We notice here that the fact that the partner is a separate person with a separate life is no delight to these lovers, but a permanent obstacle to the fulfillment of their deepest wish.

This account of love's aim must be understood in connection with the accompanying diagnosis of love's false beliefs about its object. Why does love want to incorporate or devour this person, and no other? Because this person is seen to be perfect, divine, the only one, the one he has to have. Lucretius repeatedly shows how many poetic clichés of the beloved woman as a goddess, a 'Venus,' inform male experience. Each natural property is transformed into a mythological perfection. The lover's perception, guided by stories and poetic myths, looks for a Venus in the real woman who is before him. Glimpsing a few signs, he makes up 'attributes,' the rest (1154), 'blind with desire' (1153). Thus he hardly looks at the actual person before him, nor does he accurately note the aims and goals she has, the real qualities she possesses. The lover's desire for complete possession and incorporation can now be seen as a desire to possess something of the more than human, to devour the divine.

This complex illusion. Lucretius now argues, has many bad consequences, both external to the erotic relationship and within it. The external consequences are familiar from the tradition's arguments against love: waste of strength, and force; loss of control over the rest of one's life; damage to one's fortune: damage to political activity; damage to reputation (1121–32). The internal consequences are more striking. The aim to possess the other, and its inevitable frustration, produce in the lovers a continual sense of frustration and non-fulfillment. Even at the moment of greatest sexual pleasure, 'some bitterness rises up to torment them even in the flower of their enjoyment' (1134). This bitter feeling, we see, is caused by the discrepancy between the cultural fantasy and natural reality. To these torments are added the frustrations of jealousy. For love's aim is intolerant of the other person's separate life; and glances, smiles at others, all remind the lover of his incomplete possession. This leads, in turn, to suspicious behavior that is injurious to the other person, and, in general, to a disregard of the other's real existence and separate needs.

Finally, Lucretius argues, such a lover, armed with such aims, and with the overestimation of the loved one that goes with them, will prove unable to tolerate the evidence of the woman's everyday bodily existence. This passage is extremely important for any understanding of his views concerning the cultural construction of love, and its philosophical therapy.

> But let her be as fine of face as she can be, still . . . she does just the same in everything, and we know it, as the ugly, and reeks, herself, poor wretched thing, of foul odors, and her housemaids flee, far from her and giggle in secret. But the tearful lover, turned away from her door, often smothers the threshold with flowers and garlands, and anoints the proud doorposts with marjoram, and plants kisses, poor wretch, on the door. Yet if he were finally let in, and if just one whiff of that smell should meet him as he came in, he would think up some good excuse to go away, and his deep-drawn lament, long planned, would fall silent, and on the spot he would condemn his stupidity, because he sees that he has attributed to her more than it is correct to grant to any mortal. Nor are our Venuses in the dark about this. That's why they are all the more at pains to conceal the backstage side of their lives from those whom they want to keep held fast in love. All for nothing, since you can still drag it all into the light in your mind, and look into the reasons for all this laughing, and, if she has a good mind and is not spiteful, overlook all this in your turn, and yield to human life (*humanis concedere rebus*). (1171, 1174–91)

The passage begins as a piece of satirical unmasking. It asks the lover to look behind love's radiant appearance to see what is really there. It tells him that if he does so he will find that things are not as godlike and glamorous as they seem. We now have a stock scenario from Latin love poetry: the lover standing outside his mistress's door. In front of the door the lover places sweet-smelling flowers on the posts and kisses the door his divine mistress has touched. Inside we find foul odors and knowing giggles.

What is going on here? In my longer analysis (Nussbaum, 1986, ch. 7), I have argued that the most likely explanation of the scene is that the woman is having her period. The man, who has formed the habit of thinking of her as more than mortal (has 'attributed' to her more than is right to grant to any mortal) would be expected to react to this ordinary bodily event with disillusionment, disgust, and repudiation. In this way, Lucretius continues, male illusions force the female to live a dishonest life, staging herself as in a theater and concealing the stage machinery. Since this lover has been brought up on myths of Venus, a Venus is what he must see. And so the poor human women ('our Venuses' says Lucretius with irony) must strain to give him what he wants, even if it means concealing themselves.

But it is the ending of the passage that we must now try to understand. We might expect that the reaction of the disappointed lover would be rejection of the woman, and disgusted scorn. But, clearly, that is not where Lucretius' therapeutic argument ends. The argument now takes a sudden and surprising turn, moving the pupil beyond disgust as well, to an attitude altogether new: 'If she has a good mind and is not spiteful, overlook all this in your turn, and yield to human life' (*humanis concedere rebus*). What is the nature of the transition to this advice, from the moment of unmasking and disillusionment? And what does the advice itself mean?

What has happened, I think, is that Lucretius, by writing a surprise ending to the lover's story, has forced us to reflect on the oppositions contained within the story. He invites us to recognize that these opposites depend on one another. If there is not illusion, there is no moment of disillusionment. If there is no glamorous on-stage show, there is no backstage that looks, by contrast, mean and poor. If the loved one is not turned into a goddess, there is no surprise and no disgust at her humanity. The really cured state would not be the state of the disgusted lover. It would be a condition beyond both obsession and disgust, in which the lover could see the beloved clearly as a separate and a fully human being, accurately take note of the good properties she actually does possess, and accept both her humanity and his own. The fantasies of love taught through love poetry and in the culture more generally constrain and enclose both men and women, dooming the former to an exhausting alternation between worship and hatred, the other to a frantic effort of concealment and theater, accompanied by an equal hatred of everyday human things.

Lucretius does not repudiate altogether the social element in desire. By itself, social teaching and shaping is neither good nor bad: it all depends on the character of the social teaching involved. Without any social element, he shows us in Book V of the poem, human sexual life would be conducted 'in the manner of the beasts' (*more ferarum*), and there would be no room for the experience of desire mingled with tender concern, or for the careful concern with mutual pleasure, that would characterize human society at its best. (In fact, Book IV concludes with an emphatic insistence on the importance of female pleasure, and with an account of a good marriage, based on mutual respect and on the accurate perception of one another's characteristics.) On the other hand, the myths concerning sexuality in his own society seemed to him to be pernicious and constraining, dooming all participants to an alternation between unfulfillable expectation and a disgust with perceived reality. It is his belief that the social teaching lies very deep: it shapes experience itself, not just belief about experience. And it affects what we experience not only in moments of conscious control, but also in our dream-life and fantasy-life, in ways not directly accessible to rational persuasion.

And yet, Lucretius also believes that these illusions can be therapeutically treated by philosophical argument; and that such teaching, repeatedly and skillfully applied, will result in a beneficial transformation of experience, even at the unconscious level. We learn from his poem to be skeptical of the social constructions that shape our thinking; and through its rhetorical and satirical elements we learn to distance ourselves from them, to begin to laugh at them. Longer and fuller experience of studying such arguments, and of looking at life in their light, can be expected, he claims, to form new habits of attention, new patterns of desire.

IV

This Lucretian argument, and the entire ancient debate that I have all too briefly sketched here, seems to me philosophically convincing, and highly relevant to current debates about the 'social construction of sexuality.' I think that these arguments show that, while sexual desire does have an important biological dimension, the beliefs we are brought up with, the stories we know, the terms and distinctions we use, all shape not only our discourse about desire, but also the experience of desire itself. These beliefs are not always evident to us as pieces of social learning, since they are very habitual, lie very deep, and frequently inform our entire language, in such a way that alternatives are hard to see, and our own current way looks like the only way. But history, anthropology, and philosophy, working together, can make them visible. And one of the most valuable consequences of the new scholarship on Greek homosexuality is that it is doing just that for our understanding of what we now tend to call homosexual desire. By confronting us with the reality of other possibilities, it forces us to confront what is historically made in our own discourse and experience. And once we have confronted some of our deepest beliefs and patterns of perception as contingent, as culturally constructed, we are then in a position to ask the questions that the Stoics and Epicureans asked about those constructions, and to subject them to critical philosophical 'therapy' if we find that they are inimical to human flourishing.

As we undertake that project, the arguments I have described here have much assistance and insight to offer. This is so above all because they are good arguments—because the proposals about therapy are anchored to a deep and elaborate philosophical conception (or really, conceptions) of emotion and desire, defended with good arguments against rival conceptions. Thus they will help us link our accounts of sexual desire to our inquires concerning fear and grief and anger, and to pursue the investigations of rival conceptions in all these areas with rigor that is sometimes lacking from the contemporary debate.

There are three areas, in particular, in which I think we can profit from a close study of Lucretius' arguments and their relative. First, in the area of cultural relativism. For, the ancient debate seems to me to show a promising way of striking the balance between what is culturally specific and what is likely to be shared, in one or another form, by all human beings. As Lucretius's reader readily sees, the concrete experience of love that is depicted in the poem is in certain ways peculiarly Roman. Cultural constructions are transmitted not in lofty abstractions, but in concrete ways of putting things—for example in the particular poetic clichés in which lovers think of love. And Lucretius' lover thinks about love in some characteristically and concretely Roman ways, imagining the woman as a Venus—with all the baggage of concrete mythology that entails. He also imagines love with metaphors of battle and combat, and with a number of other concrete images that give the experience a particularly Roman texture. (As the large number of Greek words in this section of the poem attests, this Roman experience, being mediated though literature, is also culturally eclectic, and this fact cannot help affecting the lover's self-perception as well, and affecting the ways in which life is experienced differently by different social classes, with their differing degrees of connection to Greek culture.) Loving is not simply the acceptance of a set of propositions, it is taking on and living out of a whole scenario, or set of stories—and these narratives are in many ways culturally specific.

Nonetheless, as the larger shape of the ancient debate informs us, there is likely to be much overlap among cultures with respect to the emotions and desires. For they are all, as Stoic arguments emphasize, grounded in the recognition that things outside us, things that we do not ourselves control, have great value. This very general belief—which, to be sure, always turns up in some culturally specific form—is the sufficient basis for a whole family of emotions. One cannot wipe out grief, fear, anger, and pity, without getting rid of it completely, in every form. Thus the ancient writers feel justified, while offering particular therapeutic arguments to culturally specified interlocutors, in claiming that some such problem is the problem of every human being, and some such argument is an argument that needs to be heard by every human being. Seneca's *On Anger* is careful to attend to the interlocutor's particular Roman experience of anger, and to focus on examples that depict the family, military obligations, etc., in a concretely Roman way. Still, it is obvious that the work is at the same time addressed to any and every human being; for anyone who has not become convinced by Stoicism or some view like it will have some external attachments that can give cause for anger and resentment. The contemporary debate seems to me to err, by contrast, by taking up positions that are too simple and unsubtle to accommodate the delicate interplay between the shared and the local. Some writers on emotions and desire—many, for example, in psychoanalysis, and cognitive psychology—tend to speak as if anger, love, fear, and sexual desire are cultural universals, neglecting the ways in which different societies set things up rather differently. The anthropological literature, on the other hand, and the part of the philosophical literature influenced by a certain reading of Foucault, speaks very often as if there is no overlap among the different societies with respect to emotional experience, no such thing as a human common ground. The ancient debate will help, I suggest, in clarifying what we shall want to say on this question.

Second, the ancient debate suggests ways in which we might do justice to the importance of both social learning and individual's personal history, when thinking about the formations of emotion and desire. Once again, here the contemporary literature usually focuses on either one or the other—on the individual in psychoanalysis, on general cultural forces in Foucault and in anthropology. The Epicureans and Stoics forcefully argue that good therapeutic argument is searchingly personal, dedicated to a scrutiny of the entirety of the individual pupil's thought and desiring, capable, therefore, of eliciting from the pupil 'acknowledgment' or 'confession' of deep and sometimes unconscious desires. On the other hand, they do not forget the fact that the unconscious, while deep 'inside,' is in many respects a social artifact. Lucretius's patient dreams in the language of Roman love-lyric, just as his lawyers dream in the language of the courts. Seneca insists that all Romans need to examine themselves for certain difficulties connected with anger and aggression; and yet his own process of 'confession,' as he describes it, is searchingly personal, going through all idiosyncrasies of his own daily history and individual responses. The material suggests how much illumination might come out of an intelligent conversation between contemporary psychoanalysis and anthropology, if conducted with the philosophical rigor of these ancient conversations.

Finally, the ancient arguments, with their emphasis on therapy and their interest in radical personal and social change, offer us promising paradigms for ways in which we ourselves might ask society and ourselves to change, if we should discover, through argument, that our own ways of constructing the discourse of desire are at odds with other things we wish and hope for ourselves, with our ideas of what it takes for human beings to flourish. The ancient arguments illustrate that even in an extremely corrupt society one can frequently find a healthy part of the pupil's beliefs to appeal to, find a conception of flourishing that will be agreed to express the wishes of that healthy part, even though it may conflict with many other things that the pupil says and does. Many modern arguments of the 'social-construction' kind suggest that there is no place in human life for change. We are the more or less passive constructs of forces larger than we are, and about the most we can do is to realize the nature of the ways of thinking that have bound, bind, and will continue to bind us. This way of thinking is especially common in the area of sexual desire. It is rare to find an anti-racist who believes that racist belief and feelings can never in any way be changed by any process of rational 'therapy.' And yet it does seem to be the positions of some leading figures in the debate on the 'social construction' of sexuality that we will never be able to stop thinking of ourselves under the categories of 'sexuality' made for us by nineteenth-century science—even if we decide, by argument, that they are arbitrary, unhelpful, and inimical to human flourishing.

Frequently such social determinisms trace their origin to Nietzsche, who is taken to hold that we can never escape from the categories in which we were raised, although we can perhaps come to see their contingent and arbitrary character. But Nietzsche, who was profoundly influenced by Hellenistic philosophy, who published his first article on a topic in that area, and who repeatedly taught and reflected on Stoic ethics, is, I believe, closely allied with Stoicism and Epicureanism on this point. For he does appear to hold that there is a healthy element in the human being that can flourish if, and only if, certain deep cultural conventions are criticized. The 're-valuation of values' begins by noticing that the values we believed to be necessary and essential are actually contingent and to some extent arbitrary. But once this perception is accepted, things can never be the same: for to admit this much opens the door to a new question: 'What do these values do for us? How do they serve or impede life?' And this second phase of re-evaluation, closely modeled on Hellenistic therapies, does not leave things in place. People who accept the fact that god is dead do not live on as before, with just a little more awareness. Or rather, they do that only if they would really rather not have this knowledge and are determined merely to pay it lip-service. Lucretius already spoke eloquently about such people: people who mouth philosophical arguments about death but do not allow the arguments to enter in and to change them. Suppose, on the other hand, one really goes through the therapeutic argument in a thoroughgoing way. Then one will emerge, Nietzsche claims, with a view of oneself as an artist—not one who plays around, does anything she likes, throws all discipline and all history to the winds, but one who exercises an intelligent and disciplined freedom with respect to her own cultural heritage, refusing it the tyranny over her thought and experience that it otherwise would have exercised.

It is this sort of radical criticism of convention, and this sort of human freedom, that I find eloquently portrayed and exemplified in the Hellenistic tradition of writing about emotion and desire. And this is why it was the belief of the Hellenistic philosophers that philosophical education and philosophical argument were the instruments of freedom for the individual, and, for the community, the bases of universal citizenship in a truly rational society.

Notes

1. See Kenneth J. Dover, *Greek Homosexuality* (Cambridge, Mass.: Harvard University Press, 1989), 61 ff. Especially interesting is a passage from Xenophon's *Hiero*, in which the poet Simonides and the morally worthy Hiero both refer to Hiero's passion for a young man as a constraint deriving from nature—using the category 'natural,' for an inclination that our own society has frequently judged 'contrary to nature'.
2. See John J. Winkler, *The Constraints of Desire: The Anthropology of Sex and Gender in Ancient Greece* (New York: Routledge, 1990).
3. Martha Nussbaum, *Therapy of Desire* (Princeton: Princeton University Press, 1994); Martha Nussbaum, 'Platonic Love and Colorado Law: The Relevance of Ancient Greek Norms to Modern Secular Controversies', in *Virginia Law Review*, 80:1515–1651 (1994); and Martha Nussbaum, 'Eros and the Wise: The Stoic Response to the Cultural Dilemma', in *Oxford Studies in Ancient Philosophy* (1995).
4. Martha Nussbaum, 'Constructing Love, Desire and Care', in D. Estlund and M. Nussbaum (eds.), *Sex, Preference and Family: Essays in Law and Nature* (New York: Oxford University Press, 1997), 17–43; and Martha Nussbaum, *Upheavals of Thought: A Theory of the Emotions* (Cambridge: Cambridge University Press, 1997).
5. See Malcolm Schofield, *The Stoic Idea of the City* (Cambridge: Cambridge University Press, 1991).
6. Compare Cyril Bailey: '... not continuous drinkings and revellings, nor the satisfaction of lusts, nor the enjoyment of fish and other luxuries of the wealthy table'.
7. For general treatments of the subject see Dover, *Greek Homosexuality*; Foucault, *Le Souci de soi* (Paris: Gallimard, 1984); Michel Foucault, *L'Usage des plaisirs* (Paris: Gallimard, 1984); David Halperin, *One Hundred Years of Homosexuality and Other Essays on Greek Love* (New York: Routledge, 1990); David Halperin, 'The Democratic Body', *Differences*, 2: 1–29 (1990); John J. Winkler, '*Phallos Politikos:* Representing the Body Politic in Athens', *Differences*, 2: 29–46 (1990); Winkler, *The Constraints of Desire*; and David Konstan, 'Love in the Greek Novel', *Differences*, 2: 186–204 (1990).
8. The work is especially valuable for its judicious treatment of evidence of many difference kinds, including oratory, comedy, and vase-painting.
9. See Foucault, *Le Souci de soi* and by the same author, *L'Usage des plaisirs*; and Halperin, *One Hundred Years of Homosexuality*.
10. See especially, Foucault, *Le Souci de soi* and by the same author, *L'Usage des plaisirs*, and David Halperin, *One Hundred Years of Homosexuality*.
11. This is the theme of Martha Nussbaum in her *Therapy of Desire*.
12. For a variety of examples of this, see Amélie Rorty (ed.), *Explaining Emotions* (Berkeley: University of California Press, 1980); Catherine Lutz, *Unnatural Emotions* (Chicago: University of Chicago Press, 1988); Rom Harré (ed.), *The Social Construction of Emotions* (Oxford: Blackwell, 1986); Melanie Klein, *Love, Guilt, and Reparation and Other Works 1921–1945* (London: Hogarth, 1975); and Ronald de Sousa, *The Rationality of Emotion* (Cambridge: Mass.: MIT Press, 1987).

13. On anger in Aristotle, see *EN* IV.5 1378a31 ff. See also Nussbaum, *Therapy of Desire*, 359–401.
14. See Aristotle, *Rhet.* 1382a21 ff. *Poet.* 1453a4–5; see Martha Nussbaum, *The Fragility of Goodness: Luck and Ethics in Greek Tragedy and Philosophy* (Cambridge: Cambridge University Press, 1986), 378–95.
15. See Aristotle, *Rhet.* 1385b13 ff. *Poet.* 1453a3, and Nussbaum, *The Fragility of Goodness*, 378–95.
16. See Nussbaum, *The Fragility of Goodness*, Chs. 11–12.
17. For references and discussion, see Martha Nussbaum, 'Therapeutic Arguments: Epicurus and Aristotle', in M. Schofield and G. Striker (eds.), *The Norms of Nature: Studies on Hellenistic Ethics* (Cambridge; Cambridge University Press, 1986), 31–74.
18. For these and other references, see Nussbaum, 'Therapeutic Arguments', in Schofield and Striker (eds.), *The Norms of Nature.*
19. For the standard definitions, see J. Von Arnim (ed.), Stoicorum Veterum Fragmenta, 4 Vols. (Stuttgart: Teubner, 1964).
20. See Nussbaum, *The Fragility of Goodness*, Ch. 7, and also Anthony Price, *Love and Friendship in Plato and Aristotle* (Oxford: Clarendon Press, 1989).
21. What follows is a brief summary of the reading of Lucretius presented in Nussbaum, *Therapy of Desire.*

Part III. Rereading Seventeenth-Century Philosophers: Minds, Bodies, and Passions

6 The Passions and Philosophy

Susan James*

In 1649 the Earl of Monmouth published an English translation of a popular French work by Jean François Senault entitled *The Use of the Passions.* Monmouth's Letter to the Reader includes a story about the Count of Gondomar, who, we are told, was wont to say, 'If you make a small inconsiderable present to any great man of the court, or to your mistress, you may do well to steer it in with some preamble, whereby to excuse the meanness, and make the fancy or workmanship thereof plead acceptance; marry, if you will present him or her with a thing of real value, as (for that it was he instanced in) with a bag of gold amounting to some three or four thousand pound, you need not use any circumlocutions, but bring it in, lay it down, and say, "Take it, there it is." The thing itself will purchase its welcome.'[1] Nowadays, the place and analysis of the passions in seventeenth-century philosophy needs, perhaps, to be steered in with some preamble, since its value, unlike that of a bag of gold, has darkened with time and grown opaque. We tend to forget that philosophers of this era worked within an intellectual milieu in which the passions were regarded as an overbearing and inescapable element of human nature, liable to disrupt any civilized order, philosophy included, unless they were tamed, outwitted, overruled, or seduced.

The power and capriciousness of the emotions made them the subject of an array of testing problems that spread through the various branches of philosophy and could not be ignored. As Thomas Wright explained in *The Passions of the Mind in General*, first published in 1604, natural philosophy deals with 'the actions and operations of the passions'.[2] His view is confirmed by Edward Reynolds, the Bishop of

* Susan James, 'The Passions and Philosophy', extract from Introduction to her *Passion and Action: The Emotions in Seventeenth Century Philosophy* (Oxford: Oxford University Press, 1997), 1–26. Reprinted by permission of the author and publisher.

Norwich whose 1640 *Treatise of the Passions and Faculties of the Soul of Man* was dedicated to the Princess Elizabeth of Bohemia with whom, a few years later, Descartes corresponded on the same subject. Natural philosophy, according to Reynolds, investigates the 'essential properties' of the passions, their 'ebbs and flows, springings and decays, the manner of their several impressions, the physical effects which are wrought by them, and the like',[3] whereas the task of moral philosophy is to explain how these inordinate appetites can and must be bridled,[4] and how 'the indifference of them is altered into good or evil by virtue of the domination of right reason, or the violence of their own motions; what their ministry is in virtuous, and what their power and independence in irregular, actions; how they are raised, suppressed, slackened and governed according to the particular natures of those things which require their motion'.[5] Finally, according to some accounts, civil philosophy revealed 'how they may be wrought upon and impressed, and how, and on what occasion, it is fit to gather and fortify, and to slack and remit them; how to discover, or suppress, or nourish, or alter, or mix them, as may be most advantageous; what use may be made of each man's particular age, nature or propension; how to advance our just ends, upon the observance and the character of these, whom we are to deal withal'.[6] Though distinct, natural and moral philosophy are mutually supportive within this scheme, each enabling the other. It is moral philosophy that 'makes philosophers, and purifying their understanding, makes them capable of considering the wonders of nature'.[7] But a grasp of the passions as natural phenomena contributes to the ability to control and direct them, and this is in turn a prerequisite of fruitful reflection on moral and political questions. The substance of philosophy here encompasses the philosopher, whose own practice becomes a subject of reflection and enquiry.

The interest in the emotions that so pervades seventeenth-century philosophy is itself part of a broader preoccupation in early-modern European culture with the relations between knowledge and control, whether of the self or others.[8] The contribution of the passions to this theme is starkly portrayed in some of the advice books to princes written in this period,[9] and in a closely related genre of works which offer to teach 'the art to know men',[10] construed as including the art to know oneself. To rule successfully, a prince must be able to control his own passions so that he does not, for example, forfeit his subjects' loyalty by doing something unjust while he is in a rage. Equally, he must be able to read and manipulate the passions of those around him, to detect and play on the ambition, envy, fear, or esteem of courtiers, counsellors, and citizens. The extreme vulnerability of a prince makes these kinds of knowledge vital to his survival; but he also symbolizes the qualities needed in any figure of authority, and draws attention to the social relevance of the branch of moral philosophy that teaches the control of the passions. According to Senault, who was the General of the Oratory in Paris, ''Tis she that instructeth politicians and teacheth them by governing their passions to govern their kingdoms; 'tis she that makes fathers of families, and who managing their inclinations teacheth them to bring up their children and command their servants; so that she is to Philosophy the same as foundations are to buildings'.[11]

This wider concern with the importance of directing the passions is reflected in works aimed not specifically at rulers, but at a broader and predominantly male élite who occupy, or will occupy, positions of power.[12] Taking over an ancient tradition, these treatises tend to identify the acquisition of self-knowledge with the ability to master and manipulate passion, and to associate both with a process of cure. Therapy, self-control, and power over others are blended to produce an image of healthy dominion, the elements of which are clearly, if crudely, assembled and displayed by Senault's translator. In his Epistle Dedicatory, Senault himself emphasizes his therapeutic aspirations, praying that his book will help to make men virtuous by showing 'how passions are raised in them, how they rebel against reason, how they seduce the understanding and what sleights they use to enslave the will. . . . When I have known the malady, teach me the remedy that I may cure it.' Monmouth, however, combines this ideal with the will to power by adding an introductory verse:

> If to command and rule o're others be
> The thing desired above all worldly pelf,[13]
> How great a prince, how great a monarch's he
> Who govern can, who can command himself.
> If you unto so great a power aspire
> This book will teach how you may it acquire.[14]

Since the control of the emotions is held to be so transformative, and to unlock such potential, enquiry into this domain is not confined to philosophers. On the contrary, the passions are approached and analysed from many angles: by divines who explicate their place in God's creation and in the history of humankind; by Christian orators who work to arouse them in their congregations; by devout Christians who bridle them to attain quietness of mind; by magistrates who seek to understand their subjects; and by civil gentlemen who must avoid being 'so appassionate in affections that their company [is] to most men intolerable'.[15] Extending Thomas Wright's list, we could add poets, musicians, painters, playwrights, doctors, lawyers, and teachers, all of whom take a professional interest in the arousing and calming of the emotions and investigate them against a background of common assumptions and overlapping legacies. To appreciate the philosophical discussions of the passions that are the subject of this book, [Ed's note: *Passion and Action*] we therefore need first to be aware of some of the shared understandings that mould early-modern conceptions of what the passions are, and of the key questions to which they give rise. Immediately, and still more as we go on, we shall find that even the most deeply entrenched positions are contested; but they are nevertheless the comparatively still points around which debate turns and evolves.

Passions, then, are generally understood to be thoughts or states of the soul which represent things as good or evil for us, and are therefore seen as objects of inclination or aversion. When Eurydice sees the snake gliding towards her, she recognizes it as venomous and feels the passion of fear; when she meets Orpheus in the Underworld, she feels (perhaps among several emotions) the passion of love. Like other animals, humans are subject to passions because we are naturally disposed to assess our surroundings and our own states as advantageous or harmful, and because the evaluations we make are not merely a matter of realizing that things have certain properties, such as being dangerous or attractive, but are emotions which move us and guide our actions. Passions, it is agreed, have intrinsic physical manifestations which bridge emotion and action and are written on the body in facial expressions, blushings, trembling, and postures. Eurydice does not merely perceive the life-threatening snake, but is afraid, pales, and tries to avoid it; nor does she simply register that Orpheus has arrived, but yearns to be close to him. Most of our everyday experience is suffused with passions, which are a fundamental aspect of our nature, one of the basic ways in which we interpret the world around us. But while this rough characterization is generally agreed, the repertoire of the passions is a subject of greater controversy. Seventeenth-century thinkers inherit and elaborate a long and palimpsestic tradition of attempts to provide a comprehensive classification of key emotions in terms of which all variants can be analysed; and while they do not arrive at any final consensus, they work with and sustain the view that certain passions are central. Love and fear, for example, are understood to be of this type, as are their opposites, hatred and hope.

The sense that these passions are of particular importance, so that no classification would be complete without them, derives in part from an informal understanding of the emotional responses that predominate. But this understanding is in turn shaped by various more-or-less articulated conceptions of what the passions are and how they operate, which are themselves expressed in different systems of classification. To opt for a classification is, to some extent, to opt for a broader theory of the passions, and any theory will be measured against existing typologies to see how well it deals with particular cases and configurations. One influential source in this dialectical process is the comparatively informal lists of passions compiled by Aristotle. In his *Rhetoric*, for example, Aristotle cites as passions anger and mildness, love and hatred, fear and confidence, shame and esteem, kindness and unkindness, pity and indignation, envy and emulation;[16] in *The Nicomachean Ethics* he picks out appetite, anger, fear, confidence, envy, joy, love, hatred, longing, emulation, pity, 'and in general the feelings that are accompanied by pleasure and pain'.[17] Some seventeenth-century authors continue to use and build on these enumerations;[18] but others, drawn by their philosophical ambitions to a more structured approach, are impressed by Cicero's claim (itself borrowed from the Greek Stoics) that there are only four fundamental passions: distress and pleasure (*aegritudo* and *laetitia*), and fear and desire (*metus* and *libido*).[19] Continuing the ancient habit of subjecting these cardinal passions to diverse interpretations, some authors held to Cicero's own view that each of these passions is a separate state with its own object.[20] *Laetitia* is a kind of delight at something believed to be a present good, *libido* is a desire for a supposed good. *Metus* is a feeling of fear at what is believed to be a threatening evil, *aegritudo* is distress at a present thing held to be evil. Other theorists, however, gave priority to desire and fear and interpreted joy and distress as states of mind resulting from them. For example, when we fail to get what we want, or are confronted by things we fear, we experience distress, whereas when we attain the objects of our desires, or avoid the things we are afraid of, we are delighted. In this latter and more economical interpretation, the objects of our desires are characterized in a particular way, as bringing us delight or removing distress. Desire itself is thus seen as directed toward *laetitia* and away from *aegritudo*, as a disposition to seek out one state and avoid the other.[21]

Jostling up against the spare lines of this antique typology was a flamboyant Christian reworking of it—Augustine's Neoplatonic reinterpretation of the passions as species of love. In *The City of God* Augustine adhered to Cicero's view that there are four basic passions,[22] but he analysed each of them in terms of a single overarching prototype. '[A] love which strains after the possession of the loved object is desire; and the love which possesses and enjoys that object is joy. The love that shuns what opposes it is fear, while the love that feels that opposition when it happens is grief.'[23] By unifying the passions, Augustinianism answered, as we shall see, to a strong synthesizing urge within seventeenth-century philosophy, and exerted a decisive influence on thinking about the epistemological implications of the passions. In addition, the reduction it advocated acquired a place in theological disputes, as Senault indicates when he compares the failure of philosophers to appreciate the unity of the passions to the failure of pagans to recognize the unity of God. 'But as amongst the infidels every perfection of God hath passed for a several deity, so among the philosophers the different qualities of love have been taken for different passions.'[24] Augustine's position had to compete, however, with the more elaborate and compartmentalized typologies worked out within the Scholastic Aristotelian tradition, particularly with that of Thomas Aquinas, who identified no fewer than eleven basic passions. Aquinas's classification continued to be used in the seventeenth century, and provided the organizing categories for numerous treatises[25] which identify as the central passions love and hatred (*amor* and *odium*), desire and aversion (*desiderium* and *fuga*), sadness and joy (*dolor* and *delectatio*), hope and despair (*spes* and *desperatio*), fear and daring (*timor* and *audacia*), and finally anger (*ira*), the only passion that has no contrary.[26]

These overlapping maps of emotional possibility furnish an understanding of the range of the passions, distinguish central from marginal cases, and offer ways to get a grip on the infinite variety of particular emotions that people experience. At the same time, they delineate a central set of oppositions. Our affective life is portrayed as for the most part a susceptibility to pairs of positive and negative emotions, which are variously characterized in terms of inclination and aversion, and of unity and separation. It is worth noting at the outset that these typologies include, alongside states that are nowadays classed as emotions, the passion of desire. For early-modern writers, desire—and feelings such as love, anger, or sadness—are all states of a single kind, and all answer to the rough definition of passion outlined above. In holding this view, seventeenth-century theorists differ sharply from contemporary philosophers, who tend to distinguish desires and emotions.[27] Although early-modern writers recognize that the role played by desire in reasoning and action differs in certain ways from that played, for example, by fear, they regard the similarities between these states as more significant than the differences. Consequently, their category of passions does not coincide with modern interpretations of the category of emotion, from which desire is excluded. Some early-modern writers use the terms 'passion' and 'emotion' synonymously.[28] But in following their practice, we need to remember that their sense of these terms diverges from common contemporary usage.

The classificatory schemes just sketched are designed, in part, to specify key passions to which everyone is prone. But this attempt to grasp the range of human emotions is counterbalanced by a lively awareness of the vast variety and diversity of passions to be found in different individuals, sexes, classes, nationalities, professions, and so forth. At an individual level, our passionate dispositions begin to be moulded at the moment of conception, as Pierre Charron explained in some detail in his popular work *La Sagesse*, which first appeared in 1601 and was frequently reprinted during the first half of the century. Urging prospective fathers to take care that their seed is of the right temperature to engender children of a good physical and psychological temper, Charron offers them some practical advice. To beget male children that are sound, wise, and judicious, a man must not couple with a woman of vile, base, or dissolute condition, or of a naughty or vicious composition of body; he must abstain from copulation for seven or eight days; during this time he must nourish himself with wholesome victuals, more hot and dry than otherwise, and must use more than moderate exercise. When the great day arrives, he must apply himself to his encounter on an empty stomach, and not near the monthly term of the woman but six or seven days before or as much afterward.[29] This regime, however, is only a beginning, for the passions continue to develop in the womb, where we share our mothers' griefs and joys, some of which may become indelibly imprinted on our characters.[30] Once we are born, our emotions develop with our nurse's milk, our first education, and with a host of individual experiences. Traumas leave their mark, so that 'this man sweats at the presence of a cat; that falls into an agony by casting his eye upon a frog or a toad; another man can never be reconciled to oysters'.[31] Vivid sights and sounds, chance associations, and idle conversations all shape our passions,[32] which continue to be formed and altered by the whole range of our experience.

While differences in people's lives account for the diversity of passions in any human population, biological and environmental factors explain patterns of distribution. In the first place, 'divers complexions are inclined to divers passions', a truth borne out, Thomas Wright tells us, by an old Italian proverb:

> If little men were patient
> And great men were valiant
> And red men were loyal,
> All the world would be equal.[33]

Another rhyme quoted by Wright affirms that this variability is as much a feature of women as of men;[34] but belief in the correlation between physical type and emotional temperament is more generally associated with the conviction that the bodily differences between the sexes are systematically reflected in their passions. Women are held to be more impressionable than men because their brains are softer, to resemble children in the inconstancy of their feelings, and to be susceptible to different passions,[35] and, according to Charron, are particularly liable to the effeminate emotions of vengefulness and sadness.[36] In addition, the changing conceptions that women and men have of their own bodies affect their sense of power, so that passions alter with age. For example, while the physical strength of young men makes them proud, the weakness of old men and women makes them covetous.[37]

Complementing and cross-cutting these divisions are a number of environmental factors, many of which are widely held to contribute to our characters. Climate, first of all, determines our internal heat, and this in turn produces spiritual differences.

> For the southerners, by reason of their cold temperature, are melancholic and therefore staid, contemplative, ingenious, religious, wise . . . From the melancholy temperature it likewise cometh that the southerners are unchaste, by reason of their frothy, fretting, tickling melancholy, as we commonly see in hares; and cruel, because this fretting sharp melancholy do violently press the passions and revenge. The northerners are of a phlegmatic and sanguine temperature quite contrary to the southern, and therefore have contrary qualities save that they agree in this one, that they are likewise cruel and inhumane, but by another reason, that is, for want of judgement, whereby like beasts they know not how to contain and govern themselves.[38]

Education, too, forms our dispositions, as Wright attests in his pathetic picture of the results of English discipline.

Our English youths are brought up with too much fear and terror. . . . The Italians and Spaniards, contrariwise, by bringing up their children with more liberty, enlarge their hearts with boldness and audacity in such sort, as usually you shall see them at sixteen or seventeen years of age, as bold and audacious as ours of thirty; and contrariwise, ours at sixteen or seventeen, drooping with fear and timidity, as if they were so many chickens drawn out of a well.[39]

Finally, then as now, European writers delight in sensational national stereotypes. Wright, for example, assures his readers that, 'I have seen by experience, there is no nation in Europe that hath not some extraordinary affection, either in pride, anger, lust, incontinence, gluttony, drunkenness, sloth or such like passion.'[40]

As assessments of the benefit or harm that things may cause us, the passions are vital to our life. Without them we would lack both the dispositional wariness that alerts us to danger, and anything beyond a basic, instinctive urge to improve our condition, and would be infinitely more helpless and vulnerable than we already are. 'No mortal man', Burton declares in *The Anatomy of Melancholy*, 'is free from these perturbations; or if he be so, sure he is either a god or a block.'[41] Since divine invulnerability is not an option, the alternative to the passions seems to be blockhood, a prospect that puts their functional traits in perspective. Whatever their limitations—and there are many—the passions are a prerequisite of everyday human existence. Explanations of their functional character interpret them simultaneously as a natural adaptation of species to environment and as evidence of God's beneficence. According to the first view, the passions promote our well-being as embodied creatures; according to the second, this goal dovetails neatly with our spiritual well-being so that, sometimes in spite of appearances, all passions are for our good. Senault, an enthusiastic promoter of this latter view, credits God with a homoeopathic talent for distilling antidotes out of poisons.

Thou employest fear to take off a covetous man from those perishable riches which possess him; thou makest a holy use of despair to withdraw from the world a courtier, whose youth had been mis-employed in the service of some prince; thou makest an admirable use of disdain to extinguish therewith a lover's flames, who is enslaved by a proud beauty. . . . In fine, thou makest claims of all our passions to unite our wills to thine.[42]

Even among less sanguine writers we encounter the view that, since God has equipped us with passions, and since he is benevolent, there must be something to be said for them. And in exploring what this might be, most authors fix on their role in promoting our well-being, where this is conceived not simply as a matter of survival and basic comfort, but more ambitiously in terms of a complex intermingling of pleasures and pains which give texture to our lives. Our passions do more than incite us to avoid danger; they also create our attachments and aspirations. They are the stuff of our responses to the course of events, so that it is hard (though not impossible) to imagine life without them. This point is forcefully made by the Dominican bishop Nicolas Coeffeteau in his *Tableau des passions humaines* of 1630. 'Would not a mother be inhuman', he asks rhetorically, 'if she were to see her child in the grip of wild beasts . . . or only seized by a violent illness, without feeling her heart filled with sadness?'[43]

Natural and theological defences of the functional character of the passions are therefore central to their interpretation. But these are not nearly so strident as the litany of complaint and lamentation about the imperfection of human nature that runs through the literature, creating the impression that the passions are an unmitigated burden. In the Epistle Prefatory to the *Natural History of the Passions*, for example, Walter Charleton mourns the fact that, 'Our inordinate affections be the bitter fountain whence . . . our practical errors, and by consequence most of the evils we suffer, flow.'[44] An initial sense of uneasiness and trouble is reflected in the rich vocabulary used to describe the passions. In *The City of God*, Augustine had noted that there are various Latin translations of the Greek term *pathe*, of which he favours the literal *passiones*, the term eventually taken over in French and English. Like the related deponent verb *patior*, this combines the idea of passivity with that of suffering, a sense nowhere more vividly conveyed than in the story of Christ's Passion. But two other translations listed by Augustine have more volatile connotations. *Pathe* is also rendered, he reminds us, as *perturbationes* (notably by Cicero) and as *affectiones* or *affectus*.[45] The view that these terms are all roughly synonymous quickly became fixed, and Augustine's discussion continued to be widely invoked and reiterated. Aquinas cites it,[46] and a range of English and French authors of the seventeenth century either replicate Augustine's list or unselfconsciously employ the range of terms it contains. Wright, for instance, remarks that the passions are also called affections or perturbations of the mind, as well as motions and affects.[47]

The passivity of passions and the stirrings of perturbations may initially seem at odds with one another: the one at rest, the other in motion; the one inactive, the other driving. But these two descriptions are brought together in an understanding of the passions as forces that are at once extremely powerful and actually or potentially beyond our control. They perturb the economy of soul and body in ways that we are sometimes unable to prevent, and in the most extreme cases can overwhelm a person so completely that they die. The Cambridge Platonist Henry More, for instance, regards it as 'a known and granted truth that passion has so much power over the vital temper of the body as to make it an unfit mansion for the soul' and attributes the deaths of both Sophocles and Dionysius the Sicilian tyrant to the sudden news of a tragic victory.[48] These characteristics are captured in a sequence of long-standing and ubiquitous metaphors. The passions are rebels who rise up against reason and understanding, make secessions, raise mutinies,[49] 'brawl with one another and so cause riots and tumults'.[50] Charmed by the sensible realm, they often prove deaf to the voice of reason, and, casting off their yoke of allegiance, 'aspire to unbounded licence and dominion'.[51] As opponents they are cunning, resilient, and insatiable; 'they are Hydras which thrust up as many heads as are cut off, they are so many Antaeuses who gather strength from their weakness and who rise up stronger after they have been beaten down; all the advantage one can expect from such subjects is to clap irons upon their hands and feet, and leave them no more power than is requisite for the service of reason'.[52] To be subject to such tyrants is, moreover, a peculiarly terrible fate, since one cannot escape servitude by running away. The passions are part of us, and we are condemned to drag our chains along, carrying our masters with us.[53] The same image is also used, moreover, to portray the aspiration to reverse this state of affairs by bringing down our despotic emotions and enslaving them in their turn. On the frontispiece of the English translation of Senault's book, Aquinas's eleven principal passions form a chain-gang. With the exception of Love, who is held by both wrists to prevent him firing his bow, each is manacled at the ankle and attached to the wrist of Reason. Sitting on her throne, she controls them by loosening and tightening the chain, assisted by Grace, who offers her advice, and also by a small dog which stands by, ready to round up any strays (see Pl. 1).

Images of civil strife within the soul are matched by a view of the passions as natural disorders—as storms, torrents, tempests. They are winds that put the mind in tumult, sweeping us along like ships in a gale,[54] and as storms disturb the harmony of nature, passions are discordant and jangling. In these metaphors passion is understood as

PLATE. 1 Frontispiece to J. F. Senault, *The Use of the Passions*, trans. Henry Earl of Monmouth (1649). Reproduced by kind permission of the British Library.

motion, an interpretation which spreads into a wider range of descriptions. The passions are turbulent, they are furious reboundings, they are violent and rash sallies, they are accessions and recessions of folly.[55] As such, they are often portrayed in addition as diseases, pathological states to which we easily succumb and of which we need to be cured, since to neglect these illnesses would be little short of suicidal, 'as if a blind man who hath not the power of directing his own feet should be permitted to run head-long, without wit or moderation, having no guide to direct him'.[56]

The passions, then, 'trouble wonderfully the soul'.[57] They induce blindness of understanding, perversion of the will, alteration of the humours, and by these means maladies and disquietness.[58] In early-modern writing, our constitutional inability to govern our emotions is often attributed to the Fall; as punishment for Adam's sin, God removed from us the capacity to control, moderate, and direct them, creating the inward chaos that is the lot of all but a very few exceptional people. But even writers who do not agree with, or do not emphasize, this Christian interpretation of our distress, nevertheless share with their Christian counterparts an understanding of its painful consequences. Our passions, they concede, make us false, foolish, inconstant, and uncertain.[59] They are the flaws that trip us up and the stuff of which tragedy is made. When Lodovico asks wonderingly about Othello,

> Is this the nature
> Whom passion could not shake, whose solid virtue
> The shot of accident nor dart of chance
> Could neither graze nor pierce?[60]

he registers a common amazement at the capacity of affect to defeat a mature and settled character and destroy social order. Because passion eats into us, making us wayward and obsessed, it renders us intensely vulnerable. At the same time, it has the destructive habit of feeding its own restlessness by setting us off on courses of action that fail to satisfy us and further damage our well-being. Shakespeare knows this, too, of course, and allows the Player King to lay out the problem before the troubled Claudius.

> What to ourselves in passion we propose,
> The passions ending, doth the purpose lose,
> The violence of either grief or joy
> Their own enactures with themselves destroy.
> Where joy most revels, grief doth most lament;
> Grief joys, joy grieves, on slender accident.[61]

These elements combine to produce a common understanding of what the passions are, and why they are important, which spans the culture of seventeenth-century Europe and creates a frame within which more specialized debates are conducted. But perhaps the most striking fact about the images outlined here is their equivocality: on the one hand the passions are functional characteristics essential to our survival and flourishing; on the other hand they are painful and destructive impulses which drive us to pursue the very ends liable to do us harm. God's benevolence in fitting us for our environment is tempered by his penalty for our first disobedience, so that our passions, which are among the most intense forces shaping our lives, condemn us to misery and error. This ambivalence poses problems that preoccupy and inspire writers of many kinds. Prominent among them are those philosophers who rise, unwisely perhaps, to the challenge of devising theories capable of reconciling these conflicting tendencies, and of situating the passions within systematic analyses of the mind and body, the moral community, the polity, and the history of humankind. Aspects of this project are undertaken by many writers who now belong to the established canon of seventeenth-century philosophers: Hobbes, Descartes, Locke, Pascal, Malebranche, and Spinoza are all, in different ways, profoundly interested in the passions, which play a major part in shaping both the philosophical problems they address and the solutions they propose.

Precisely because the passions are so central, and bear on such a wide range of issues, my discussion of them in this book [Ed's note: *Passion and Action*] will necessarily be selective. I shall not, on the whole, discuss particular passions, or the typologies in which they are embedded. Nor shall I focus directly on the ethical character of our affections or the part they play in a virtuous life.[62] My aim is rather to explore the place of the passions in seventeenth-century interpretations of the body and mind, and to understand the roles they play in reasoning and action. Since the investigation of these neglected themes bears most directly on problems usually allocated to metaphysics, the philosophy of mind, and epistemology, these areas of philosophy will figure largely in this book. Many of the views I shall discuss point invitingly to early-modern ethics, politics, and aesthetics, and many discoveries remain to be made about the connections between these fields. Meanwhile, however, an appreciation of the centrality of the passions to seventeenth-century conceptions of our grasp of ourselves and the world is significant for at least three reasons, one of them bearing specifically on the history of early-modern philosophy, the other two raising questions about contemporary philosophical practice.

Philosophers have tended in the first place to neglect the fact that their early-modern ancestors wrote about the passions.[63] This may partly be due to the influence of Hume and other Enlightenment thinkers, who represented the seventeenth century as an era dominated by dogmatic, religious values in which a proper appreciation of sentiment was suppressed. But the neglect also stems in the twentieth century from a preoccupation with philosophy as a scientific and secular form of enquiry distinct from psychology, a conception which has shaped our understanding of historical texts and led us to read them as mainly addressing the metaphysical, scientific and epistemological issues that now tend to be seen as the core of the subject. While not necessarily mistaken, the resulting interpretations are partial in several ways: they skip over topics, such as the passions, that are perceived as marginal or irrelevant to a particular interpretation of what philosophy is; they focus on philosophers whose work most easily answers to the preconceptions created by this interpretation; they select from the works of favoured philosophers those which strike them as most relevant and coherent; and having thus shaped the subject, they string philosophers together into schools and traditions. This process yields maps of the past which are, from the perspective of certain contemporary issues and problems, highly informative. But for travellers of a more historical bent, it is as though the contour lines were missing. The landscape is flattened, stripped of many of the vistas and surprises that enliven a journey, and deprived of the singularity and complexity that makes a region distinctive. Such a map is not only misleading but—to many people, at least—less enticing than it might be, for although flat lands have their charm, they are also monotonous.

The fact that cartographics of early-modern philosophy have tended to leave out the passions of the soul is, I believe, a significant loss. As well as obliterating a deeply fascinating set of configurations, this practice has impoverished our awareness of the territory as a whole. The passions are not, for seventeenth-century philosophers, embellishments to be tacked on to the back of a treatise once the real work is done, or added to a map when the surveying and measuring are completed. They are integral to the landscape, vital to a philosophical grasp of our own nature and our power to comprehend and negotiate the natural and social environments in which we live. Unless we realize this, we are liable to read over the connections that seventeenth-century philosophers draw between the passions and other problems or arguments that strike us more forcibly, and are also prone to construct anachronistic links of our own. On a map without contours, two communities cut off from one another by an impassable mountain may appear as close neighbours; comparable misunderstandings can arise from a map without passions. Misunderstandings of this type have actually arisen and the study of the passions can in consequence substantially revise our views about the character and achievements of philosophy in the seventeenth century.

The cumulative effect of investigating the passions serves, not merely to vindicate their importance within early-modern philosophy but to revise some currently influential conceptions of this area and its relation to the philosophical positions that we associate with the Enlightenment. However, some of the assumptions and standpoints that it encourages us to give up have had an impact beyond the confines of avowedly historical enquiry, and form part of a picture of the history of philosophy that shapes all kinds of current work. The view, for example, that Descartes made an absolute distinction between states of the body and states of the soul and allowed nothing to cross it, has long been a mainstay of the philosophy of mind,[64] but it is a mainstay that will not stand up once the Cartesian account of the passions is taken into account. More recently, the claim that Descartes divided reason from emotion, and banished the latter to the body, has gained currency among a wide range of philosophers concerned to reassess the relation between thinking and feeling; but this too fails to take account of an important Cartesian distinction between passions and so-called intellectual emotions. On a larger scale, the seventeenth century continues to be portrayed as the dawn of modernity, the cradle of a culture in which man becomes set over against nature and nature takes on a purely instrumental significance, and in which a range of emotional responses to the natural world give way to dispassionate calculations of utility.[65] This interpretation rests, it seems to me, on an oversimplification both of the tensions between function and dysfunction within the passions, and of a sequence of debates about how this is to be resolved, as well as underestimating the complexity of early-modern debates about the self.[66]

If none of these interpretations can be sustained without a great deal of qualification, it becomes interesting to ask why they are so widely accepted and reiterated. In part, they serve as a backdrop against which contemporary positions are shown off and displayed, and hence as a reassuring sign of philosophical progress. By demonizing aspects of our own philosophical past, we are able to bask in our own purportedly dispassionate originality and insight. By branding our most celebrated predecessors as incompetent, we release ourselves from the obligation to look as sensitively and creatively as we can at their philosophies, and fend off the possibility of having to acknowledge that sometimes they were there before us. This strategy will clearly not go away. It is part of an Oedipal struggle between philosophy and its past without which the subject would come to a standstill, and is a stage in a longer dialectical pattern of rejection and recovery. But it is nevertheless a strategy about which it is helpful to be self-conscious. A second reason for studying what early-modern philosophy has to say about the passions is therefore that it provides both an exemplification of, and a commentary on, this approach, and offers us an opportunity to consider some of the ways in which it has most recently been used.

This line of enquiry is particularly relevant in relation to feminist philosophy, one of the most innovative areas in contemporary philosophical research. During the last few years, a group of exceptionally original authors have shown how deeply embedded interpretations of the differences between men and women are reflected in some of the most central of our philosophical categories. In certain ways, oppositions such as those between reason and passion, or mind and body, carry connotations of male and female, and mirror the power-relations of a patriarchal society in which women are dominated by men. Taking up the widespread view that modern philosophy begins with Descartes, some feminist writers have also argued, or assumed, that the patriarchal character of philosophy was clinched and consolidated in the seventeenth century: the emergence of a clear division between body and mind served to attach women more firmly to the physical world, and a comparable split between reason and passion condemned them to the realm of affect.[67]

These interpretations belong, on the one hand, to a not-yet-completed stage in which the patriarchal face of philosophy as it has traditionally been practised has been boldly, if sometimes crudely, outlined. In breaking with the past, exponents of these views have relied on the familiar technique of discrediting its key figures, and have achieved the intended effect of enabling people to see them differently. The fact that many of these interpretations are partial in the ways I have mentioned is therefore not altogether a criticism. But feminist research has now reached a point at which the insights yielded by the demonizing approach have been absorbed, and it is safe—and indeed necessary—to muddy the picture by looking more critically at the strategy of vilification. By condemning our forebears as empiricist, rationalist, Christian, or patriarchal, we generate the access of enthusiasm and hope that comes from starting afresh. But at the same time we enact one of the passionate strategies that philosophers such as Hobbes, Malebranche, or Spinoza identify as a flaw in self-knowledge and an obstacle to understanding.

To cast the luminaries of the early-modern canon as villains is to mimic the treatment that many seventeenth-century philosophers meted out to the ancients. For example, when Descartes and Spinoza assured their readers that no one before them had written anything to rival their own analyses of the passions,[68] they joined a chorus of condemnation of classical and Scholastic philosophy in which a break with the past was artfully constructed. While almost all philosophers were anxious to distance themselves from at least some aspects of their history and were not too intellectually fussy about how they did it, there was at the same time a sophisticated awareness of the dangers inherent in the use of this device. Reflection on its character and limitations was not usually applied directly to the practice itself; but the two existed side by side, so that the connection between them was there to be made. One interpretation of our disposition to condemn other people and erase our debts, as Hobbes runs down Aristotle or some feminist philosophers run down Descartes, was attributed to a concern with grandeur that is deeply etched into human nature. Our craving for esteem, and the enviousness and anxiety that this breeds, shapes our intellectual life and makes us prone to the demonizing strategy, which, by diminishing others, serves to augment our sense of our own value. In addition, as Hobbes explains, our undirected passions tend to fix on particular objects, so that antipathy or frustration can focus on a philosopher or a tradition. This process may be driven more by a desire to order and legitimate our emotions than by careful judgement, and may yield states in which belief merges with pacifying fantasy. But once this has occurred, it becomes more difficult to reconsider the evaluations we have reached, and to ask ourselves whether a position is really as obtuse as we have made out.

This self-reflective strand within seventeenth-century philosophy has been obscured by the contention that the mind came to be regarded, during this period, as transparent to itself. Recovering this line of thought gives us an opportunity both to reassess this interpretation and to reflect on the way we ourselves have used it. At the moment, this change of stance is particularly germane to feminist philosophy, where a history organized around rigid oppositions is in the process of giving way to finer grained studies of the cross-cutting conceptions of masculinity and femininity that run through early-modern debate.[69] But because the demonizing strategy is so common, it is also of wider relevance.

A third reason for studying seventeenth-century treatments of the passions relates more directly to current philosophical work, much of which is designed to overcome the rather narrow approaches to the topic which became entrenched around the middle of the present century. In its heyday, analytical philosophy tended to place the emotions in an unduly cramped and restrictive frame, so that the questions asked about them, and the range of answers discussed, now seem to have missed an awful lot out. This was partly because the compartmentalization of philosophy, psychology, and some of the other social sciences meant that questions previously considered philosophical came to be seen as lying outside the boundaries of the subject. For instance, the variation in emotions from place to place and group to group which fascinated seventeenth-century writers came to be regarded as psychological or anthropological. The constriction also occurred because analytical philosophy was itself dominated by theories of knowledge and action—and also to a great extent by ethical and political theories—in which emotion played at best a marginal role, and whose hold over the subject made it difficult to see that the emotions raise important and central philosophical problems. For example, an emphasis within epistemology on criteria for knowledge left little room for discussion of the role of emotion in the processes by which we come to know things;[70] an emphasis on meta-ethical issues left little room to explore the emotional dimensions of virtue.[71] Finally, analytical philosophy's rather narrow approach to the emotions stemmed not just from the character of its interests, but also from its adherence to a set of standards and distinctions which made it hard to incorporate the emotions into a broader account of our experience. Among the conditions that proved problematic was the requirement that a satisfactory analysis of emotions should be applicable to all central cases. Not an unreasonable demand, to be sure, but one that proved difficult to meet and led in some cases to stipulative conclusions.[72] Another debate, shaped by a powerful distinction between cognitive and non-cognitive mental states, concerned the cognitive status of the emotions. William James's view that these are our experience of bodily changes caused by perceptions[73] was rejected by a series of philosophers who interpreted our passions as more or less rational judgements.[74] While their analyses reflected a wish to maintain a clear distinction between the cognitive and non-cognitive, they also imposed a conception of the passions which obscured some of their distinctive characteristics and helped to keep them on the fringe of the mental phenomena studied by philosophers.[75] Only gradually has it become possible to acknowledge the complexity and diversity of the emotions, and to use this insight to reconsider their part in our mental life and behaviour.[76]

As a result of these and comparable developments, there is now an established sense among the inheritors of the analytical tradition that the study of the emotions provides a fruitful standpoint from which to question the terms in which mental states are analysed, and, independently, that the emotions are a richer topic than had been allowed. This shift has been particularly marked and successful in ethics. In other areas it remains more hesitant, as though, while agreeing that our philosophical predilections have been too tightly laced for our own good, we remain tempted to maintain the outline of old-fashioned respectability and elegance. Nevertheless a change is under way, and this puts us in a stronger position to integrate the passions into areas of philosophy in which they have had little or no place.

This book [Ed's note: *Passion and Action*] is intended as a contribution to the reinstatement of the emotions within philosophy, to the gathering tide of opinion that we need to take account of our emotional life if we are to understand, among other topics, moral motivation and growth, the springs of action (rational and otherwise), and the nature of reasoning. The philosophy of the seventeenth century remains a crucial moment from which we trace our own origins, and an appreciation of the significance accorded to the passions during this period can serve us as a model and a source. It can help us to see how problems related to the passions pervade many areas of philosophy. They are not merely ethical or merely psychological, but spread through the whole subject. It can also enable us to find in the history of philosophy itself insights and perspectives to inspire us; for it is not only in the ecological domain that recycling, and the transformations that go with it, are vital to our well-being.

Many of the most celebrated innovations introduced by seventeenth-century philosophers were provoked by the conviction that Scholastic Aristotelianism suffered from terminal deficiencies and needed to be replaced. While the initial dissatisfactions prompting this change were concerned mainly with physics and the metaphysics underpinning it, the failures of Aristotelianism that attracted most attention also bore on Scholastic interpretations of the passions. These interpretations are accordingly introduced in Part I of this book [Ed's note: *Passion and Action*]. Writers who aspired to produce systematic philosophies free from the taint of Aristotelianism were therefore committed to articulating uncontaminated analyses of the passions, and this motivation partly accounts for a series of original and sometimes piercing treatments of the subject, notably those of Hobbes and Descartes. However, as in other areas of philosophy, any suggestion that there is a clean break between Aristotelianism and the New Philosophy needs to be handled with care. The break is real enough, but it is offset by several sorts of continuity, both in the works of writers dedicated to leaving Scholasticism behind, and in the philosophical culture at large.[77]

First and most obviously, Aristotelianism did not collapse all at once, and throughout the seventeenth century many writers continued to adhere to one or other of its numerous variants. In the case of the passions, Aquinas's analysis of the states of the tripartite soul (among which the passions are included) remained particularly influential, and the transition to a post-Scholastic philosophical psychology was extremely protracted. This was partly because the planks of the vast and cumbersome Aristotelian ship could not all be replaced simultaneously. But the urge to scrap it was also tempered by the eclecticism of many philosophers, who were content to salvage a doctrine here or a principle there and incorporate them into purportedly more seaworthy vessels. While some of the resulting craft appear extraordinary to our eyes, the disposition to save and modify arose in many cases from the belief—inherited from Renaissance humanism and expressed in the use of the dialogue—that all the philosophical schools had arrived at truths which could be amalgamated into a single complete and correct system.[78] This approach was widespread, but is particularly well exemplified by the Cambridge Platonists. While such writers as Cudworth and More accord priority to the divine Plato, they also appeal to a much wider and more varied range of authorities. In his posthumously published *Treatise concerning Eternal and Immutable Morality*, Cudworth imaginatively welds together a sequence of pagan and Christian traditions and legitimates the mechanical philosophy by tracing it back to the dawn of the historical record.

> If we may believe Posidonius the Stoic, who, as Strabo tells us, affirmed this mechanical philosophy to have been ancienter than the times of the Trojan War, and was first invented and delivered by one Moschus a Sidonian, or rather a Phoenician . . . Now what can be more probable than that this

Moschus the Phoenician, that Posidonius speaks of, is the very same person with that Moschus the physiologer that Jamblichus mentions in the Life of Pythagoras, where he affirms that Pythagoras, living some time at Sidon in Phoenicia, conversed with the prophets that were the successors of Mochus physiologer, and was instructed by them . . . And what can be more certain than that both Mochus and Moschus the Phoenician and philosopher was no other than Moses, the Jewish lawgiver, as Arcerius rightly guesses.[79]

Less extravagantly, but eclectically none the less, More's *Enchyridion Ethicum*, first published in 1667, which contains his most sustained discussion of the passions, appeals to numerous sources: to Plato and Plotinus, to Cicero and Marcus Aurelius, to Aristotle and Aquinas, to Epictetus and sundry Pythagoreans.[80] In these texts, and in others like them, Aristotle appears as one philosopher among others, an authority who had some useful and some not-so-useful ideas, rather than as The Philosopher who must be either revered or rejected.[81]

A second kind of continuity is created by the rejection of Aristotelianism itself. Searching for something to replace it with, philosophers of a systematic bent were drawn to reconsider alternative classical traditions, to see whether, or how, they could be adapted and used. Gassendi, for example, embarked on a wholehearted revival and modification of Epicurean atomism, which had a considerable impact on natural philosophy.[82] And although Epicureanism was not much favoured by seventeenth-century theorists of the passions, they were strongly influenced by the revival of Stoicism which had been undertaken in the same wholehearted spirit by Lipsius.[83] It would be a drastic oversimplification, however, to interpret interest in the Stoics as fuelled simply by the need to find an alternative to Scholastic orthodoxy. While the study of natural philosophy had been effectively dominated by Aristotelianism, so that its demise threatened to create a gulf in this region of philosophy, the situation facing theorists of the passions was less desperate. Enquiry in this field had for a long while been spread between a Scholastic Aristotelian tradition and a Roman one, both of which had a place in standard educational curricula. As well as reading commentaries on Aristotle and Aquinas, students learned about the place of the passions in rhetoric, as discussed by Aristotle, Cicero, and Quintilian, and about their moral and political significance, as discussed by Cicero and Seneca among others.[84] This training made certain strands of Stoicism available; and these had in turn been taken up by writers, including Lipsius, who were dedicated to reviving a Christianized version of its ethical doctrine, a fortitude and tranquility deriving from a recognition of the futility of worldly existence and the greatness of the life to come. Stoicism therefore formed part of the intellectual background of seventeenth-century philosophers writing on the passions, and was correspondingly widely discussed and criticized. As Aristotelianism declined, it seemed to some philosophers to offer solutions to certain outstanding problems: Hobbes and Spinoza, for example, draw on its metaphysical doctrines to develop their accounts of the passions.

Running alongside these pagan philosophies are a number of strands of Christian thought, each with its own continuities and discontinuities, of which two are, perhaps, particularly important to our concerns. On the one hand, Aquinas's immense and continuing influence is partly due to the fact that he embeds the passions in a familiar and orthodox world-view, and explains them as a function of the position of humanity within this all-encompassing scheme. On the other hand, the figure of Augustine towers over philosophers of various denominations. His conception of the passions as modifications of a will that may be rightly or wrongly directed remains central to Catholic doctrine and is, for example, never far from the mind of authors such as Malebranche or Senault. His impact on Luther ensures that this view is taken up within Protestantism, where it is reflected in the emphasis placed by Puritan writers on the need for self-abasement and the constructive role of passions such as self-hatred and despair. In addition, Augustine's influence on Jansen, who entitled his *magnum opus Augustinus*, in turn shapes the work of authors such as Pascal and Nicole.

In this book [Ed's note: *Passion and Action*], I focus on a period in which philosophers appeal to a variety of traditions in order to challenge and displace the understanding of the passions embedded in Scholastic Aristotelianism. Although there is no determinate point at which this process begins, and no moment at which one can say that Aristotelianism is finally left behind, I argue that the need to replace it preoccupies philosophers throughout the seventeenth century, and that during this time they not only formulate a post-Aristotelian conception of the passions and their place in the mind, but also begin to come to terms with its implications. For all its complexity and equivocality, the urge to transcend the perceived limitations of Aristotelianism remains a central philosophical motivation. Rather than trying to assess the contribution of traditions such as Stoicism or Platonism to an altered understanding of the passions, I approach this theme through the work of individual philosophers. Some of them are nowadays obscure figures, and my aim in discussing them is to illustrate the place of the passions in the broader philosophical culture of the period. On the whole, however, I concentrate on the seventeenth-century philosophers whose names are most familiar. This is not because of any profound attachment to the established canon. However, by exploring the work of acknowledged giants, I aim to show that the study of the passions is a central topic even within the accepted heartland of early-modern philosophy.

Notes

1. *Use of the Passions*, trans. Henry Earl of Monmouth (London, 1649), sig. A 3^{v}–4^{r}. On Senault see A. Levi, *French Moralists: The Theory of the Passions 1585 to 1649* (Oxford, 1964), 213–24; P. Parker, 'Définir la passion: Corrélation et dynamique'. *Seventeenth-Century French Studies*, 18 (1996), 49–58.
2. (2nd edn., 1604), ed. W. W. Newbold (New York, 1986), 90.
3. *Treatise of the Passions and Faculties of the Soul of Man* (London, 1640), 41.
4. Wright, *Passions of the Mind*, 90.
5. Reynolds, *Treatise of the Passions*, 41.
6. Ibid. 43. Reynolds cites Aristotle's *Politics* as his source for this division of the study of the passions. On changing strategies for dealing with the passions see A. O. Hirschman, *The Passions and the Interests: Political Arguments for Capitalism before its Triumph* (Princeton, 1977), esp. 12–35.
7. Senault, *Use of the Passions*, sig. C 1^{v}.
8. Influential exponents of the view that the New Philosophy embodies a novel aspiration to control the natural world include C. Merchant, *The Death of Nature: Women, Ecology and the Scientific Revolution* (San Francisco, 1980); G. Lloyd, *The Man of Reason: 'Male' and 'Female' in Western Philosophy* (London, 1984), 10–17; E. Fox Keller, *Reflections on Gender and Science* (New Haven, 1985), 33–66; C. Taylor, *Sources of the Self* (Cambridge, 1989), 143–58. For a parallel concern with self-control see S. Greenblatt, *Renaissance Self-Fashioning from More to Shakespeare* (Chicago, 1980); M. Meyer, *Le Philosophe et les passions* (Paris, 1991).
9. See e.g. François La Mothe le Vayer, *De l'instruction de Monseigneur le Dauphin*, in *Œuvres*, 2 vols. (2nd edn., Paris, 1656), i; Pierre Nicole, *De l'éducation d'un prince* (Paris, 1670).
10. 'L'art de connaître les hommes'. Marin Cureau de la Chambre, *Les Caractères des passions* (Paris, 1648), Advis necessaire au lecteur; trans. J. Holden as *The Characters of the Passions* (London, 1650), sig. a 2^{r}. On Cureau de la Chambre see A. Darmon, *Le Corps immatériels: Esprits et images dans l'œuvre de Marin Cureau de la Chambre* (Paris, 1985).
11. *Use of the Passions*, sig. C I^{r}.
12. The works already cited by Wright, Senault, and Cureau de la Chambre are good examples of this genre.
13. i.e. wealth or possessions.
14. *Use of the Passions*, sig. B 6^{r}.
15. Wright, *Passions of the Mind*, 92.
16. In *The Complete Works of Aristotle*, ed. J. Barnes (Princeton, 1984), vol. ii,

1378^{a}31–1388^{b}31. See also *On the Soul*, in *Complete Works*, ed. Barnes, vol. 1, 403^{a}16–18.
17. In *Complete Works*, ed. Barnes, vol. ii, 1105^{b}21–3.
18. See e.g. Thomas Hobbes, *The Elements of Law*, ed. F. Tönnies (2nd edn, London, 1969), 36–48. On the relation between Hobbes's classifications and those of Aristotle see G. B. Herbert, *Thomas Hobbes: The Unity of Science and Moral Wisdom* (Vancouver, 1989), 92 f.
19. Cicero, *Tusculan Disputations*, trans. J. E. King (Harvard, Mass., 1927), iii. 24–5.
20. e.g. Antoine Le Grand, *Man without Passions: Or the Wise Stoic according to the Sentiments of Seneca*, trans. G.R. (London, 1675), 77.
21. This interpretation derives from Stobaeus. See A. A. Long and D. N. Sedley, *The Hellenistic Philosophers* (Cambridge, 1987), 411. Seventeenth-cent. authors tended to condense his interpretation still further by combining *libido* and *metus* into one passion—desire—which is understood to include aversion. See Ch. 11 [of *Passion and Action*].
22. Ed. D. Knowles (Harmondsworth, 1972), 14. 6.
23. Ibid. 14. 7.
24. *Use of the Passions*, 26.
25. See e.g. Nicolas Coeffeteau, *Tableau des passions humaines, de leurs causes et leurs effets* (Paris, 1630), 17 f; Jean Pierre Camus, *Traité des passions de l'âme*, in *Diversitez* (Paris, 1609–14), viii. 96 f; La Mothe le Vayer, *Morale du Prince*, 850; Cureau de la Chambre, *Characters of the Passions*, sig. a 5$^{r–v}$; Henry More, *An Account of Virtue or Dr. More's Abridgment of Morals put into English*, trans. E. Southwell (London, 1690), 850. On Coeffeteau, Camus, La Mothe le Vayer, and Cureau de la Chambre, see A. Levi, *French Moralists: The Theory of the Passions 1585–1649* (Oxford, 1964). On Henry More see Ch. 10 [of *Passion and Action*].
26. Aquinas, *Summa Theologiae*, ed. and trans. by the Dominican Fathers (London, 1964–80), 1a, 2ae. 23.
27. The dominance of this view is reflected in textbooks—e.g. S. Guttenplan (ed.), *A Companion to the Philosophy of Mind* (Oxford, 1994)—and is particularly evident in contemporary discussions of agency, where desires, along with beliefs, are habitually singled out as the antecedents of action. E.g. see P. Pettit, *The Common Mind* (Oxford, 1993), 10–24; M. Hollis, *Models of Man* (Cambridge, 1977), 137–41; F. Jackson, 'Mental Causation', *Mind*, 105 (1996), 377–409. This assumption also underlies the theory of rational choice. See J. Elster (ed.), *Rational Choice* (Oxford, 1986), 12–16.
28. See e.g. René Descartes, *The Passions of the Soul*, in *The Philosophical Writings of René Descartes*, ed. J. Cottingham *et al.* (Cambridge, 1984–91), i. 27–8. For further discussion of his view see Ch. 5 [of *Passion and Action*].
29. Charron, *Of Wisdome*, trans. S. Lennard (London, 1608), 7; see also 438 f. On Charron see M. Adam, *Études sur Pierre Charron* (Bordeaux, 1991) and 'L'Horizon philosophique de Pierre Charron', *Revue philosophique de la France et de l'Étranger*, 181 (1991), 273–93.
30. See Ch. 10 [of *Passion and Action*].
31. Walter Charleton, *A Natural History of the Passions* (London, 1674), 75–6.
32. On these aspects of our vulnerability see esp. P. Nicole, 'Discours où l'on fait voir combien les entretiens des hommes sont dangereux', in *Essais de Morale*

(Paris, 1672), ii. 241–64. On Nicole see E. D. James, *Pierre Nicole, Jansenist and Humanist: A Study of his Thought* (The Hague, 1972).

33. *Passions of the Mind*, 121.
34. 'Faire and foolish, little and lowde | Long and lazy, black and prowde | Fatte and merrie, leane and sadde | Pale and pettish, redde and bad.' Ibid. 120.
35. Nicolas Malebranche, *De la Recherche de la Vérité* (2nd edn.), ed. G. Rodis Lewis in *Euvres complètes*, ed. A. Robinet (Paris, 1972), i. 266. For an Eng. trans. see *The Search after Truth*, trans. T. M. Lennon and P. J. Olscamp (Columbus, O., 1980), 130–1.
36. *Of Wisdome*, 85–6, 90.
37. Wright, *Passions of the Mind*, 117.
38. Charron, *Of Wisdome*, 156–7.
39. *Passions of the Mind*, 83–4.
40. Ibid. 92. On national character as a topos in early-modern Europe see L. Van Delft, *Littérature et anthropologic: Nature humaine et caractère à l'âge classique* (Paris, 1993), 87–104.
41. Ed. T. C. Faulkner *et al.* (Oxford, 1989–94), i. *Text*, 249. On Burton see B. C. Lyons, *Voices of Melancholy: Studies in Literary Treatments of Melancholy in Renaissance England* (London, 1971), 113–48; E. P. Vicari, *The View from Minerva's Tower: Learning and Imagination in The Anatomy of Melancholy* (Toronto, 1989).
42. *Use of the Passions*, sig. B 2[r–v].
43. p. 133.
44. (1674), sig. A 4[r].
45. *City of God*, 9. 4.
46. *Summa*, 1a, 2ae 22.
47. *Passions of the Mind*, 94.
48. *The Immortality of the Soul*, ed. A. Jacob (Dordrecht, 1987), 168. The same claim is made by Reynolds, *Treatise on the Passions*, 73, and Wright, *Passions of the Mind*, 136.
49. Francis Bacon, *The Advancement of Learning*, ed. G. W. Kitchin (London, 1973), 147.
50. Wright, *Passions of the Mind*, 141.
51. Charleton, *Natural History of the Passions*, 58.
52. Senault, *Use of the Passions*, 90. Antaeus was a giant killed by Hercules.
53. Ibid. 96.
54. Bacon, *Advancement of Learning*, 171; Baruch Spinoza, *Ethics*, in *The Collected Works of Spinoza* ed. E. Curley (Princeton, 1985), vol. i, III. 59 s; Charleton, *Natural History of the Passions*, 69.
55. Charron, *Of Wisdome*, 213.
56. Reynolds, *Treatise of the Passions*, 45.
57. Wright, *Passions of the Mind*, 94.
58. Ibid. 125.
59. Charron, *Of Wisdome*, 215–16.
60. William Shakespeare, *Othello*, in *The Complete Works*, ed. S. Wells and G. Taylor (Oxford, 1988), iv. i. 844.
61. William Shakespeare, *Hamlet*, in *Complete Works*, ed. Wells and Taylor, III, ii. 672.

62. For a survey of these issues see S. James, 'Ethics as the Control of the Passions', in M. Ayers and D. Garber (eds.), *The Cambridge History of Seventeenth-Century Philosophy* (Cambridge, 1997), vii. 5.
63. Among important exceptions to this generalization see Levi, *French Moralists*; Meyer, *Le Philosophe et les passions*; M. Nussbaum, *The Therapy of Desire: Theory and Practice in Hellenistic Ethics* (Princeton, 1994); A. O. Rorty, 'From Passions to Emotions and Sentiments', *Philosophy*, 57 (1982), 159–72; J. Cottingham, 'Cartesian Ethics: Reason and the Passions', *Revue internationale de philosophie*, 50 (1996), 193–216; D. Kambouchner, *L'Homme des passions: Commentaires sur Descartes* (Paris, 1996).
64. This interpretation seems to have solidified in the 19th cent., alongside a conception of Descartes as an epistemologist. See B. Kuklick, 'Seven Thinkers and How They Grew' in R. Rorty *et al.* (eds.), *Philosophy in History* (Cambridge, 1984), 130; S. Gaukroger, *Descartes: An Intellectual Biography* (Oxford, 1996), 2–7. Its influence on the 20th-cent, analytical tradition owes much to G. Ryle, *The Concept of Mind* (London, 1949) and it remains prominent in histories of philosophy—e.g. R. Scruton, *From Descartes to Wittgenstein* (London, 1981)—and in surveys of the philosophy of mind—e.g. P. Smith and O.R. Jones, *The Philosophy of Mind: An Introduction* (Cambridge, 1986); G. McCulloch, *The Mind and its World* (London, 1995).
65. For this type of analysis of modernity see Lloyd, *Man of Reason*, esp. 10–18; Taylor, *Sources of the Self*, 143–58; P. A. Schouls, *Descartes and the Enlightenment* (Montreal, 1989); S. Toulmin, *Cosmopolis: The Hidden Agenda of Modernity* (New York, 1990); R. B. Pippin, *Modernity as a Philosophical Problem: On the Dissatisfactions of European High Culture* (Oxford, 1991), 16–45. For a measured interpretation see H. Blumenberg, *The Legitimacy of the Modern Age*, trans. R. M. Wallace (Cambridge, Mass., 1983), esp. ii.
66. See S. James, 'Internal and External in the Work of Descartes', in J. Tully (ed.), *Philosophy in an Age of Pluralism* (Cambridge, 1994), 7–19.
67. See Lloyd, *The Man of Reason*; S. Bordo, *The Flight to Objectivity: Essays on Cartesianism and Culture* (Albany, NY, 1987) and 'The Cartesian Masculinisation of Thought', in S. Harding and J. O'Barr (eds.), *Sex and Scientific Enquiry* (Chicago, 1987), 247–64; N. Scheman, 'Though this be method yet there is madness in it: Paranoia and Liberal Epistemology', in L. M. Anthony and C. Witt (eds.), *A Mind of One's Own: Feminist Essays on Reason and Objectivity* (Boulder, Colo., 1993), 145–70; N. Tuana, *The Less Noble Sex: Scientific, Religious and Philosophical Conceptions of Women's Nature* (Bloomington, Ind., 1993), 60–4. The view that it was Descartes who succeeded in separating mind from body and passion from reason is taken for granted by a wide range of feminist writers. See e.g. E. Fox Keller, 'From Secrets of Life to Secrets of Death', in *Secrets of Life: Essays on Language, Gender and Science* (London, 1992), 39; J. Flax, 'Political Philosophy and the Patriarchal Unconscious: A Psychoanalytic Perspective on Epistemology and Metaphysics', in N. Tuana and R. Tong (eds.), *Feminism and Philosophy* (Boulder, Colo., 1995), 227–9; E. Grosz, *Volatile Bodies* (Bloomington, Ind., 1994), 6–10; S. Benhabib, *Situating the Self: Gender, Community and Postmodernism in Contemporary Ethics* (Cambridge, 1992), 207.
68. See Descartes, *Passions of the Soul*, 68 (though compare the more concessive view in his letter to Princess Elizabeth, 21 July 1645, in *Philosophical Writings*,

ed. Cottingham, *et al.*, iii. *Correspondence* 256); Spinoza, *Ethics*, pref. to prt. III, 491. On ancients and moderns see S. Gaukroger (ed.), *The Uses of Antiquity* (Dordrecht, 1991); B. P. Copenhaver and C. B. Schmitt, *Renaissance Philosophy* (Oxford, 1992), 285–328; T. Sorell (ed.), *The Rise of Modern Philosophy* (Oxford, 1993).

69. Outstanding examples of a more fruitful approach to 17th-cent. philosophy include M. Atherton, 'Cartesian Reason and Gendered Reason', in Antony and Witt (eds.). *A Mind of One's Own*, 19–34, and G. Lloyd, 'Maleness, Metaphor and the "Crisis" of Reason', Antony and Witt (eds.), *A Mind of One's Own*, 69–83.
70. Though on this issue see M. Stocker, 'Intellectual Desire, Emotion and Action', in A. O. Rorty (ed.), *Explaining Emotions* (Berkeley and Los Angeles, 1980), 323–38; A. Jagger, 'Love and Knowledge: Emotion in Feminist Epistemology', in A. Garry and M. Pearsall (eds.), *Women, Knowledge and Reality* (Boston, 1989), 129–56; J. Benjamin, *The Bonds of Love* (London, 1990), T. Brennan. *History after Lacan* (London, 1993).
71. This position has recently changed. See the surveys by J. R. Wallach, 'Contemporary Aristotelianism', *Political Theory*, 20 (1992), 613–41, and J. Oakley, 'Varieties of Virtue Ethics', *Ratio*, 9 (1996), 128–52.
72. See e.g. R. C. Roberts, 'What an Emotion Is: A Sketch', *Philosophical Review*, 97 (1988), 184–5. Roberts acknowledges that his analysis will not cover various states which other philosophers regard as emotions, but does not regard this as an objection to his view.
73. *The Principles of Psychology* (Cambridge, Mass, 1983), 1,065.
74. See e.g. R. C. Solomon. *The Passions* (Notre Dame, Ind., 1983).
75. On this debate see P. Greenspan, *Emotions and Reasons: An Inquiry into Emotional Justification* (London, 1988), 3–36, C. Armon Jones, *Varieties of Affect* (London, 1991).
76. See Jones, *Varieties of Affect*, J. Oakley, *Morality and the Emotions* (London, 1992), 6–37.
77. For this continuity in interpretations of the passions see Levi, *French Moralists*, 329–38; Van Delft, *Moraliste classique*, 129–37.
78. For syncretists who held this view see C. B. Schmitt and Q. Skinner (eds.), *The Cambridge History of Renaissance Philosophy* (Cambridge, 1988): on Vernia, 494; on Pico, 494, 578; on Ficino, 675.
79. *A Treatise concerning Eternal and Immutable Morality With A Treatise of Freewill*, ed. S. Hutton (Cambridge, 1996), 38–9.
80. Trans. and abridged as *An Account of Virtue or Dr. Henry More's Abridgment of Morals* (London, 1690).
81. On Renaissance antecedents of this approach see B. Copenhaver and C. Schmitt, *Renaissance Philosophy*, 75–126.
82. See L. S. Joy, *Gassendi the Atomist* (Cambridge, 1987); M. J. Osler (ed.), *Atoms,* Pneuma *and Tranquility: Epicurean and Stoic Themes in European Thought* (Cambridge, 1991).
83. On aspects of early-modern Stoicism see L. Xanta, *La Renaissance du Stoicisme au XVI*[e] siècle (Paris, 1914); C. Chesnau, 'Le Stoïcisme en France dans la première moitié du XVIIe siècle: Les Origines', *Études franciscaines*, 2 (1951), 384–410; J. L. Saunders, *Justus Lipsius: The Philosophy of Renaissance Stoicism* (New York, 1955), 492–519; Levi, *French Moralists*; on Du Vair, M. Fumaroli,

L'Âge d'éloquence (Geneva, 1980); G. Oestreich, *Neostoicism and the Early-Modern State* (Cambridge, 1982); G. Monsarrat, *Light from the Porch: Stoicism and English Renaissance Literature* (Paris, 1984); A. Chew, *Stoicism in Renaissance English Literature* (New York, 1988); Osler, *Atoms,* Pneuma *and Tranquility*; M. Morford, *Stoics and Neo-Stoics: Rubens and the Circle of Lipssus* (Princeton, 1991).

84. On changing curricula in the English universities see J. Gascoigne, *Cambridge in the Age of the Enlightenment: Science and Religion from the Restoration to the French Revolution* (Cambridge, 1989); on English grammar schools see Q. Skinner, *Reason and Rhetoric in the Philosophy of Hobbes* (Cambridge, 1996), 19–40; on France see L. W. B. Brockliss, *French Higher Education in the Seventeenth and Eighteenth Centuries* (Oxford, 1987); on the Jesuit curriculum see F. de Dainville, *L'Education des Jèsuites* (Paris, 1978).

7 Selections from *The Flight to Objectivity*[1]

Susan Bordo*

On November 10, 1619, Descartes had a series of dreams—bizarre, richly imaginal sequences manifestly full of anxiety and dread. He interpreted these dreams—which most readers would surely regard as nightmares—as revealing to him that mathematics is the key to understanding the universe. Descartes's resolute and disconcertingly positive interpretation has become a standard textbook anecdote, a symbol of the seventeenth-century rationalist project. That project, in the official story told in most philosophy and history texts, describes seventeenth-century culture as Descartes described his dreams: in terms of intellectual beginnings, fresh confidence, and a new belief in the ability of science—armed with the discourses of mathematics and the 'new philosophy'—to decipher the language of nature.

Recent scholarship, however, has detected a certain instability, a dark underside, to the bold rationalist vision. Different writers describe it in different ways. Richard Bernstein speaks of the great 'Cartesian anxiety' over the possibility of intellectual and moral chaos (1980, 762); Karsten Harries speaks of the (Cartesian) 'dread of the distorting power of perspective' (1973, 29); Richard Rorty reminds us that the seventeenth-century ideal of a perfectly mirrored nature is also an 'attempt to escape' from history, culture, and human finitude (1979, 9). Looking freshly at Descartes's *Meditations*, one cannot help but be struck by the manifest epistemological anxiety of the earlier Meditations and by how unresolute a mode of inquiry they embody; the dizzying vacillations, the constant requestioning of the self, the determination, if only temporary, to stay within confusion and contradiction, to favor interior movement rather than clarity and resolve.

* Susan Bordo, 'Selections from *The Flight to Objectivity*', from Susan Bordo (ed.), *Feminist Interpretations of René Descartes* (University Park: Pennsylvania State University Press, 1999), 48–69; *The Flight to Objectivity* was originally published by Albany: State University of New York Press, 1987. Reprinted by permission of the publisher.

All that, of course, is ultimately left behind by Descartes, as firmly as his bad dreams (as he tells his correspondent, Elizabeth of Bohemia) were conquered by the vigilance of his reason. The model of knowledge that Descartes bequeathed to modern science, and of which he is often explicitly described as the father, is based on clarity, dispassion, and detachment. Yet the transformation from the imagery of nightmare (the *Meditations*'s demons, dreamers, and madmen) to the imagery of objectivity remains unconvincing. The sense of experience conveyed by the first two Meditations—what Karl Stern calls the sense of 'reality founded on uncertainty' (1965, 99)—is not quite overcome for the reader by the positivity of the later Meditations. Descartes's critics felt this in his own time. Over and over, the objection is raised: given the power of the first two Meditations, how can you really claim to have extricated yourself from the doubt and from the dream?

Drawing on the work of Margaret Mahler and Jean Piaget, I will undertake a cultural reexamination of Cartesian doubt and of Descartes's seeming triumph over the epistemological insecurity of the first two Meditations. I will suggest that in an important sense the separate self, conscious of itself and of its own distinctness from a world outside it, is born in the Cartesian era. This was a *psychocultural* birth—of 'inwardness,' of 'subjectivity,' of locatedness in time and space—generating new anxieties and, ultimately, new strategies for maintaining equilibrium in an utterly changed and alien world. In interpreting those anxieties and strategies, I propose, much can be learned from those theorists for whom the concepts of psychological birth, separation anxiety, and the defenses that may be employed against such anxiety, are central to a picture of human development. Such theories provide an illuminative framework for a fresh reading of the *Meditations.*

I will suggest that we view the 'great Cartesian anxiety,' although manifestly expressed in epistemological terms, as anxiety over separation—from the organic female universe of the Middle Ages and the Renaissance. The Cartesian reconstruction, correspondingly, will be explored as a *re*birthing of nature (as machine) and knowledge (as objectivity), a 'masculine birth of time,' as Francis Bacon called it, in which the more intuitive, empathic, and associational elements were exorcised from science and philosophy. The result was a 'super-masculinized' model of knowledge in which detachment, clarity, and transcendence of the body are all key requirements.

SEPARATION AND INDIVIDUATION THEMES IN THE *MEDITATIONS*

The need for God's guarantee, in the *Meditations*, is a need for a principle of continuity and coherence for what is experienced by Descartes as a disastrously fragmented and discontinuous mental life. For Descartes, indeed, discontinuity is the central fact of human experience. Nothing—neither certainty, nor temporal existence itself—endures past the present moment without God. Time—both external and internal—is so fragmented that 'in order to secure the continued existence of a thing, no less a cause is required than that needed to produce it at the first' (Haldane and Ross 1961, 1:56 [hereafter referred to as HR]). This means not only that our continued existence is causally dependent on God (HR 1:158–59), but that God is required to provide continuity and unity to our inner life as well. That inner life, without God, 'is always of the present moment'; two and two may equal four right now, while we are attending to it, but we need God to assure us that two and two will always form four, whether we are attending to it or not. Even the most forcefully experienced insights—save the *cogito*—become open to doubt once the immediacy of the intuition passes:

> For although I am of such a nature that as long as I understand anything very clearly and distinctly, I am naturally impelled to believe it to be true, yet because I am also of such a nature that I cannot have my mind constantly fixed on the same object in order to perceive it clearly, and as I often recollect having formed a past judgement without at the same time properly recollecting the reasons that led me to make it, it may happen meanwhile that other reasons present themselves to me, which would easily cause me to change my opinion, if I were ignorant of the facts of the existence of God, and thus I should have no true and certain knowledge, but only vague and vacillating opinion. (HR 1:183–84)

This strong sense of the fragility of human cognitive relations with the object world is closely connected to the new Cartesian sense (which Descartes shared with the culture around him) of what Stephen Toulmin has called 'the inwardness of mental life' (1976): the sense of experience as occurring deeply within and bounded by a self. According to many scholars of the era, such a sense was not prominent in the medieval experience of the world:

> When we think casually, we think of consciousness as situated at some point in space . . . even those who achieve the intellectual contortionism of denying

that there is such a thing as consciousness, feel that this denial comes from inside their own skins . . . This was not the background picture before the scientific revolution. The background picture then was of man as a microcosm within the macrocosm. It is clear that he did not feel himself isolated by his skin from the world outside to quite the same extent that we do. He was integrated or mortised into it, each different part of him being united to a different part of it by some invisible thread. In his relation to his environment, the man of the middle ages was rather less like an island, rather more like an embryo. (Barfield 1965, 78)

During the Renaissance, as Claudio Guillen argues, European culture become 'interiorized' (1971). It is in art and literature that the change is most dramatically expressed. For the medievals and the early Renaissance, there is no radical disjunction between the 'inner' reality and outward appearance, but rather 'a close relation between the movement of the body and movement of the soul' (Baxandall 1972, 60). Now, the portrayal of the 'inner life'—both as a dramatic problem and as a subject of literary exploration—becomes an issue. In Shakespeare, a new theme emerges: the 'hidden substance' of the self—the notion that the experience of individuals in fundamentally opaque, even inaccessible to others, who can only take the 'outer' view on it. ''Tis not . . . all forms, moods, shapes of grief, that can denote me truly,' Hamlet bemoans, '. . . For they are actions that a man might play, / But I have within which passes show; / These but the trappings and the suits of woe.' In Montaigne, the inner life becomes an object of voluptuous and unrestrained introspection: 'I turn my gaze inward, I fix it there and keep it busy . . . I look inside myself; I continually observe myself, I take stock in myself, I taste myself . . . I roll about in myself' (1963, 273). 'Myself' here is neither the public self, a social or familial identity, nor even the voice of personal conscience, belief, or commitment. It is an experiential 'space,' deeply interior, and at the same time capable of objectification and examination.

In philosophy, the interiorization of the self is marked by a change from the notion of 'mind-as-reason' to the notion of 'mind-as-consciousness' (Rorty 1979, 53). For Aristotle, there had been two modes of knowing, corresponding to the two ways that things may be known. On the one hand, there is *sensing*, which is the province of the body, and which is of the particular and material; on the other hand, there is *thought* (or reason), which is of the universal and immaterial. For Descartes, both these modes of knowing become subsumed under the category of *penser*, which embraces perceptions, images, ideas, pains, and volitions alike: 'What is a thing which thinks? It is a thing which doubts, understands, [conceives], affirms, denies, wills, refuses, which also imagines and feels' (HR 1:153). The characteristic that unites all these states is that they are all *conscious* states: 'Thought is a word which covers everything that exists in us in such a way that we are immediately conscious of it. Thus all the operations of will, intellect, imagination, and of the senses are thoughts' (HR 2:52).

'Consciousness' was a new categorical umbrella which was at once to suggest the appropriateness of new imagery and metaphors. Whereas 'Reason,' for the Greeks and medievals, was a human faculty, resisting metaphors of locatedness, neither 'inside' nor 'outside' the human being, 'consciousness,' for Descartes, was the quality of a certain sort of event—the sort of event distinguished from all other events precisely by being located in inner 'space' rather than in the external world. The *Meditations*, in both form and content, remains one of the most thorough-going and compelling examples we have of exploration of that inner space. Augustine's *Confessions* embody a stream of consciousness, to be sure, but they very rarely confront that stream as an object of exploration. Descartes provides the first real phenomenology of the mind, and one of the central results of that phenomenology is the disclosure of the deep epistemological alienation that attends the sense of mental interiority: the enormous gulf that must separate what is conceived as occurring 'in here' from that which, correspondingly, must lie 'out there.'

Consider, in this connection, the difference between the Greek and medieval view of the nature of error and the Cartesian view. The principal form that error takes, for Descartes, is in the judgment that the ideas that are in me 'are similar or conformable to the things which are outside me' (HR 1:160). For the Greeks and medievals, such a formulation would have made no sense. Completely absent in their thought is the image of an unreliable, distorting inner faculty; rather, there are two worlds (for Aristotle, it might be more correct to say two aspects of the same world) and two human faculties—intellect and sense—appropriate to each. Error is the result of confusion *between* worlds—the sensible and the unchanging—not the result of inner misrepresentation of external reality. For Descartes, contrastingly, the central inquiry of Meditation 2, and the first formulation of what was to become *the* epistemological question for philosophers until Kant, is 'whether any of the object of which I have ideas *within me* exist *outside of me*' (HR 1:161, emphasis added). Under such circumstances, *cogito ergo sum* is, indeed, the only emphatic reality, for to be assured of its truth, we require nothing but confrontation with the inner stream itself. Beyond the direct and indubitable 'I am,' the meditation on the self can lead to no other truths without God to bridge the gulf between the 'inner' and the 'outer.'

The profound Cartesian experience of self as inwardness ('I think, therefore I am') and its corollary—the heightened sense of distance from the 'not-I'—inspires a deeper consideration of the popular imagery that describes the transition from the Middle Ages to the early modern period through metaphors of birth and infancy. 'The world did in her Cradle take a fall,' mourned Donne in the *Anatomy of the World* (1611), grieving for a lost world as well as for Elizabeth Drury. Ortega y Gasset describes the 'human drama which began in 1400 and ends in 1650' as a 'drama of parturition' (1958, 184). Arthur Koestler compares the finite universe to a nursery and, later, to a womb: 'Homo sapiens had dwelt in a universe enveloped by divinity as by a womb; now he was being expelled from the womb' (1959, 218). Such imagery may be more appropriate than any of these authors intended. As individuals, according to Margaret Mahler, our true psychological birth comes when we begin to experience our separateness from the mother, when we begin to individuate from her. That process, whose stages are described in detail by Mahler, involves a slowly unfolding reciprocal delineation of self and world (1972). For Mahler (as for Piaget, in describing cognitive development), as subjectivity becomes ever more internally aware, so the object world (via its principal representative, the mother) becomes ever more external and autonomous. Thus, the normal adult experience of 'being both fully "in" and at the same time basically separate from the world out there' is developed from an original state of unity with the mother (Mahler 1972, 333).

This is not easy for the child, for every major step in the direction of individuation revives an 'eternal longing' for the 'ideal state of self' in which mother and child were one, and recognition of our ever increasing distance from it. 'Side by side with the growth of his emotional life, there is a noticeable waning . . . of his [previous] relative obliviousness to the mother's presence. Increased separation anxiety can be observed . . . a seemingly constant concern with the mother's whereabouts' (Mahler 1972, 337). Although we become more or less reconciled to our separateness, the process of individuation and its anxieties 'reverberates throughout the life cycle. It is never finished, it can always be reactivated' (33).

I offer these insights not in the service of a 'developmental' science of Western history (such as that, for example, that Piaget has proposed). Theories of separation and individuation describe *individual* development on the level of *infant* object relations, and arguable within a particular cultural milieu and a particular form of family life. The categories and developmental schema presented by Mahler cannot simply be transposed into a grand narrative of historical change or evolutionary development. But they *do* offer a way of seeing the Cartesian era empathically, psychologically, and 'personally.' They enable us to ask whether separation anxiety might not 'reverberate,' too, on the cultural level. Perhaps, for example, some cultural eras *compensate* for the pain of personal individuation better than others, through a mother imagery of the cosmos (such as was dominant throughout the Chaucerian and Elizabethan eras) that assuages the anxiety of our actual separateness as individuals. On the other hand, during periods in which long-established images of symbiosis and cosmic unity *break down* (as they did during the period of the scientific revolution), may we not expect an increase in self-consciousness, and anxiety over the distance between self and world—a constant concern, to paraphrase Mahler, over the 'whereabouts of the world'? All these are central motifs in the *Meditations.*

Recall, in this connection, Descartes's concern over the inability of the mind to be 'constantly fixed on the same object in order to perceive it clearly' (and thus, without God's guarantee, to be assured only of 'vague and vacillating opinion'; HR 1:183–84). The original model of epistemological security (which Descartes knows cannot be fulfilled—thus the need for God) is a constant state of mental vigilance over the object; in the absence of that, nothing can be certain. To put this in more concrete terms; no previously reached conclusions, no past insights, no remembered information can be trusted. Unless the object is present and immediately in sight, it ceases to be available to the knower.

Consider this epistemological instability in connection with Piaget's famous experiments on the development of 'permanent object concept' (or objectivity) in children (1954). That development is from an egocentric state, in which the self and world exist on an unbroken continuum and the child does not distinguish between events occurring in the self and events occurring in the world, to one in which the sense of a mutually juxtaposed self and world is distinct, firm, and stable. At first, the developing child does not perceive objects as having enduring stability, 'firm in existence though they do not directly affect perception.' Instead, the object world is characterized by 'continuous annihilations and resurrections,' depending upon whether or not the object is within the child's perceptual field. When an object leaves the child's sight, it (effectively) leaves the universe (103).

In a sense, this is Descartes's dilemma, too, and the reason he needs God. Neither the self nor objects are stable, and the lack of stability in the object world is, indeed, experienced as concern over the whereabouts of the world. This is not, to say that Descartes saw the world as a child does. He, of course, had 'permanent object concept.' In speaking of perceiving objects, he is talking not about rudimentary perception but of the intellectual apprehension of the essences of things. The structural similarity between his 'doubt by inattention' (as Robert Alexander calls it [1972, 121]) and the developing child's perceptual deficiencies is suggestive, however. At the very least, such similarities open up the imagination to a consideration of the thoroughly *historical* character of our modern structuring of the relation between self and world. They urge us to entertain the notion that the categories that we take for granted as experiential or theoretical 'givens'—subjectivity, perspectivity, inwardness, locatedness, and objectivity (all 'moments' of the subject/object distinction)—may not be universals, but specific to the history of dominant Western norms of consciousness, each with its own birth, life, and decline.

Without my making any unsupportable claims about how medievals 'saw' the world, it seems clear that for the medieval aesthetic and philosophical imagination, the categories of self and world, inner and outer, human and natural were not as rigorously opposed as they came to be during the Cartesian era. The most striking evidence for this comes not only from the organic, holistic imagery of the cosmos and the animistic science that prevailed until the seventeenth century, but from medieval art as well. That art, which seems so distorted and spatially incoherent to a modern viewer, does so precisely because it does not represent the point of view of a detached, discretely located observer confronting a visual field of separate objects. The latter mode of representation—that of the perspective painting—had become the dominant artistic convention by the seventeenth century. In the medieval painting, by contrast, the fiction of the fixed beholder is entirely absent; instead, the spectator, as art historian Samuel Edgerton describes the process, is invited to become 'absorbed within the visual world ... to walk about, experiencing structures, almost tactilely, from many different sides, rather than from a single, overall vantage' (1975, 9). Often, sides of objects that could not possibly be seen at once (from one perceptual point of view) are represented as though the (imagined) movement of the subject in relating to the object—touching it, considering it from all angles—constitutes the object itself. The re-created experience is of the world and self as an unbroken continuum.

Owen Barfield suggests that the reason that perspective was not discovered before the Renaissance was because people did not need it: 'Before the scientific revolution the world was more like a garment men wore about them than a stage on which they moved. In such a world the convention of perspective was unnecessary . . . It was as if the observers were themselves in the picture. Compared with us, they felt themselves and the objects around them and the words that expressed those objects, immersed together in something like a clear lake of—what shall we say?—of "meaning", if you choose' (Barfield, 1965, 94–95). By extreme contrast, consider Pascal's despair at what seems to him an arbitrary and impersonal 'allotment' in the 'infinite immensity of spaces of which I know nothing and which know nothing of me. . . . There is no reason for me to be here rather than there, now rather than then. Who put me here?' (Pascal 1966). Pascal's sense of homelessness and abandonment, his apprehension of an almost personal indifference on the part of the universe, is closely connected here to an acute anxiety at the experience of personal boundedness and locatedness, of 'me-here-now' (and *only* 'here-now'). A similar anxiety, as I have suggested, is at the heart of Descartes's need for a God to sustain both his existence and his inner life from moment to moment, to provide a reassurance of permanence and connection between self and world. Once, such connection had not been in question.

THE CARTESIAN REBIRTH AND RECONSTRUCTION

> Descartes envisages for himself a kind of rebirth. Intellectual salvation comes only to the twice-born.
>
> —Harry Frankfurt, *Demons, Dreamers, and Madmen*

If the transition from Middle Ages to Renaissance can be looked on as a kind of protracted birth—from which the human being emerges as a decisively separate entity, no longer continuous with the universe with which it had once shared a soul—so the possibility of objectivity, strikingly, is conceived by Descartes as a kind of *re*birth, on one's own terms, this time.

Most of us are familiar with the dominant Cartesian themes of starting anew, alone, without influence from the past or other people, with the guidance of reason alone. The product of our original and actual birth, childhood, being ruled by the body, is the source of all obscurity and confusion in our thinking. For, as body, we are completely reactive and nondiscriminative, unable to make the most basic distinctions between an inner occurrence and an external event. One might say, in fact, that the distinction has no meaning at all for the body. This is why infancy—when the mind, 'newly united' to the body, was 'swamped' or 'immersed' within it (HR 1:237)—is for Descartes primarily a period of egocentrism (in the Piagetian sense): of complete inability to distinguish between subject and object. It is this feature of infancy that is responsible for all the 'childhood prejudices' that later persist in the form of adult philosophical confusion between primary and secondary qualities, the 'preconceptions of the senses,' and the dictates of reason. As children, we judged subjectively, determining 'that there was more or less reality in each body, according as the impressions made [on our own bodies] were more or less strong.' So, we attributed much greater reality to rock than air, believed the stars were actually as small as 'tiny lighted candles,' and believed that heat and cold were properties of the objects themselves (HR 1:250). These 'prejudices' stay with us, 'we quite forget we had accepted them without sufficient examination, admitting them as though they were of perfect truth and certainty'; thus, 'it is almost impossible that our judgments should be as pure and solid as they would have been if we had had complete use of our reason since birth and had never been guided except by it' (HR 1:88).

It is crucial to note that it is the lack of differentiation between subject and object, between self and world, that is construed here as the epistemological threat. The medieval sense of relatedness to the world had not depended on such 'objectivity' but on continuity between the human and physical realms, on the interpenetrations, through meanings and associations, of self and world. Now, a clear and distinct sense of the boundaries of the self has become the ideal; the lingering of infantile subjectivism has become the impediment to solid judgment.

The precise form of that subjectivism, as we have seen, is the inability to distinguish properly what is happening solely 'inside' the subject from what has an external existence. 'Swamped' inside the body, one simply did not have a perspective from which to discriminate, to examine, to judge. In *Meditation* 1, Descartes re-creates that state of utter entrapment by luring the reader through the continuities between madness, then dreaming—that state each night when each of us loses our adult clarity and detachment—and finally to the possibility that the whole of our existence may be like a dream, a grand illusion so encompassing that there is no conceivable perspective from which to judge its correspondence with reality. This, in essence, is the Evil Demon hypothesis—a specter of complete enclosedness and entrapment within the self. The difference, of course, is that in childhood, we assumed that what we felt was a measure of external reality; now, as mature Cartesian doubters, we reverse that prejudice. We assume nothing. We refuse to let our bodies mystify us: 'I shall close my eyes, I shall stop my ears, I shall call away all my senses' (HR 1:157). We begin afresh.

For Descartes, then, the state of childhood *can* be revoked, through a deliberate and methodical reversal of all the prejudices acquired within it, and a beginning anew with reason as one's only parent. This is precisely what the *Meditations* attempts to do. The mind is emptied of all that it has been taught. The body of infancy, preoccupied with appetite and sense-experience, is transcended. The clear and distinct ideas are released from their obscuring material prison. The end result is a philosophical reconstruction that secures all the boundaries that in childhood (and at the start of the *Meditations*) are so fragile between the 'inner' and the 'outer,' between the subjective and the objective, between self and world.

The Cartesian reconstruction has two interrelated dimensions. On the one hand, the ontological blueprint of the order of *things* is refashioned. The spiritual and the corporeal are now two distinct substances that share no qualities (other than being created), permit of interaction but no merging, and are each defined precisely in opposition to the other. *Res cogitans* is 'a thinking and unextended thing'; *res extensa* is 'an extended and unthinking thing.' This metaphysical reconstruction has important epistemological implications, too. For the mutual exclusion of *res cogitans* and *res extensa* makes possible the conceptualization of complete intellectual independence from the body, *res extensa* of the human being and chief impediment to human objectivity.

Descartes, of course, was not the first philosopher to view the body with disdain. Nor was Descartes the first to view human existence as bifurcated into the realms of the physical and the spiritual, with the physical cast in the role of the alien and impure. For Plato, the body is often described via the imagery of separateness from the self: It is 'fastened and glued' to me, 'nailed' and 'riveted' to me (*Phaedo*, 66c). Images of the body as confinement from which the soul struggles to escape—'prison,' 'cage'—abound in Plato, as they do in Descartes. For Plato, as for Augustine later, the body is the locus of all that which threatens our attempts at control. It overtakes, it overwhelms, it erupts and disrupts. This situation becomes an incitement to battle the unruly forces of the body. Although less methodically than Descartes, Plato provides instruction on how to gain control over the body, how to achieve intellectual independence from the lure of its illusions and become impervious to its distractions. A central theme of the *Phaedo*, in fact, is the philosopher's training in developing such independence from the body.

But while dualism runs deep in our traditions, it is only with Descartes that body and mind are *defined* in terms of mutual exclusivity. For Plato (and Aristotle), the living body is permeated with soul, which can only depart the body at death. For Descartes, on the other hand, soul and body become two distinct substances. The body is pure *res extensa*—unconscious, extended stuff, brute materiality. 'Every kind of thought which exists in use,' he says in the *Passions of the Soul*, 'belongs to the soul' (HR 1:33). The soul, on the other hand, is pure *res cogitans*—mental, incorporeal, without location, *bodyless*: 'in its nature entirely independent of body, and not in any way derived from the power of matter' (HR 1:118). Plato's and Aristotle's view that 'soul' is a principle of life is one that Descartes takes great pains to refute in the *Passions of the Soul*. The 'life' of the body, he insists, is a matter of purely mechanical functioning: 'We may judge that the body of a living man differs from that of a dead man just as does a watch or other automation (i.e., a machine that moves of itself), when it is wound up and contains in itself the corporeal principle of those movements for which it is designated along with all that is requisite for its action, from the same watch or other machine when it is broken and when the principle of its movement ceases to act' (HR 1:333).

While the body is thus likened to a machine, the mind (having been conceptually purified of all material contamination) is defined by precisely and only those qualities that the human being shares with God: freedom, will, consciousness. For Descartes there is no ambiguity or complexity here. The body is excluded from all participation, all connection with God; the soul alone represents the godliness and the goodness of the human being. In Plato and Aristotle, the lines simply cannot be drawn in so stark a fashion. In the *Symposium*, we should remember, the love of the body is the first, and necessary, step on the spiritual ladder that leads to the glimpsing of the eternal form of beauty. For the Greek philosophers, the body is not simply an impediment to knowledge; it may also function as a spur to spiritual growth. Its passions may motivate the quest for knowledge and beauty. Moreover, since soul is inseparable from body except at death, any human aspirations to intellectual purity during one's lifetime are merely wishful fantasy. 'While in company with the body the soul cannot have pure knowledge,' Plato unequivocally declares in the *Phaedo* (Plato 1953, 121).

For the Greeks, then, there are definite limits to the human intellect. For Descartes, on the other hand, epistemological hubris knows few bounds. The dream of purity is realizable during one's lifetime. For given the right method, one can transcend the body. This is, of course, what Descartes believed himself to have accomplished in the *Meditations.* Addressing Gassendi as 'O flesh!' he describes himself as 'a mind so far withdrawn from corporeal things that it does not even know that anyone has existed before it' (HR 2:214). Such a mind, being without body, would be unaffected by distracting disruption and 'commotion' in the heart, blood, and animal spirits. It would see through the deceptiveness of the senses. And it would be above the idiosyncrasies and biases of individual perspective. For the body is the most ubiquitous reminder of how *located* and perspectival our experience and thought are, how bounded in time and space. The Cartesian knower, on the other hand, being without a body, not only has 'no need of any place' (HR 1:101) but actually *is* 'no place.' He therefore cannot 'grasp' the universe—which would demand a place 'outside' the whole. But, assured of his own transparency, he can relate with absolute neutrality to the objects he surveys, unfettered by the perspectival nature of embodied vision. He has become, quite literally, '*objective.*'

In the new Cartesian scheme of things, neither bodily response (the sensual or the emotional) nor associational thinking, exploring the various personal or spiritual meanings the object has for us, can tell us anything about the object 'itself.' *It* can only be grasped, as Gillispie puts it, 'by measurement rather than sympathy' (1960, 42). It now became inappropriate to speak, as the medievals had done, in anthropocentric terms about nature, which for Descartes is 'totally devoid of mind and thought.' Also, the values and significances of things in relation to the human realm must be understood as purely a reflection of how we feel about them, having nothing to do with their 'objective' qualities. 'Thus,' says Whitehead, in sardonic criticism of the 'characteristic scientific philosophy' of the seventeenth century, 'the poets are entirely mistaken. They should address their lyrics to themselves, and should turn them into odes of self-congratulation . . . Nature is a dull affair, soundless, scentless, colourless; merely the hurrying of material, endlessly, meaninglessly' (1967, 54). But this colorless impersonality, for the Cartesian model of knowledge, is the mark of truth. Resistant to human will, immune to every effort to the knower to make it what he would have it be rather than what it 'is,' purified of all 'inessential' spiritual associations and connections with the rest of the universe, the clear and distinct idea is both compensation for and conqueror of the cold, new world.

THE CARTESIAN 'MASCULINIZATION' OF THOUGHT

> If a kind of Cartesian ideal were ever completely fulfilled, i.e., if the whole of nature were only what can be explained in terms of mathematical relationships—then we would look at the world with that fearful sense of alienation, with that utter loss of reality with which a future schizophrenic child looks at his mother. A machine cannot give birth.
>
> —Karl Stern, *The Flight from Woman*

The Cartesian reconstruction may also be described in terms of separation from the *maternal*—the immanent realms of earth, nature, the authority of the body—and a compensatory turning toward the *paternal* for legitimization through external regulation, transcendent values, and the authority of law. For the medieval cosmos whose destruction gave birth to the modern sensibility was a *mother*-cosmos, and the soul which Descartes drained from the natural world was a *female* soul. Carolyn Merchant, whose groundbreaking interdisciplinary study, *The Death of Nature*, chronicles the changing imagery of nature in this period, describes the 'organic cosmology' that mechanism overthrew: 'Minerals and metals ripened in the uterus of the Earth Mother, mines were compared to her vagina, and metallurgy was the human hastening of the living metal in the artificial womb of the furnace. . . . Miners offered propitiation to the deities of the soil, performed ceremonial sacrifices . . . sexual abstinence, fasting, before violating the sacredness of the living earth by sinking a mine' (1980, 4).

The notion of the natural world as *mothered* has sources, for the Western tradition, in both Plato and Aristotle. In Plato's *Timeaus*, the formless 'receptacle' or 'nurse' provides the substratum of all determinate materiality. The 'receptacle' is likened to a mother because of its receptivity to impression: the father is the 'source or spring'—the eternal forms that 'enter' and 'stir and inform her.' The child is the determinate nature that is formed through their union: the *body* of nature (1949, 4). In this account, the earth is not a mother, but is itself a child of the union of 'nurse' and forms. The notion that the earth *itself* mothers things, for example, metals and minerals, required the inspiration of the Aristotelian theory of animal reproduction. In that theory, the female provides not only matter as 'substratum,' but matter as sensible 'stuff': the *catamenia*, or menstrual material, which is 'worked upon' and shaped by the 'effective and active' element, the semen of the male (729a–b).

In the fifteenth and sixteenth centuries, the Aristotelian account of animal generation was 'projected' onto the cosmos. A 'stock description' of biological generation in nature was the marriage of heaven and earth, and the impregnation of the (female) earth by the dew and rain created by the movements of the (masculine) celestial heavens (Merchant 1980, 16). The female element here is *natura naturata*, of course—passive rather than creative nature. But passivity here connotes *receptivity* rather than inertness; only a living, breathing earth can be impregnated. And indeed, for Plato most explicitly, the work *has* a soul—a female soul—which permeates the corporeal body of the universe. In the seventeenth century, as Merchant argues, that female world-soul died—or more precisely, was *murdered*—by the mechanist re-visioning of nature.

The re-visioning of the universe as a *machine* (most often, a clockwork) was not the work of philosophers alone. Astronomy and anatomy had already changed the dominant picture of the movements of the heavens and the processes of the body by the time the *Meditations* was written. But it was philosophy, and Descartes in particular, that provided the cosmology that integrated these discoveries into a consistent and unified view of nature. By Descartes's brilliant stroke, nature became *defined* by its lack of affiliation with divinity, with spirit. All that which is God-like or spiritual—freedom, will, and sentience—belong entirely and exclusively to *res cogitans*. All else—the earth, the heavens, animals, the human body—is merely mechanically interacting matter.

The seventeenth century saw the death, too, of another sort of 'feminine principle'—that cluster of epistemological values, often associated with feminine consciousness and that apparently played a large and respected role in Hermetic philosophy and, it might be argued, in the prescientific orientation toward the world in general. If the key terms in the Cartesian hierarchy of epistemological values are *clarity* and *distinctness*—qualities that mark each object off from the other and from the knower—the key term in this alternative scheme of values might be designated (following Gillispie's contrast here) as *sympathy*. Various writers have endeavored to articulate such a notion. Henri Bergson names it 'intellectual sympathy,' and argues that the deepest understanding of that which is to be known comes not from analysis of parts but from 'placing oneself within' the full being of an object and allowing *it* to speak. 'Sympathetic' understanding of the object, according to Karl Stern, is that which understands it, through 'union' with it (1965, 42) or, as James Hillman describes it, through 'merging with' or 'marrying' it. To merge with or marry that which is to be known means, for Hillman, to grant personal or intuitive response a positive epistemological value, even (perhaps especially) when such response is contradictory or fragmented (1972, 293).

For sympathetic thinking, the objective and subjective *merge*, participate in the creation of meaning. This does not necessarily mean a rejection, but rather a *re-visioning* of 'objectivity.' Sympathetic thinking, Marcuse suggests, is the only mode that *truly* respects the object, that is, that allows the variety of its meanings to unfold without coercion or too focused interrogation (Marcuse 1972, 74). More recently Evelyn Fox Keller has offered the conception of 'dynamic objectivity':

> Dynamic objectivity is . . . a pursuit of knowledge that makes use of subjective experience . . . in the interests of a more effective objectivity. Premised on continuity, it recognizes difference between self and other as an opportunity for a deeper and more articulated kinship. The struggle to disentangle self from other is itself a source of insight—potentially into the nature of both self and other. It is a principle means for divining what Poincaré calls 'hidden harmonies and relations.' To this end, the scientist employs a form of attention to the natural world that is like one's ideal attention to the human world: it is a form of love. (1985, 117)

Various writers, including Keller, have argued that 'sympathetic' thinking was a valued mode of knowledge in the pre-Renaissance world. Morris Berman finds such thinking in the 'common denominators' of medieval consciousness (whether Aristotelian or Hermetic)—

the doctrines of *resemblance, sympathy, antipathy*—which connect all domains of the universe through a network of shared meanings. More specifically, the alchemical and magical traditions—the 'hermetic wisdom'—are 'dedicated to the notion that real knowledge occurred only via the union of subject and object, in a psychic-emotional identification with images rather than a purely intellectual examination of concepts' (1981, 73). In contrast, Cartesian objectivity has as its ideal the rendering *impossible* of any such continuity between subject and object. The scientific mind must be cleansed of all its sympathies toward the objects it tries to understand. It must cultivate absolute *detachment*.

Recognizing the centrality of such ideals to modern science has led writers such as Sandra Harding to characterize modern science in terms of a 'super-masculinization of rational thought.' Similarly, Karl Stern has said that '[what] we encounter in Cartesian rationalism is the pure masculinization of thought' (1965, 104). The notion that modern science crystallizes masculinist modes of thinking is a theme, too, in the work of James Hillman: 'The specific consciousness we call scientific, Western and modern,' says Hillman, 'is the long sharpened tool of the masculine mind that has discarded parts of its own substance, calling it "Eve," "female," and "inferior"' (1972, 250). What these writers have in mind in describing modern science as masculine is *not* the fact that science has been male dominated, or that it has had problematic attitudes toward women. Science has, of course, a long history of discrimination against women, insisting that women cannot measure up to the rigor, persistence, or clarity that science requires. It also has its share of explicitly misogynist doctrine, as do its ancient forefathers, Aristotle and Galen. What Harding, Stern, and Hillman are criticizing, however, are not these features of science, but a dominant *intellectual* style required of men *and* women working in the sciences today. In the words of Evelyn Fox Keller: 'The scientific mind is set apart from what is to be known, i.e., from nature, and its autonomy is guaranteed . . . by setting apart its modes of knowing from those in which the dichotomy is threatened. In this process, the characterization of both the scientific mind and its modes of access to knowledge as masculine is indeed significant. Masculine here connotes, as it so often does, autonomy, separation, and distance . . . a radical rejection of any comingling of subject and object' (1985, 79).

The remarkable and provocative notion that knowledge *became* masculinized at a certain point in our intellectual history suggests that it is misleading to view the history of philosophy as consistently and obsessively devoted to the exclusion or transcendence of those qualities identified as or associated with the feminine. Although men have been the cultural architects of our dominant scientific and philosophic traditions, the structures they have built are not 'male' in the same way in all eras and cultures—for what it has meant to *be* male (or scientific) has historically and culturally varied dramatically. The images, language, and principles central to the Hermetic science that mechanism dethroned in the seventeenth century are precisely those traditionally associated with the feminine; moreover, they were attacked as such by the opposition. Medieval philosophy, too, for all its retreat from sexuality, did *not* disparage the body's role in knowledge, nor was it especially impressed with distance and detachment as paths to understanding. Rather, it is precisely *because* all that was changed by the scientific and intellectual revolutions of the seventeenth century that we can today find meaning in describing those revolutions as effective some sort of masculinization of thought.

Such notions, moreover, are not unique to contemporary thought. According to Francis Bacon, the new scientific and philosophic culture of the seventeenth century inaugurated 'a truly masculine birth of time.' Similarly and strikingly, Henry Oldenberg, secretary of the Royal Society, asserted in 1664 that the business of that society was to raise 'a masculine philosophy.' Kellers pays very serious attention to such historical associations of gender and 'cognitive style,' which we might have thought to belong to a peculiarly contemporary mentality, but which in fact crop up frequently in Royal Society debates. As she reads them, the controversies between Bacon and Paracelsus become an explicit contest between masculine and feminine principles: head versus heart, domination over versus merging with the object, purified versus erotic orientation toward knowledge, and so forth (1985, 43–54). Bacon's own deepest attitudes, Keller suggests, were more complicated and ambivalent than his oft-reproduced and notorious images of male seduction, penetration, and rape of nature may indicate. But what emerges with clarity, despite any subtleties in the attitudes of individual thinkers, is that the notion of science as masculine is hardly a twentieth-century invention or feminist fantasy. The founders of modern science consciously and explicitly proclaimed the masculinity of science as inaugurating a new eıa. And they associated that masculinity with a clearer, purer, more objective, and more disciplined epistemological relation to the world.

Psychoanalytic theory urges us to examine that which we actively repudiate for the shadow of a loss we mourn. Freud, in *Beyond the Pleasure Principle*, tells the story of an eighteen-month-old-boy—an obedient, orderly little boy, as Freud describes him—who, although 'greatly attached to his mother,' never cried when she left him for a few hours.

> This good little boy, however, had an occasional disturbing habit of taking any small objects he could get hold of and throwing them away from him into a corner, under the bed, and so on, so that hunting for his toys and picking them up was often quite a business. As he did this he gave vent to a loud, long-drawn-out 'o-o-o-o,' accompanied by an expression of interest and satisfaction. His mother and the writer of the present account were agreed in thinking that this was not a mere interjection but represented the German word '*fort*' ('gone'). I eventually realized that it was a game and that the only use he made of any of his toys was to play 'gone' with them. . . . [T]he complete game [was] disappearance and return. . . . The interpretation . . . became obvious. It was related to the child's great cultural achievement—the instinctual renunciation (that is, the renunciation of instinctual satisfaction) which he had made in allowing his mother to go away without protesting. He compensated himself for this, as it were, by himself staging the disappearance and return of the objects within his reach. . . . Throwing away the object so that it was 'gone' might satisfy an impulse of the child's, which was suppressed in his actual life, to revenge himself on his mother for going away from him. In that case it would have a defiant meaning: 'All right, then, go away! I don't need you. I'm sending you away myself.' (1959, 33–35)

The 'fort-da' game and Freud's interpretation of it places the Cartesian facility for transforming anxiety into confidence, loss into mastery, in a striking new perspective. The Cartesian reconstruction of the world can be seen as a 'fort-da' game—a defiant gesture of independence from the female cosmos, a gesture that is at the same time compensation for a profound loss. The sundering of the organic ties between person and nature—originally experienced as epistemological estrangement, as the opening up of a chasm between self and world—is reenacted, *this* time with the human being as the engineer and architect of the separation. Through the Cartesian 'rebirth,' a new masculine theory of knowledge is delivered, in which detachment from nature acquires a positive epistemological value. A new *world* is reconstructed, too, one in which all generativity and creativity fall to God, the spiritual father, rather than to the female 'flesh' of the world.

With the same masterful stroke—the mutual opposition of the spiritual and the corporeal—the formerly female earth becomes inert matter and the objectivity of science is insured. 'She' becomes 'it'—and 'it' can be understood and controlled. Not through sympathy, of course, but by virtue of the very *object*-ivity of the 'it.' At the same time, the 'wound' of separateness is healed through the *denial* that there 'was' any union: For the mechanists, unlike Donne, the female world-soul did not die—rather the world is dead. There is nothing to mourn, nothing to lament. Indeed, the 'new' epistemological anxiety is evoked, not over loss, but by the 'memory' or suggestion of *union*; sympathetic, associational, or bodily response obscures objectivity, feeling for nature muddies the clear lake of the mind. The 'otherness' of nature is now what allows it to be known.

Note

1. In selecting a piece of my own work for this collection, [*Feminist Interpretations of René Descartes*] the simplest thing would have been to reprint 'The Cartesian Masculinization of Thought,' which originally appeared in *Signs* and has since been reprinted in a number of collections. 'The Cartesian Masculinization of Thought' was drawn from *The Flight to Objectivity*, and does focus on the gender dimensions of Cartesianism. I have found, however, that this article—for a variety of reasons—is too frequently misinterpreted as an historical application of Nancy Chorodow's work. I admire Chodorow's work, but, as discussed in the Introduction to this volume, the point of my argument is different from that of Chodorow and other 'gender difference' theorists. As I write in the introduction to *Flight*, 'My use of developmental theory focuses, not on gender difference, but on very general categories—individuation, separation anxiety, object permanence—in an attempt to explore their relevance to existential changes brought about by the dissolution of the organic, finite, maternal universe of the Middle Ages and Renaissance' (6–7). In order to avoid perpetuating further misunderstandings of my project, I have chosen to construct a new piece, culled from both the article and other sections of the book, but which puts greater emphasis on the argument that I believed myself to be making in the book. My apologies for any gaps or points that seem to be made too swiftly in the interests of an accurate 'precis' of the argument.

References

Alexander, Robert. 1972. 'The Problem of Metaphysical Doubt and Its Removal.' In R. J. Butler, ed., *Cartesian Studies*, 106–22. New York: Barnes & Noble.

Aristotle. 1941. *Basic Works.* Edited by Richard McKeon. New York: Random House.

Barfield, Owen. 1965. *Saving the Appearances: A Study in Idolatry.* New York: Harcourt Brace Jovanovich.

Baxandall, Michael. 1972. *Painting and Experience in Fifteenth-Century Italy.* Oxford: Oxford University Press.

Berman, Morris. 1981. *The Re-enchantment of the World.* Ithaca: Cornell University Press.

Bernstein, Richard. 1980. 'Philosophy in the Conversation of Mankind.' *Review of Metaphysics* 33, no. 4: 745–75.

Descartes, René. 1969. *Philosophical Works.* Vols. 1 and 2. Edited by Elizabeth Haldane and G. R. T. Ross. Cambridge: Cambridge University Press.

—— 1976. *Conversations with Burman.* Translated by John Cottingham. Oxford: Clarendon Press.

Easlea, Brian. 1980. *Witch-hunting, Magic, and the New Philosophy.* Atlantic Highlands, N.J.: Humanities Press.

Edgerton, Samuel, Jr. 1975. *The Renaissance Rediscovery of Linear Perspective.* New York. Harper and Row.

Farrington, Benjamin. 1951. *Temporis Partus Masculus: An Untranslated Writing of Francis Bacon.* N.p.: Centaurus I.

Frankfurt, Harry. 1970. *Demons, Dreamers, and Madmen.* New York: Bobbs-Merrill.

Freud, Sigmund. 1959. *Beyond the Pleasure Principle.* New York: Bantam.

Furth, Hans. 1969. *Piaget and Knowledge.* Englewood Cliffs, N.J.: Prentice-Hall.

Gibson, James J. 1950. *The Perception of the Visual World.* Boston: Houghton Mifflin.

Gillispie, Charles. 1960. *The Edge of Objectivity.* Princeton: Princeton University Press.

Guillen, Claudio. 1971. 'On the Concept and Metaphor of Perspective.' In *Literature as System.* Princeton: Princeton University Press.

Harries, Karsten. 1973. 'Descartes, Perspective, and the Angelic Eye.' *Yale French Studies*, 49: 28–42.

Hillman, James. 1972. *The Myth of Analysis.* New York: Harper and Row.

Keller, Evelyn Fox. 1985. *Reflections on Gender and Science.* New Haven: Yale University Press.

Koestler, Arthur. 1959. *The Sleepwalkers.* New York: Grosset & Dunlap.

Lewis, C. S. 1964. *The Discarded Image.* Cambridge: Cambridge University Press.

Mahler, Margaret. 1972. 'On the First Three Subphases of the Separation-Individuation Process.' *International Journal of Psychoanalysis* 53: 333–38.

Marcuse, Herbert. 1972. *Counter-Revolution and Revolt.* Boston: Beacon.

Merchant, Carolyn. 1980. *The Death of Nature.* San Francisco: Harper and Row.

Montaigne, Michel de. 1963. *Essays.* Translated and edited by Donald Frame. New York: St. Martin's Press.

Ortega Y Gasset, Jose. 1958. *Man and Crisis.* New York: W. W. Norton.

Pascal, Blaise. 1966. *Pensées.* Translated by A. J. Krailsheimer. Harmondsworth, U.K.: Penguin.

Piaget, Jean. 1954. *The Construction of Reality in the Child.* New York: Random House.

Plato. 1949. *Timeaus.* Translated by Benjamin Jowett. Indianapolis: Bobbs-Merrill.

—— 1953. *Phaedo. The Dialogues of Plato.* Translated by Benjamin Jowett. 4th edition, rev. Oxford: Clarendon Press.

—— 1957. *Theatetus and Sophist.* Translated by Francis Cornford. New York: Library of Liberal Arts.

Popkin, Richard. 1979. *History of Scepticism from Erasmus to Spinoza.* Berkeley and Los Angeles: University of California Press.

Rorty, Richard. 1979. *Philosophy and the Mirror of Nature.* Princeton: Princeton University Press.

Shakespeare, William. 1946. *Hamlet.* New York: Appleton-Century-Crofts.

Stem, Karl. 1965. *The Flight from Woman.* New York: Noonday.

Toulmin, Stephen. 'The Inwardness of Mental Life.' *Critical Inquiry* 6 (Autumn 1976): 1–16.

Whitehead, Alfred North. (1933) 1967. *Adventures of Ideas.* New York: Collier Macmillan.

—— (1925) 1967. *Science and the Modern World.* Toronto: Collier Macmillan.

Princess Elisabeth and Descartes: The Union of Soul and Body and the Practice of Philosophy

Lisa Shapiro*

It is difficult to talk about Elisabeth without subordinating her to her correspondent, Descartes. That is, it is difficult to talk about Princess Elisabeth of Bohemia as a philosopher *in her own right.*[1] This is, of course, largely due to the fact that all we have of her philosophical writing is her correspondence with Descartes. And in this correspondence, Elisabeth assumes the role of a reader of Descartes: she raises objections to and asks for clarification of Descartes's claims but does not seems to advance any philosophical program of her own. This is not to say that Elisabeth's comments do not influence Descartes. On the contrary, it seems to me quite certain that they do. In particular, her challenges move Descartes to think more carefully about the union of the soul and body, and it is at her request that he undertakes to write a work on the passions of the soul. Equally, we might tend to read Elisabeth's letters in this way—that is, as simply responsive to, and so as interesting only for shedding some light on, Descartes's philosophy—because she herself seems to take that as her role. In her correspondence she consistently denigrates her own intellectual contribution to their exchanges, and she looks to Descartes as someone who can help her to remedy the weaknesses of her own mind. Or at least it seems that way at first.

Despite these considerations, it seems inappropriate to leave things at that—with Elisabeth as simply a student and reader of Descartes. For one, Descartes does not seem to share Elisabeth's opinion of herself. In the dedication of his *Principles of Philosophy*, he quite eloquently praises her as someone whose virtue 'springs solely from a comprehension of what is right' and within whom is to be found 'the

* Lisa Shapiro, 'Princess Elisabeth and Descartes: The Union of Soul and Body and the Practice of Philosophy', *British Journal for the History of Philosophy*, 7/3 (1999), 503–20. Reprinted by permission of Taylor and Francis, Ltd.

keenest sort of intellect and greatest zeal for knowing the truth along with the firmest will to act rightly' (AT VIIIA 2–3; MM xv).[2] According to Descartes, only Elisabeth has understood equally well his geometry and his metaphysics, and for him this is evidence not simply of her value to him but also of the quality of her mind. He writes: 'I know of no mind but yours to which all things are equally evident, and which I therefore deservedly term incomparable' (AT VIIIA 4; MM xv). Moreover, thinking of Elisabeth as a kind of sounding board whose reflection helps Descartes to clarify his thoughts leaves her with little independent intellectual life. In fact, what she writes to Descartes reveals that she does have her own ideas about things.

The problem one has in wanting to take Elisabeth seriously as a philosopher is that there is nothing ready-to-hand in which she offers a systematic treatment of her philosophical position: we cannot turn to other works of hers—we cannot even turn to other correspondence—to get clear on what she herself thinks. What I would like to do here is see if we can't use her correspondence with Descartes to trace out a line of thought proper to Elisabeth *herself*. The line of thought in which I am particularly interested is that concerning the nature of the union of soul and body.[3] I want to look at how Elisabeth's own thought about this metaphysical question develops from the objection she is most famous for raising—that regarding the notion of the union available to Descartes given his dualist commitment of the *Meditations*—to her later objections to his rather neo-Stoic advice about how she would do best to regulate her passions. In the course of this development, I will argue, Elisabeth traces out for us a unique philosophical position: she defends neither a reductionist materialism nor a substance dualism, but rather wants to find a way of respecting the autonomy of thought without denying that this faculty of reason is in some essential way dependent on our bodily condition. I think it is particularly interesting that Elisabeth is able to put forward her own position in a way that proves compelling in the context involving the passions, and in particular one involving her own passions and well-being. And so, once I have told a story about the evolution of Elisabeth's thoughts on the soul–body union, I want to conclude by reconsidering Elisabeth's practice of philosophy in this personal context and the lack of a systematic treatment of philosophical issues on her part.

THE EARLY OBJECTION TO DESCARTES'S ACCOUNT OF THE UNION OF SOUL AND BODY

Perhaps the most well known part of Elisabeth's correspondence with Descartes is that in which she wonders how it is possible, given Descartes's dualist commitments, for him to still maintain that soul and body affect one another.[4] She writes:

> tell me please how the soul of a human being (it being only a thinking substance) can determine the bodily spirits and so bring about voluntary actions. For it seems that all determination of movement is made either by the impulsion of the thing moved, or it is pushed either by that which moves it or else by the particular qualities and shape of the surface of the latter. Physical contact is required for the first two conditions, extension for the third. You entirely exclude the one from the notion that you have of the soul, and the other appears to me incompatible with an immaterial thing.
>
> (16 May 1643; AT III 661)

Elisabeth is here asking Descartes just how, for him, soul and body can interact: How can something immaterial and non-extended move something material and extended?

Descartes's reply is less than satisfying. While he does point out that the interaction between soul and body should not be conceived as if it were between two bodies—implicitly suggesting that all the options Elisabeth considers for understanding the union turn on this misconception—the only alternative he presents is the kind of union the Scholastics maintain exists between the real quality of heaviness and bodies.

Elisabeth is quite rightly dissatisfied with this answer to her question. In her next letter, she writes that she is unable

> to understand the idea through which we must judge how the soul (non-extended and immaterial) is able to move the body, that is, by that idea through which you have at another time understood heaviness; nor why this power to carry a body towards the center of the earth, which you falsely attributed to a body under the name of a quality, must now persuade us that a body can be pushed by something immaterial.
>
> (20 June 1643; AT III 684)

And so she is left admitting that 'it would be easier for me to concede matter and extension to the soul, than the capacity to move a body and be moved by it to an immaterial thing' (AT III 685).

Focussing on these passages had led interpreters to take Elisabeth to be posing the mind–body problem in its interactionist form. She can seem to be asking simply: How is it possible for two really distinct substances to interact causally with each other? And it is not only these two letters which support this reading. In the last letter of this particular series—that of 1 July 1643—Elisabeth concedes Descartes's point (in his reply to her of 28 June 1643) that the senses show us that the soul moves the body (and presumably she will also concede that they show us that the body moves the soul), but she insists that they 'do not teach us anything (no more than do the understanding and imagination) about the means by which it does so' (AT IV 2). It is *this* question—that of *how* the soul is supposed to move the body—which concerns her.

However, Elisabeth's questions of Descartes go beyond this problem of interaction. We can begin to see this by looking a little more closely at these three letters. In the letter of May 16, in which she originally asks about how we are to conceive the interaction of mind and body, Elisabeth assumes that Descartes *does* have an account of the way in which soul and body can interact with one another, and she asks for clarification on what he takes the soul to be. She takes it that, since she cannot get clear on how soul and body are supposed to interact, she must also be unclear about the way in which the soul and body are two distinct substances. She writes:

> This is why I ask you for a more precise definition of the soul than you give in your *Metaphysics*, that is to say, of its substance, separated from its action, from thought.
>
> (AT III 661)

Thus, Elisabeth does not simply search for an account of the causal relation which stands between these two distinct substances. Rather, it seems she wants to arrive at an account of the way mind and body are able to affect one another by revisiting the question of the way in which soul and body are meant to be two really distinct things, and in particular that of what constitutes the mind as substance.

This concern about the nature of the Real Distinction between mind and body carries over into her next letter. There, Elisabeth tries to spell out her worry, and the examples she invokes to do so can help us begin to see her point. She contends, noted just above, that it is easier for her to entertain the idea of the soul's having matter and extension than it conceive of the interaction of an immaterial thing and a material one. And this would seem to imply that she can see only two alternatives to conceiving the relation between soul and body. On the one hand, one can be a substance dualist, as Descartes seems to be, and be left with an apparently intractable problem of interaction. On the other hand, one can be a reductionist materialist, perhaps like Hobbes, and claim that the 'activities' of our soul are just manifestations of a particular sort of bodily state. And indeed, seeing things in these terms is quite reasonable, for it is precisely the way much criticism of Cartesian dualism proceeds. But the way in which Elisabeth supports her contention could well suggest something more. She asks Descartes how he can account for the fact that the soul,

> after having had the faculty and the custom of reasoning well, can lose all that by some vapors and that, being able to subsist without the body, and having nothing in common with it, it [the soul] is still so governed by it.
>
> (20 June 1643; AT III 685)

Elisabeth thus grounds her worry about the Real Distinction in the sorts of cases in which people who would otherwise have full use of their faculty of reason fall ill—they have a touch of the vapors, say—and thereby lose the ability to think clearly. Perhaps they become delusional, or are muddle-headed, or in some other way lose the capacity to see things as they are or to draw inferences properly. Elisabeth does not see how a substance dualist like Descartes could accommodate these sorts of phenomena. For it would appear, on a strong dualist line, that even if we do have a touch of the vapors we should still in principle be able to think clearly: the soul, after all, on that line, subsists completely independently of the body, and so it should be able to exercise its power of thought no matter what the condition of the body in which it finds itself. Elisabeth's thought is that this principle of independent subsistence is belied by the phenomena. However, in order to explain such cases. Elisabeth need not hold a reductionist materialist account of mind; she need not like Hobbes want to maintain that everything, including thought, is material and so explain these sorts of episodes in terms of some workings of the brain. Rather than taking Elisabeth to be promulgating such a materialist line here, we might equally understand her to be struggling with a way to preserve the intuition behind Descartes's substance dualism—that is, the intuition that thought is not a mere matter of bodily motions—while at the same time acknowledging that this faculty of reason is still in some way dependent on the body. That is, she could be taken to be gesturing towards a third sort of alternative for understanding the relation between mind and body.

This latter reading can be supported by the next of her letters to

Descartes. There, in her July 1 letter, she traces out this position as follows:

> Even though extension is not necessary to thought, being not at all repugnant to it, it [that is, extension] could suit some other function of the soul, which is no less essential to it.
>
> (1 July 1643; AT IV 2)

Here Elisabeth seems to be toying with an idea that the soul could be distinct from body with regards to thought—extension does not determine our thought and so is not necessary to it—while at the same time being dependent on it in another way. But at this stage of the discussion, this is all Elisabeth can say, and though we do not have any record of Descartes's reply, we might imagine that he would not have understood what she is trying to say. There are many questions to ask: What other function does the soul have besides thought? How does extension, or body, particularly suit the soul's performing that function? What is the middle ground between being not repugnant and not necessary? Answers to these questions are needed if Elisabeth is to distinguish her position both from the reductionist materialist one and Descartes's own apparent strong dualist position of the *Meditations.*

At this point the record of this particular exchange between Descartes and Elisabeth stops. But we can see them resuming discussion on this topic almost two years later. And this time, I will argue, Elisabeth is able to articulate her position more fully. Interestingly their approach to this issue of the relation of soul and body and of the sense in which the soul is an independent thing is quite different. It is to this later exchange which I turn now.

ELISABETH'S ILLNESS AND DESCARTES'S REMEDY: THE UNION OF SOUL AND BODY REVISITED

The exchange on which I will presently focus is often neglected, even by those who do take Descartes's and Elisabeth's correspondence seriously. I suppose this is because on its face it does not seem to be of any philosophical import. (Indeed Descartes's letter beginning the exchange is omitted from the CSMK collection of Descartes's philosophical correspondence.) In it Descartes and Elisabeth discuss her persistent illness of the Summer of 1645. I think, however, that in looking at this particular exchange we will find Elisabeth and Descartes once again engaged in clarifying the relation between mind and body. But they do so not through a straightforward investigation of the metaphysical consistency of Descartes's position but rather through consideration of the passions, the way in which they affect us, and our ability to regulate them.

The discussion begins with Descartes's letter of 18 May 1646. Descartes has learned that Elisabeth 'has had, for three or four weeks, a low-grade fever, accompanied by a dry cough, and that after having been delivered from [this indisposition] for five or six days, the illness returned' (AT IV 201),[5] and he proceeds to offer his diagnosis.[6] We can assume that Descartes does not think that whatever ails Elisabeth has a primarily physiological aetiology, for he does not tell her, as her physicians have, to visit the Spa, nor does he direct her toward any of the other purgatives and astringents that constituted the standard prescriptions of the day. He asserts rather that 'the most common cause of a low-grade fever is sadness' and suggests that the many crises that have befallen her house, and the publicity these events have been accorded, are the 'principle cause of your indisposition' (AT IV 201). Indeed, his diagnosis does make good sense, for apparently, at this time, one of Elisabeth's brothers had challenged either her mother's or her sister's suitor (the story varies depending on whose biography one reads) to a duel which was then suspended. The day after the duel had been scheduled, however, her brother stabbed the suitor in public; the problems associated with this incident only compounded Elisabeth's other family worries, for they had been exiled to the Netherlands from Bohemia upon her father Frederick's losses in war, and the repeated attempts to regain the realm had failed. Moreover, her uncle Charles I of England faced political problems (a civil war!) of his own, which in turn cut off the family's primary source of income. It is no wonder she should be distressed.[7]

Descartes prescribes for Elisabeth a typically neo-Stoic remedy. She ought, he suggests, to reflect on her soul, to take comfort in her own strength, and thereby to become happy. Even while he claims that he is 'not at all like those cruel philosophers, who want their sage to be insensible' (AT IV 201–2), thus distancing himself from the Stoics, he does seem to espouse other paradigmatically Stoic beliefs in his contrasting of vulgar and great souls (Elisabeth, of course, has a great soul, 'the most noble and elevated I know'). While the vulgar let themselves be carried away by the things they come across, those with great souls subject their feelings to reason, and if nothing else, gain strength, and even a sort of pleasure from their ability to support the misfortunes that may befall them.[8] And indeed these same great souls have so perfected their intellect that it is no longer swayed by any thought it may have arrived at solely by its involvement with the body to which it is joined.

What is Elisabeth's reaction to this diagnosis and prescription? It is very curious. Although Elisabeth does seem to appreciate Descartes's awareness of the stresses in her life—something her doctors are blind to—she is skeptical about his proposed remedy. But not in the way one expects. In light of what she had written two years earlier and the questions she had raised about the Real Distinction of soul and body, one expects Elisabeth to challenge the general validity of Descartes's neo-Stoic prescription. In particular, one expects her to take issue with the sort of dualist picture underlying his neo-Stoicism. Descartes's prescription presupposes that even while under the influence of the passions, we will be able to think clearly about our own worth. But, just as our ability to think clearly can be compromised by a touch of the vapors, so could it be by the physiological motions causing a passion such as sadness. And in so far as the physiology of the passions could compromise our reason in this way, Descartes's Stoic remedy would prove ineffective: while melancholic, we would not be able to think clearly enough to administer the remedy. But Elisabeth does not raise this sort of objection directly. Instead, she says something quite remarkable:

> Know this, that I have a body imbued with a large part of the weaknesses of my sex, so that it [my body] very easily feels the afflications of the soul and has none of the strength to recover with it [my soul], being of a temperament subject to obstructions.
>
> (24 May 1645, AT IV 208)

What is the significance of this remark? Why does Elisabeth introduce her nature as a female at this point? There are two ways of reading this remark. On the one hand, we might understand Elisabeth's remark as expressive of her internalization of a kind of sexist attitude. On the other hand, we might see a note of irony in what she writes. Each of these readings, however, seems to rest on an understanding of the soul–body union akin to the one Elisabeth gestured towards in the earlier exchange.

Let us first consider the reading which takes Elisabeth to have internalized a kind of sexism. There are reasons to take Elisabeth's remark in this way: I have already alluded to Elisabeth's own devaluation of her intellectual capacity; also, in a later letter, without provocation, she regrets that she cannot pay Descartes a visit because of the 'curse of my sex' (AT IV 234);[9] while most likely she offers her menses as a medical reason preventing her visit, her choice of expression suggests that here too she sees her biology as fating her to some evil. While such an interpretation might tempt us simply to dismiss the remark, it is worth considering the assumptions which underlie it. On this line, she seems to be maintaining that women are so closely tied to their bodies that they are subject to them, and thereby incapable, in virtue of their sex alone, of becoming fully rational. That is, Elisabeth wants to deny that Descartes's neo-stoic remedy will work *on her*. But in doing so, she is implicitly admitting that we can in principle regulate our bodily disposition just by using our faculty of reason, by thinking thoughts other than those we find ourselves having. Thus, she also implicitly admits that the soul has a sort of autonomy from the body: it can have these other thoughts at will. With her denial, however, Elisabeth seems to be suggesting that there are certain limits to or conditions on the soul's autonomy. In particular, she seems to suggest her very femaleness proves to be too chronic a condition to overcome; it is akin to a touch of the vapors. Thus, Elisabeth seems to be suggesting that she cannot manage to get beyond her biology and that she has an inability to maintain control of her emotions (the 'afflictions of the soul') through reason: her being a female—a bodily state, if you will—prevents her from achieving the Stoic contentment Descartes recommends to her. And so, while she accepts a certain aspect of Descartes's philosophical position—that the mind has a certain *autonomy* which allows it to maintain control over its own thoughts—she also wants to deny that *her* mind is fully autonomous, that she has that kind of control: she suggests that her bodily condition—simply being female—deprives it of that freedom.

This same point about the autonomy of the mind also emerges if we understand Elisabeth's remark here in the other way—as sounding a note of irony. Read in this way, Elisabeth is not so much denigrating herself as trying to point up what she may have assumed was a kind of misogyny on Descartes's part. He does after all assume that whatever ails her rests in a certain emotional incontinence; she would never recover, he suggests, if only her reason would be master. Her response might then be an ironic one, meant to bring Descartes's own assumptions to the surface—that he offers the diagnosis he does because she is a woman, and that, in prescribing the remedy he does, he is suggesting that she effectively deny that she is a woman and be more like a man—

for she is pointing out that she cannot help but be female. There is just as much textual evidence for this reading, for later in the letter, after running through a litany of the crises she has faced through the year, she states quite frankly that

> if my life were entirely known to you, you would find it more strange that a mind as sensible as my own, has conserved itself for so long, through so many hardships, in a body so weak, without any advice besides that of its own reasoning, and without any consolation but that of its conscience, than you would find strange the cause of the present malady.
>
> (24 May 1645; AT IV 209)

Her point here seems to be that she has had to maintain her sanity in the face of incredible difficulty, and that she has managed to do so should deflate Descartes's pop-psychology.[10] But in taking this line, she must still be read both as accepting the principle of the autonomy of the mind—the view that one has control over one's thoughts—and as insisting that this power of thought is in some way contingent on our bodily state. While on this reading, Elisabeth is maintaining that she *does* have her full faculty of thought, she still notes that this very fact is surprising. Her poor health and weak condition, might well have obscured or otherwise impeded her ability to reason. And in addition, she does not want to deny that her femaleness affects her thought: her making a remark of this kind at all suggests that she is unwilling to deny that she is female and moreover that this fact of her embodiment figures in who she is and in her ability to reason.[11] What she does deny is that her femaleness is in any way *debilitating* to her power of thought.

No matter which of these readings of this passage we prefer, then, we can see Elisabeth as adhering to a certain position on the relation of mind and body. On this position, the mind is autonomous: it has its own proper activity—thought—which allows us to have control over what we think. If we find ourselves burdened with many hardships, we need not dwell on them: we can think of other things. But Elisabeth also wants to suggest that the mind's being autonomous in this way, its ability to engage in this activity, is dependent on the condition of the body in which it finds itself. The difference between the two readings of Elisabeth's remark lies in the details of this dependence.

In order to assign Elisabeth this position, I have had to do a bit of interpretive work; Elisabeth's philosophical commitments lie beneath the surface of her remarks. But with what follows in this exchange, we can see Elisabeth herself coming to explicate this position, and so to read this whole exchange as a new effort on her part to clarify the relation between the soul and the body, both how they are distinct and the way in which the body does have a bearing on thought. That is, we can read Elisabeth as here working towards an intermediary position, one between the substance dualism she originally identified with Descartes's own and the materialism which she then seemed to take to be the only alternative to that dualism. In this regard, it is interesting that in her reaction to Descartes's Stoic advice, Elisabeth does not seem to even entertain the problem of interaction which concerned her in the earlier discussion, even though it would seem that that problem should still be alive: how can the thoughts we have affect our bodily state? Instead, the other problem—that of the relation between mind and body, and of the nature of the soul as substance—has come to the fore. Let us look at that ensuing discussion.

Descartes, in his response, quite pointedly insists upon the *general* application of his diagnosis and remedy. While acknowledging the particular pressures on Elisabeth, he wants to claim that everyone, men and women alike, though each may be affected by their peculiar circumstances, can and must maintain the mastery of reason. He says:

> I can readily understand how many things continually distress Your Highness, and I know that they are more difficult to overcome when they are of such a kind that true reason does not command us to oppose them directly or try to remove them. They are domestic enemies with whom we are forced to keep company, and we have to be perpetually on guard lest they injure us.
>
> (AT IV 218, CSMK 249)

He thus persists in pursuing his psychological diagnosis, and he repeats his neo-Stoic prescription, 'so far as possible to distract our imagination and senses from them, and when obliged by prudence to consider them [these difficulties], to do so with our intellect alone' (Ibid.). Descartes then proceeds to illustrate the effectiveness of his proposed remedy for *anyone.* Each person, he claims, has his own bodily disruption, whether to happiness or to sadness or to some other affective state, and in order to overcome a poor disposition each needs only to avoid thinking of, say, sad things while making every effort to consider objects which would 'furnish contentment and joy' (Ibid.). He goes so far as to maintain that thinking such happy thoughts is alone 'capable of restoring [someone with such a poor disposition] to health, even if his spleen and lungs were already in poor condition because of the bad condition of the blood caused by sadness' (AT IV 219–20; CSMK 250). He even maintains that an application of this remedy to *himself* was enough to cure him of a disease he purports to have inherited from his mother, and so to foil the doctors who all believed that he would die young. Descartes thus seems simply to be reiterating his position. He does not respond directly to Elisabeth's observations about her femaleness, for he does not here argue that femaleness is not a chronic condition. Rather, he implicitly assimilates her femaleness to any other bodily 'condition' and propounds again his view that *all* bodily dispositions can be overcome by reason alone. And so Descartes still seems committed here to a strong separation of mind and body: for him our capacity for thought is in no way contingent or otherwise dependent on our physical condition.

The correspondence continues in this neo-Stoic vein; indeed Descartes proposes that they read Seneca's *De Vita Beata*, undoubtedly thinking that such a study will help Elisabeth overcome her illness. But Descartes finds the work less than rigorous, and Elisabeth is still skeptical about Stoicism. She, in turn, comes to frame her objection in a slightly different way. And here is where her insight about the nature of the soul-body union becomes explicit. The reformulated objection comes in response to Descartes's discussion of *la béatitude*—happiness or Stoic contentment. While Descartes is not particularly clear about the content of this concept, at its center is the notion of willing, the act of resolving to do something, for Cartesian virtue consists of nothing but 'a firm and constant resolution to carry out whatever reason recommends' (AT IV 265; CSMK 257–8). Elisabeth remarks upon this relation of will and reason as she raises her objection. She writes:

> I still do not know how to rid myself of doubt that we can arrive at the happiness of which you speak, without the assistance of that which does not depend absolutely on the will, because *there are some diseases which altogether take away the power of reasoning, and by consequence that of enjoying a reasonable satisfaction, others which diminish its* [reason's] *force*, and prevent our following maxims that good sense would have forged, and which render the most moderate person subject to letting themselves be carried away by her passions, and less capable of untangling herself from the accidents of fortune, which require a prompt resolution.
>
> (16 August 1645; AT IV 269; emphasis mine)

Elisabeth here is finally able to articulate the view I have argued is implicit in her raising the issue of her femaleness. For she here claims both that our faculty of reason essentially involves a kind of control over our thoughts and that our physical condition can affect that faculty. This time, however, she frames her objection in more general terms: she objects that our bodily condition affects our ability to think otherwise, that is to will and to reason. Her point is not obscured by the consideration of whether her being female precludes her being fully rational.

In seeing Elisabeth's position laid out before us, we can begin to see the significance of her original questions to Descartes in her letters of 1643. There, recall, she asked Descartes to distinguish further the soul's activity from its substance, and to explain more clearly his concept of substance. Descartes, recall, ignored this question. Now we can see that she might have been driving at just this way of understanding the relation of mind and body. In this correspondence of the summer of 1645, Elisabeth points out that reason is intimately tied to our bodily condition: in order to think properly, we need to be in a state of good health. That is, while thought itself is an activity through which the mind demonstrates its essential autonomy from the body—through the mind alone, we determine our thoughts—still our capacity to engage in this activity, our rational faculty, depends on our being in a certain state physiologically. That is, the body enables the mind to be what it is. In making this sort of claim about the relation between mind and body, Elisabth need not take up a reductionist materialist position; she need not claim that all our thoughts are just bodily states, and so maintain, that our thoughts are essentially beyond our control, determined by the causal laws governing material things; that is, she need not maintain that thought is entirely subject to the body. That our being in a certain sort of bodily state enables us to achieve rationality in this way need not compromise the *autonomy* of thought—the activity of thought—from the body. But in insisting that *we* determine our thoughts, neither need Elisabeth be committed to the kind of substance dualism that Descartes appears to espouse. For maintaining that thought is an autonomous activity does not require us to claim that it is an independent *substance*; we need not think of thought as an *entity subsisting in and by itself.* Elisabeth's insight, I take it, is to draw this distinction between autonomy and the sort of independence that makes something a substance.

It is interesting that Descartes concedes Elisabeth's point this time around:

> You observe very truly that there are diseases which take away the power of reasoning and with it the power of enjoying the satisfaction proper to a rational mind. This shows me that what I said in general about every

person should be taken to apply only to those who have the free use of their reason and in addition know the way that must be followed to reach such happiness.

(1 September 1645: AT IV 281–2; CSMK 262)

Descartes, in his initial response to Elisabeth, implicitly acknowledges that being female is no different than any other individual-specific bodily disposition, but at this point in the correspondence he was not yet clear on the degree to which we can exert our will over our bodies: he claims he is not a Stoic while prescribing a pragmatically Stoic remedy. Perhaps his commitment to the even distribution of good sense to all human beings blinds him to Elisabeth's more general point, for in his second response, once Elisabeth has gone on from her own experience as a woman to home in on her philosophical position, he no longer endorses a strongly Stoic line, and he perhaps even tempers his substance dualism. It is interesting that in the *Passions of the Soul*, a work written at Elisabeth's request as a result of this portion of their correspondence, Descartes wants to distinguish the functions of the soul from those of the body, but he does not refer to them as two distinct substances. The line Elisabeth presses shows Descartes that in claiming that critical reflection is at the core of reason, he need not deny that the way we find ourselves in the world will very much affect our thought. Indeed, our embodiment might well be understood to be an integral part of reason itself, for if Elisabeth is right, our bodily health, our physiological integrity, enables us to exercise our own proper faculty of thought. This insight too gains expression in the *Passions*, for in that work more than any other of his, Descartes respects the fact that we are embodied—the passions all find their source in our bodies for him, and interestingly *générosité*, through which we are to remedy the disorders of our passions, has its own proper physiological state for him, for it is a *passion* as well as a virtue—while at the same time, in his consideration of the regulation of the passions, he adheres to the Stoic notion of the centrality of the will. This double aspect of the passions gains its first considered expression in the part of his correspondence with Elisabeth I have been discussing.

Through considering a more extended portion of their correspondence, I hope to have shown that Elisabeth is not merely a critic of Descartes but also has philosophical views of her own. I have argued that we can see in her correspondence with Descartes the development of a position of the nature of the human mind. First, in the early part of their correspondence, Elisabeth begins to carve out a logical space for an alternative metaphysics which is neither a substance dualism nor a reductionist materialism. Then, as she and Descartes turn to discuss how her passions affect her, she comes to articulate just what this metaphysics is. In her view, the mind is autonomous—we are agents in our thinking and determine our own thoughts. Nevertheless, in order to be autonomous in this way, the mind depends upon the good health of the body. In so far as the body enables the mind's proper functioning in this way, it is necessary to the mind. We might still want to ask questions about the nature of the union of mind and body on Elisabeth's account. On one front, we might want a more complete account of the way in which our bodily state enables our thought. What does it take to be a 'disease' which impedes our faculty of reason? How does Elisabeth ultimately—and rightly—distinguish between being a female and a genuine 'disease' which does affect our rationality? What is it about these 'diseases' which make us unable to think freely? Would she want to say that the passions are such diseases? Or that perhaps only certain passions, such as deep melancholy or anger, are? We could accept the union as Elisabeth outlines it—accept that our bodily state is an enabling condition of thought—and ask where that leaves us: How does Elisabeth avoid a specious form of epiphenomenalism? That is, how is this understanding of the relation between mind and body supposed to explain our having the particular sensations, or perceptions, of things that we do have? What might Elisabeth have to say about the immortality of the soul, if she wants to insist that the body is an enabling condition of rationality?

These are all I think relevant and interesting questions to pursue, and doing so would involve engaging with Elisabeth as a philosopher in her own right. I cannot undertake to do this at all adequately here. However, I do want to make a few brief points. First, let me say right out that if Elisabeth does indeed want to maintain that the condition of the body enables the soul to be rational, I do not see how she can maintain that the soul is immortal, so long as it is to remain a rational soul in its immortality. Second, Elisabeth can avoid charges of epiphenomenalism. For in insisting that the mind is autonomous she need not claim that the mind is in a realm of its own—suspended causally from the body and the world. She might admit that the power we have over our thoughts does have causal efficacy; she might, for instance, subscribe to Descartes's psychotherapy as a cure for her physical maladies. In doing so, she will, of course, face a new challenge—that of explaining just how changes of mind can affect changes of body. And this question is related to that about how we come to have the particular sensations we do. It seems that there are several ways the answers to these questions could go. For one, it does not seem to me that an interactionist explanation is ruled out on this model as we are no longer faced with the problem of getting two really distinct substances to meet. But nor does it seem that such an interactionist resolution is the only way to go. Elisabeth might well prefer to adopt a more Aristotelian alternative to explain our perceptions and intentional actions. Finally, that Elisabeth does not fully articulate what counts as a bodily condition enabling rationality might count in her favor. For to do so would amount to defining what counts as a full-fledged human being, and that is surely a politically charged endeavor. In remaining silent, Elisabeth seems to err on the side of inclusion in the class of humans rather than exclusion, and so she manages to avoid struggles like those Locke has in considering monsters and changelings.

Rather than pursue these lines, however, I want to return to consider briefly Elisabeth's practice of philosophy. Does this investigation into this portion of her correspondence with Descartes give us any insight into why she never systematically presents a philosophical position? Is there an explanation of why Elisabeth *is* more able to articulate her philosophical position in the context she does? I am not sure that I have any answers to these questions, but I do want to consider them in light of Elisabeth's philosophical style.

ELISABETH'S PHILOSOPHICAL STYLE

I remarked at the beginning of this paper that part of the difficulty in taking Elisabeth as a philosopher in her own right lies in the lack of a systematic presentation of her philosophical position. And I hope that the effort required to extract a positive philosophical position from her letters has borne out this claim. We might well ask ourselves why this is so. Why does she not promulgate a philosophical theory of her own? There are of course many sorts of answers one might try to give to this question—most obviously, one might offer a social-historical argument appealing to the opportunities available to women in the mid-seventeenth century: perhaps it was acceptable for them to correspond with the great (male) intellects of their time and not to write anything of their own. Presumably, one could also appeal to the details of Elisabeth's life and circumstances and come up with more personal reasons preventing her from writing her own work. In this regard, the context provided by the series of letters I have been considering may prove quite useful. But, while I think there is much to learn in pursuing these avenues, they are not the routes I want to take here. Instead, I want to ask another question: Why should we be bothered by the absence of any systematic presentation of a philosophical position on Elisabeth's part? Does her not having one make her any less of a philosopher?

It may well be true that Elisabeth's philosophical activity consists largely in her raising objections to what she reads. But there are two ways of raising objections. One way is to attend to details, to catalogue lists of inconsistencies and counter-examples. Certainly this way of practising philosophy is important and useful, for it is in response to these sorts of objections that a philosopher clarifies his or her position. Elisabeth is sometimes engaged in this sort of activity with respect to Descartes. In letters I have not considered here, she points to apparent inconsistencies in the physics he puts forward in the *Principles* (see her letter of 1 August 1644, acknowledging his dedication of that book to her), and she certainly draws on her wealth of practical experience in the later letters, taking Descartes to task for making being virtuous seem like an easy matter. And it can seem as if her appeal to the sorts of diseases which seem to take away our faculty of reason is an objection of the same order: Elisabeth might well be read as simply raising a counter-example to press Descartes to further articulate his own position. In so far as Elizabeth raises these sorts of objections, she should count as a philosopher, but it is easy to see how she might fade into the background as a thinker: her work is that of a helper, and she does not have a program of her own.

There is, however, another way of raising objections. The second sort of objection takes the same form as the first—it involves pointing up inconsistencies and invoking counter-examples—but it has a very different impact. These second sort of questions do not demand answers which serve to articulate the details of a position. Rather, they are incisive questions, going straight to the assumptions on which the philosophical position rests. It is this sort of question—the incisive one—which typifies Elisabeth's philosophical style in the letters I have examined here. And this sort of question, while it need not involve putting forward theses of one's own as an alternative (though I have suggested that Elisabeth's questions do have a view in their background), serves a central role in the practice of philosophy as the systematic presentation of positive philosophical programs. These questions are more momentous; they force a philosopher either to take a stand, or to revise, his or her views. And insofar as these questions are challenging, they play a more direct role in the arrival at a position, and so the questioner deserves a bit more recognition. Indeed, often times the questioner is pressed to offer a coherent alternative to make the point come home, and so ends up being a philosopher in a positive sense.

Now, that Elisabeth is asking particularly incisive questions is not readily apparent, at least not to Descartes. For he initially treats her questions as though they were of the former kind: in his answers he sets about explaining his own view more thoroughly without ever calling into question his basic presuppositions. It is not until quite late in their discussion that he feels the force of her questions, and sets about reconsidering his position. But this is the nature of the incisive question: the person to whom such questions are directed must be in a frame of mind which allows them to reconsider the value of what is most dear to them.

These are two things I would like to note in this regard. The first is about the relation of Elisabeth's way of doing philosophy to her own self-conception. The second is about the appropriateness of both Elisabeth's insights and Descartes's arising in the context in which they do. First, often the very questions which challenge the presuppositions of a given problem are those which on their face seem most naïve. That is, they can seem like stupid questions; it can appear that one does not understand what is supposed to have been obvious, especially before the person to whom they are addressed feels their force. To persist in asking these naïve questions either requires an almost incredible degree of self-effacement—one needs to be completely comfortable with the possibility that one may look foolish—or an incredible degree of confidence—one needs to be sure that one is right in asking these questions. By considering both of these possibilities, I think, we can begin to understand Elisabeth's own self-devaluation: we might see her persistent self-effacement either as arising from her philosophical temperament or as said with some irony, and so revealing the confidence of one who is trying to get her correspondent to see her point.

Second, it seems appropriate to me that the insights Elisabeth and Descartes have about the union of soul and body arise out of a quite personal discussion of the emotions. For one, the passions are a topic suitable to the content of the insight. They, more than sensations, show us just how our bodies do affect us, and in particular affect our capacity to think clearly about things. The way we feel about things often does color our perceptions and leaves us with certain prejudices. But equally, we can regulate our passions, and do so just by considering the reasons *not* to feel the way we do, and this very possibility of their being regulated in this way suggests that they do, at least most often, leave our faculty of reason intact. But sometimes, our emotions do get the better of us: anger and sadness are notorious for their ability to cloud our judgement. The passions thus provide just the right sort of context for Elisabeth's making the point she does about the soul–body union. They serve to illustrate her thesis about the relation between mind and body.

But also the personal nature of the discussion serves as an appropriate context for challenging one of Descartes's most fundamental tenets. The focus of their discussion is *not* Descartes's metaphysics but rather Elisabeth's depression. Descartes is trying to help Elisabeth to feel differently, and for him that requires that she sees things differently. Feeling differently, for him, involves taking stock of what we think and what we take to be important to us, and sometimes this involves asking ourselves hard questions, and being willing to answer them. For her part in this discussion, Elisabeth is willing to do just this, and her willingness to engage with him in these very personal matters I suspect goes some way towards her facilitating her own recovery. Equally, we might think that Elisabeth's own openness encourages a similar attitude in Descartes. He responds to her trust in his good will with an equal trust in hers, and so he is finally able to hear what she is trying to say. In this way, Elisabeth is not simply a reader of Descartes. She is a friend, and a good friend, as he is to her. And we might understand her as engaging Descartes philosophically, and displaying her own philosophical talents, in just this way. As a friend, she asks and presses him to answer the hard questions, directly engaging with one whose thoughts she finds interesting, challenging him to clarify his position. And it is as a friend that Descartes responds, for he in turn, if he does not always understand, still is receptive to her thoughts and so challenges her to articulate and clarify her own views about philosophical topics. This way of doing philosophy might not lend itself easily to a systematic presentation of one's view, but it still strikes me as both a legitimate and a good way of doing philosophy.[12]

Notes

1. Some biographical details about Elisabeth may be useful. What follows owes much to Beatrice Zedler's synthesis of various sources in her 'Three Princesses', *Hypatia*, 4, 1, 1989. In addition to the sources cited by Zedler, see Baroness Blaze de Bury. *Memoirs of the Princess Palatine, Princess of Bohemia* (London: Richard Bentley, 1853).

   Elisabeth was born at Heidelberg in December 1618, the daughter of Frederick V of Bohemia and Elizabeth Stuart, daughter of James I of England. Her uncle was thus Charles I, who was beheaded in the English Civil War. In November 1620 her father lost in battle not only the throne of Bohemia but also his own land. The family went into exile, first in Germany and then in the Hague. Elisabeth had several siblings, six brothers, the oldest of whom died when she was eleven, and three sisters, perhaps the most famous of whom was the youngest, Sophie, who became Electress of Hanover and corresponded with Leibniz, as did her daughter, Sophie Charlotte. Elisabeth was the eldest of her siblings.

   Elisabeth was taught etiquette, Scripture, mathematics, history, the sciences, jurisprudence, and several languages including Latin and Greek. Perhaps as part of her schooling, she read the *Meditations* in Latin (in 1642), and a meeting between her and Descartes was facilitated by Pollot. Thence begins their contact with one another.

   In 1667, Elisabeth entered a Protestant convent at Herford in Westphalia, where she eventually became abbess. As abbess she offered refuge to those whose religious beliefs were less than orthodox, including Jean Labadie and his followers (including Anna Maria von Schurmann, a friend of Elisabeth's from Holland, who undoubtedly organized the Labadists' stay), and William Penn and other Quakers. Elisabeth died in February 1680.
2. I use the following abbreviations in parenthetical citations to Descartes's works and their translations. The translations of Elisabeth's letters are my own.

   AT *Oeuvres de Descartes*, Adam and Tannery (eds), Vrin, 1996. 'AT' is followed by volume and page number.

   MM *Principles of Philosophy*. Miller and Miller (trs), Kluwer, 1991, 'MM' is followed by page number.

   CSMK *The Philosophical Writings of Descartes. Vol. III.* Cottingham, Stouthof, Murdoch and Kenny (trs), Cambridge, 1991. 'CSMK' is followed by page number.
3. Andrea Nye, in her 'Polity and Prudence: the Ethics of Elisabeth, Princess Palatine' in *Hypatia's Daughters*, Linda Lopez McAlister (ed.), Bloomington: Indiana UP, 1996, also aims to set out Elisabeth's own philosophical view. As the title suggests, she is concerned with Elisabeth's ethics, whereas I will be concerned with her metaphysics.
4. There has been much attention to Elisabeth's contribution to Descartes's philosophical program in these letters. See Ruth Mattern, 'Descartes's Correspondence with Elisabeth: Concerning Both the Union and Distinction of Mind and Body' in Michael Hooker (ed.). *Descartes: Critical and Interpretive Essays*, Johns Hopkins UP, 1978; Daniel Garber, 'Understanding Interaction: What Descartes Should Have Told Elisabeth', *Southern Journal of Philosophy*, 21, Supplement (1983). What I am interested in exploring here, however, is Elisabeth's own philosophical position.

5. It is this letter which is missing from CSMK. The translations of this and subsequent passages from this letter are my own.
6. He feels justified in doing so because Elisabeth had solicited and accepted his medical advice the summer before.
7. Indeed, it is widely recognized that Elisabeth was plagued by family troubles. I have already mentioned the death of her eldest brother (see fn. 1 above). With the death of her father in 1632, when Elizabeth was 13, the family was left financially dependent on others. Despite support from the English and Dutch governments, they were always in debt. The English Civil War exacerbated an already bad financial situation, while at the same time undoubtedly causing great personal pain. And then there is the other incident which surrounds the correspondence under consideration here. Shortly before this period, in November 1645, another brother, Edward, renounced his Protestant faith to become a Catholic and marry Anne of Gonzaga. Elisabeth was clearly upset by this, as she writes to Descartes, himself a Catholic, to complain (see AT IV 335).
8. Those with great souls

   have such strong and such powerful reasonings, that even while they have passions, and sometimes feel them even more violently than normal, their reason nevertheless always remains mistress, and makes it that even these afflictions serve them and contribute to the perfect felicity which they enjoy in this life. . . . The greatest of souls, of which I speak, have the satisfaction in themselves, of the things which happen to them, even the most unfortunate and insupportable. Thus, feeling the pain in their bodies they exert themselves to support it patiently, and this test that they make of their strength is agreeable to them. Thus, seeing their friends in some large affliction, they sympathize with their trouble, and do all that is possible to deliver them from it, and do not even fear exposing themselves to death, for this purpose, if it is necessary.

   (AT IV 202f)

9. Elisabeth to Descartes, 22 June 1645. It is remarkable just how enduring this expression has been.
10. Despite the self-assurance that such an ironic tone of voice may reveal, it also seems clear that Elisabeth is less than confident: she presses the point of her own weakness, both physical and intellectual, again and again, in this letter and in others, and consistently chastises herself for failing to understand and for asking what she takes to be stupid questions. Such language could of course be simply polite deference to Descartes, a testament to her manners, rather than a reflection of her opinion of herself. For another somewhat equivocal statement of self-esteem on Elisabeth's part, see her later letter to Descartes of 4 December 1649: 'Do not think that such an advantageous description [of Queen Christina] gives me anything to be jealous about; rather it leads me to esteem myself a little more than I did before she gave me an idea of a person so accomplished, which liberates our sex from the imputation of imbecility and weakness which the pedants want to give it' (AT V 452). I do not think any part of my discussion rests on how we read Elisabeth's self-denigratory remarks.

11. Neither does Elisabeth adopt the essentialist position. That is, she does not make the strong claim that she, because she is female, thinks differently.
12. A version of this paper was originally presented at the Conference on Seventeenth Century Women Philosophers held at the University of Massachusetts at Amherst in November 1997. I would like to thank the organizers, Vere Chappell. Eileen O'Neill and Robert Sleigh, for the occasion to think more about Elisabeth as a thinker in her own right. The comments and questions of the audience there and at William Paterson University were also very helpful.

Spinoza on the Pathos of Idolatrous Love and the Hilarity of True Love

Amélie Oksenberg Rorty*

In memory of Laszlo Versenyi
Hungary, 1929–Williamstown, Mass., 1988

> ['In reflecting on love], I was led far beyond my individual life and time, to the point where . . . [I] became no more than an accidental focal point of something much larger; a mere vantage point for seeing and ranging over a landscape that has no clear boundaries.'
>
> Laszlo Versenyi, *Going Home*

Differ as we do about its nature, its causes and effects, its proper objects, we all agree that love is—or can be—the beginning of wisdom. But wisdom about what? Spinoza wrote not only truthfully but wisely about love, about its travails and dangers, about its connection to knowledge and power, about individuality and the disappearance of the self. To understand what is vital and what is mortifying about the passions, to trace the movement from the bondage of passivity to the freedom of activity, we could do no better than follow his investigations. In the nature of the case, each of us necessarily understands him—as we do all else—from the partiality of our own perspectives. We shall follow Ariadne's thread, into the heart of the labyrinth, first speaking with the vulgar, telling fragmentary tales about appearances. Then we must follow the thread out again, thinking with the learned, gaining scientific understanding of what we really are; and finally we must put these two—vulgar appearance and scientific explanation—together to tell the real story, the story of reality.

* Amélie Oksenberg Rorty, 'Spinoza on the Pathos of Idolatrous Love and the Hilarity of True Love', from Robert C. Solomon and Kathleen M. Higgins (eds.), *The Philosophy of (Erotic) Love* (Lawrence: University Press of Kansas, 1991), 352–71. Reprinted by permission of the publisher.

SPEAKING WITH THE VULGAR ABOUT APPEARANCES: FRAGMENTARY IMAGES OF PASSIVITY, IDOLATRY, PARTIALITY

Spinoza is, first and last, a particularist: The world is composed wholly and entirely of particular individuals, so interrelated that they form a complex individual, a unified system. To understand the pathos of love, we must therefore begin with a particular story; it will, of course, be merely a fragmentary image, only partially true, because it is, perforce, only part of the story. Nevertheless, following it where it must go will bring us to an increasingly adequate understanding of love, of the characters in our story, and of ourselves, as we love.

Ariadne loves Echo, loves him, as she thinks, for the subtlety of his interpretation of Spinoza, for his wry speech, the precision and delicacy of his courtesy, his way of looking at her with those eyes of his, and perhaps most important of all, as is the way of these things, for she knows not what.

As Spinoza would see it, Ariadne's love is an elation—a sense of well-being—that she thinks Echo brings her. She feels herself more fully herself, freer to write clearly and fluently, to move gracefully because of him. ('Love is elation accompanied by the idea of an external cause' [III. app. D. 6].)[1] But if she thought that her University or a particular landscape were the causes of her elation—her exhilarated enhancement—she would love her University or that landscape. Although each love—indeed each moment of love—is unique, there are as many types of love as there are types of individuals. ('There are as many kinds of . . . love . . . as there are kinds of objects by which we are affected. Any affect of one individual differs from that of another in the extent that the essence of one individual differs from the essence of the other' [III. 56–57].) The elation of love is the ideational or psychological expression of a change in Ariadne's bodily thriving. Indeed every 'affect is a modification of the body by which the body's power is increased or diminished, assisted or checked, together with the ideas of these modifications. If we are the adequate cause of an affect, then the affect is active; if we are not, it is passive' (III. D. 3). So in truth, Ariadne's love is her body's elation, psychologically expressed. To the extent that she thinks of this elation as externally caused, her affect is passive; to the extent that she thinks of it as a function of her own nature, her love is active.

Spinoza's *affectus*—usually translated as 'affect' or 'emotion'—is obviously a much broader and more encompassing notion than the contemporary class of *emotions* that is commonly contrasted to *beliefs* and *desires*. Affects include desires, wishes, a sense of health or debility: They are ideational indicants of bodily thriving or declining. A condition is passive when its cause is (regarded as) external, active when internal, to the body. So, for instance, a healing process which is a function of the body's own 'internal' defensive immune system is a modification of the body, registered in the mind as an active affect; a healing process 'externally' produced by medication is a modification of the body, registered in the mind as a passive affect.

So far, so good: Love is a particular sense of health, with a diagnosis of its cause. But troubles soon begin. Elation is an active contrast to a previous state; it must, in its very nature, escalate. ('Elation is . . . a passage or transition from a state of less to a state of greater perfection or vitality' [III. app. D. 2].) Ariadne will try to secure Echo for herself in whatever ways she can, acting to preserve her elation and to oppose or to destroy whatever might bring dejection. ('We endeavour to bring about whatever we imagine to be conducive to elation; [and] endeavor to remove or destroy whatever we imagine to be opposed to it and conducive to dejection' [III. 26–28].) One of the ways Ariadne will attempt to secure him is to think of him a lot. When Echo is not actually around discussing Spinoza with her, she will have fantasies of their increasing intimacy, an intimacy that would still further enhance and elate her. But she will—she must—go further than fantasy: She will attempt to control Echo so that those aspects of his character that enhance her are strengthened, those that debilitate her are weakened. There is nothing special about love in this; all psychological conditions are active, relational, and dynamic. Thoughts and passions alike are individuated in a field of forces. Each individual is so constituted as to attempt to perpetuate and enhance his nature, in relation to other individuals. ('Everything . . . endeavors to persist in its own being . . . The mind endeavors as far as it can to think of those things that increase or assist the body's power of activity' [III. 6–9, 12].) Indeed, the details of all an individual's activities in self-preservation, taken together, constitute its *conatus*, its essential nature. A person's thoughts and passions are the traces—the expressions and reflections—of all this activity.

Of course the satisfaction of Ariadne's desires will depend on her psychological canniness, on how well she understands Echo and herself. If Echo does not reciprocate her affections—if that way of looking at her turns out to be nearsightedness, if the intricacies of his interpretations are merely constructed to impress Ariadne in her persona as department head—her love will be short-lived, likely to be replaced by hatred for someone who has diminished her sense of herself. But would Spinoza expect their apparent happiness to continue if Echo returns her affections? The natural story of the best of such love relatively quickly leads to ambivalence, confusion, unhappiness. ('Emotional distress and unhappiness have their origin especially in excessive love towards anything subject to considerable instability, a thing which we can never completely possess. For nobody is disturbed or anxious about any thing unless he loves it, nor do wrongs, suspicions, enmities, etc. arise except from love towards things which nobody can truly possess' [V. 20. S].) Ariadne and Echo are complex people, with complex relations to others. She has her work, he has his; she has one set of friends, he has another. Their relations to one another are necessarily affected by the constant and subtle changes in their interactions with the rest of the world. If their friends and acquaintances endorse their mutual esteem, their love will, for a time, be reinforced. But if their common acquaintances do not respect Echo, Ariadne's love will be weakened. If, on the other hand, he is commonly thought to be too good for her, she will begin to fear—and to perceive—a change in his attentions. When his affection fluctuates, her sense of assurance falters, her grace and style crack. She will sense herself diminished and her estrangement will begin.

In loving Echo, Ariadne comes to redefine her relations to the rest of the world: Her interactions with others will be mediated, skewed by how she imagines they affect Echo and above all by how they affect Echo's relation to her. She will love what she believes enhances his love for her, hate what endangers it, become jealous of what draws his attentions away from her, envy those whom Echo envies. It is this feature of love—that it generates tangential, perspectivally fragmented relations to the world—that makes it especially blinding. The bondage of Ariadne's passive love ramifies beyond her perspectivally distorted perceptions of the complexities of Echo's qualities to similar distortions about the complex qualities of all that interacts with Echo.

For their happiness to continue, their constant changes must remain in harmony. Each must exactly register and adapt to the constant transformations in the other, and those transformations must remain mutually enhancing. Ariadne's growing reputation must somehow stand in continuous harmony with the changes that affect Echo, the reviews of his commentary on Spinoza, the adoration of his women students. As we fill in the familiar details of such stories, it becomes harder and harder to imagine the two continuing to enhance one another. How do they perceive one another's attentions to the rest of the world? Every unshared moment of delight becomes the occasion for fear, envy, and jealousy. Every shared moment introduces a subtle struggle for power. But even if all goes well—and of course if it does, we have moved from a familiar story to a fairy story—things are at best precarious. Every moment of love occurs within a larger context. But since affects that are accidentally associated remain associated, the elation of love readily becomes linked with a sense of debility. ('Anything can accidentally be the cause of elation, dejection or desire' [III. 15]. 'If the mind has once been affected by two passions at the same time, when it is later affected by one it will also be affected by the other' [III. 14].) For instance, if Ariadne tended Echo during an illness, comforted him during some disappointment, or protected him from his crippling sense of insecurity, his affection will remind him of debilities that he naturally prefers to forget. It gets harder and harder to prevent elation from sliding to ambivalence, and ambivalence from sliding to the disintegration that is associated with erratic and vacillating impulsive movements. Any love that focuses on a particular individual is idolatrous; and because idolatrous love is fetishistic and partial, it inevitably brings ambivalence and frustration.

Ariadne's natural vitality will combat disintegration; she straightway moves to preserve herself, to overcome pathology in whatever way she can. Of course she has ways to combat debility; indeed she'd have disintegrated long ago if she'd not been naturally constructed and organized in such a way as to overcome debility, to preserve her integrity. Ariadne could not be cured of envy, jealousy, fear, just by trying to stop loving Echo. After all, every chance joy and enhancement brings love with it. She must in some way go to the root of the matter of her dreadful and tiresome tendency to fall in love, always and invariably, time and again, to fall in love. Nor—however tempting that might seem—will it help her to attempt to transform her love to contempt, disdain, hate. As love is a sense of enhancement, of elation, hate is a sense of dejection, accompanied by an idea of its cause (III. app. D. 7). But no one can be enhanced by an affect that is itself an expression of a variety of diminution.

Ariadne can only redirect her passive love through a more powerful emotion. ('An affect or emotion cannot be checked or destroyed except by a contrary emotion which is stronger than the emotion to be checked' [IV. 7].) It will not help Ariadne to love a more powerful person, (say) Abraham, or to acquire a more dominating passion, for (say) fame, or a passion for a more stable object, (say) Sung vases. All idolatry—any focus on a single object—brings the miseries of pathology in its wake. Love is love, with the same structure and the same consequences, even if each moment of elation is uniquely determined by the details of that moment. If she is astute, Ariadne will know that she cannot avoid the disintegration of one pathological love by finding another.

THINKING WITH THE LEARNED ABOUT THE STRUCTURE OF APPEARANCES: FROM THE BONDAGE OF PASSIVITY TO THE FREEDOM OF ACTIVITY

Let us suppose that Aridane is psychologically canny, that she has considerable natural endowments—some of them constitutional, some acquired by the fortune of her upbringing. Central among them is a certain capacity for and energy toward clarity in reflection. She knows that idolatrous love, focused on a particular individual, necessarily involves misperception. Not that Echo wasn't what he seemed: He did have a wry turn of mind; he did have a sound understanding of Spinoza. But in fact the elation he first brought her was not just a function of *his* character: it was, rather, the expression of the fit between his traits *and* hers. Had she been the star of a hardrock music group, she'd not have been charmed by Echo's charms. Since she is canny—and this is just what it means to be canny, neither more nor less—she has a hunger for further explanations, an active passion for understanding. In fact her hunger for further explanation is another way of expressing her activity in integration, her moving from the debilities of love and its consequences. That hunger, her reflections, her drive to integrity are all different ways of describing the same thing: the active energies exercised in preserving and enhancing her existence.

Explanation-hungry as she is, Ariadne has also come to realize a number of things about herself and Echo: that she and Echo—and anyone or anything else she might love—are complex, constantly changing, compounded entities. Every aspect of their individuality is affected by their interactions with other equally historically conditioned, dynamic individuals. The details of all these interactions are themselves expressions and reflections of the details of their past history, the active traces, as it were, of many different layers of previous interactions, stretching far beyond their individual lives. Echo's interest in Spinoza expresses his grandmother's attitudes toward the world; his eyes and the look of his eyes reflect his biological inheritance. Ariadne's own penchant for fellows with a wry turn of mind derives from some of her childhood attachments, and the timbre of her voice reflects not only her constitution but also her family's passion for folksongs. Gradually, Ariadne comes to see herself and Echo in a different light. In fact, she begins to suspect—though she has as yet no way of making this suspicion anything but a vague hunch—that she and Echo just *are* the active traces of all that has happened to them, stretching far backward before their births, and far outward to distant interactive individuals. She gives up her idolatrous modes of thinking about Echo and herself as 'closed and bounded entities' and instead comes to think of all individuals as complex, dynamic compounds, individuated by their history and their interactions. By changing her thoughts in this way. Ariadne's image-ideas have become reflective ideas, ideas which, besides including their direct objects, also include reflections on the relations between the idea of their direct objects and other ideas. So in thinking of Echo, Ariadne now thinks of the interrelations between her ideas of Echo and her ideas of her brother, his grand-parents, folksongs of a certain era; in thinking of herself, she now thinks of her ideas of Echo, of her grandmother, and so on.

All of these reflections give her some relief from ambivalence and its inevitably erratic behavior. Because she has traced the disparate sources of the various strands that have formed Echo, she has dispersed the intensity of her attachment. Since she now sees Echo as a mediating transmitter rather than as a Substance, her idea of the causes of her elation has correspondingly changed. The train of associated passions—fear, envy, jealousy—is deflected by this change. Her greater understanding gives her an increased sense of her own powers: and her new sense of power gives her a new source for elation. She has, for one thing, turned inadequate ideas—images—into increasingly adequate ideas. In following her own nature, in affirming the truth about its history and constitution, she has become active rather than passive. She is, in fact, active in exactly the degree to which her ideas are adequate rather than inadequate. Instead of imagining herself to be the recipient of the benefits of Echo's charms, she actively identifies herself with the system of interactive causes that have determined her. In so affirming her identity, she recognizes that what she had thought of as a passive passion, a modification produced by an external cause, actually in part also proceeds from her own nature. ('Insofar as the mind has adequate ideas, it is necessarily active; insofar as it has inadequate ideas, it is necessarily passive' [III. 1]. 'We are active when something takes place in us or externally to us of which we are the adequate cause, that is, when it follows from our nature . . . We are passive when something takes place in us, of which we are only the partial cause' [III. D. 2]. 'The more active a thing is, the more perfect it is' [V. 40].)

It now seems as if Ariadne's original passive elation—her love of Echo—is as nothing in comparison to the active elation she has in discovering the real nature of individuals, in understanding how she and Echo came to interact as they did. ('The greater the number of causes that simultaneously concur in arousing an emotion, the greater the emotion' [V. 8].) There is no better cure for idolatry than the analysis of its causes and objects, no better cure for the fetishism of idolatry than its dispersed and ramified redistribution. But the movement that locates the particular in its place in a pattern loses neither the particularity nor love: It transforms inadequacy into adequacy, passivity into activity.

We've talked as if Ariadne's discoveries and reflections are things *she* did in attempting to persevere, to integrate herself. In a way that is right; Ariadne's nature just is of this kind: She is psychologically canny and historically reflective. Her researches, inquiries, and reflections are, however, just as much an expression of—a determination of—her constitution and her history as are the timbre of her voice and her taste for wry minds. Her insight has—and does not have—a special status. In one sense, she neither generates nor controls it; for it, too, follows from the interactive nexus of individuals. Even her insight is nothing more (or less) than the complex and dynamic active traces of her genetic constitution and personal history. Still, if she is so fortunate as to be an active inquirer, her insight is more expressive of her nature than is the timbre of her voice or her taste for wry minds. The centrality of insight is not (alas) assured because insight lasts longer than the timbre of a voice. Treated as facts, both are timeless and unchangeable; treated as properties, both are contingent, susceptible to disease and debility. Insight does not cure or prevent senility; nor does it empower an individual mind by elevating it to transcendent objects. It is nothing more (or less) than the detailed activity of integrating ideas. It consists of painstakingly putting two and two together, and then tracing the functions of four in the system of natural numbers. There is nothing more mystical to it than that: The power of a mind is expressed in its comprehensive activity in integration.

In pursuing her liberation from the pathology of love, Ariadne is not a *homuncula* somewhere at the center of her essence, willing herself to be whole and intact, directing the strategies designed to free her from the disintegrative suffering of love. Ariadne knows better; she knows that she does not will the direction of energy. Just as Echo is not the only begetter of her elation, so too she is not the only begetter of her liberation. All these active reflections are just the fortune of her history and interactions, working in and through her. Even her realization that she necessarily is (no more and no less) than the totality of the accidents of her history and her interactions is the fortune of her history and interactions. If she has the good fortune to identify herself *with* and *as* all those dynamic interactions which have made her who she is, she will no longer think of herself as having been formed *by* them, as if she could mysteriously have been the same essential core, with a different history. Her characteristics will follow from her nature because they *are* her nature. This reflection is not a further thought; it is just the self-conscious realization of the connected significance of all the thoughts that she is.

Ariadne's conception of herself—her idea of her mind as a structure of ideas—is exactly coordinate with her conception of the boundaries that distinguish her essence from those of other individuals. It therefore exactly defines the scope of her passive affects, those she imagines to be externally caused, in contrast to her active affects, those that she thinks of as following from her nature. A person's passions are functions of her conceptions of her essential nature. It is ambiguous and misleading to say that a person bent on liberation from the pathology of passion must transform and enlarge her conception of her individuality. It suggests that there are two distinct lines of thought, one's conception of oneself on the one hand, and the range of one's affects on the other. But these are different ways of describing the same thing. To have a clearer conception of oneself just *is* to have turned and to be turning passive into active affective states, seeing them as parts of one's nature rather than as invasions. To recommend a better conception of oneself misleadingly suggests that there is a core person deciding to correct her self-image. But these processes of correction are just the various strands in the person's complex nature, expressing themselves in the many ways a complex *conatus* acts to persist in its own nature.

As we have told it so far, the story of Ariadne's increased awareness of the complex dynamic relations between herself and Echo is, in every sense of the word, a vulgar story. But in her larger understanding, Ariadne sees that there is a tale of necessity within every vulgar story. The vulgar story of love—with its trials and tribulations—is told in a very confused and as we might say, provisional language, within the realm of *imaginatio.* It is partial, fragmentary. Even Ariadne's increased self-awareness is, as the story first unfolds, a case of narrative discovery, tracing more and more of the vast expanding network of the historical and relational details that determine Echo and herself. The language of psychological canniness, even that of historical astuteness is still quite inadequate to express the deeper structures of these appearances. If Ariadne follows Spinoza's therapeutic recommendations in liberating herself from passive love, she detaches her love from her confused imagistic thought of Echo, and concentrates instead on understanding how her emotions formed an interdependent pattern. First she might think of family histories and family resemblances; then she begins to form rough generalizations about academics and men, about the relation between love and dependence, weakness and fear, envy and jealousy. ('The power of the mind over the emotions consists in . . . detaching the affect from the thought of their external cause, which we imagine confusedly; and in . . . knowing the . . . order and connection among the affects' V. 20. S.) Actively engaging in this sort of sociopsychological investigation helps Ariadne become less prey to the demons of associated passive affects. She becomes actively thoughtful. Although such rough generalizations are, to be sure, genuinely central to understanding Ariadne's condition, we—and if she is fortunate, she—can get further.

Ariadne's active elation in the power of her psychological and historical understanding can be still further enhanced by her understanding of biology and eventually of mathematical physics. Before we have a full understanding of Ariadne's love, and before we return the particularity of Ariadne's love to her, we must stop speaking with the vulgar and leave appearances and the language of appearances behind. In truth, Ariadne and Echo are human bodies, organisms delicately and dynamically structured in such a way as to conserve and preserve their continuing complex activities in their interactions with other bodies surrounding them. Organic processes are themselves expressions of the activities of basic entities, the simple particulars (*corpora simplicissima*) of which the world is composed, no more, no less. The organization and activity of human bodies—the interactions between Ariadne, Echo, and other bodies—are functions of the dynamic interactions among the *corpora simplicissima* that compose them (II. 13).

In truth, then, Ariadne and Echo (it is now more appropriate to ignore their individual histories and to call them *A* and *E*) are compound bodies whose properties are functions of the character of extension. Their individual minds—that is, their ideas of themselves and of one another—are ideas of the ideas of their bodies. More fully and adequately understood, the order of Ariadne's ideas—the rationale of her thoughts and affects—is the same as the order of the properties of bodies. ('The order and connection of ideas is the same as the order and connection of things. . . . The . . . human mind is basically nothing else but the idea of an individual actually existing thing. . . . The object of the idea constituting the human mind is the body, a definite mode of extension, and nothing else. . . . The idea which constitutes . . . the human mind is nothing simple, but composed of very many ideas' [II. 7, 11–13, 15].) What *A* knows of herself—in contrast to what she may imagine—is a set of ideas of the condition of a compound body (vulgarly called *hers*) which is itself a reflection of the interaction between her compound body and other sections of extension, including that compound vulgarly called Echo. What she knows of the world, she knows only through her body; her ideas are just the intellectual articulations of bodily states. Yet Spinoza's psychophysicalism is not reductive, but co-relative. Relations among ideas are the articulations of the relations among parts of extension; and the relational properties of extension are the expressions—the spatial projections—of the relational structures of ideas. The properties of extension can only be characterised, can only be expressed as relations among ideas; but the relations among ideas are just the expressions of the dynamic properties of extension, nothing more and nothing less. Spinoza's insistence on the relational and dynamic character of both thought and extension preserves him from sliding into a reductivist position, either on the side of materialism or on that of idealism.

For all its graces, *A*'s mind is nothing special. All her ideas—including her love and other affects or emotions—are articulations, expressions of the activities of her body. But that body—that relatively self-preserving organism—is, like every other extended individual, an active nexus of *corpora simplicissima* interrelated, concatenated in such a way that they preserve a particular ratio of motion and rest. Some of the central properties of *A*'s body are properties which she has in common with all other bodies: They are properties that are as attributable to any part of her as they are to the whole of her, attributable to any part of extension as they are to the whole of extension (II. 37). Now since the order of extension is necessarily expressed in ideas, *A*'s mind necessarily has (is in part composed of) self-evident ideas of these common properties of extension. Her body is composed of these properties; and her ideas are ideas of the properties of her body. Since such common ideas are not fragmentary or perspectival, not qualified by their dependence on other ideas—since they are ideas of the properties of *every* body—they are adequate, necessarily and self-evidently true (II. 38–40). Like every idea, common ideas are relational, determined by their interconnection in the system of ideas. But since common ideas are universally instantiated, the ideas which determine them are identical to them. The grounds or conditions for common ideas are therefore represented within them; and since they are the bearers of their own determination, they are self-evident. Since *A*'s power and activity is a function of the adequacy of her ideas, her power—her elation—is increased by her knowledge of the unqualifiedly necessary properties of bodies.

Every individual mind has (is partially composed of) a set of adequate ideas of extension, the common notions that express 'her' body, as they do every body. To the extent that she focuses on these adequate ideas, *A* has a more adequate understanding of her relation to *E* than she has from her psychological and historical understanding, which at best forms a contingent narrative, a set of generalizations from likely stories. The common notions of mathematical physics take *A* beyond psychological and historical insight to *ratio*, to a necessary and deductive scientific demonstrative science of extension. All that was particular—that is, all that was merely conditional and perspectival—about Echo and herself, and all the sound but incomplete generalizations of folk psychology and history can now be supplemented by a rigorously deductive science. *A* now has a much more powerful idea of her own mind, because she now has placed her idea of her mind in a system of interrelated ideas: She knows *what it is to be a mind.* In focusing on these adequate ideas, in bringing them to light, she has in a sense enlarged her mind; she not only has a clear idea of how things are, but also why they are like that. She now has two quite different types of explanations of the phenomena. The first was afforded by the reflections that moved her from confused images to psychological and historical generalizations. The second is afforded by the rationally demonstrative science of extension.

In a sense *A* is no longer merely the passive person she was. As a mind which has realized her adequate ideas of itself, she affirms what necessarily follows from her nature. As a psychological historian, she affirmed herself as the active traces of all that made her what she is: acknowledging herself as identical with what—the world being what it is—she was caused to become. But as a mathematical physicist, *A* is the active expression of principles much more powerful than the relatively finite temporal incidents in the life of Ariadne and Echo, even as they might be extended to their ancestors and their communities. Her idea of herself—which was in any case nothing more than the idea of the nexus of her ideas of her body (II. 15)—now includes an idea of herself as a systematically organized set of adequate ideas. Her idea of her mind is still exactly correlated with her idea of its 'boundaries.' Insofar as she is a mind composed of adequate ideas of the properties common to every part of extension, she does not conceive of anything falling outside her boundaries, her nature. Although all properties—including those that are universally instantiated—are relational, the interdependence of common properties does not make them conditional; they interact with properties that are exactly identical to them. It is for this reason that, despite their place in the nexus of ideas, adequate ideas can be self-evident. They are conditional on something identical with them.

A is active to the extent—but only to the extent—that she identifies herself as a mind composed of adequate ideas. What a powerful and integrated system of adequate ideas (and their logical consequences) she now is! The crude psychological egoism with which Ariadne began—the egoism sketched in the first, preliminary accounts of *conatus*—is by now strikingly modified, reinterpreted. The power of Ariadne's *conatus* is expressed in its actively expanding its original, narrow, and necessarily defensive conception of its boundaries. The more narrowly defined is an individual's conception of her boundaries, the more readily is she overcome by the vast number of external forces. But the more broadly she identifies herself with other free rational minds, the more actively powerful she becomes: Her nature is not then bounded by, but agrees with others (IV. 35–37). 'It is of first importance to [men] to establish close relationships [with other rational men] and to bind themselves together . . . unite[d] in one body . . . to act in such a way as to strengthen friendship' (IV. app. 12).

Compared to the exhilaration of *this* rationally extended sense of her activity and action, the elation of Ariadne's original relation to Echo—even as it became extended to her activities as an inquirer into the constitution and history—was really child's play. What elation can Echo bring to *A*, who identifies herself with other free, rational citizens who recognize universal and timeless truths about the basic structure of Nature? After all, modestly speaking, without any trace of megalomania, she now sees that as part of an aspect of God, she cannot be enhanced or diminished by the flotsam and jetsam of *la vie quotidienne.*

We have skipped and condensed quite a bit, but in any case, we are far from through. First of all there is the extremely difficult question of just how *A* came to realize her adequate ideas, how she came to have a more adequate idea of herself as a mind composed of both adequate ideas and a history of confused ideas. After all, what is self-evident—even what is demonstrated as self-evident—is not always obvious. Even if *A* timelessly was the person she—as we confusedly say—came to be, how did the timeless story come to be just what it always was, a timeless story that seems to have *befores* and *afters* and *becauses*? Even if Ariadne's intellectual biography provides a psychohistorical answer to that question, can there be a properly scientific answer to it? It is all very well to say that *A*'s complex condition can be explained backward historically, and outward by a nexus of interactive causes. Can it also be generated downward from adequate ideas of common properties? Having fully adequate ideas, can *A* demonstrate the particular set of events that caused and constituted her loving Echo? Can she have adequate ideas about such contingent, conditional matters, rather than relatively vague generalizations about the nature of love in this or that historical era? Evidently not, for it is impossible to deduce particular temporal events from ideas that are by definition common to absolutely every event. But doesn't this mean that the promise of explanation—and therefore the promise of freedom—was false, a misleading confused promise? To answer these rhetorical questions, we must move from *ratio* to *scientia intuitiva*, the highest level of knowledge that grasps the interconnections of individual essences within one unified system.

HAVING IT ALL: BACK TO LOVE WITH VULGARITY AND LEARNING

What happened to the confusions of the imagination, perceptions, rough generalizations, passive affects? Have they utterly disappeared? How do we preserve the particularity of appearances with which we began? What happened to individual essences and the essence of individuality? If confused ideas of the boundaries among individuals are necessary, isn't there a sense in which a timeless understanding of the order of things—of the whole of reality—must include a timeless understanding of these partial and confused appearances? And what happened to love, to the promised *hilaritas* of true love?

Ariadne has not, thank god, been intransformed into a pure abstract mind, a divine geometer, not Spinoza's Ariadne, at any rate. She is, was, and will be the *particular* very finite collection of ideas reflecting a particular body. All *A*'s mathematical knowledge of the *corpora simplicissima* is knowledge of the properties that are *common* to all bodies. Those properties—and the ideas of those properties—are still particular. What distinguishes them from other particular ideas is simply their universality and their self-evident necessity. So in having adequate ideas, in becoming actively affected, *A* is still Ariadne, and she still loves. For that matter she still loves Echo; but her active love is a far, far better love than she has ever loved before. It is, of course, not better in being purer or more self-sacrificing; nor scandalously, is it more perfect. Indeed on the contrary, far from being purer, it is more comprehensive in every sense of that term. Not only does she love Echo, but she loves Echo-as-a-particular-expression-of-the-vast-network-of-individuals that have affected him; through him, she loves all that has made him. Far from being self-sacrificing, her active love of Echo—now more truly, adequately understood by her—is self-expressing. In loving him, she loves herself. Nor is her truthful love more perfect, because *the idea of perfection is an inadequate idea*, formed from a fragmented, particular perspective.

It is time to unwrap Spinoza's irony. Ariadne's liberation has been described as a movement to greater perfection. That's vulgar talk. (In truth 'Men are accustomed to call natural things perfect or imperfect more from prejudice than from true knowledge of those things. . . . Nature does nothing on account of an end. . . . Perfection and imperfection are only modes of thinking, that is, notions we are accustomed to feign when we compare individuals of the same species to one another. . . . Insofar as we attribute something to them that involves negation,—like a limit, and end or lack of power—, we call them imperfect, because they do not affect our mind as much as those we call perfect, not because something is lacking in them which is theirs' [IV. Preface]. 'Nothing happens in nature which can be attributed to a defect in it' [III. Preface].) The idea of perfection is a mote in the eye of the perceiver, an idea which—like all other ideas—is a reflection of the order of things. But it is a confused and partial idea. In truth, since each thing is what it must be, nothing is, in and of itself, either less or more than it is or can be. Seen in this way, Ariadne's pathological love, necessitated as it was by the order of things, could not have been a *defect* in her.

All along Ariadne is, even with her transformation into a psychohistorian and mathematical physicist, a particular interactive finite body, a particular finite system of ideas. Now we saw that rational demonstration—the system that expresses the relations among adequate ideas—is not hospitable to such variables as *Ariadne*, let alone *Ariadne's love of Echo at a particular time*. How can the *corpora simplicissima* that compose *A* and *E* rub together to produce the explosion of a particular love? Increasing the number of *corpora* to form compounds does not increase their explanatory power, nor does increasing the complexity of the relations between their respective ratios of motion and rest. There can be no mathematical demonstration that concludes with Ariadne's love for Echo. Yet she did passively love Echo, and that passive love was interactively necessitated. ('Inadequate and confused ideas follow by the same necessity as adequate or clear ideas' [II. 36].) Although *A*'s rational knowledge as a mathematician gives her necessary knowledge of what she has in common with all other bodies, it cannot, in the nature of the case, provide a demonstration of the necessity of her confused, inadequate, partial, perspectival ideas. ('Whatever ideas follow in the mind from adequate ideas are also adequate' [II. 40].) It should not be surprising that we cannot derive the dynamic, relational, historical particular from what is timeless, necessary, and invariant.

Fortunately there is, besides psychohistorical knowledge and mathematical physics, yet another knowledge—*scientia intuitiva*—which combines the other two in a single active act of understanding. *Scientia intuitiva* involves apprehending the vast system, the network of particular individuals (including of course all the properties they have in common) as a unified individual. Since there is no such thing as abstract Being as such, *scientia intuitiva* is not mystical insight into the abstract nature of Being. On the contrary, this insight preserves all particularity: Reflective ideas—ideas of ideas—retain their particularity when they are systematically inter-connected to form the increasingly more encompassing particular that is *A*'s individual mind. (As, for instance, the *corpora simplicissima* of which *A*'s body is composed retain their particularity even though they are organized to form another individual, Ariadne's body.) *A* cannot have an adequate idea of Echo, treated merely as a finite mode, an isolated fragment of the world; but since she can have increasingly adequate ideas of him as part of the system of ideas, and since she can treat the system of her ideas as a particular, she can have *scientia intuitiva* of the unified system of which Echo is a fragment. (Compare: While there is no *ratio* [scientific knowledge] of a particular corpuscle of hemoglobin, taken in isolation as a fragment of extension, there is scientific knowledge of hemoglobin, treated as a functional part of organic systems. Going beyond the *ratio* of discursive biochemistry, *scientia intuitiva* fuses all that is discretely encompassed by *ratio*, recognizing that it forms a unity, a particular individual.)

How does intuitive insight—psychohistorical knowledge and demonstrative rationality all wrapped into a bundle and seen as a unified, self-sustaining, self-evident whole—free us? It is, as are all ideational states, the expression of a bodily condition, one in which the body is, as it were, enlarged because 'the individual body' is no longer artificially separated as a bounded, separate entity. Nevertheless, each condition of any 'particular part' of extension necessarily has the properties it has, by virtue of its interconnections with all other parts. So the sense of boundary—Ariadne's experiencing herself as a bounded particular individual—is *itself* the necessary outcome, the expression of all that exists, no more and no less. Ariadne's passivity and defensiveness are, despite their being confused and conditional ideas, necessary (II. 36). When she realizes this, she actively rather than passively preserves all the details of her individuation because she recognizes that those details, too, follow from her nature (V. 27). Ariadne actively expresses rather than passively suffers whatever follows from the necessities of her nature; so Ariadne does not *suffer* the pathology of love, the Goyaesque furies of any passive passion. Does that mean that she will not suffer ambivalence, envy, fear, despair? Well, yes, she will not passively suffer the Goyaesque furies; but, depending on her circumstances and condition, she may nevertheless enact some of them.

Like all Stoics, including Freud, Spinoza speaks with forked tongue about whether those who have reached the most active and comprehensive knowledge have no passive love, ambivalence, and the rest of the furies. On the one hand, those passions are, even in their experienced passivity, *necessary* natural events. On the other hand, 'The truth shall make you free' is absolutely true; and there is, in principle, absolutely no barrier between any individual and truth. Affects that follow from adequate ideas are not passive, and at least some affects only follow from inadequate ideas. An individual is free and active just to that degree that she has adequate ideas. ('If we remove an agitation of the mind, or emotion, from the thought of its external cause and join it to other thoughts, then . . . the vacillations that arise from these affects will be destroyed. . . . There is no affection of the body of which we cannot form a clear and distinct conception' [V. 2, 4].) Can Ariadne turn all her inadequate ideas into fully adequate ideas? It seems not; but if she is fortunate, she can make them more adequate, and if she is even more fortunate, she can focus primarily on her adequate ideas. ('[If *scientia intuitiva*] does not absolutely remove passive affects, it at least brings it about that they constitute the smallest part of the mind' [V. 20. S].)

But we have in a way been dodging the real question. Does knowledge always liberate us from suffering? What are we to make of all our wise friends whose love is passive and who suffer in loving? Here Spinoza reveals his Socratic face: Not all those who mouth knowledge genuinely have it. In the first place, *being able to discourse fluently* isn't necessarily *knowing*. Only knowledge that pervades a person's psychology and that expresses an appropriate bodily state counts as real knowledge. Knowledge is not an attitude toward propositional content: To know *p* is to engage in a vast number of activities of integrating *p* within a system of ideas, beliefs, desires. Unless an intellectual attitude really transforms the way a person thinks and acts, it does not qualify as knowledge. (Compare: Knowing a mathematical technique is not merely a matter of being able to state and defend it clearly. To qualify as knowing a technique, one must actually use it in constructions and proofs.)

In the second place, not everyone who wishes to know, not everyone who dreams of *scientia intuitiva* is in a position—a constitutional, and psychohistorical position—to have it. Whether or not a particular bit of understanding succeeds in being knowledge at any given time is—like everything else—a function of person, time, and circumstance. It is not only our own activity, but our activity in dynamic relation to what surrounds us that determines our condition. ('The force and growth of any passion, . . . are not defined by the power by which we strive to persevere in existing, but by the power of an external cause compared with our *own*' [IV. 5]. 'It is necessary to come to know both our nature's power and its lack of power to determine what reason can do—and what it cannot do—in moderating the affects' [IV. 17. Scholium].) In any case, even our wisest friends are finite individual minds, composed of a mixture of adequate and inadequate ideas. ('The human mind does not involve an adequate knowledge of the component parts of the body . . . [or] of an external body' [II. 24–31]. 'Desire which arises from knowledge of good and evil insofar as it concerns future . . . or contingent things . . . can be easily restrained by desires for things which are present' [IV. 16–17].) Starkly, not even *A*—that superb mathematical physicist—is, at any and every moment of her life, focused only on her adequate ideas, let alone engaged in *scientia intuitiva.* Although compared individually adequate ideas and active passions are much more powerful than inadequate ideas and their corresponding passive passions, a large number of inadequate ideas and passive passions can deflect the directions of active desires.

In the third place, we should not confuse suffering with *suffering.* When Spinoza contrasts activity with passivity, freedom with bondage, he does not identify—though he does associate—passivity and bondage with *pain.* To begin with, many passive affects are delightful. And by Spinoza's lights, however uncomfortable they may be, healthy growing pains are not *sufferings,* unless an adolescent thinks of his body as an external cause of his condition. Similarly, the hardships of difficult thought are not sufferings, unless a scholar thinks of himself as invaded or obsessed by them.

But what, you may ask, is the point of being free? Why isn't mucking along in trouble and travail, in ambivalence and uncertainty, in the pathology of idolatry, fragmentation, and fetishism good enough? Since that is what the particularity of life is, and since there is nothing but particularity, why want more? Maybe life is not directed to the hilarity of integration, but just to living. In a way Spinoza agrees. It is not a question of striving for a better, nobler form of life. We each live according to the life force within us. Those whose constitution and circumstances make them relatively vulnerable to forces they experience as external to them will indeed suffer love and hate. Others are, by the fortune of their situation, capable of what liberation their circumstances allow. In any case, both those who are relatively passively weak and those who are relatively actively strong alike attempt to live as fully as they can. There is no teleology in the matter, no salvation, and in a way, no liberation. We are what we are no matter what. We *are* the extent and manner of our striving toward harmonic integration.

Still, be that as it must be, Spinoza thinks that liberated love is superior to bonded love: Wise lovers are not only more joyous, but more effective and beneficent than unenlightened lovers. How do the wise act on behalf of those they love? To be sure, they desire to unite with what they love. But that is, according to Spinoza, a consequence rather than the essential definition of love (III. app. D. 6, Explication).

In any case that desire does not define any particular action; it might, for instance, generate civic as well as sexual unity and harmony. Ariadne's desire to unify herself with Echo is a desire to conjoin her own welfare with his to form a single well-structured whole (IV. 35–37, 62–66). But passive love generates a desire to control, rather than to act on behalf of a common good. Promoting the real—rather than the partial and imagined—welfare of an extended self properly arises from a rational recognition of interdependence (IV. 73). Since passive love is ambivalent, mingled with hate and envy, disdain, and fear, the behavior that expresses it will be erratic, each moment undermining the next. Well-formed action arises only from well-formed attitudes, from adequate ideas.

And the hilarity, the promised hilarity of true love? True love is the elation that comes of true knowledge, an intuitive grasp of the world, seen as a whole, immanent within one's ideas. Because such love is the expression of an individual's most vital activity, it carries the greatest possible self-realization. But an elation that affects the individual as a whole *is* hilarity (III. 11. Scholium). Like true knowledge, hilarity can never be excessive; when it is seen as actively following from an individual's own nature, it can never bring bondage in its wake (IV. 42).[2]

Notes

1. I have used two translations, turning sometimes to E. M. Curley, *The Collected Works of Spinoza* (Princeton, N.J.: Princeton University Press, 1985) and sometimes to Samuel Shirley, *The Ethics*, ed. Seymore Feldman (Indianapolis: Hackett, 1982). But I have also substituted some translations of my own. Rather than following Shirley's *pleasure* or Curley's *joy*, I render *laetitia* as *elation* because I believe that it better captures Spinoza's view that love, like other affects, is an expression of a *change*, an increase, in the body's powers or vitality. Spinoza distinguishes two varieties of *laetitia*: *titillatio* and *hilaritas*. Titillation involves an increase of activity or power in one part of the body more than in another (the early stages of sexual excitation, for example): *hilaritas* marks an increase in vitality that affects all parts of the body equally (radiant health, for example). The corresponding distinctions for varieties of *tristitia*, which I translate as *dejection* (rendered by Shirley as *pain* and by Curley as *sadness*), are *dolor* (pain), a change which affects one part of the body more than another (a wound, for example), and *melancholia*, a change which affects all parts equally (anemia, for example). Spinoza undertakes to show that all affects arise from the three basic affects of elation, dejection, and desire (III. 11. S).
2. I am grateful to Alan Hart for detailed, incisive comments, to Tom Cook and Genevieve Lloyd for many illuminating conversations. This paper was

prepared for a conference on 'Theoretical Perspectives on Love and Friendship' at the National Center for the Humanities. I enjoyed and benefited from Tom Hill's acute and searching discussions. Annette Baier helpfully suggested some issues that needed elaboration: Spinoza's avoidance of both reductive materialism and reductive idealism, and the problem of how the adequate ideas of common notions can be both relational and self-evident. Martha Nussbaum pressed me to give an account of the directions—and the limits—of what she sees as Spinoza's psychological egoism.

Part IV. Rereading Eighteenth-Century Philosophers: Reason, Emotion, and Ethics

10 Hume, the Women's Moral Theorist?

Annette C. Baier*

In his brief autobiography, David Hume tells us that 'as I took particular pleasure in the company of modest women, I had no reason to be displeased with the reception I met with from them.' This double-edged remark is typical of Hume's references to women. Suggesting as it does that what pleased Hume was the women's pleasure in his pleasure in *their* company, it both diminishes the significance of their welcome to him, since 'whoever can find the means either by his services, his beauty, or his flattery to render himself useful or agreeable to us, is sure of our affections,'[1] and makes us wonder about the sources of his particular pleasure in their company. Pleasure in the ample returns he got for a little flattery? Yet his flattery of women in his writings is itself double-edged, as much insult as appreciation. Women's 'insinuation, charm and address,' he tells us, in the section on justice in his *Enquiry Concerning the Principles of Morals*, will enable them to break up any incipient male conspiracy against them. His archness of tone in 'Of Love and Marriage' and his patronizing encouragement of the greater intellectual effort of reading history instead of romances in 'Of the Study of History' were reason enough for him to suppress those two essays (as he did, but for unclear reasons, and along with the more interesting and more radical 'Of Moral Prejudices,' in which he describes a man who is totally dependent, emotionally, on his wife and daughter, and a woman who makes herself minimally dependent on the chosen father of her child).[2] It is not surprising that despite his popularity with the women, modest and less modest, who knew him, his writings have not met with a very positive reception from contemporary feminists. They fix on his

* Annette C. Baier, 'Hume, the Women's Moral Theorist?', from *Moral Prejudices: Essays on Ethics* (Cambridge, Mass., and London: Harvard University Press, 1994), 51–75; original version in Eva Kittay and Diane T. Meyers (eds.), *Women and Moral Theory* (Totowa, NJ: Rowman and Littlefield, 1987), 37–55. Reprinted by permission of the publisher.

references to the 'fair' and the 'weak and pious' sex and on his defense in the essay 'The Rise and Progress of the Arts and Sciences' of the claim that male gallantry is as natural a virtue as respect for one's elders, both being ways of generously allaying others' well-founded sense of inferiority or infirmity: 'As nature has given *man* the strength above *women*, by endowing him with greater strength both of mind and body, it is his part to alleviate that superiority, as much as possible, by a studied deference and complaisance for all her inclinations and opinions.' Hume's 'polite' displays of concern for the sex that he saw to be weaker in mind and body are not likely to encourage feminists to turn to him for moral inspiration any more than Kant's exclusion, in the *Metaphysical Elements of Justice*, §46, of all women from the class of those with 'civil personality,' fit to vote, will encourage them to look to him.

My main concern here is not with feminism, however, but with the implications, for ethics and ethical theory, of Carol Gilligan's findings about differences between males and females both in moral development and in mature versions of morality. Whether those differences reflect women's weakness, their natural inferiority to men in mind and body, or their social inferiority, or their superiority, is not my central concern. I am focusing here on the concept of morality many women have and the sort of experience, growth, and reflection on it that leads them to develop it. My interest in a moral theory like Hume's in this context, then, is primarily with the extent to which the version of morality he works out squares or does not square with women's moral wisdom. Should the main lines of his account prove to be true to morality as women conceive of it, then it will be an ironic historical detail if he showed less respect than we would have liked for those of his fellow persons who were most likely to find his moral theory in line with their own insights. And whatever the root causes of women's moral outlook, of the tendency of the care perspective to dominate over the justice perspective in their moral deliberations, now that we have, more or less, social equality with men, women's moral sense should be made as explicit as men's moral sense and as influential in structuring our practices and institutions. One way, not of course the only or the best way, to help make it explicit is to measure the influential men's moral theories against it. That is what I propose to do with Hume's theory. This can be seen as a prolegomenon to making wise women's theories influential. Then, once I have examined Hume's theory and its fit or misfit with women's moral wisdom, I shall briefly return to the question of how his own attitude toward women relates to his moral theory.

As every student of the history of philosophy knows, Hume was the philosopher Kant set out to 'answer,' and both Kant's theory of knowledge and his ethics stand in significant contrast to Hume's. And Kant's views, through their influence on Jean Piaget and John Rawls, are the views which are expressed in Lawrence Kohlberg's version of moral maturity and the development leading to it, the version which Gilligan found not to apply to girls and women as well as it did to boys and men. We may wonder, therefore, whether other non-Kantian strands in Western ethics, as developed in the philosophical tradition, might prove less difficult to get into reflective equilibrium with women's (not specifically philosophical) moral wisdom than the Kantian strand. For there certainly is no agreement that Kant and his followers represent the culmination of all the moral wisdom of our philosophical tradition. Alasdair MacIntyre's attacks on the Kantian tradition and all the controversy caused by attempts to implement in high schools the Kohlberg views about moral education have shown that not all men, let alone all women, are in agreement with the Kantians. Since the philosopher Kant was most notoriously in disagreement with was Hume, it is natural to ask, after Gilligan's work, whether Hume is more of a women's moral theorist than is Kant. We might do the same with Aristotle, Hegel, Marx, Mill, MacIntyre, with all those theorists who have important disagreements with Kant, but a start can be made with Hume.

He is inviting, for this purpose, in part because he did try to attend, for better or worse, to male–female differences and in his life did, it seems, listen to women; and also because he is close enough in time, in culture, and in some presuppositions to Kant for the comparison of their moral theories to hold out the same hope of the reconciliation that Gilligan in *In a Different Voice* wanted to get between men's and women's moral insights. There are important areas of agreement as well as of disagreement or difference of emphasis. I should add two more personal reasons for selecting Hume—I find his moral theory wise and profound, and I once, some years ago, in an introductory ethics course where we had read a little Aristotle, Aquinas, Hume, Kant, Mill, then Rawls and Kohlberg, had my students try to work out what each of our great moral theorists would have said in answer to Kohlberg's test question about whether Heinz should steal the drug which he cannot afford to buy and which might save his dangerously ill wife.[3] By hypothesizing how each philosopher would answer that question, and support his answer, we tried to measure *their* stage of moral development by the Kohlberg method.[4] Hume seemed to check out at as merely second level, stage three, with some stage four features, just as did most of Gilligan's mature women. So I have, since then, thought of Hume as a second 'conventional' level challenger of Kohlberg's claims about the superiority of the third postconventional level over the second, or as an exemplar of a fourth level, gathering up and reconciling what was valuable and worth preserving in both the conventional and the postconventional Kohlberg levels—a fourth level which we could call 'civilized,' a favorite Humean term of approbation. For this reason, when I read Gilligan's findings that mature, apparently intelligent and reflective women 'reverted' to Kohlberg's stage three (lower stage of level two, the conventional level), my immediate thought was 'perhaps we women tend to be Humeans rather than Kantians.'

I shall list some striking differences between Kant's and Hume's moral theories, as I understand them, then relate these to the differences Gilligan found between men's and women's conceptions of morality.

First, Hume's ethics, unlike Kant's, make morality a matter not of obedience to universal law but of cultivating the character traits which give a person 'inward peace of mind, consciousness of integrity' (*E.*, p. 283) and at the same time make that person good company to other persons. Hume uses 'company' in a variety of senses, ranging from the relatively impersonal and 'remote' togetherness of fellow citizens, to the more selective but still fairly remote relations of parties to a contract, to the closer ties among friends, family members, lovers. To become a good fellow-person one doesn't consult some book of rules; one cultivates one's capacity for sympathy, or fellow feeling, and also stands ready to use one's judgment when conflicts arise among the different demands that such sympathy may lead us to feel. Hume's ethics requires us to be able to be rule followers in some contexts, but does not reduce morality to rule following. Corrected (sometimes rule-corrected) sympathy, not law-discerning reason, is the fundamental moral capacity.

Second, Hume differs from Kant regarding the source of the general rules he does recognize as morally binding—the rules of justice. Where Kant sees human reason as the sole author of these moral rules, and sees them as universal, Hume sees them as authored by self-interest, instrumental reason, custom and tradition, and rationally 'frivolous' factors such as historical chance and human fancy and what it selects as salient. He sees these rules, such as property rules, not as universal but as varying from community to community and as changeable by human will as conditions, needs, wishes, or human fancies change. His theory of social 'artifice,' and his account of justice as obedience to the rules of these social artifices, formed by 'convention' and subject to historical variation and change, stands in stark opposition to rationalist accounts, such as Aquinas's and Kant's, of justice as obedience to laws of pure practical reason, valid for all people at all times and places. Hume has a historicist and conventionalist account of the moral rules which we find ourselves expected to obey and which, on reflection, we usually see it to be sensible for us to obey, despite their elements of arbitrariness and despite the inequalities their working usually produces. He believes it is sensible for us to conform to those rules of our group which specify obligations and rights, as long as these do redirect the dangerous destructive workings of self-interest into more mutually advantageous channels, thereby giving all the 'infinite advantages' of increased force, ability, and security (compared with what we would have in the absence of any such rules), although some may receive *more* benefits of a given sort, say, wealth or authority, than others, under the scheme we find ourselves in. So Hume's ethics seems to lack any appeal to the universal principles of Kohlberg's 'higher' stages. The moral and critical stance Hume encourages us to adopt toward, say, the property rules of our society, before seeing the rights which those rules recognize as *moral* rights, comes not from our ability to test them by higher, more general rules but from our capacity for sympathy, from our ability to recognize and share sympathetically the reactions of others to that system of rights, to communicate feelings and understand what our fellows are feeling, and so to realize what resentments and satisfactions the present social scheme generates. Self-interest and the capacity to sympathize with the self-interested reactions of others, plus the rational, imaginative, and inventive ability to think about the likely human consequences of any change in the scheme, rather than an acquaintance with a higher law, are what a Humean appeals to at the postconventional stage.

This difference from Kantian views about the role of general principles in grounding moral obligations goes along in Hume with a downplaying of the role of reason and a playing up of the role of feeling in moral judgment. Agreeing with the rationalists that when we use our reason we all appeal to universal rules (the rules of arithmetic, or of logic, or of causal inference) and failing to find any such universal rules of morality, as well as failing to see how, even if we found them, they should be able, alone, to *motivate* us to act as they tell us to act, he claims that morality rests ultimately on sentiment. This is a special motivating feeling we come to have once we have exercised our capacity for sympathy with others' feelings and also learned to overcome the emotional conflicts which arise in a sympathetic person when the wants of different fellow persons clash, or when one's own wants clash with those of one's fellows. Morality, on Hume's account, is the outcome of a search for ways of eliminating contradictions in the 'passions' of sympathetic persons who are aware of both their own and their fellows' desires and needs, including emotional needs. Any moral progress or development a person undergoes will be, for Hume, a matter of 'the correction of sentiment,' where what corrects it will be contrary sentiments plus the cognitive-cum-passionate drive to minimize conflict both between and within persons. Reason and logic are indispensable 'slaves' to the passions in this achievement, because reason enables us to think clearly about consequences or likely consequences of alternative actions, to foresee outcomes and avoid self-defeating policies. But 'the ultimate ends of human actions can never, in any case, be accounted for by *reason*, but recommend themselves entirely to the sentiments and affections of mankind, without any dependance upon intellectual faculties' (*E.*, p. 293). A lover of conflict will have no reason, since he will have no motive, to cultivate the moral sentiment, nor will that man of 'cold insensibility' who is 'unaffected with the images of human happiness or misery' (*E.*, p. 225). A human heart, as well as human reason, is needed for the understanding of morality, and the heart's responses are to particular persons, not to universal principles of abstract justice. Such immediate responses may be corrected by general rules (as they will be when justice demands that the good poor man's debt to the less good miser be paid) and by more reflective feeling responses, such as dismay and foreboding at unwisely given love and trust or disapproval of excessive parental indulgence. But what controls and regulates feeling will be a wider web of feelings, which reason helps us apprehend and understand, not any reason holding authority over all feelings.

The third point to note is that Hume's version of what a typical human heart desires is significantly different from that of both egoists and individualists. The 'interested passion,' or self-interest, plays an important role, but so do sympathy and concern for others. Even where self-interest is of most importance in his theory, in his account of justice, it is the self-interest of those with fairly fluid ego boundaries, namely, family members, concerned with 'acquiring goods and possessions for ourselves and our nearest friends' (*T.*, pp. 491–492). This is the troublesome passion that needs to be redirected by agreed rules, whereby it can control itself so as to avoid socially destructive conflict over scarce goods. Its self-control, in a society-wide cooperative scheme which establishes property rights, is possible because the persons involved in it have already learned, in the family, the advantages that can come both from self-control and from cooperation (*T.*, p. 486). Had the rough corners of 'untoward' and uncontrolled passions, selfish or unselfish, not been already rubbed off by growing up under some parental discipline, and were there no minimally sociable human passions such as love between man and woman, love of parents for their children, love of friends, sisters, and brothers, the Humean artifice of justice could not be constructed. Its very possibility as an artificial virtue depends upon human nature's containing the natural passions, which make family life natural for human beings, which make parental solicitude, grateful response to that, and the restricted cooperation thereby resulting, phenomena that do not need to be contrived by artifice. At the very heart of Hume's moral theory lies his celebration of family life and of parental love. Justice, the chief artificial virtue, is the offspring of family cooperativeness and inventive self-interested reason, which sees how such a mutually beneficial cooperative scheme might be extended. And when Hume lists the natural moral virtues, those not consisting in obedience to agreed rules and doing good even if not generally possessed, his favorite example is parental love and solicitude. The good person, the possessor of the natural virtues, is the one who is 'a safe companion, an easy friend, a gentle master, an agreeable husband, an indulgent father' (*T.*, p. 606). We may deplore that patriarchal combination of roles—master, husband, father—but we should also note the virtues these men are to display—gentleness, agreeability, indulgence. These were more traditionally expected from mistresses, wives, and mothers than from masters, husbands, and fathers. Of course they are not the only virtues Humean good characters show; there are also due pride, or self-esteem, and the proper ambition and courage that that may involve, as well as generosity, liberality, zeal, gratitude, compassion, patience, industry, perseverance, activity, vigilance, application, integrity, constancy, temperance, frugality, economy, resolution, good temper, charity, clemency, equity, honesty, truthfulness, fidelity, discretion, caution, presence of mind, 'and a thousand more of the same kind' (*E.*, p. 243).

In Hume's frequent lists of virtues, two are conspicuous by their absence, or by the qualifications accompanying them, namely, the martial 'virtues' and the monastic or puritan 'virtues.' Martial bravery and military glory can threaten 'the sentiment of humanity' and lead to 'infinite confusions and disorders . . . the devastation of provinces, the sack of cities' (*T.*, p. 601), so cool reflection leads the Humean moral judge to hesitate to approve of these traditionally masculine traits. The monastic virtues receive more forthright treatment. Celibacy, fasting, penance, mortification, self-denial, humility, silence, solitude 'are everywhere rejected by men of sense, but because they serve to no manner of purpose . . . We observe, on the contrary, that they cross all these desirable ends, stupify the understanding and harden the heart, obscure the fancy and sour the temper' (*E.*, p. 270). Here speaks Hume the good companion, the one who enjoyed cooking for supper parties for his Edinburgh friends, the darling, or perhaps the intellectual mascot, of the pleasure-loving Parisian salons. Calvinist upbringing and the brief taste he had in youth of the military life seem to have left him convinced of the undesirability of such styles of life; and his study of history convinced him of the dangers for society both of religious dedication, 'sacred zeal and rancor,' and of military zeal and rancor. His list of virtues is a remarkably unaggressive, uncompetitive, one might almost say womanly list.

Although many of the virtues on his list are character traits that would show in a great range of contexts, most of those contexts are social contexts, involving relations to others, and many of them involve particular relationships such as parent–child, friend to friend, colleagues to each other, fellow conversationalists. Even when he tries to list virtues that are valued because they are useful and agreeable to their possessor rather than valued primarily for their contribution to the quality of life of the virtuous person's fellows, the qualities he lists are ones involving relations to others—the ability to get and keep the trust of others, sexual self-command and modesty as well as sexual promise, that is, the capacity to derive 'so capital a pleasure in life' and to 'communicate it' to another (*E.*, p. 245), temperance, patience, and sobriety, are virtues useful (long term) to their possessor; while among those he lists as immediately agreeable to their possessor are contagious serenity and cheerfulness, 'a proper sense of what is due to one's self in society and the common intercourse of life' (*E.*, p. 253), friendliness and an avoidance of 'perpetual wrangling, and scolding and mutual reproaches' (*E.*, p. 257), amorous adventurousness, at least in the young, liveliness of emotional response and expressive powers—all agreeable traits which presuppose that their possessor is in company with others, reacting to them and the object of their reactions. There may be problems in seeing how a person is to combine the various Humean virtues—to be frugal yet liberal, to be sufficiently chaste yet show amorous enterprise, to have a proper sense of what is due one yet avoid wrangling and reproaches. Hume may, indeed, be depending on a certain sexual division of moral labor, allocating chastity to the women and amorous initiative to the men, more self-assertion to the men and more avoidance of wrangling to the women, but we should not exaggerate the extent to which he did this.

The title page of Book Three of the *Treatise* invokes Lucan's words referring to the lover of difficult virtue, and Humean virtues may be difficult to unify. Only in some social structures, indeed, may they turn out to be a mutually compatible set. Some investigation, not only into what virtue is and what the true virtues are but into the social precondition of their joint exemplification, may be needed in the lover of difficult virtue. Indeed everything Hume says suggests that these are not independent enterprises. What counts as useful and agreeable virtues will depend in part on the social and economic conditions in which their possessors live, just as the acceptability of those social and economic conditions depends on what sort of virtues can flourish there and how they are distributed within the population. Hume points out that the usefulness of a trait such as a good memory will be more important in Cicero's society than in his own, given the lesser importance in the latter of making well-turned speeches without notes, and given the general encouraged reliance there on written records in most spheres of life. The availability, accessibility, and portability of memory substitutes will vary with the customs and the technological development of a society, and Hume is aware that such facts are relevant to the recognition of character traits as functional virtues. The ease of simulation or perversion of such traits will also affect the recognition of virtues—in an age when private ambition is easily masked as public spirit, or tax exemption as benevolence, the credit given to such easily pretended virtues may also understandably sink. The status of a character trait as a virtue need not be a fixed matter, but a matter complexly interrelated with the sort of society in which it appears. This makes good sense, if moral virtues are the qualities that enable one to play an acceptable part in an acceptable network of social roles, to relate to people in the variety of ways that a decent society will require, facilitate, encourage, or merely permit.

The fourth point I want to stress in Hume's moral theory is that in his attention to various interpersonal relations, in which our Humean virtues or vices show, he does not give any special centrality to relationships between equals, let alone between autonomous equals. Because his analysis of social cooperation starts from cooperation within the family, relations between those who are necessarily unequals, parents and children, are at the center of the picture. He starts from a bond which he considers 'the strongest and most indissoluble bond in nature' (*E.*, p. 240), 'the strongest tie the mind is capable of' (*T.*, p. 352), the love of parents for children, and in his moral theory he works out, as it were, from there. This relationship, and the obligations and virtues it involves, lacks three central features of relations between moral agents as understood by Kantians and contractarians—it is intimate, it is unchosen and it is between unequals. Of course the intimacy need not be 'indissoluble,' the inequality may be temporary, or later reversed, and the extent to which the initial relationship is unchosen will vary from that of unplanned or contrary-to-plan parenthood to intentional parenthood (although not intentional parenting of a given particular child) to that highest degree of voluntariness present when, faced with an actual newborn child, a decision is taken not to let it be adopted by others or, when a contrary decision is taken by the biological parent or parents, by the decision of adoptive parents to adopt such an already encountered child. Such fully chosen parenthood is rare, and the norm is for parents to *find themselves* with a given child, perhaps with any child at all, and for parental affection to attach itself fairly indiscriminately to its unselected objects. The contractarian model of morality as a matter of living up to self-chosen commitments gets into obvious trouble with the duties both of young children to their unchosen parents, to whom no binding commitments have been made, and of initially involuntary parents to their children. Hume has no problem with such unchosen moral ties, because he takes them as the paradigm moral ties, one's giving rise to moral obligations more self-evident than any obligation to keep contracts.

The last respect in which I wish to contrast Hume's moral philosophy with its more Kantian alternative is in his version of what problem morality is supposed to solve, what its point is. For Kantians and contractarians, the point is freedom; the main problem is how to achieve it, given that other freedom aspirants exist and that conflict between them is likely. The Rousseau–Kant solution is obedience to collectively agreed-to general law, where each freedom seeker can console himself with the thought that the legislative will he must obey is as much his own as it is anyone else's. For Hume, the problem of the coexistence of would-be unrestrained self-assertors is solved by the invention of social artifices and the recognition of the virtue of justice, namely, of conformity to the rules of such mutually advantageous artifices. But the problem morality solves is deeper; it is as much intrapersonal as interpersonal. It is the problem of contradiction, conflict, and instability in any one person's desires, over time, as well as conflict among persons. Morality, in theory, saves us from internally self-defeating drives as well as from self-defeating interpersonal conflict. Nor is it just an added extra to Hume's theory that the moral point of view overcomes contradictions in our individual sentiments over time. ('Our situation, with regard to both persons and things, is in continual fluctuation; and a man, that lies at a distance from us, may, in a little time, become a familiar acquaintance' [*T.*, p. 581].) His whole account of our sentiments has made them intrinsically reactive to other persons' sentiments. Internal conflict in a sympathetic and reassurance-needing person will not be independent of conflicts among the various persons in his or her emotional world. 'We can form no wish, which has not a reference to society. A perfect solitude is, perhaps, the greatest punishment we can suffer. Every pleasure languishes when enjoy'd a-part from company, and every pain becomes more cruel and intolerable. Whatever other passions we may be actuated by; pride, ambition, avarice, curiosity, revenge, or lust; the soul or animating principle of them all is sympathy; nor wou'd they have any force were we to abstract entirely from the thoughts and sentiments of others' (*T.*, p. 363).

I have drawn attention to the limited place of conformity to general rules in Hume's version of morality; to the historicist conventionalist account he gives of such rules; to his thesis that morality depends upon self-corrected sentiments, or passions, as much or more than it depends upon the reason that concurs with and serves those passions; to the nonindividualist, nonegoistic version of human passions he advances; to the essentially interpersonal or social nature of those passions which are approved as virtues; to the central role of the family, at least at its best, as an exemplar of the cooperation and interdependency morality preserves and extends; to the fact that moral cooperation, for him, includes cooperation in unchosen schemes, with unchosen partners, with unequal partners, in close intimate relations as well as distanced and more formal ones. And finally, I emphasized that the need for morality arises for Hume from conflicts within each person as well as from interpersonal conflict. It is a fairly straightforward matter to relate these points to at least some of the respects in which Gilligan found girls' and women's versions of morality to differ from men's.[5] Hume turns out to be uncannily womanly in his moral wisdom. 'Since the reality of connection is experienced by women as given rather than as freely contracted, they arrive at an understanding of life that reflects the limits of autonomy and control' (*D.V.*, p. 172). Hume lived before autonomy became an obsession with moral and social philosophers, or, rather, he lived while Rousseau was making it their obsession, but his attack on contractarian doctrines of political obligation, his clear perception of the given-ness of interconnection in the family and beyond, his emphasis on our capacity to make others' joys and sorrows our own, on our need for a 'seconding' of sentiments, and on the inescapable mutual vulnerability and mutual enrichment that the human psychology and the human condition, when thus understood, entail, make autonomy not even an ideal, for Hume. A certain sort of freedom, freedom of thought and expression, is an ideal, but to 'live one's own life in one's own way' is not likely to be among the aims of persons whose every pleasure languishes when not shared and seconded by some other person or persons. 'The concept of identity expands to include the experience of interconnection' (*D.V.*, p. 173).

The women Gilligan studied saw morality as primarily a matter of responsibilities arising out of their attachment to others, often stemming from originally given rather than chosen relations. The men spoke more of their rights than of their responsibilities, and saw those rights as arising out of a freely accepted quasi-agreement between self-interested equals. Hume does in his account of justice have a place for quasi-agreement-based rights serving the long-run interests of those respecting them, but he also makes room for a host of responsibilities which presuppose no prior agreement or quasi-agreement to shoulder them. The responsibilities of parents are the paramount case of such duties of care, but he also includes cases of mutual care and duties of gratitude where 'I do services to such persons as I love, and am particularly acquainted with, without any prospect of advantage; and they may make me a return in the same manner' (*T.*, p. 521). Here there is no right to a return, merely the reasonable but unsecured trust that it will be forthcoming. (There may even be something of an either/or, duck-rabbit effect between his 'artificial virtues,' including justice, and his 'natural virtues,' including mercy and equity, in all those contexts where both seem to come in to play.)

Hume's conventionalism about the general rules we may have to obey to avoid injustice to one another has already been mentioned as dooming his theory of justice to mere 'stage four' moral marks, if to get any critical appraisal of customary rules one must have moved on to social contracts or universal principles. Hume is a realist about the historical given-ness and inevitable arbitrariness of most of the general rules that there is any chance of our all observing. Like Gilligan's girls and women, he takes moral problems in concrete historical settings, where the past history as well as the realistic future prospects for a given group are seen as relevant to their moral predicaments and their solutions. Even the fairly abstract and ahistorical social artifices of the *Treatise* are given a quasi-historical setting, and they give way in the *Essays* and *History of England* to detailed looks at actual concrete social and moral predicaments, in full narrative depth.

For Kohlberg, the distrust of abstract ahistorical principles, the girls' need to fill out Kohlberg's puzzle questions with a story before answering them, led to the suspicion that this poor performance on the application of universal principles to sketchily drawn particular cases, shorn of full narrative context, showed that their 'reason' was less well developed than the boys' (*D.V.*, p. 28). But the performance might rather have indicated, as it did in Hume's case, a conviction that this was a false model of how moral judgments are made. He endorses the emotional response to a fully realized situation as moral reflection at its best, not as one of its underdeveloped stages, and he mocks those rationalists who think abstract universal rules will ever show why, say, killing a parent is wrong for human beings but not for oak trees (*T.*, pp. 466–467).

At this point it may be asked whether Hume's account allows for any version of stages of moral development, whether it is not one of those 'bag of virtues' accounts Kohlberg derides. Can one who thinks morality is a matter of the passions find room for any notion of individual moral progress or development? The answer is yes. Although he does not give us such a theory for the individual, Hume does speak of a 'correction of sentiment' and of a 'progress of sentiments,' especially where 'artificial' virtues are concerned. Since morality depends for him on a *reflective* sentiment, and on self-corrected self-interest and corrected sympathy, it is plain that more experience and more reflection could lead an individual through various 'levels' of moral response. The interesting questions are those of what the outlines of such an alternative developmental pattern might be. Clearly this is not a matter that can be settled from a philosopher's armchair, and psychological research of the sort Gilligan is doing would be needed to find out how human passions do develop and which developments are seen as moral progress by those in whom they occur, and by others. Some features of women's development, features which would not necessarily show up on the Kohlberg tests, are indicated in the latter chapters of *In a Different Voice.* In the chapter 'Concepts of Self and Morality' Gilligan describes transitions from self-centered thinking (which presumably is likely in women reacting to being let down by the fathers of the fetuses the women interviewed were considering aborting, rather than a natural starting point for a girl or woman) to a condemnation of such 'selfishness' (or an alternation between 'selfish' and 'unselfish' impulses) to what is seen as a clearer perception of the 'truth' concerning the human relations in which they are involved, leading perhaps to a cool or even ruthless determination to protect themselves from further hurt and exploitation, then later to a revised version of what counts as their own interests, to a realization that those interests require attachment to and concern for others (see especially *D.V.*, p. 74).

If alternatives to Kohlberg's rationalist scenario are to be worked out in detail, probably some guiding moral as well as psychological theory will be needed, as well as empirical tests. There will be a need for something to play a role like that which Rawls's and Kant's moral theory played in getting Kohlberg to look for certain particular moral achievements, and to expect some to presuppose other earlier ones. It might even be that, once we had a nonrationalist yet dynamic moral theory, and an expected developmental pattern accompanying it, empirical tests would show it to be true not merely of women but of men. The gender difference may be not in the actual pattern of development of passions, nor in our reasoning and reflection about the satisfaction of our passions, but merely in our intellectual opinions, as voiced in interviews, as to whether this is or is not *moral* development. For both Gilligan's and Kohlberg's tests have so far looked at verbally offered versions of morality, at intellectual reflection on morality, not at moral development itself, at motivational changes and changed emotional reactions to one's own and others' actions, reactions, and emotions. As I understand it, only in Gilligan's abortion study were people interviewed while actually in the process of making a moral decision—and those women may not have been a representative sample of women decision makers, since they were selected for their apparent indecisivness, for what was judged their need to think and talk more about their decision. The clear-headed or at least the decisive women simply did not get into this study (*D. V.*, p. 3).

We should not equate a person's moral stance with her intellectual version of it, nor suppose that a person necessarily knows the relative strength of her own motives and emotions. To test people's emotional and motivational growth, we would need emotion and motive experiments, not thought experiments, and they can be tricky to design safely. Hume said, 'When I am at a loss to know the effects of one body upon another in any situation, I need only put them in that situation and observe what results from it. But should I endeavour to clear up after the same manner any doubt in moral philosophy, by placing myself in the same case with that which I consider, 'tis evident this reflection and premeditation would so disturb the operation of my natural principles, as must render it impossible to form any just conclusion from the phaenomenon' (*T.*, p. xix). By moral philosophy, here, he means simply the investigation of human nature, in both its unreflective and its more reflective operations. Moral psychology, as he understands it, is indeed a matter of letting reflection and premeditation make a difference to the operation of natural motives and passions, so moral experiments, in the narrow sense of 'moral,' would not necessarily be contaminated by the reflection or self-consciousness that the self-experimentation would involve. Knowing that when we react in a given situation, what we are doing is being treated as a display of moral character, as a test of moral progress, might merely encourage that progress, not lead to its misrepresentation. But the 'experiments' Hume is thinking of are real-life ones, not either our own, after-the-fact versions of them or our responses, intellectual or emotional, to merely imagined situations, in which one knows one is not really involved. Not only are these too thin and sketchy, as Gilligan's girls clearly felt in the story of Heinz and the expensive medicine, but even if a fully worked out fictional narrative were given—a whole novel, let us say—there is still no reason to think that one's response to a fictional situation is a good indicator of what one's own response would be, were one actually in a predicament like that of a novelist's character. Reading good novels and attending or acting in good plays may be the most harmless way to prepare oneself for real-life moral possibilities, but this isn't moral 'practice.' There is no harmless practicing of moral responses, no trial run or dress rehearsal. Children's play, the theater, novels, knowledge about and sympathy with friends' problems may all play a useful role in alerting us to the complexities of moral situations, but one's performance there is no reliable predictor of what one's response to one's own real-life problems will be. As Aristotle said, the only way to learn to be morally virtuous is to perform virtuous actions—real ones, not fantasy ones. And only from one's moral practice, not from one's fantasy moral practice or rationalized versions of past moral practice, can we learn the stage of moral development a person actually exhibits. As Hume said, it seems that only a cautious observation of human life, of 'experiments' gleaned as they occur in the 'common course of the world' in people's behaviour in company, in affairs, and in their pleasures' (ibid.) can found any empirical science of moral development.

Let me repeat that I am not saying that knowledge that one is being observed is what would spoil the results of contrived moral 'tests'; what would spoil them, rather, would be the knowledge that the tests are fantasy ones, not real-world ones. I do not want to deny that what one takes to be one's sincere beliefs about what morality demands, as they might be expressed in an interview with a psychologist or in a reaction to a fictional situation, have some connection with one's actual moral choices. But I agree with Gilligan in wondering how close the connection is, especially for reactions to sketched fictional situations. The old question 'How can I know what I think until I see what I write?' can be adapted for moral convictions: 'How can I know what I judge right until I see what decisions I make and how I then live with them?' But even that may be too optimistic about our ability to size up how we are living with our past decisions—we naturally tend either to avoid recognizing bad conscience or to exaggerate and self-dramatize it in our own follow-up reactions to a moral decision. We tend to interpret our own pasts deceptively, as possibly displaying tragedy or demonic wickedness, but not moral error, stupidity, or ordinary vice. We glaze our own pasts over with the pale cast of self-excusing or, in some cases, self-accusing, self-denigrating, self-dramatizing thought. I see no nonsuspect way, by interviewing people about other people's actual or hypothetical decisions or even about their own past actual ones, to gauge what are or were their *effective* moral beliefs.

I resume my exploration of what sort of pattern of development one might expect as experience of the common course of the world changes our passions as well as the thoughts that guide them when they motivate our actions. Two things that several of the Gilligan women *say* happened to them are that they developed a sense of their own competence to control their lives and affairs and that their attitudes toward selfishness and unselfishness underwent change. Clearly both these dimensions, of general competence at and confidence in responsible decision making and of understanding the relations between self-concerned and other-concerned passions, are ones along which one would expect change and variation, as experience deepens and opportunity widens. A child's opportunity for responsible decision making is small, and yet the child's experience of having to live with others' decisions, to react to inconsiderate decisions, or to be willing to discern, protest, understand, or forgive decisions by superiors which affect her badly is a vital preparation for later responsible decision making. The person who has forgotten what it was like to be the relatively powerless one, the decided-for and not the decision maker, is not going to be able even to anticipate the protests or grievances his or her own decisions produce, let alone be a wise or compassionate decision maker. So development along what we could call the sympathy and memory dimensions—development and enrichment of the ability to understand others' reactions—will be something one hopes will occur in normal development.

Recent studies by Judith A. Hall and Robert Rosenthal and their associates[6] have shown, interestingly enough, that women typically are better readers of other people's *nonverbal* communications of feelings (in facial expression, 'body language,' and tone of voice) than are men, and that women also are more easily read. It seems to make good evolutionary sense to suppose that there is an innate basis for such superiority, since women have been the ones who had both to communicate with infants and to interpret their communications before the child has learned a natural language. Not only may women's moral voice be different from men's and often unheard by men, but women's *tone* of voice and nonverbal expression may be subtler, more expressive, and understood more easily by other women than by men. Both in the Humean virtue of 'ease of expression' and in facility in recognizing expressed feelings, women seem to outperform men.

The second dimension of expected change and development concerns the weight a person gives to the understood preferences of the various others involved in her decision, when she decides. How one sees their interests in relation to one's own will also change as experience grows. Even if infant egoism is where we all start, it seems to be infant egoism combined with infant trust in parents and with faith in the ease of communication of feelings. In parent–child and other intimate relations, Hume says, the other 'communicates to us all the actions of his mind; makes us privy to his inmost sentiments and affections; and lets us see, in the very instant of their production, all the emotions, which are caus'd by any object' (*T.*, p. 353). Where we start, in infancy, seems to be in optimism about ease of mutual understanding, even without language, and about harmony in wills. What we may have to learn, by experience, is that conflict of wills is likely, that concealing one's feelings can be prudent, and that misunderstanding is frequent. Hume's own versions of childhood attitudes in, for example, the *Treatise*, Book Two, the section 'Of the Love of Relations,' show an incredibly strong and dominant memory or fantasy of such parent-child trusting and harmonious intimacy. Parents and children are seen to take pride in one another's achievements and successes, and not to compete with one another for eminence. 'Nothing causes greater vanity than any shining quality in our relations' (*T.*, p. 338). But this idyll of shared interests, concerted wills, and shared pride or self-assertion must soon be interrupted by experience of what Hume calls 'contrariety,' and that 'comparison' or competition which interferes with sympathy and cooperation. A most important dimension of the moral development one would look for on a Humean moral theory would be this one, the interplay of what he calls the opposed principles of sympathy and comparison. Although on his account sympathy is what morality chiefly depends upon, the opposed principle of comparison, a due sense of when our interests are or would be in conflict with those of others, and of what is then our due, also plays a not unimportant role in the generation of a sense of the virtue of justice, as he describes it. But the interpersonal problem to which various versions of morality give better or worse solutions, on Hume's account, is the problem of how to *minimize* opposition of interests, how to arrange life so that sympathy, not hostile comparison, will be the principle relating our desires to those of our fellows. Where, on the more contractarian model, morality regulates and arbitrates where interests are opposed, on a Humean view, as on Gilligan's girls', morality's main task is to rearrange situations so that interests are no longer so opposed.

There is, for Hume, an intimate interplay between the operation of sympathy and the sense of what are one's own interests. It may seem that only relative to some already fixed sense of which desires are and are not my own desires could I recognize any reaction of my own as sympathy with another's desires. But in fact, as Hume describes the workings of sympathy, they serve as much to determine, by outward expansion as well as by reinforcement of the inner core, what counts as 'my interests.' Since he believes that every human desire languishes unless it receives sympathetic reverberation from another (*T.*, p. 363), then unless someone sympathizes with my 'selfish' pleasures they will not persist. But that another does so sympathize both makes that pleasure less purely selfish, more 'fertile' for others, and also evokes in me a sympathy with the other's sympathy for me—a 'double reverberation'—and a grateful willingness to sympathize with that one's pleasures, as long as sympathy is not drowned by comparison of our respective social statuses. Hence Hume can say that 'it seems a happiness in the present theory that it enters not into that vulgar dispute concerning the *degrees* of benevolence or self-love, which prevail in human nature' (*E.*, p. 271).

Hume has a famously fluid concept of the self, and the fluid ego boundaries that allows work interestingly in his moral psychology. One could say that, on a Humean version of moral development, the main task is to work to a version of oneself and one's own interests which both maximizes the richness of one's potential satisfactions and minimizes the likely opposition one will encounter between one's own and others' partially overlapping interests. This is both an individual and a social task—a matter of the social 'artifices' which divide work so as to increase, not decrease, the real ability of all workers, which conjoin forces so that not just the collective power but each person's power is augmented, and which arrange that 'by mutual succour we are less expos'd to fortune and accidents' (*T.*, p. 485). The additional force, ability, and security which acceptable social institutions provide, he later says, must be a 'system of actions concurr'd in by the whole society, . . . infinitely advantageous to the whole and to every part' (*T.*, p. 498). This may seem an absurdly high demand to make, one which no set of social institutions has yet met. But if we remember those endless added satisfactions which sympathetic enlargement of self-interest can bring to Humean persons, then we can see that a set of institutions that really did prevent oppositions of interest might indeed bring 'infinite' or at least indeterminately great increase of power of enjoyment (such as that he described at *T.*, p. 365). Whether these increased satisfactions in fact come about will depend not just on the nature of the institutions but on the individuals whose lives are structured by them—'a creature absolutely malicious and spiteful' or even a man of 'cold insensibility or narrow selfishness' (*E.*, pp. 225–226) will not receive infinite advantages from even the best institutions. Hume, perhaps overoptimistically, thinks that given halfway decent institutions and customs of upbringing, these nasty creatures will be 'fancied monsters' (*E.*, p. 235), not real possibilities (he excuses Nero's actions by citing his grounds for fear, Timon's by his 'affected spleen').

One dimension of moral development, then, for a Humean version of morality, will be change in the concept of one's own interest. 'I esteem the man whose self-love, by whatever means, is so directed as to give him a concern for others, and to render him serviceable to society' (*E.*, p. 297). But equally important, and perhaps slower to develop in women in our society, is a realistic sense of whether or not one's agreeable moral virtues are being exploited by others, whether or not there is any 'confederacy' of the more narrowly selfish and of the sensible knaves, free-riding on the apron strings of those whose generous virtues they praise and encourage but do not envy or emulate. Due pride is a Humean virtue, and one cannot be proud of tolerating exploitation. Still, a realistic appraisal of the relative costs and benefits of cooperative schemes to their various participants and an unwillingness to tolerate second-class status require a realistic estimate of just how much real gain the 'narrowly selfish' get from their exploitation of others' more generous other-including self-love. By Hume's accounting, the sensible knaves and the narrowly selfish don't do better than their victims—they are 'the greatest dupes.' The very worst thing the exploited can do to improve their situation is to try to imitate the psychology of their exploiters. The hard art is to monitor the justice of social schemes, to keep an eye on one's rights and one's group's rights, without thereby contracting one's proper self-love into narrow selfishness in its 'moralized' version—into insistence on one's rights, even when one gains nothing, and others lose, by one's getting them. A sense of what is due one can easily degenerate into that *amour propre* which is the enemy of the sort of extended sociable and friendly *amour-de-soi* which Hume, like Rousseau, sees as the moral ideal for human beings.

Will there be anything like Kohlberg's level-difference in the moral development of Humean passions, if we see this as a change in concepts of self in relation to others, in our capacity to understand facts about likely and actual conflicts, and in our capacity to sympathize with others' reactions, developed through experience and maturation? For Hume a defining feature of a moral response is that it be a response to a response—that it be a matter of a 'reflexion,' that it be a sentiment directed on sentiments. One can postulate a fairly clear difference between levels of 'reflection,' parallel to Kohlberg's jumps in critical ability, if one distinguishes the mere ability to sympathize (and to react negatively to others' feelings) which young children show, a sort of proto-moral response, from that more legitimized version of it which comes when we sympathize with others as right-holders in some conventional scheme and sympathize with their resentments at insult or injury (a level two response), achieving a sort of officially 'seconded' sympathy, comparison, sense of self, and recognition of recognized conflicts of interest. One would reserve the title of really moral response to the reflexive turning of these capacities for sympathy, for self-definition, and for conflict recognition onto themselves, to see if they can 'bear their own survey.' Doing this would involve the sympathetic comparative evaluation of different styles of self-definition, styles of watching for and managing conflicts, of inhibiting or cultivating sympathy. The Humean concept of 'reflexion' performs the same sort of job as Kantian reason—it separates the mature and morally critical from the mere conformers. A moral theory which developed Gilligan's women's moral strengths could make good use of Hume's concept of reflection.

I end with a brief return to the question of how this wise moral theory of Hume's could allow its author to make the apparently sexist remarks he did. Now, I think, we are in a position to see how harmless they might be, a display of his social realism, his unwillingness to idealize the actual. Women in his society *were* inferior in bodily strength and in intellectual achievement. Neither of these, however, for someone who believes that reason should be the slave of reflective and moralized passions, is the capacity that matters most. What matters most, for judging moral wisdom, are corrected sentiments, imagination, and cooperative genius. There Hume never judges women inferior. He does call them the 'timorous and pious' sex, and that is for him a criticism, but since he ties both of these characteristics with powerlessness, his diagnoses here are of a piece with his more direct discussions of how much power women have. In those discussions he is at pains not just to try to point out the subordination of their interests to those of men in the existing institutions (marriage in particular) but also to show women where their power lies, should they want to change the situation.

As he points out, a concern for 'the propagation of our kind' is a normal concern of men and women, but each of us needs the cooperation of a member of the other sex to further this concern, and 'a trivial and anatomical observation' (*T.*, p. 571) shows us that no man can know that his kind has been propagated unless he can trust some woman either to be sexually 'faithful' to him or to keep track of and tell him the truth about the paternity of any child she bears. This gives women great, perhaps dangerously great, threat advantage in any contest with men, a power very different from any accompanying the 'insinuation, address and charms' (*E.*, p. 191) that Hume had invoked as sufficient to break any confederacy against them. The non-self-sufficiency of persons in reproductive respects that he goes on in the next paragraphs to emphasize, and the need of the male for a trustworthy female in order to satisfy his postulated desire for offspring he can recognize as his (a desire Hume had emphasized in the *Treatise* section 'Of Chastity and Modesty'), put some needed iron into the gloved hands of the fair and charming sex. Hume gives many descriptions in his *History* and *Essays* of strong independent women, and he dwells on the question of whether the cost of their iron wills and their independence is a loss of the very moral virtues he admires in anyone but finds more often in women than in men—the 'soft' nonmartial compassionate virtues. Need women, in ceasing to be timorous and servile, cease also to be experts at care and mutual care? His moral tale of a liberated woman who chooses to be a single mother (in 'Of Moral Prejudices') suggests not—that avoidance of servile dependence on men can be combined with the virtues of caring and bearing responsibility, that pride and at least some forms of love can be combined.

POSTSCRIPT

This essay was written before Carol Gilligan had clarified and slightly revised her views about women and the care perspective. Indeed this essay was written for the conference at which Gilligan made the clarification.[7]

I now find a slight distortion or oversimplification of Hume's views at one place (p. 248) in this essay. I would not now say that his characterization of the 'good' person as 'a safe companion, an easy friend, a gentle master, an agreeable husband, an indulgent father' is intended to summarize the person with all or even the most important natural virtues, but merely to characterize the person who has that subset of them which confers moral 'goodness,' as distinct from moral 'greatness' and moral 'ability.' Hume, as I go on to say here, recognizes a great variety of natural virtues, and he subdivides them in various ways. One way is by varying the narrowness and width of the circle of others with whom the moral judge must sympathize, in order to judge the impact of the character trait on its possessor's fellows. Gentleness typically affects those in the 'narrow circle' of family, friends, and workmates. But the general's courage and the diplomat's wisdom may affect very wide circles. These traits therefore have a special moral 'importance and weight' (*T.*, p. 613). Hume writes that some natural virtues make their possessor amiable while others make her estimable (*T.*, p. 608). 'Goodness' tends to be a term reserved by him for those virtues which make their possessor lovable rather than estimable, qualities which favorably affect the narrow circle around her rather than affecting the 'great confederacy of mankind.'

This point of Hume's linguistic usage is of interest primarily to Hume interpreters rather than to moral philosophers more generally. It does, however, raise a deeper question concerning just how we can be sure how widely the effects of a given character trait spread their beneficial or baneful influence. The gentle parent may not influence the fate of empires in his lifetime in the way that the great national leader does, but the gentle parent may influence not only his children but also his children's children, just as the violent parent tends to bring about the replication of his own vices in his victims. Hume notes the special degree of shame which attaches to diseases that 'affect others,' for instance, any venereal disease that 'goes to Posterity' (*T.*, p. 303). Most of the natural vices which prevent a person from being 'good,' in Hume's sense, are ones that may well 'go to posterity,' and so do have weight and moment. The line between the 'great' and the 'good,' the estimable and the amiable, may be difficult to draw. The 'narrow circle,' over several generations, can widen out quite dramatically.

My usage of the term 'natural vices' may be un-Humean, since Hume requires of a natural virtue that it be the norm, not the exception, in a human population (*T.*, p. 483). All the vices which are opposed to these virtues therefore become in one sense 'unnatural.' I have discussed elsewhere some of the problems that this makes for Hume.[8]

Notes

1. David Hume, *A Treatise of Human Nature*, ed. L. A. Selby-Bigge and P. H. Nidditch (Oxford: Clarendon Press, 1978), p. 348. References in the text will be given as *T.* Other works by Hume referred to in the text are *Enquiries*, ed. L. A. Selby-Bigge and P. H. Nidditch (Oxford: Clarendon Press, 1975), to be given as *E*; and *Essays: Moral, Political and Literary*, ed. Eugene F. Miller (Indianapolis, Ind.: Liberty Classics, 1985), to be given as *Es.* I also refer to *History of England*, any edition.
2. The three essays referred to in this section were published by Hume in the first edition of *Essays Moral and Political* (1741–42), but were removed by him in

subsequent editions. They can be found in David Hume, *Essays: Moral, Political and Literary*, ed. Eugene F. Miller (Indianapolis, Ind.: Liberty Classics, 1985) in the appendix 'Essays Withdrawn and Unpublished.'

3. Lawrence Kohlberg, *The Philosophy of Moral Development* (San Francisco, Calif.: Harper & Row, 1981), p. 12. See also Kohlberg, *Collected Papers on Moral Development and Moral Education* (Cambridge, Mass.: Harvard University, Moral Education Research Foundation, 1971).
4. See Introduction to Eva Kittay and Diana Meyers, eds., *Women and Moral Theory* (Lanham, Md.: Rowman & Littlefield, 1987). I discuss Kohlberg's theory in Essay 2, pp. 21–22.
5. Carol Gilligan, *In a Different Voice: Psychological Theory and Women's Development* (Cambridge, Mass.: Harvard University Press, 1982), pp. 25 ff. Future references to this work will be given in the text as *D.V.*
6. Robert Rosenthal, J. A. Hall, M. R. DiMatteo, P. L. Rogers, and D. Archer, *Sensitivity to Nonverbal Communication: The PONS Test* (Baltimore, Md.: Johns Hopkins University Press, 1979). See also Judith A. Hall, *Non-Verbal Sex Differences* (Baltimore, Md.: Johns Hopkins University Press, 1984). Immanuel Kant, *The Metaphysical Elements of Justice*, trans. John Ladd (Indianapolis, Ind.: Bobbs-Merrill, 1965).
7. Carol Gilligan, 'Moral Orientation and Moral Development,' in *Women and Moral Theory*, ed. Kittay and Meyers, pp. 19–33.
8. 'Natural Virtues, Natural Vices,' *Social Philosophy & Policy*, 8, Ethics, Politics, and Human Nature (Autumn 1990): 24–34.

11 Agency, Attachment, and Difference

Barbara Herman*

It is for no trivial reason that Kant's ethics is the standard model of an impartial ethical system. Persons have moral standing in virtue of their rationality, and the morally dictated regard we are to have for one another reflects this deep sameness: we are never to fail to treat one another as agents with autonomous rational wills. This yields impartial treatment of persons and impartial judgment across cases. Although these features of Kant's ethics have traditionally been a source of its appeal, in many recent discussions just this sort of impartiality has come to stand for a kind of vice—mostly a vice of theory.[1] To the extent, however, that persons embody the values of impartiality, it is sometimes thought to be in them, if not quite a vice, then a lack or limit or defect of moral sensibility.[2]

In this essay I want to examine a cluster of criticisms of Kantian ethics associated with its impartiality. They arise from concern for the moral standing of relationships of attachment between persons and extend to claims for the nonrational nature of the moral agent and the moral relevance of difference. Each strand of criticism has this form: because of its commitment to impartiality (or one of the grounds of impartiality, such as rationality), Kantian ethics fails to make room for *x*, where *x* is something no acceptable moral theory can ignore. Without making a general argument in praise of impartiality, I want to see whether its Kantian instantiation really fails to accommodate things no moral theory can afford to omit.

Relationships of attachment pose a serious problem for Kantian ethics, if attachment is a source of distinctive moral claims that

* Barbara Herman, 'Agency, Attachment, and Difference', from her *The Practice of Moral Judgment* (Cambridge, Mass., and London: Harvard University Press, 1993), 184–207; original version in *Ethics*, 101 (1991), 775–97. Reprinted by permission of University of Chicago Press.

impartiality disallows or if the features of persons that support and express attachment are devalued by its conception of moral agency. While friends of Kantian ethics have described ways to accommodate the concerns that motivate the criticism, *what* has to be accommodated has to a large extent been accepted in the critics' terms. It is among my purposes here to initiate a more independent examination of the value of partiality.

It is important to say at the outset that I do not intend this essay in the spirit of endless defense of a favorite system. The cluster of criticisms are worth attention because they do point to important matters that have been omitted or ignored by Kantian theorists, though whether by Kant himself is another matter. Moral theories should not be static. As we discover (or uncover) things a theory as formulated did not know about or attend to, we have occasion to further elaborate or develop the theory in the light of what we now know. Sometimes a theory can absorb new things; sometimes not. Whichever, we do best if we make the effort and see what happens to the theory under strain. Its success may suggest we have misunderstood the theory all along. Its failure can only instruct if we are scrupulous in finding the source of the fault. The fact that a theory as traditionally understood omits something should be the beginning, not the end, of inquiry.

I

Impartiality per se is the requirement that like cases be treated alike. As a requirement on justification, it is not trivial. Differential treatment or judgment requires the demonstration of relevant difference. But as a substantive moral requirement, impartiality by itself demands little. Do we violate impartiality when we favor friends over strangers in the distribution of some good? Does impartiality show that if pregnancy is accorded the status of a disability, employment law will not be impartial between men and women? Because there is nothing in the idea of impartiality to indicate when or in what terms cases are alike, it can seem that impartiality is an empty (or uninstructive) moral value. It is then hard to see what all the fuss could be about.

There is an interesting asymmetry here. For if impartiality is empty, partiality (in its different manifestations) is the stuff our lives are said to be about: *my* life, *my* loves, *my* ideals. Then to the extent that impartiality defines the moral perspective, partiality creates tension with and within morality. When I attend specially to the needs of my children and friends because I am partial to them, either I have acted as I ought not (morality requires that I count their needs no more than others'), or I have done what I ought to do, because there are obligations to one's children and friends, but I have done it the wrong way: my actions were expressions of my partiality, not of my moral understanding and commitment. Partiality is then either a sign or an occasion of moral failure, or a value that morality cannot acknowledge in a direct way. Those unhappy with this will say: impartial ethics does not allow room (or the right sort of room) for the relationships and structures of attachment that constitute good or normal human lives. It devalues the affective life—the life constituted by feeling, intimacy, connection. And if affect-grounded connection creates partiality of attachment, then impartial ethics pushes us away from such attachments.

I want to think more about this claim and about the nature of what makes it disturbing. Of special interest is the argument that takes a positive moral attitude toward feelings to be the basis for asserting the disvalue of impartiality as a moral norm for relationships. What I want to show is that much of the conflict between concerns of partiality and impartial ethics is caused by a misunderstanding of the requirements of both.

Let us first survey the kind of room that Kantian ethics provides for actions motivated by care and concern for the other—what I will call 'motives of connection.' As we see where reasonable grounds for complaint remain, we will have the issues that need attention. In Chapter 2 I argued that Kantian ethics does not block the satisfaction of certain obligations from motives of connection as they are available or appropriate, so long as the agent's volition (her maxim) is regulated by the motive of duty functioning as a secondary motive or limiting condition. That is to say: in acting from a motive of connection I must also recognize that I am in circumstances in which action is morally required, be willing and able to act even if connection wavers, and act only on the condition that the particular action I am moved to take is permissible. But permitting action from motives of connection does not fully resolve the problem. Even though there is nothing wrong with acting from a motive of connection in circumstances of obligation, the Kantian is likely to insist that action so motivated has no moral worth. The Kantian position is that the value signaled by moral worth is action done from a motive that tracks morality (the motive of duty): only then is there a maxim of action with moral content. A dutiful action done from a motive of connection has a maxim with a different content. The critic of Kantian ethics objects to the fact that no moral value is assigned to maxims or motives of connection. Toleration is not enough.

There are countermoves the Kantian may make at this point. One may note that in most cases the actions at issue are ones required by 'imperfect duties.' What one is required to do is adopt morally required ends *from* the motive of duty. That leaves open how (from what motive) one acts for that end. An agent may act for a morally required end from motives of connection. Indeed, a helping action guided by connection may be more successful than one done from the moral motive working alone. The agent's complete maxim then includes not only the motive of connection but also the underlying moral commitment to the required end (from the motive of duty).[3] The complete maxim has moral content. If this treatment secures moral worth to the agent acting from motives of connection, it still fails to accord moral value to these motives, except indirectly. The motives of connection are placed among those that can lend support to a morally required end, but the moral value of connection remains in question.

One might try to argue that since there is an indirect duty to maintain one's happiness (to secure stability for moral character), and since attachments are necessary to human happiness, then the motives of connection have moral value as they are means to happiness.[4] But this will not really satisfy those who find the issue in the need to justify the motives of connection in the first place. Nor should it. This way of arguing the value of connection or attachment depends on its role in supporting the 'mental health' of the moral agent.[5]

Perhaps we should have asked first: why should it matter that maxims of connection do not have *moral* value? Why can't we say: morality is one kind of value, connection another? Not everything that matters to us must have moral value. A reason for caring about this might turn on the relative value weight of connection, especially if one thought that regulative priority implied value priority. That is, if morality (impartial morality) trumps connection, the value of connection is diminished. But, of course, even assigning moral value to motives of connection would not resolve the priority issue unless we thought that the moral value of connection was at least sometimes greater than the value associated with the motive of duty. And this the Kantian cannot accept.

There is an additional worry. Given the association in Kantian ethics between morality and rationality, on the one hand, and connection with affect and feeling on the other, the assignment of (at best) subordinate value to the motives of connection supports the idea that our affective nature is not essential to our moral agency, or at least the idea that our moral agency would remain intact in the absence of the grounds of connection. We will return to this concern later.

Does regulative priority translate into value priority? I think not. When we require that belief and argument meet standards of theoretical rationality, we are hardly committed to the thought that we thereby care more about rationality than we care about the substance of our inquiry. Regulative rules may serve what we value. We think that caring about theoretical rationality is part of caring about our other projects because rationality has instrumental value.[6] But of course sometimes it does not—as when we may recognize that false belief will facilitate some important activity. However we diagnose the tension in such cases, the very fact that there is tension would seem to undermine any automatic translation from regulative to value priority.

If theoretical rationality draws authority from its relation to conditions of success in action and belief, perhaps the problem with impartial morality is that it does not serve our purposes. So it cannot just be part of caring about what we care about. An instrumental claim is made on behalf of morality by some contract theorists.[7] But it is hard to see how such a claim could be supported in Kantian ethics, given its rejection of heteronomous (subjective, interest-based) foundations and its commitment to there being substantive moral questions about ends. Morality can be seen as the expression of a highest-order rational interest (as it is in Rawls), but that does not join the question of the relations between morality and interests per se, and motives of connection in particular.

One might argue that, just as theoretical rationality and prudential practical rationality have their authority based in the fact that we are interest and truth pursuers, so morality has its authority based in some equi-primordial fact—say, of our sociality. We need not take the Humean circumstances of justice to be the full terms that define the moral agenda for success as a human being among others (of our kind, language, culture).[8] Along these lines, morality would be necessary (and in that sense instrumental) given the complex of requirements needed to support acceptable or suitable conditions of sociality. There is much to find attractive in this way of proceeding. And if sociality involved connection (as partiality) in an essential way, it would certainly ease the tension between morality and connection. But it is not clear what sociality in this role involves.

And it is not in any case a form of argument that is readily available to the Kantian.

Where does this leave us? I want to accept that it is reasonable to expect a moral theory to give noninstrumental expression to the role that sociality and the partiality of connection play in a human life. To show that and how Kantian ethics does this, we must restart the discussion taking instruction from the fact that the affective life is not in general independent of various norms of rationality. This creates space for the claim that connection itself could be partially dependent on or a function of moral value.

II

We begin then with acknowledgment that intimacy and connection are necessary not just to a happy human life but to the form of life we call human. (This is to be understood in the sense that deprivation of the possibility of intimacy and connection threatens a person's humanity—thus the peculiar violence of solitary confinement.[9]) And the relationships between parents and children, between friends, lovers, neighbors, are essentially partial. It is because someone is *my* neighbor, lover, or child that I have reasons for action of a certain sort. Having these relationships is to have these reasons. They are reasons of considerable strength and priority, and they are reasons such that acting on them (and not on other reasons that can produce the same outcomes) is important to maintaining the relationships that generate them. The importance of these reasons derives from connections of feeling, familiarity, love.

If my child is among those who are at risk, I do not act for my child as a moral agent but as a mother. That is to say, even when morality permits mothers to act for their children first among others (and it will not always do this), I do not act for my child because morality permits it, but because I am his mother. To be a parent is to be a person constituted by a set of motives and reasons for action. This is a matter of personal identity. The strength of these reasons, their priority and the fact that acting on them gives expression to constitutive commitments, all add to the sense that moral reasons—reasons that do not arise directly from the natural affective connection between parent and child—are out of place here.[10]

There have been different philosophical responses to these facts.[11]

Some suppose they show the limits of morality as regulative of our concerns.[12] Not only are moral reasons not ubiquitous, but they must stand aside when they conflict with personal commitments that are constitutive of selves. Others do not find in the facts reason to question the authority of morality but rather the claim of impartial morality to be the paradigm of moral concern. So, it may be claimed, just these sorts of reasons, with their grounding in feeling and connection, provide the model for a 'morality of care' or, as some have argued, for the distinctive moral perspective of women.[13] With either response, any claim for the priority of impartial morality is rejected as a devaluing of constitutive human concerns.

Such arguments against impartial morality are based on the feeling that our commitments and relationships of connection are sometimes of greater or deeper importance than those of impartial morality. But because it feels this way is a reason to take such feelings seriously, not a reason to give their claims automatic authority. For example, part of what growing up as a parent involves is the recognition of the place and point of such feelings. I think it is generally true that you feel like hurting anyone who causes your child undeserved pain, but that is not sufficient reason to do it. That someone close to you may suffer terribly in failing to get what he wants is not reason to make it happen when that is inappropriate. Sometimes it is the welfare of the loved one that is jeopardized by what one would do out of feeling. So the feeling needs to mature (or we who have the feeling need to mature); we need to be able to ask whether a particular expression of love is good for the one loved. And we sometimes need to let changes in those we love change our feelings (or what will count as expression of those feelings).

Since accepting limits set by autonomy, maturation, and change do not necessarily interfere with the way our supporting actions give expression to our connection with others, why should we be so easily disposed to accept that morality will interfere? We mistake the nature of feelings and their role in constituting our character to think that they are 'original existences' whose modification cannot or should not be tolerated.

Let us look a little closer at the moral dimension of a relationship of connection. In addition to involving a deep bond of connection, parent-to-child is a relationship of *trust* between unequals: an essential kind of moral relationship that Annette Baier has argued cannot be expressed in impartial morality. Trust, as Baier describes it, is a noncontractual moral relationship between persons where there is vulnerability on the one hand and an implied reliance on good will and caring on the other (explicit or not, conscious or not). Because they are centered on cool, voluntary relationships between equals, Baier contends that moral theories such as Kant's cannot provide guidance in these regions. Yet, as we must agree, 'a complete moral philosophy would tell us how and why we should act and feel toward others in relationships of shifting and varying power asymmetry and shifting and varying intimacy.'[14]

If there is tension between trust and the morality of impartiality, there is no secure alliance between trust and partiality.[15] From the fact that my child trusts that my concern for him will lead me to guard and preserve his well-being as I can, it does not follow that I violate his trust if I refrain from doing some things that will benefit him (because they are wrong or unfair) or if I act for someone else first, as when I tend to the younger child hurt in the playground or expend finite resources on a needier sibling. What my son has reason to trust is that I am committed to his well-being: among the things that matter to me most and that will determine how I act is that he do well and flourish. But, as I must often remind him (and myself), his interests are not the only ones I care about (there are not only my friends, my spouse, my students, and myself, but sometimes complete strangers or causes that claim my attention and resources), and further he will do fine, indeed he will often do better, if he relies on me less and if my life is increasingly separate from his.[16] Because I care about him, he can trust that I will count his well-being as among the basic facts that determine what I do, not as special reasons at work when I have to choose between his and someone's equal or greater claim, but as a set of changing needs that will partially determine the shape of my life.

How we understand the role of impartial morality here depends on how we represent its place in deliberation. I want to suggest that failure to recognize two quite different models of practical concern and deliberation leads to serious distortion of the problem thought to be posed by impartial morality to concerns of trust and connection. I will call them, for reasons that should become clear, the 'plural interest' and the 'deliberative field' models.

According to the plural-interest model, where there is connection, there are those I care about, and the effect of my caring is to give their interests greater deliberative weight: for me. They matter more. And they matter more to me because I care about them. When I need to balance or weigh interests—should I do some good for my son or his friend—my son counts more. Of course I have a variety of interests and concerns, and they have different weights (as I care about them and as they matter directly or instrumentally). The interests of my child weigh more than the next career step, which weighs more than my enjoyment of movies, and morality (if it has regulative priority) weighs more than all of the above. Deliberation involves further weighing and balancing. Interinterest comparisons of various sorts will be necessary. The descriptions of interests will often need to be more qualified and situationally explicit: a minor desire of my child won't count against going to a film I've waited years to see. There will be tension between looking to get the most interests satisfied and getting the most important interests satisfied. Over all these differently weighted interests loom the requirements of impartial morality in which I am not only supposed to have an interest, but an interest sufficient to support its supremely regulative role.[17]

On the plural-interest model, when morality contends with attachments it forces one against the grain, attacking the immediacy of connection. It would be natural to feel hostile to or alienated from the requirements of morality if they in this way denied a deeply felt claim of partiality. I do not mean to suggest that one would necessarily feel alienated whenever one acts for morality in a context in which connection draws you in a different direction. There are many times, especially with children, when the fact that a choice must be made impartially provides the occasion for useful moral lessons. In such circumstances, acting impartially expresses trustworthiness. The problem arises when it looks like 'over here' is what I most care about, what I want to happen (and cannot not want to happen), but 'over there' is what impartial morality demands. There is then deep conflict and tension. And when impartial morality wins, it is not only at the expense of what I most care about, but it provides no deliberative space even to acknowledge my concerns. The fact that I care about my son in no way affects the deliberative outcome.

If this is the way I see it, I can learn to take these losses, even to believe they are necessary. They are the price you pay for . . . and then some account of the role of morality that presumably justifies such losses by pointing to greater gains elsewhere. What other kind of justification of morality could work, given the imposition of losses? And if I am unmoved by the greater gains to be had elsewhere, often gains to be had by those other than myself or those I care about—not because I am selfish, but because of who I am (a person who cares about such and such)—then my life will not seem to be valued from the moral point of view. I will act either morally badly or against myself. Clearly, so long as we stick with the plural-interest model, we will have difficulty negotiating the terrain between impartial morality and attachment.

Among the elements of a full moral theory, we should find an account of how one is to integrate the requirements of morality into one's life. One could be someone whose interest in morality was an interest (if a very strong or strongest interest) among others. But such a connection to morality is not in itself morally neutral; it will follow from the substantive nature of moral requirements. There is no unique atheoretic model of a morally serious or committed moral agent. Depending on how this feature of a moral theory is elaborated, there will be more than one answer to the question of the effects of moral requirements on the motives of connection. Since on the plural-interest model, commitment to morality is at the expense of other commitments, especially attachments, there will be reason to favor a different model if it is better able to integrate these elements in a morally good life.

On the second model, deliberation addresses a field only partially shaped by those commitments, concerns, and relationships that determine my conception of the good. They stand there as myself—as interests that I need no further or instrumental reason to care about. It is not that I care about my son and therefore, when interests are to be weighed, his weigh more. Rather, because I care about my son—because of the way I care about my son—his interests (his good) are part of my good: *the* good as I see it. But just as I know in advance that I cannot do whatever will promote my own well-being, so I know in advance and as part of my caring that I may not be able to promote his good in circumstances where it is inappropriate to determine the effective practical weight of interests by how much I care about them.

According to this deliberative-field model, the practical self does not have as its major task negotiating a settlement among independent competing claims. Insofar as one has interests and commitments, one is a human self. But a human life is not the result of a 'bundle' of competing interests (among which is an interest in morality). One's interests are present on a deliberative field that contains everything that gives one reasons. Thus, in addition to interests and attachments, there are also grounds of obligation, principles of prudential rationality, and, depending on the individual, a more or less complex conception of the Good. Not everything that may seek a place on my deliberative field is good for me to have there: bad habits, destructive relationships, incompatible goals and projects. And if there is a real question about what enters (or remains on) the deliberative field—this is often a question about ends—the conditions for accepting desires or interests as ends may (and often will) shape the result.

An agent with a deliberative field partly constructed by moral principles recognizes from the outset, in the adoption of ends, that pursuit of important goals may unforeseeably lead one to means that are morally inappropriate (not permissible). The commitment to pursue an end is always conditional; this is so whether the ends are ends of interest or necessary ends. In this way ends are absorbed into a moral structure as they enter the deliberative field.

This resetting of ends in the deliberative field is not unique to moral requirements. Something analogous occurs because of potential practical conflict between different nonmoral goals. Wanting both to have a career and a family, I can pursue both and hope for the best, or I can give one end priority (absolute or weighted) over the other, or I can make action on one conditional on noninterference with the other. With other ends—say, teaching and writing—I have additional possibilities, including the revision of each of these ends to include aspects of the other (I value my teaching as an integral part of the process that leads me to successful writing, or vice versa). These need not be once and for all decisions: my sense of the relative importance of ends may change, the likelihood of conflict may diminish, still other relevant interests may come on the scene. But having set ends in a complex deliberative framework, my sense of loss on abandoning one is different than it would be if I thought of myself simply as acting for diverse and separate goals, having to give up or limit or frustrate one for the sake of another. Acting from a deliberative framework, I am in a better position to accept the outcome. This is not a matter of resignation so much as acknowledgment. Without such a framework, the decision will seem more contingent—more a matter of bad luck—and the outcome arbitrary.[18]

To make sense of the deliberative-field model (and so, I believe, of Kantian ethics[19]), we must resist the tendency to think of the Good—an agent's conception of what is good—as a composite cluster of objects of desire, perhaps structured by priority principles and other success-oriented practical devices external to the ends we have because of the desires we have. This leaves the desire-object relation too much intact, with the agent passive with respect to her bundle of desires. Desires do not give reasons for action: they may explain why such and such is a reason for action, or even why something can be an effective reason for action, but the desire itself is not a reason. One can take the fact of a desire to be a reason, but that just is to hold that desire, or this desire, is good.[20] Nor is it, enough to replace desire with 'end that it is rational or good to have.' That still suggests discrete sets of interests and ends. What is missing—what you are supposed to learn as a maturing agent—is the integration and transformation of the ends in light of one another, of one's practical situation, and of one's conception of place and importance understood through the regulative principles—aesthetic, moral, prudential—one accepts. One has, or tries to have, a good life.

We will be inclined to view deliberation differently as we take ourselves to be either active or passive with respect to our desires. If we take the paradigmatic deliberative situation to be either means-end calculation or the resolution of conflict between ends, it will look as if our starting point is the pursuit of discrete goods (the objects of desires or interests) whose compatibility is a matter of luck. Now sometimes this is just the way things are. Circumstances can sharpen conflict, as they can make deliberation look like a search for the least costly compromise. But focusing on these cases reinforces a sense of our passivity as agents: what Kant meant, I believe, by a heteronomy of the will.

Our sense of things is different if we look instead at the ways we are or can be active with respect to our desires. We have desires we do not want to act on; we have desires we act on but do not value; we come to discover that some of what we want is caused by needs that would be better met some other way (as when an underlying insecurity leads to placing excessive demands on others). Refusing desires of the last two types is importantly not like restraining one's desire for sweets: a kind of desire we like to think we can turn our back on at will (or fail at controlling because of 'weakness of will,' a kind of muscular insufficiency). Activity involves more than effective second-order wants.

When, for example, I hear my mother's parental anxieties in my own voice as I criticize my son, I cannot resolve the problem I discover just by abandoning some end or disowning some desire, however much distress I feel about what I am doing. Part of what I discover in these moments is who I am—or who I am as a parent. I listen and find out what I desire. But then it is not enough to say that I do not want to act on these desires, and also not enough to say that I do not want to have them. I want them not to have a place in the complex of desires and thoughts that constitute myself as a parent. This may be no easy thing, for the very desires I would disavow may hold together things I like about myself as a parent.

Someone who is otherwise a good friend cannot come through when there is illness involved; he simply cannot see what there is to do. Suppose he comes to believe that he acts inadequately in these circumstances. What can he do? He wants to act as a good friend. He has the relevant ends. The problem is that illness makes him panic. Perhaps as a child he was made to feel responsible for a sick parent. Now, confronted with illness in others, he feels inadequate; he withdraws in the face of what he feels will be certain failure.

When we discover that with our children or our friends we are acting in ways that do not match our values or ideals, the practical task involves special difficulties, in the sense that we must come to see why we would do what we do not seem to want to do (this is *not* weakness of will). Success at this task may still leave us trying to figure out what to do with, or what we are able to do with, what we find. This is a function of what we might think of as the enmeshedness or even geology of desire.

Encountering (or more often stumbling against) such a complex, we may be enlightened or transformed, or moved to therapy, or despair. Affective disorders alert us to inertial features of character. We cannot just choose to care (about some things), and we cannot just prize out an unwanted desire by identifying and rejecting its object. So also we come to see that you cannot just add ends: not only because there may be conflict in realizing ends but also because the adoption of some ends resonates in the deliberative field. For the good friend to lose his panic in the face of illness, he may have to revise his relations with his mother (now and in the past).

The point here is not to argue for therapy or discuss the relative merits of deep versus shallow psychological change, but to let the difficulty of these matters direct us to a different picture (or set of pictures) about the Good as the complex object not of desire, but of practical agency.

If the attempt to abandon ends may draw us into more complexity than expected, we should not suppose that adopting an end is any simple matter. Ends are not adopted in isolation from one another. It is not only that their joint pursuit may not be possible. Adopting an end is (or can be) wanting some interest to be effective in my life. This may alter other ends I already have and affect what ends I may come to have. Wanting friendship to play a greater role in my life does not just mean creating more time for friends (and so less for the pursuit of other ends). It may make me see in my present attachment to other ends a lack of concern for others. Or vice versa: coming to take my work more seriously may reveal a will to distraction in my absorption with others. (When everything works for the best, this kind of insight need not lead to conflict with friendship: it can make me a better friend.)

Because of the complexity of relations among ends, it can be difficult to predict the outcome of deliberation—for another agent, but equally sometimes for ourselves. We may not know in advance what impact circumstances will have on ends. When situations are new or complex, what an agent wants can depend on her response to the situations she finds herself in and on the way she makes use of whatever knowledge and sensitivity she can bring to bear. Some deliberative outcomes will reshape ends; others can lead her to see the world in a different way. Deliberation itself will then reshape or reconfigure the deliberative field.

Deliberation structured by *substantive* regulative principles involves still more. If in all of my relationships I am to treat people as ends, then as this conception has deliberative priority, what is possible for me in relationships will be different. My ends of friendship and intimacy will not be what they would have been otherwise. It is not that I must replace motives of connection with moral motives; I will have *different* motives of connection. Perhaps I will be more sensitive to problems of exclusion or of fairness. Perhaps I will be less tempted to interfere 'for the best.' It does not follow from the interpenetration of motives of connection with moral concerns that these will be the changes: what the changes are will depend on what I discover about the structure and tendencies of my relationships.

This transformational process does not go only one way. Commitment to treat others as ends (or in accordance with the dictates of some moral conception or ideal) does not by itself guide deliberation. As I come to understand more of what is involved in friendship and intimacy, so I also come to see more of what the moral requirement amounts to. Without knowledge of how intimacy engages vulnerabilities, I cannot see that or how certain behaviors which could be acceptable among strangers are impermissibly manipulative among intimates, and vice versa. Where power and inequality mix with intimacy, questions of exploitation and abuse are raised. Such questions are not part of the concept of treating persons as ends. They are what we discover treating persons as ends amounts to, given what human relationships tend to be like, or what particular relationships involve. Without such knowledge, moral judgment is not possible.[21]

*

Let us briefly retrace our steps. The sense of conflict and loss that we think follows from the regulation of relationships and attachments by impartial moral principles might instead be a function of the way we understand the connection between ends and deliberative principles. My discussion of the difference between activity and passivity with respect to our desires and ends was aimed, on the one hand, to defeat a picture of an autarchy of ends slotted into a legalistic or merely formal deliberative framework and, on the other hand, to replace that picture with the idea of the Good as a constructed object of practical agency.[22] Locating attachments in a deliberative field, we uncover a mutual practical dependence between formal moral principle (as it applies to us) and the structure of attachment.

Some resistance to this move may come from a presumed tension between moral and personal reasons that follows from a split in the practical between the moral and the natural. There is the thought that personal attachments—and especially what is good in them—are in some special way natural or spontaneous or pure. So one might worry that moral transformation might involve loss of this natural good. This concern is to be met with the reminder that 'natural' relationships are, among other things, the locales of abuse, infantilization, exploitation, and other sins of intimacy. Intimacy may be a natural need, or arise from natural motives, but the relationships among adults usually are, when healthy, complex and mediated descendants of spontaneous or natural attachments.

When there is moral criticism of a relationship, we should not think that morality aims to replace the structure of attachment. Love for another may be necessary to change a relationship whose premises or practices are morally faulty. Morality alone can do no more than indicate the fault and give reason not to accept terms of relationship in which the fault is embodied; it cannot by itself direct the parties to a satisfactory resolution *within* the framework of intimacy.

As our conception of the Good becomes increasingly complex (involving morality but also work and children and the various kinds of intimacy), our understanding of our activities and attachments should reflect that complexity. This is not a loss of innocence that we have reason to reject (or rationally regret).

If the deliberative field were empty[23] until the agent brought to it—from outside, as it were—her interests, projects, and commitments, looking to use its principles to maximize satisfaction while attending to the demands of morality, one could safely predict the frustration of one for the satisfaction of the other. If the deliberative field is not empty at the outset, things look different. The alternative, or Kantian, model suggests that we think of an agent's deliberative field as containing representations of her interests, projects, and commitments that have been 'normalized' to varying degrees to the principles of practical agency, both moral and nonmoral. Kantian deliberation requires the prior processing of the material it takes up. Maxims and ends we know to be impermissible, if attractive, are represented as such; tasks we would take up as means toward desired goals are not represented as independently valuable (unless they also are); and so on. The normalization of the material of interest and desire to the principles of practical agency minimizes the degree to which deliberation and choice must involve sorting and weighing things of incommensurable or conflicting value.

Desires and interests are normalized to beliefs and values as well. Take a nonmoral example. Suppose it is normal (given certain patterns of up-bringing, socialization, and such) that, faced with certain kinds of situations, people have sharply competitive reactions. For one sort of person, these reactions may be taken as the direct and natural response to a challenge, and so give reason to act competitively. Someone else may have a view about the etiology of such reactions in herself (anxiety, status hunger, aggression) that leads her to conclude that they should not be taken at face value: in and of themselves they are not reason-giving. If one describes the effects of such psychological facts as introducing a deliberative problem when circumstances provoke the reaction in question, the second person is misdescribed in an important way. Suppose, in addition to recognizing the origins of the competitive impulse in herself, the second person believes that the kinds of action it generates are by and large counterproductive (or just contrary to what she holds is good). She need not be faced with a choice each time the reaction occurs, for she does not regard the reaction as making a claim or having automatic reason-giving status. One might say that the impulse to competition enters her deliberative field already discounted, if it enters at all.

Discounted impulses need not be entirely counted out. The agent in the second case may believe that letting a competitive response regulate action can sometimes be useful. But even when it is, the impulse to competition is normalized in the agent's deliberative field to the discounted value. (That is, it is indulged for a special purpose; acting on it is not, in the usual way, an expression of competitiveness.) One could, I suppose, think that such impulses are held in check and then in special circumstances set free. But it seems truer to the pattern of increased and practically effective self-knowledge that the desires themselves be modified, or at least be under principled constraint in the way they are given access to the deliberative field. It is not just the pressure they exert that gains them entry.[24]

The advantage gained from taking natural motives to be normalized to the principles of practical agency is that it eliminates the deliberative quandary of having always to choose between natural motives and moral motives (or even motives of prudence). Without this, the tension between natural and moral concerns seems unavoidable: the tension will recur within the domain of the moral between virtues and moral requirements insofar as the virtues rely on natural motives (like compassion). If the natural motive of compassion has as its object the well-being of another, normalized compassion—concern for another framed by a practical awareness of the place of compassion in the moral life (suppose this is right)—would not shift the object of compassionate concern. It is still the welfare of the other that is sought in acting. What would change is the impact of the motive in the deliberative field. A natural motive is as effective as it is strong. A normalized motive is effective as a function of its place in the deliberative field: expressing more than the natural impulse at its origin, standing aside (not pressing its claim) as there are more important concerns present, but also drawing strength from its place in overall practical conception.[25]

There is great complexity here. Motives can be embedded in or connected to other motives. Some concerns can absorb deep constraints without damage, others are fragile. Requiring civility while doing the grocery shopping introduces no grave distortions in the activity. A demand that one justify all nonnecessary expenses from the point of view of world hunger might well interfere with reasonable enjoyments. But this is a problem, if it is, of a substantive moral requirement. It does not follow from the formal fact that motives (or interests or concerns) are normalized to impartial moral principles.

Let me be clear about what I am *not* trying to say. The normalization of a natural motive does not eliminate the possibility of conflict with other moral considerations and claims. This discussion has been about the *structure* of deliberative commitments. The likelihood that the world will throw up difficulties is not diminished, though perhaps one will be, in a manner of speaking, better prepared when they occur.

Still one might worry that too little is left for deliberation to do because the process of 'normalizing' has covertly usurped its work. If one thinks that deliberation brings its principles to bear on raw data, this would be so. Part of what I have wanted to present here are reasons for thinking this not true to experience. Two larger theoretical concerns give me confidence that this way of treating deliberation is appropriate. First is the fact that Kantian deliberation, if it in any way engages with the CI procedure, applies to maxims, and maxims require exactly the normalized input I have described.[26] Second is a view about what a practical commitment to morality amounts to. The moral agent (certainly the Kantian moral agent) is not one who has some set of desires and interests and then introduces an onlay of controlling principles and rules (with a new motive to get the regulative authority right). She is rather someone who takes the fact of morality to be constitutive of herself (or her identity as a moral person) and for whom the normalization of desires and interests is a way of making them her own.

Deliberation is not called for unless the agent finds reasons in her circumstances of action or choice to believe that normal moral constraints should not apply. So, for example, in cases of threat or danger or pressing need, one may need to deliberate to determine whether such facts ground a rebuttal of the moral prohibition on, say, deceit. But such facts ground a rebuttal, if they do, not because of the degree of one's concern but because they mark the presence of additional moral facts in an agent's deliberative field.

The upshot of this discussion for the questions with which we started can be put somewhat simply. When understood within the deliberative-field model, the regulative or transformative priority of impartial morality does not cause the loss or corruption of motives of connection. We can resist the idea that any constraint of a natural motive, any move to relocate it in a structure of justification, gives it a new object. Once attachment is moved into the deliberative field, however, we must acknowledge that strength or intimacy of attachment alone does not provide grounds to rebut the demands of moral requirement.

If in deliberation moral requirement is not external to other motives, and if our understanding of morality and attachment are mutually transformative, then the motives of connection themselves can come to express the fact that attachment takes place in a world that attachment alone does not create.

III

Having argued that there is no obvious or necessary incompatibility between impartial ethics and the value of attachment, we still need to consider arguments that Kantian ethics is inimical to a sound notion of the person as moral subject.

A typical argument goes this way. In Kantian ethics, we are moral agents insofar as we have practical reason (an autonomous will). Other facts about us—what we feel, how we are connected to others, that we are empirically, socially, and historically situated—are not what make us moral agents. Since 'Kantian' persons have moral value insofar as they are moral agents, the moral value of persons does not reflect their situation or attachments (neither that we in general have them nor how, in particular, having them makes a difference). If these omitted features are central to our ideas of what a person is (and of the good for persons), then the substantive normative claims of Kantian ethics are derived from an inadequate and impoverished concept of the person as moral agent.[27] If this is true, it is a serious problem. For even if, as argued in section II, moral deliberation is informed by the facts of our attachments, interests, and specific needs, the moral principles that construct the deliberative field have their source in the 'pure' autonomous self.

Kantian autonomy is the property that the rational will has of being self-legislating. This is a metaphysical claim about the nature of rational agency. Its role is to explain both the possibility and the authority of morality. Nothing follows from it to the effect that persons are radically separate, nor that insofar as we take the moral point of view, we are not to pay attention to the distinctive features of other persons. As I need not, because I am an agent with interests, look out at the world and others from a fortress of own-interests and desires, so equally, as a moral agent, I do not look out on a world of featureless moral agents because I have an autonomous will. Whether I am preoccupied with myself or engaged with others and sensitive to differences depends on my circumstances and my conception of the Good. Perhaps it is this last bit that is the source of the problem.

Kantian ethics constrains a conception of the Good by requiring that one's deliberative field be given a certain structure (a structure implied by the nature of rational agency itself). In particular, we are never to act on a maxim that we cannot will all rational beings to act on. But, it is argued, this cannot be the right way to derive moral principles for persons, since filtering for what is possible for all rational beings (or even all human beings) cannot tell the full moral story about fully embodied and socially connected persons in specific historical settings.

We can see some of the force of this concern by looking at a second kind of criticism of Kantian autonomy. The identification of Kantian autonomy as the property of a rational will seems to ignore morally important ways in which we judge that human beings are or can fail to be autonomous. If one has Kantian autonomy as a rational being (able to act on self-given principles), Kantian autonomy may be a necessary but not a sufficient condition for 'real' moral autonomy. Ordinarily, we have reason to think that the autonomous person is not merely one who can act on principles but is, rather, the person whose situation or upbringing yields not only a character capable of practically effective critical reflection but also a character moved by desires and interests that are in some important sense her own: desires and interests that are neither the result of coercion nor the products of institutionalized oppression.[28] Lack of autonomy in this sense is compatible with Kantian autonomy. The question then is whether the Kantian conception of autonomy obscures a real issue of human autonomy, and, if it does, whether it implies that oppression cannot interfere with the most important kind of human freedom.

I want to argue that the Kantian conception of the autonomous agent neither elevates rationality to the only thing that really counts about persons nor forces us to deny that agency is compromised by the circumstances of oppression. It is true that the 'worth beyond price' of the Kantian agent is in her autonomous will. This is the ground of the claim that persons are not to be valued only for use. The contested question is whether the constraints on action that follow from this ignore the real circumstances and full nature of persons.

The best way to answer the question is to look carefully at the way specific constraints work. What I will offer here is a summary examination of the restrictions on deceit and coercion: actions that are the archetypes of impermissible use of another. What the restrictions show is that the subject of moral protection is the fully situated human agent.

Deceit is an attempt to control how another will choose to act through the introduction of relevant false beliefs into her deliberative circumstances. In coercion, threats or force alter deliberative circumstances by evoking or strengthening desires that will bring the victim to act as the coercer wills. In both cases, the impermissible actions constitute an assault on the situated integrity of the victim's agency. You would not, for what deceit or coercion do to you, cease being an autonomous agent. Deceit and coercion invade the morally supported boundaries between autonomous agents in that the aggressor regards the *situated* will—the will as it draws reasons from beliefs and desires—as a possible means to her ends.

This story does not quite describe the moral wrong involved in deceit, for I look to control the will of another when I introduce true beliefs to get someone to act as I will. The problem clearly is not control of the will in the sense of contributory cause to a deliberative outcome, since that is the case whether what I tell you is true or (known by me to be) false.

What others tell us is one of the normal ways we have access to the facts in our circumstances of action (and belief). This is an inescapable fact about human agency. Our reliance on what others say creates an area of vulnerability—a point of access to the will. Although what I want in telling you the truth can be the same as when what I say is false—that you do what I will—the full story about how I am acting can be, in morally important ways, different. In some cases when I say what is true, I tell the truth only as what I need to say in order to get you to do what I will. I have no commitment to telling you the truth in telling you the truth. If the truth will not bring you to do what I will, I am ready to tell you something else.[29] When, by contrast, I tell you the truth as truth, though I believe that if you know this truth you will do what I will (and I even tell it to you wanting you to act as I will), I tell you the truth as information of use to you as well as me. Insofar as I conceive of what I give you as information, the intent is not to control your will, though it is to contribute to the causal (here, deliberative) conditions of your action. On this principle of action, I would not tell you something if I believed it was not the case.

Of course things are not so simple. If I tell misleading partial truths, I am equally taking advantage of our situation in order to create a view of the circumstances of action which will lead you to act as I want. This kind of truthtelling is a kind of deceit. You take me to be giving relevant information, in part because I lead you to believe that is what I am doing, but also in part because it is a normal expectation that I know of and rely on. This expectation is for you a condition of belief formation. That is why you must not catch on that I am controlling the flow of information if I am to get you to act as I will. You are deceived in that you are brought (encouraged) to believe falsely that I have told you whatever I know that is relevant to your deliberation, choice, and action. And this is why when I tell you a partial truth I am manipulating your will.

The importance of this for our question about Kantian agency lies in the fact that what counts as deceit varies with the persons involved, the social conditions of expectations, particular practices, and so on. If impermissible actions are those that fail in respect for the value of the autonomous agent, respect for the autonomy of another person in cases where we wish to influence deliberation requires detailed attention to specific facts about them. This will include facts about relationships (where one person has authority over another, or responsibility for another, expectations are affected), as well as facts about the social world that bear on their circumstances of action.

The point of morality, one might say, is to regulate what can go on given the vulnerabilities of persons as agents—vulnerabilities we all share as human rational beings *and* vulnerabilities that are specific to our situations and relationships. Thus the constraints that morality imposes reflect the real conditions of effective human rational agency: the aspects of a person's circumstances of action (or deliberation) that are situated, historical, empirical. As I read it, Kantian morality not only does not ignore these features, but it makes them central to its 'derivation of duties.'

In effect, much of the critique of the Kantian conception of autonomy confuses autonomy and agency. Autonomy is the condition of the will that makes agency possible. If we were not rational beings, we would not have wills that could be interfered with. But *agency* is not completely described by identifying a will as rational. As human agents we are not distinct from our contingent ends, our culture, our history, or our actual and possible relations to others. Agency is situated. The empirical and contingent conditions of effective agency set the terms of permissibility because it is through effective agency that autonomy is expressed (made real). Here is a place where consequences matter.

The implications of the idea of deriving Kantian duties from the situation of real agents are far-reaching. If agency is situated, the conditions of agency will not be uniform. Certain features will remain constant: that we have vulnerable bodies, are mortal, are capable of acquiring new skills, that we are deceivable and vulnerable to duress. Other features will be a function of the social world in which a person acts. Matters of institutionalized subordination, dependency, questions of gender, class, and race, will need to be taken into account. This encourages us to move beyond the 'agent-to-agent' limitations of traditional interpretations of Kantian ethics, where everything that is morally relevant is found in the actions and intentions of single, separate persons.[30]

Suppose, for example, social circumstances are such that the range of successful activities is dramatically limited by inability to read and write (both in terms of opportunities to act but also for gaining skills and developing talents). Illiteracy prevents the acquisition of information necessary to effective action. In such circumstances, denial of opportunity to become literate could be judged an impermissible refusal (under mutual aid) to provide for agency-necessary needs. Since literacy is not normally a good that functions outside an institutional context—schools, publishers—the moral failure in providing real access to literacy skills will not be one that is best or completely described as occurring between individuals. (I think a similar argument can be made for provision of a minimal standard of health care.) It does not follow that one is committed to viewing literacy as necessarily making people better off regardless of their cultural circumstances. The point is to explain the circumstances in which literacy could become a moral requirement, the ground of a moral claim.[31]

In analogous fashion, there is room to talk about institutional or cultural assaults on the conditions of agency. If agent-to-agent coercion controls choice by manipulating desires (introducing penalties in order to block permissible choices), then when institutions penalize permissible choices, they act no less coercively. The chief difference in the moral analysis is, I think, that in the institutional case there can be coercion without specific intent. Quite apart from issues of dependency and lack of alternatives, it can be hard to understand the battered wife's refusal to leave her home, with its violence, without factoring in the effect of social pressures that measure adult success in terms of a woman's ability to maintain a marriage.[32]

On similar grounds I regard a recent controversy over the introduction of new brands of cigarettes targeted at particular, vulnerable groups as capturing the institutional variant of the wrong involved in agent-to-agent deceptive manipulation. Uptown and Dakota cigarettes were to be marketed to inner-city blacks and 'virile females,' respectively. Now the fact that advertising works by playing on beliefs and desires is not news. But since the conditions that make deceit possible vary from person to person and group to group, it is precisely the fine tuning of the ad campaign to trade on marks of social prestige among those both young and doubly disadvantaged that makes the moral case. (It is hard here not to see intent; but there will be other cases where the belief in the information conveyed is more credible. Certainly it was a stunning moment in the Uptown episode when a Philip Morris executive labeled as racist those who argued against the Uptown campaign on the grounds that it would exploit the special vulnerabilities of young blacks.)

On the basis of these brief remarks I want to offer two provisional conclusions. First, if agency is situated, then the fundamental moral equality of agents requires that we attend to difference when it affects the capacity for effective agency. Second, if agency is situated, and groups of people share vulnerabilities and needs that arise from institutional or nonuniversal cultural causes, then there are grounds for moral criticism of those causes that appeal to the same root values as ground agent-to-agent requirements.

This section began with a question about the relations among Kantian views of autonomy, rationality, and agential separateness. There has been no attempt to deny that autonomy and rationality are deeply connected and that both are the condition of our moral and practical capacities. On the other hand, the tremendous practical importance of autonomy and rationality in understanding the kind of agent we are does not force us to view ourselves as, from the moral point of view, wholly or essentially or even ideally rational. As we are practical agents—human agents—we are constituted by our needs, our interests, our beliefs, and our connections to others. Different aspects of our agency will be peculiar to our 'natural' condition, our social circumstances, and our particular histories. We will be free human agents—ones whose actions express autonomy—as the actual conditions of our agency allow us to deliberate and act according to a conception of the Good that is constructed not only by moral requirements but also by the pursuit and critical attention to interests that we understand to be part of a good life.

Notes

1. The vanguard of this complaint is to be found in the work of Bernard Williams, Michael Stocker, and Lawrence Blum.
2. Criticisms of the so-called justice perspective find fault this way. See Carol Gilligan, *In a Different Voice* (Cambridge: Harvard University Press, 1982), and her later introductory assay to *Women and Moral Theory*, ed. E. Kittay and D. Myers (Totowa: Rowman and Littlefield, 1987).
3. An agent's 'complete' maxim is the fully elaborated subjective principle of volition, including not only the motive and end of the action to be taken but

also the regulative conditions the agent accepts in acting. In the case imagined, the complete maxim reflects the agent's commitment to the morally required end of helping and her belief that the best means of acting in the circumstances is in a way that is expressive of connection.

4. See G399. Henning Jensen offers an interesting variant of this, arguing that a perfect duty to maintain the rights of humanity in ourselves entitles us to act from motives of connection *from* the motive of duty. See his 'Kant and Moral Integrity,' *Philosophical Studies* 57 (1989), 193–205.
5. We should at least mark that there is a question about why something that is slotted as of instrumental value does not bear the value of its end. This may have to do with a tendency to believe that instruments are fungible. It does not seem to be a necessary truth about value.
6. In a Humean mood, one might conjecture that what we take theoretical rationality to be is the manner of thinking that promotes our ends: the method of thinking that works.
7. David Gauthier, in *Morals by Agreement* (Oxford: Oxford University Press, 1986), offers an extremely sophisticated version of such an argument.
8. An example of such an account can be found in Stuart Hampshire, *Innocence and Experience* (Cambridge: Harvard University Press, 1989).
9. That someone might choose a solitary life or live well without intimate connection to others no more undermines this fact about human beings than extreme physical stoicism or a high pain threshold undermines the fact that physical assault interferes with successful human activity.
10. Thus Freud identifies an antisocial rather than a presocial role for the family in the 'origins of society.' But then, as he sees it, there is a primal antagonism between the partiality of family and the sociality of 'fraternal' bonds. See his *Civilization and Its Discontents* (New York: Norton, 1962), chap. 3.
11. I view them as facts about feelings we take to be reasons.
12. Williams' influential notion of constitutive 'ground projects' provides the most direct version of this view (see his 'Persons, Character and Morality,' in *Moral Luck*).
13. In addition to Gilligan and some of the essays in the Kittay and Myers volume, see also Nel Noddings, *Caring: A Feminine Approach to Ethics and Moral Education* (Berkeley: University of California Press, 1984).
14. Annette Baier, 'Trust and Anti-Trust,' *Ethics* 96 (1986), 252.
15. This is just an extension of Baier's point, reinforcing the claim that a moral theory must have the means to talk about connection, inequality, power, and such. A moral theory that cannot get it right about these relationships cannot generate the appropriate regulative norms.
16. Of course I would not have said this when he was six months old. But that is just the point.
17. It is not a necessary feature of the model that impartial morality has this role. I present it in this form because some such version of the plural-interest model is commonly introduced in preparation for criticism of the implausibility of the demands of impartial morality. Although I am primarily concerned with the limits of this model to represent that claim of morality, the causes of its failure in this area suggest more general inadequacies.
18. I do not mean to imply that desire must be understood to have its practical effect only in one of these two ways—in the deliberative field or as an

intensity-weighted reason. There are accounts of desire that build reasons into them. In the tradition of Kant criticism, however, the simpler Humean model of desire has been thought to suffice in showing the weaknesses of the Kantian account of practical activity. The deliberative-field model is intended both to describe more accurately Kantian practical deliberation and activity and to show certain limits of the Humean model.

19. Textual and other support for this claim can be found in Chapter 8 of *The Practice of Moral Judgment.*
20. I have borrowed this way of putting things from Philippa Foot (unpublished manuscript, 1988), who sees confusion about this occurring because often it is reasonable to satisfy desires. If we imagine a very different sort of creature who had desires that were not in general good (for it) to satisfy, it is not clear how we would then regard desires.
21. A more general conclusion of this sort is argued for in Chapter 4, section III of *The Practice of Moral Judgment.*
22. See John Rawls, 'Themes in Kant's Moral Philosophy,' in *Kant's Transcendental Deductions*, ed. E. Forster (Stanford: Stanford University Press, 1989), pp. 90–95.
23. Using metaphors this way will eventually—if not immediately—be misleading. But since all talk about deliberation is metaphoric (formalized versions no less so), the limits and presuppositions of the different pictures are worth exploration.
24. The psychological models that moral theorists use in these contexts are frequently unwarrantedly simple. We might want to think about sublimation or other strategies of object shifting (the mechanism of delayed gratification involves not just a willingness to wait for some often indefinite good, but also a release of focused task-oriented energy).
25. Bishop Butler's distinction between the strength and the authority of a motive might help here. See *Five Sermons* (Indianapolis: Hackett, 1983), p. 39.
26. This is argued in Chapter 4, section I of *The Practice of Moral Judgment.*
27. As one critic writes, 'Why assume that the sole form of human autonomy adequate to support our moral theory is one that an agent [has] in isolation from her contingent ends, her culture, history, and relations to others?' Sally Sedgwick, 'Can Kant's Ethics Survive the Feminist Critique?' *Pacific Philosophical Quarterly* 71 (1990), 22.
28. I do not mean to suggest that such desires are easy to identify, though at critical times they may come to the surface not only as plainly alien—not mine—but as identifiably other (certain desires for approval, dispositions to defer, and so on).
29. There are problems involving counterfactuals that we can ignore here.
30. Textual support for such a move is not wanting. In elaborating the duties of beneficence, Kant attends to the special moral situation of the recipient of charity: a person receiving charity is in a position in which his dignity and sense of self-worth is fragile. Kant recommends that charity be given in such a way that the giver 'make it felt that he is himself obliged by the other's acceptance or honored by it, hence that the duty is merely something that he owes' (DV453). And see Victor J. Seidler, *Kant, Respect, and Injustice* (London: Routledge and Kegan Paul, 1986), for a sensitive if highly critical treatment of Kant's views on these issues.

31. Kant, of course, makes both education and welfare a moral task of the state (and as such the grounds for coercion through taxation). See *Metaphysical Elements of Justice* 326.
32. Lenore E. Walker, *The Battered Woman Syndrome* (New York: Springer, 1984).

Part V. Rereading Nineteenth-Century Philosophers: Resentment, Irony, and the Sublime

12 On Hegel, Women, and Irony

Seyla Benhabib*

Das Bekannte überhaupt ist darum, weil es bekannt ist, nicht erkannt.

(The well-known is unknown, precisely because it is well-known.)

G. W. F. Hegel, *Phaenomenologie des Geistes*

SOME METHODOLOGICAL PUZZLES OF A FEMINIST APPROACH TO THE HISTORY OF PHILOSOPHY

The 1980s have been named 'the decade of the humanities' in the USA. In many institutions of higher learning a debate is underway as to what constitutes the 'tradition' and the 'canon' in literary, artistic and philosophical works worth transmitting to future generations in the last quarter of the twentieth century. At the center of this debate is the question: if what had hitherto been considered the major works of the Western tradition are, almost uniformly, the product of a specific group of individuals, namely propertied, white, European and North American males, how universal and representative is their message, how inclusive is their scope, and how unbiased their vision?

Feminist theory has been at the forefront of this questioning, and under the impact of feminist scholarship the surface of the canon of Western 'great works' has been forever fractured, its unity dispersed and its legitimacy challenged. Once the woman's question is raised, once we ask how a thinker conceptualizes the distinction between male and female, we experience a *Gestalt* shift: we begin to see the great thinkers of the past with a new eye, and in the words of Joan

* Seyla Benhabib, 'On Hegel, Women, and Irony', from Mary Lyndon Shanley and Carole Pateman (eds.), *Feminist Interpretations and Political Theory* (Oxford: Polity Press, 1991), 129–45. Reprinted by kind permission of the author and Blackwell publishers.

Kelly Gadol 'each eye sees a different picture.'[1] The vision of feminist theory is a 'doubled' one: one eye sees what the tradition has trained it to see, the other searches for what the tradition has told her was not even worth looking for. How is a 'feminist reading' of the tradition in fact possible? At the present, I see two dominant approaches, each with certain shortcomings.

I describe the first approach as 'the teaching of the good father.' Mainstream liberal feminist theory treats the tradition's views of women as a series of unfortunate, sometimes embarrassing, but essentially corrigible, misconceptions. Taking their inspiration from the example of a progressive thinker like John Stuart Mill, these theorists seek in the classical texts for those moments of insight into the equality and dignity of women. They are disappointed when their favorite philosopher utters inanities on the subject, but essentially hold that there is no incompatibility between the Enlightenment ideals of freedom, equality and self-realization and women's aspirations.

The second view I would characterize as 'the cry of the rebellious daughter.' Agreeing with Lacan that language is the symbolic universe which represents the 'law of the father,' and accepting that all language has been a codification of the power of the father, these rebellious daughters seek for female speech at the margins of the Western logocentric tradition. If it is impossible to think in the Western logocentric tradition without binary oppositions, then the task of feminist reading becomes the articulation not of a new set of categories but of the transcendence of categorical discourse altogether. One searches not for a new language but for a discourse at the margins of language.

Juxtaposed to these approaches, in this essay I would like to outline a 'feminist discourse of empowerment.' With the second view, I agree that the feminist challenge to the tradition cannot leave its fundamental categories unchanged. Revealing the gender subtext of the ideals of reason and the Enlightenment compromises the assumed universality of these ideals. Nonetheless, they should not be thrown aside altogether. Instead we can ask what these categories have meant for the actual lives of women in certain historical periods, and how, if women are to be thought of as subjects and not just as fulfillers of certain functions, the semantic horizon of these categories is transformed. Once we approach the tradition to recover from it women's subjectivity and their lives and activities, we hear contradictory voices, competing claims, and see that so-called 'descriptive' discourses about the sexes are but 'legitimizations' of male power. The traditional view of gender differences is the discourse of those who have won out and who have codified history as we know it. But what would the history of ideas look like from the standpoint of the victims? What ideals, aspirations and utopias of the past ran into a dead-end? Can we recapture their memory from the battleground of history? This essay attempts to apply such a 'discourse of empowerment' to G. W. F. Hegel's views of women.

Hegel's treatment of women has received increased attention in recent years under the impact of the feminist questioning of the tradition.[2] This feminist challenge has led us to ask, is Hegel's treatment of women merely a consequence of his conservative predilections? Was Hegel unable to see that he made the 'dialectic' stop at women and condemned them to an ahistorical mode of existence, outside the realms of struggle, work and diremption which in his eyes are characteristic of human consciousness as such?[3] Is the 'woman question' in Hegel's thought one more instance of Hegel's uncritical endorsement of the institutions of his time, or is this issue an indication of a flaw in the very structure of the dialectic itself? Benjamin Barber, for example, siding with the second option has recently written:

> What this paradox reveals is that Hegel's position on women is neither a product of contingency nor an effect of ad hoc prejudice. Rather, it is the necessary consequence of his belief that the 'Prejudices' of his age are in fact *the* actuality yielded by history in the epoch of liberation. Hegel does not have to rationalize them: because they *are*, they are already rational. They need only be encompassed and explained by philosophy. Spirit may guide and direct history, but ultimately, history alone can tell us where spirit means it to go.[4]

Judging, however, where 'history alone can tell . . . spirit' it means it to go, requires a more complicated and contradictory account of the family and women's position at the end of the eighteenth and the beginning of the nineteenth century in the German states than either Barber or other commentators who have looked at this issue so far have provided us with. I suggest that to judge whether or not the Hegelian dialectic has stopped at women, we must first attempt to define the 'discursive horizon' of competing claims and visions within which Hegel articulated his position. To evaluate the historical options concerning gender relations in Hegel's time, we have to move beyond the methodology of traditional text analysis to the 'doubled vision' of feminist theory. In practicing this doubled vision we do not remain satisfied with analyzing textual discourses about women, but we ask where the women themselves were at any given period in which a thinker lived. With one eye we see what stands in the text, and with the other, what the text conceals in footnotes and in the margins. What then emerges is a 'discursive space' of competing power claims. The discursive horizon of Hegel's views of women and the family are defined on the one hand by the rejection of political patriarchy (which mixes the familial with the political, the private with the public), and on the other by disapproval of and antagonism toward efforts of early female emancipation.

This essay is divided into two parts: by using the traditional method of text analysis in the first part I explore *the logic of oppositions* according to which Hegel develops his views of gender relations and of female subordination. In particular I focus on the complex relationship between reason, nature, gender and history. Second, having outlined Hegel's views of women in his political philosophy, I situate his discourse within the context of historical views on women and the family at the turn of the eighteenth century. I read Hegel against the grain; proceeding from certain footnotes and marginalia in the texts, I move toward recovering the history of those which the dialectic leaves behind.

WOMEN IN G. W. F. HEGEL'S (1770–1831) POLITICAL THOUGHT

In many respects Hegel's political philosophy heralds the end of the traditional doctrine of politics, and signals its transformation into social science. *Geist* which emerges from nature, transforms nature into a second world; this 'second nature' comprises the human, historical world of tradition, institutions, laws, and practices (*objektiver Geist*), as well as the self-reflection of knowing and acting subjects upon objective spirit, which is embodied in works of art, religion, and philosophy (*absoluter Geist*). *Geist* is a transindividual principle that unfolds in history, and whose goal is to make externality into its 'work'. *Geist* externalizes itself in history by appropriating, changing, and shaping the given such as to make it correspond to itself, to make it embody its own subjectivity, that is, reason and freedom. The transformation of substance into subject is attained when freedom and rationality are embodied in the world such that 'the realm of freedom' is actualized, and 'the world of mind [is] brought forth out of itself like a second nature.' The social world is *Substance*, that is, it has objective existence for all to see and to comprehend;[5] it is also *subject*, for what the social and ethical world is can only be known by understanding the subjectivity of the individuals who compose it.[6] With Hegel's concept of objective spirit, the object domain of modern social science, that is, individuality and society, make their appearance.

Does his concept of *Geist* permit Hegel to transcend the 'naturalistic' basis of gender conceptions in the modern period, such as to place the relation between the sexes in the social, symbolic, historical, and cultural world? Hegel, on the one hand, views the development of subjectivity and individuality within the context of a human community; on the other hand, in assigning men and women to their traditional sex roles, he codifies gender-specific differences as aspects of a rational ontology that is said to reflect the deep structure of *Geist.* Women are viewed as representing the principles of particularity (*Besonderheit*), immediacy (*Unmittelbarkeit*), naturalness (*Natürlichkeit*), and substantiality (*Substanzialität*), while men stand for universality (*Allgemeinheit*), mediacy (*Vermittlung*), freedom (*Freiheit*), and subjectivity (*Subjektivität*). Hegel develops his rational ontology of gender within a logic of oppositions.

The Thesis of the 'Natural Inequality' of the Sexes

On the basis of Hegel's observations on the family, women, and the rearing of children, scattered throughout the *Lectures on the Philosophy of History*, I conclude that he was well aware that differences among the sexes were culturally, symbolically, and socially constituted. For example, in the section on Egypt, Hegel refers to Herodotus' observations 'that the women urinate standing up, while men sit, that the men wear one dress, and the women two; the women were engaged in outdoor occupations, while the men remained at home to weave. In one part of Egypt polygamy prevailed; in another, monogamy. His general judgment on the matter is that the Egyptians do the exact opposite of all other peoples.'[7]

Hegel's own reflections on the significance of the family among the Chinese, the great respect that is shown to women in this culture, and his comment on the Chinese practice of concubinage again indicate an acute awareness that the role of women is not naturally but culturally and socially defined.[8]

These passages show a clear awareness of the cultural, historical, and social variations in family and sexual relations. Nevertheless, although Hegel rejects that differences between 'men' and 'women' are naturally defined, and instead sees them as part of the spirit of a people (*Volksgeist*), he leaves no doubt that he considers only one set of family relations and one particular division of labor between the sexes as rational and normatively right. This is the monogamic sexual practice of the European nuclear family, in which the woman is confined to the private sphere and the man to the public. To justify this arrangement, Hegel explicitly invokes the superiority of the male to the female while acknowledging their *functional complementarity* in the modern state.

The 'Superiority' of the Male

The most revealing passages in this respect are paragraphs 165 and 166 of the *Philosophy of Right* and the additions to them. In the Lasson edition of the *Rechtsphilosophie*, Hegel writes that 'The natural determinacies of both sexes acquire through its reasonableness *intellectual* as well as *ethical* significance.'[9] This explicit reference to the 'natural determinacies of the sexes' is given an ontological significance in the next paragraph:

> Thus one sex is mind in its self-diremption into explicit self-subsistence and the knowledge and volition of free universality, i.e. the self-consciousness of conceptual thought and the volition of the objective final end. The other sex is mind maintaining itself in unity as knowledge and volition in the form of concrete individuality and feeling. In relation to externality, the former is powerful and active, the latter passive and subjective. It follows that man has his actual substantive life in the state, in learning, and so forth, as well as in labour and struggle with the external world and with himself so that it is only out of his diremption that he fights his way to self-subsistent unity with himself. In the family he has a tranquil intuition of this unity, and there he lives a subjective ethical life on the plane of feeling. Woman, on the other hand, has her substantive destiny in the family, and to be imbued with family piety is her ethical frame of mind.[10]

For Hegel men's lives are concerned with the state, science, and work in the external world. Dividing himself (*sich entzweiend*) from the unity of the family, man objectifies the external world and conquers it through activity and freedom. The woman's 'substantial determination,' by contrast, is in the family, in the unity and piety (*Pietät*) characteristic of the private sphere. Hegel suggests that woman are not *individuals*, at least, not in the same measure and to the same extent as men are. They are incapable of the spiritual struggle and diremption (*Entzweiung*) which characterize the lives of men. In a passage from the *Phänomenologie* concerned with the tragedy of

Antigone, he indicates that for the woman 'it is not *this* man, not *this* child, but *a man* and *children in general*' that is significant.[11] The man by contrast, individuates his desires, and 'since he possesses as a citizen the self-conscious power of universality, he thereby acquires the right of desire and, at the same time, preserves his freedom in regard to it.'[12]

Most significant is the fact that those respects in which Hegel considers men and women to be spiritually different are precisely those aspects that define women as 'lesser' human beings. Like Plato and Aristotle, Hegel not only assigns particularity, intuitiveness, passivity to women, and universality, conceptual thought, and 'the powerful and the active' to men, but sees in men the characteristics that define the species as human. Let us remember that *Geist* constitutes second nature by emerging out of its substantial unity into *bifurcation* (*Entzweiung*), where it sets itself over and against the world. The process through which nature is humanized and history constituted is this activity of *Entzweiung*, followed by *externalization* (*Entäusserung*), namely the *objectification* (*Vergegenständlichung*) of human purposes and institutions in a world such that the world becomes a home for human self-expression. Women, since they cannot overcome unity and emerge out of the life of the family into the world of *universality*, are excluded from history-constituting activity. Their activities in the private realm, namely, reproduction, the rearing of children, and the satisfaction of the emotional and sexual needs of men, place them outside the world of *work*. This means that women have no history, and are condemned to repeat the cycles of life.

The Family and Political Life

By including the family as the first stage of ethical life (*Sittlichkeit*), alongside 'civil society' and 'the state,' Hegel reveals how crucial, in his view, this institution is to the constitution of the modern state. The family is significant in Hegel's political architectonic because it is the sphere in which the right of the modern individual to particularity (*Besonderheit*) and subjectivity (*Subjektivität*) is realized.[13] As Hegel often notes, the recognition of the 'subjective moment' of the free individual is the chief strength of the modern state when compared to the ancient *polis*. In the family the right to particularity is exercised in love and in the choice of spouse, whereas the right to subjectivity is exercised in the concern for the welfare and moral well-being of other family members.

The various Additions to the section on the family, particularly in the Griesheim edition of the *Philosophy of Right*,[14] reveal that Hegel is concerned with this institution, not like Aristotle in order to discipline women, nor like Rousseau to prepare the true citizens of the future, but primarily from the standpoint of the freedom of the male subject in the modern state. Already in the *Philosophy of History*, Hegel had observed that the confusion of familial with political authority resulted in *patriarchalism*, and in China as well as in India this had as consequence the suppression of the freedom of the will through the legal regulation of family life and of relations within it. The decline of *political patriarchy* also means a strict separation between the private and the public, between the moral and intimate spheres, and the domain of public law. The legal system stands at the beginning and at the end of family; it circumscribes it but does not control its internal functioning or relations. It recognizes and administers, along with the church, the marriage contract as well as legally guaranteeing rights of inheritance when the family unit is dissolved. In this context, Hegel allows women certain significant legal rights.

He radically criticizes Kant for including women, children, and domestic servants under the category of *jura realiter personalia* or *Personen-Sachen-Recht*.[15] Women are persons, that is, legal-juridical subjects along with men. They are free to choose their spouse;[16] they can own property, although once married, the man represents the family 'as the legal person against others.'[17] Nevertheless, women are entitled to property inheritance in the case of death and even in the case of divorce.[18] Hegel is against all Roman and feudal elements of the law that would either revert family property back to the family clan (*die Sippe*), or that would place restrictions on its full inheritance and alienability.[19]

The legal issue besides property rights that most concerns Hegel is that of divorce. Divorce presents a particular problem because, as a phenomenon, it belongs under two categories at once. On the one hand, it is a legal matter just as the marriage contract is; on the other hand, it is an issue that belongs to the 'ethical' sphere, and more specifically to the subjectivity of the individuals involved. Hegel admits that because the bodily-sensual as well as spiritual attraction and love of two particular individuals form the basis of the marriage contract, an alienation between them can take place that justifies divorce; but this is only to be determined by an impersonal third-party authority, for instance, a court.[20] Finally, Hegel justifies monogamy as the only form of marriage that is truly compatible with the *individuality* of personality, and the subjectivity of feeling. In an addition to this paragraph in the Griesheim lectures he notes that monogamy is the only marriage form truly compatible with the equality of men and women.[21]

Contrary to parroting the prejudices of his time, or ontologizing them, as Benjamin Barber suggests, with respect to the right of the free choice of spouse, women's property and divorce rights, Hegel is an Enlightenment thinker, who upholds the transformations in the modern world initiated by the French Revolution and the spread of the revolutionary Code Civil. According to the Prussian *Das Allgemeine Landrecht* of 1794, the right of the free choice of spouse and in particular marriage among members of the various *Stände*—the feudal stratas of medieval society—was strictly forbidden. It was legally stipulated 'that male persons from the nobility . . . could not enter into marriage . . . with female persons of peasant stock or the lesser bourgeoisie (*geringerem Bürgerstand*).'[22] If such marriages nonetheless occurred, they were declared 'null' and the judges 'were not empowered to accept their continuation.'[23] To avoid social dilemmas, the lawgivers then distinguished between 'the lesser' and 'the higher bourgeoisie.'

Hegel's position on this issue, by contrast, follows the revolutionary proclamations of the French Assembly which, codified as the 'Code Civil' in 1804, were also adopted in those parts of Germany conquered by Napoleon.[24] Social strata differences are irrelevant to the choice of spouse and must not be legally regulated: the free will and consent of two adults (as well as of their parents), as long as they are legally entitled to marriage (that is, have not been married before or otherwise have falsified their civil status), is the only relevant point of view.

Yet Hegel inserts an interesting detail in considering this issue, which is wholly characteristic of his general attitude towards modernity. Distinguishing between the extremes of arranged marriages and the wholly free choice of spouse, he argues that: 'The more ethical way to matrimony may be taken to be the former extreme or any way at all whereby the decision to marry comes first and the inclination to do so follows, so that in the actual wedding both decision and inclination coalesce.'[25] Presumably this decision can also involve such relevant 'ethical' considerations as the social background and appropriateness of the spouses involved. Consideration of social origin and wealth are now no longer legal matters to be regulated, as they were in feudal society, but personal and ethical criteria to be kept in view by modern individuals, aware of the significance, as the British Hegelian Bradley named it, of 'my station and its duties.'

While Hegel certainly was ahead of the Prussian legal practices of his time, and endorsed the general transformations brought about by the French Revolutionary Code Civil, he was, as always, reluctant to follow modernity to its ultimate conclusion and view the choice of spouse as a wholly individual matter of love and inclination between two adults. Hegel's views on love and sexuality, when placed within the larger context of changes taking place at this point in history, in fact reveal him to be a counter-Enlightenment thinker. Hegel surreptitiously criticizes and denigrates attempts at early women's emancipation and seeks to imprison women once more within the confines of the monogamous, nuclear family which they threatened to leave.

THE QUESTION OF FREE LOVE AND SEXUALITY: THE THORN IN HEGEL'S SIDE

Hegel's 1797–8 'Fragment on Love' reflects a more romantic conception of love and sexuality than the tame and domesticized view of marriage in the *Rechtsphilosophie*. Here love is given the dialectical structure of spirit; it is unity in unity and separateness; identity in identity and difference. In love, lovers are a 'living' as opposed to a 'dead' whole; the one aspect of dead matter that disrupts the unity of love is property. Property separates lovers by making them aware of their individuality as well as destroying their reciprocity. 'True union or love proper exists only between living beings who are alike in power and thus in one another's eyes living beings from every point of view . . . This genuine love excludes all oppositions.'[26]

Yet the discussion of the family in the *Philosophy of Right* is in general more conservative and criticizes the emphasis on free love as leading to libertinage and promiscuity. One of the objects of Hegel's greatest ire is Friedrich von Schlegel's *Lucinde*, which Hegel names 'Die romantische Abwertung der Ehe' ('the romantic denigration of love').[27] To demand free sexuality as proof of freedom and 'inwardness' is in Hegel's eyes sophistry, serving the exploitation of women. Hegel, in smug bourgeois fashion, observes:

> Friedrich v. Schlegel in his *Lucinde*, and a follower of his in the *Briefe eines Ungennanten*, have put forward the view that the wedding ceremony is superfluous and a formality which might be discarded. Their reason is that love is, so they say, the substance of marriage and that the celebration therefore detracts from its worth. Surrender to sensual impulse is here represented

as necessary to prove the freedom and inwardness of love—an argument not unknown to seducers.

And he continues:

It must be noticed in connexion with sex-relations that a girl in surrendering her body loses her honour. With a man, however, the case is otherwise, because he has a field for ethical activity outside the family. A girl is destined in essence for the marriage tie and for that only; it is therefore demanded of her that love shall take the form of marriage and that the different moments in love shall attain their true rational relation to each other.[28]

Taking my cue from this footnote in the text, I want to ask what this aside reveals and conceals at once about Hegel's true attitudes toward female emancipation in this period. The seemingly insignificant reference to Friedrich Schlegel's *Lucinde* is extremely significant in the context of the struggles for early women's emancipation at this time.

Remarking on the transformations brought about by the Enlightenment and the French Revolution, Mary Hargrave has written:

The close of the eighteenth and the beginning of the nineteenth centuries mark a period of Revolution for men and Evolution for women. The ideas of the French Revolution, that time of upheaval, of revaluing of values, of imperious assertion of the rights of the individual, swept over Europe like a quickening wind and everywhere there was talk of Liberty, Equality, Fraternity, realised (and perhaps only realisable) in that same order of precedence . . .

The minds of intellectual women were stirred, they became more conscious of themselves, more philosophic, more independent . . . France produced a writer of the calibre of Madame de Stäel, England a Mary Sommerville, a Jane Austen; and Germany, although the stronghold of the domestic ideal, also had her brilliant intellectual women who, outside their own country, have perhaps not become as widely known as they deserve.[29]

In this work devoted to *Some German Women and their Salons*, Mary Hargrave discusses Henriette Herz (1764–1847) and Rahel Varnhagen (1771–1833), both Jewesses, Bettina von Arnim (1785–1859), and Caroline Schlegel (1763–1809), among others. Of particular importance in this context is also Karoline von Günderode (1780–1806), the most significant woman German poet of the Romantic era, in love with Hegel's high-school friend, Hölderlin. These women, through their lives and friendships, salons and contacts, and in some cases through their letters, publications and translations, were not only forerunners of the early women's emancipation, but also represented a new model of gender relations, aspiring to equality, free love and reciprocity.

Definitive for Hegel's own contact with these women and their ideals, was the so-called Jenaer Kreis, the Jena circle, of the German Romantics, Friedrich and August Wilhelm Schlegel, Novalis, Schleiermacher, and Schelling. The journal *Athenäum* (1798–1800) was the literary outlet of this circle, frequented by Goethe as well as Hegel after his arrival in Jena in 1801. The 'Jena circle' had grown out of friendship and literary cooperation among men but counted Caroline Schlegel among its most influential members. She had extraordinary impact on the Schlegel brothers, and was the inspiration for many of Friedrich Schlegel's literary characters as well as for his views on women, marriage and free love.[30] It is widely believed that Caroline Schlegel was the model for the heroine in the novel *Lucinde.*

Born as Caroline Albertina Michaelis, in Göttingen, as the daughter of a professor of Old Testament, Caroline was brought up in an intellectual household.[31] Following traditional patterns, in 1784 she married a young country doctor Georg Böhmer and moved from Göttingen to Clausthal, a mining village in the Hartz mountains. Although she suffered from the narrowness of her new surroundings and from the lack of intellectual stimulation, she remained here until suddenly her husband died in 1788. Caroline, who was then mother of three, lost two of her children after her husband's death. With her daughter Auguste Böhmer, she returned to the parental city. At Göttingen she met August Wilhelm Schlegel, six years her junior, who fell in love with her. In 1792 she left Göttingen for Mainz, the home now of her childhood friend Teresa Forster, born Heym. In December 1792 the city fell to the French under General Custine; the aristocrats fled and the republic was proclaimed. Teresa's husband, Forster, who was an ardent republican, was made president of the Jacobin Club. His wife, no longer in sympathy with his views, left him but Caroline stayed on and worked with revolutionary circles. In the spring of the following year, 1793, a German army mustered from Rheinisch principalities, retook Mainz. Caroline was arrested and with her little daughter Auguste was imprisoned in a fortress. After some months, her brother petitioned for her release, offering his services as an army surgeon in return, and August Wilhelm Schlegel exercised what influence he could to obtain her freedom.

Caroline was freed, but was banned from the Rheinisch provinces; even Göttingen, her home town, closed its doors to her. She was now pregnant, expecting the child of a French soldier, and August Wilhelm arranged for her to be put under the protection of his brother, Friedrich, then a young student in Leipzig. A lodging outside the city had to be found for her; here a child was born, but it did not live. In 1796, urged by her family and realizing the need for a protector, Caroline agreed to become August Schlegel's wife and settled with him in Jena. She never really loved Schlegel, and with the appearance of the young Schelling on the scene in 1798 a new love started in her life. Caroline's daughter, Auguste, died in July 1800. Schlegel settled in Berlin in 1802, and the increasing estrangement between them was resolved by a divorce in 1803. A few months later, she and Schelling were married by his father, a pastor, and they lived in Jena until her death in 1809.

Hegel lived in the same house with Caroline and Schelling from 1801 to 1803, and certainly the presence of this remarkable woman, an intellectual companion, a revolutionary, a mother, and a lover, provided Hegel with a flesh and blood example of what modernity, the Enlightenment and the French Revolution could mean for women. And Hegel did not like what he saw. Upon her death, he writes to Frau Niethammer: 'I kiss a thousand times over the beautiful hands of the best woman. God may and shall preserve her as befits her merit ten times longer than the woman of whose death we recently learned here [Caroline Schelling], and of whom a few here have enunciated the hypothesis that the Devil had fetched her.'[32] A damning and unkind remark, if there ever was one!

Whether Hegel should have liked or approved of Caroline, who certainly exercised a caustic and sharp power of judgment over people, making and remaking some reputations in her circle of friends—Schiller's for example—is beside the point. The point is that Caroline's life and person provided an example, and a very close one at that, of the kinds of changes that were taking place in women's lives at the time, of the possibilities opening before them, and also of the transformation of gender relations. In staunchly defending women's place in the family, in arguing against women's education except by way of learning the necessary skills to run a household, Hegel was not just 'falling prey to the prejudices of his time.' 'His time' was a revolutionary one, and in the circles closest to Hegel, that of his Romantic friends, he encountered brilliant, accomplished and nonconformist women who certainly intimated to him what true gender equality might mean in the future. Hegel saw the future, and he did not like it. His eventual critique of Romantic conceptions of free love is also a critique of the early Romantics' aspirations to gender equality or maybe some form of androgyny.

Schlegel's novel *Lucinde* was written as a eulogy to love as a kind of union to be enjoyed both spiritually and physically. In need of neither religious sanction—Lucinde is Jewish—nor formal ceremony, such true love was reciprocal and complete.[33] In the Athäneums-Fragment 34, Schlegel had defined conventional marriages as 'concubinages' to which a 'marriage à quatre' would be preferable.[34] *Lucinde* is a critical text, juxtaposing to the subordination of women and the duplicitous sexual conduct of the times a utopian ideal of true love as completion between two independent beings. Most commentators agree, however, that *Lucinde*, despite all noble intentions, is not a text of female emancipation: Lucinde's artistic pursuits, once they have demonstrated the equality of the lovers, cease to be relevant. The letters document Julius's development as a man, his *Lehrjahre*, his movement from sexual desire dissociated from respect and equality to his attainment of the ultimate companionship in a spiritually and erotically satisfying relationship. Women are idealized journey-mates, accompanying the men on this spiritual highway. 'Seen on the one hand as the complementary opposites of men, embodying the qualities their counterparts lack, they are on the other, complete beings idealized to perfection.'[35] Although in a section of the novel called 'A dithyrambic fantasy on the loveliest situation in the world,'[36] there is a brief moment of reversal of roles in sexual activity which Julius sees as 'a wonderful . . . allegory of the development of male and female to full and complete humanity,'[37] in general in the *Lucinde*, the spiritual characteristics of the two genders are clearly distinguished.

In his earlier essays such as 'Über die weiblichen Charaktere in den griechischen Dichtern' and 'Über die Diotima' (1793–4), composed after meeting Caroline Schlegel Schelling, and being enormously influenced by her person, Friedrich Schlegel had developed the thesis—to be echoed later by Marx in the *1844 Manuscripts*—that Greek civilization decayed or flourished in proportion to the degree of equality it accorded to women. In particular, Schlegel emphasized that inequality between men and women, and the subordination of women, led to a bifurcation in the human personality, whereby men came to lack 'innocence, grace and love,' and women 'independence.' As opposed to the crudeness of male–female relations in Homer, Sophocles in Schlegel's eyes is the poet who conceives his male and female characters according to the same design and the same ideal. It is Antigone who combines the male and female personality into an androgynous ideal: she 'desires only the true Good, and accomplishes it without strain,' in contrast to her sister, Ismene, the more traditional feminine, who 'suffers in silence.'[38] Antigone transcends these stereotypes and represents a blending of male and female characteristics; she 'is the Divine.'

Read against the background of Schlegel's views, Hegel's generally celebrated discussion of Antigone in the *Phenomenology of Spirit* reveals a different message. In Hegel's version of Antigone, she and Creon respectively stand for 'female' and 'male' virtues, and forms of ethical reality. Antigone represents the 'hearth,' the gods of the family, of kinship and of the 'nether world.'[39] Creon stands for the law, for the city, human law and the dictates of politics that are of 'this world'. Their clash is a clash between equal powers; although through her acknowledgement of guilt, Antigone presents that moment in the dialectic of action and fate which Hegel considers necessary, it is eventually through the decline of the family and the 'nether world' that Spirit will progress to the Roman realm of law and further to the public light of the Enlightenment. Spiritually, Antigone is a higher figure than Creon, although even the most sympathetic commentators have to admit that what Hegel has accomplished here is 'an apologia for Creon.'[40]

Ironically, Hegel's discussion of the *Antigone* is more historically accurate in terms of the condition of Greek women, their confinement to the home, and the enormous clash between the newly emerging order of the *polis* and the laws of the extended family on which Greek society until the sixth and seventh centuries had rested than was Schlegel's.[41] But in his version of Antigone, Hegel was not simply being historically more accurate than Schlegel; he was robbing his romantic friends of an ideal, of a utopian vision. If Antigone's greatness derives precisely from the fact that she represents the ties of the 'hearth and blood' over and against the *polis*, notwithstanding her grandeur, the dialectic will sweep Antigone in its onward historical march, precisely because the law of the city is public as opposed to private, rational as opposed to corporal, promulgated as opposed to intuited, human as opposed to divine. Hegel's narrative envisages no future synthesis of these pairs of opposites as did Schlegel's; whether on a world-historical scale or on the individual scale, the female principle must eventually be expelled from public life, for 'Womankind—the everlasting irony (in the life) of the community—changes by intrigue the universal end of the government into a private end.'[42] Spirit may fall into irony for a brief historical moment, but eventually the serious transparency of reason will discipline women and eliminate irony from public life. Already in Hegel's discussion of Antigone, that strain of restorationist thought, which will celebrate the revolution while condemning the revolutionaries for their actions, is present. Hegel's Antigone is one without a future; her tragedy is also the grave of utopian, revolutionary thinking about gender relations. Hegel, it turns out, is women's gravedigger, confining them to a grand but ultimately doomed phase of the dialectic, which 'befalls mind in its infancy.'

What about the dialectic then, that locomotive of history rushing on its onward march? There is no way to disentangle the march of the dialectic in Hegel's system from the body of the victims on which it treads. Historical necessity requires its victims, and women have always been among the numerous victims of history. What remains of the dialectic is what Hegel precisely thought he could dispense with: irony, tragedy and contingency. He was one of the first to observe the ironic dialectic of modernity: freedom that could become abstract legalism or selfish pursuit of economic satisfaction; wealth that could turn into its opposite and create extremes of poverty; moral choice that would end in a trivial project of self-aggrandizement; and an emancipated subjectivity that could find no fulfillment in its 'other.' Repeatedly, the Hegelian system expunges the irony of the dialectic: the subject posits its opposite and loses itself in its other, but is always restored to selfhood via the argument that the 'other' is but an extension or an exteriorization of oneself. Spirit is infinitely generous, just like a woman; it gives of itself; but unlike women, it has the right to call what it has contributed 'mine' and take it back into itself. The vision of Hegelian reconciliation has long ceased to convince: the otherness of the other is that moment of irony, reversal and inversion with which we must live. What women can do today is to restore irony to the dialectic, by deflating the pompous march of historical necessity—a locomotive derailed, as Walter Banjamin observed—and by giving back to the victims of the dialectic like Caroline Schlegel Schelling their otherness, and this means, in true dialectical fashion, their selfhood.

Notes

Some of the material in this essay formerly appeared as Seyla Benhabib and Linda Nicholson, 'Politische Philosophie und die Frauenfrage,' in Iring Fetscher and Herfried Münkler, eds, *Pipers Handbuch der politischen Ideen*, vol. 5 (Munich/Zurich: Piper Verlag, 1987), pp. 513–62. I would like to thank Linda Nicholson for her agreement to let me use some of this material in the present article.

1. Joan Kelly Gadol, 'Some Methodological Implications of the Relations Between the Sexes,' *Women, History and Theory* (Chicago: University of Chicago Press, 1984), pp. 1 ff.
2. Cf. Genevieve Lloyd, *The Man of Reason: 'Male' and 'Female' in Western Philosophy* (Minneapolis: University of Minnesota Press, 1984); Patricia J. Mills, *Woman, Nature and Psyche* (New Haven: Yale University Press, 1987); Benjamin Barber, 'Spirit's Phoenix and History's Owl,' *Political Theory*, 16(1), 1988, pp. 5–29.
3. Cf. Heidi Ravven, 'Has Hegel Anything to Say to Feminists?', *The Owl of Minerva*, 19(2), 1988, pp. 149–68.
4. Barber, 'Spirit's Phoenix and History's Owl,' p. 20. Emphasis in the text.
5. Hegel, *Hegel's Philosophy of Right*, trans. and ed. T. M. Knox (Oxford: Oxford University Press, 1973), para. 144, p. 105.
6. Ibid., para. 146, pp. 105–6.
7. G. W. F. Hegel, *Vorlesungen über die Philosophie der Weltgeschichte*, in *Hegels Sämtliche Werke*, ed. G. Lasson, vol. 8 (Leipzig, 1923), p. 471. English translation by J. Sibree, *The Philosophy of History* (New York: Dover, 1956), p. 205. Since Sibree's translation diverged from the original in this case, I have used my translation of this passage.
8. *Philosophy of History*, trans. Sibree, pp. 121–2.
9. I have revised the Knox translation of this passage in *Hegel's Philosophy of Right*, para. 165, p. 114, in accordance with Hegel, *Grundlinien der Philosophie des Rechts*, ed. Lasson, para. 165, p. 144. Emphasis in the text.
10. *Hegel's Philosophy of Right*, ed. Knox, para. 166, p. 114.
11. G. W. F. Hegel, *Phänomenologie des Geistes*, ed. J. Hoffmeister, Philosophische Bibliothek, vol. 114 (Hamburg, 1952), p. 326. English translation by A. V. Miller, *Hegel's Phenomenology of Spirit* (New York: Oxford University Press, 1977), p. 274. Emphasis in the text.
12. Ibid.
13. *Hegel's Philosophy of Right*, ed. Knox, paras. 152, 154, p. 109.
14. Cf. the excellent edition by K. H. Ilting, prepared from the lecture notes of K. G. V. Griesheim (1824–5), *Philosophie des Rechts* (Stuttgart: Klet-Cotta, 1974), vol. 6.
15. *Hegel's Philosophy of Right*, ed. Knox, para. 40 Addition, p. 39; cf. also Griesheim edition, para. 40 Z, pp. 180–1.
16. *Hegel's Philosophy of Right*, ed. Knox, para. 168, p. 115.
17. Ibid., para. 171, p. 116.
18. Ibid., para. 172, p. 117.
19. The one exception to this rule is the right of primogeniture, that is, that the oldest son among the landed nobility receives the family estate. It has long been observed that here Hegel indeed supported the historical interests of the landed Prussian gentry against the generally bourgeois ideology of free and unencumbered property and commodity transactions, which he defended in the rest of his system. However, on this issue as well Hegel is a modernist insofar as his defense of primogeniture among the members of the landed estate is justified not with reference to some family right but with reference to securing an independent income for the eldest son of the family, who is to function as a political representative of his class. Cf. *Hegel's Philosophy of Right*, ed. Knox, para. 306 and Addition, p. 293.

20. Ibid., para. 176, p. 118.
21. *Philosophie des Rechts*, Griesheim edition, para. 167 Z, p. 446.
22. Hans Ulrich Wehler, *Deutsche Gesellschaftsgeschichte* (Darmstadt: C. H. Verlag, 1987), vol. 1, p. 147.
23. Ibid.
24. Emil Friedberg, *Das Recht der Eheschliessung* (Leipzig: Bernhard Tauchnitz, 1865), pp. 593 ff.
25. *Hegel's Philosophy of Right*, ed. Knox, para. 162, p. 111.
26. G. W. F. Hegel, 'Love,' in his *Early Theological Writings*, trans. T. M. Knox (Philadelphia: University of Pennsylvania Press, 1971, p. 304).
27. *Hegel's Philosophy of Right*, ed. Knox, para. 164 Addition, p. 263; cf. Griesheim edition, p. 436.
28. *Hegel's Philosophy of Right*, ed. Knox, para. 164, p. 263.
29. Mary Hargrave, *Some German Women and their Salons* (New York: Brentano, n.d.), p. viii.
30. Cf. ibid., pp. 259 ff; Kurt Lüthi, *Feminismus und Romantik* (Vienna: Harmann Böhlaus Nachf., 1985), pp. 56 ff.
31. Cf. ibid., pp. 251 ff.
32. G. W. F. Hegel, *The Letters*, trans. Clark Butler and Christiane Seiler (Bloomington: Indiana University Press, 1984), p. 205.
33. Friedrich Schlegel, *Friedrich Schlegel's Lucinde and the Fragments*, trans. and intro. Peter Frichow (Minneapolis: University of Minnesota Press, 1971); cf. Sara Friedrichsmeyer, *The Androgyne in Early German Romanticism*, Stanford German Studies, vol. 18 (New York: Peter Lang, 1983), pp. 151 ff.
34. Schlegel, *Lucinde and the Fragments*, p. 165.
35. Friedrichsmeyer, *Androgyne*, p. 160; cf. also, Lüthi, *Feminismus und Romantik*, pp. 95ff.
36. Schlegel, *Lucinde and the Fragments*, pp. 46 ff.
37. Ibid., p. 49.
38. Cited in Friedrichsmeyer, *Androgyne*, p. 120.
39. Hegel, *Phenomenology of Spirit*, p. 276.
40. George Steiner, *Antigones* (New York: Oxford University Press, 1984), p. 41.
41. Hegel's reading of Antigone is more inspired by Aeschylus, who in his *Oresteia* exposed the clash between the early and the new orders as a clash between the female power of blood and the male power of the sword and the law. The decision to speak Orestes free of the guilt of matricide is signalled by an astonishingly powerful statement of the clash between the maternal power of birth and the paternal power of the law. Athena speaks on behalf of Orestes: 'It is my task to render final judgement: / this vote which I possess / I will give on Orestes' side / For no mother had a part in *my* birth; / I am entirely male, with all my heart, / except in marriage; I am entirely my father's. / I will never give precedence in honor / to a woman who killed her man, the guardian of her house. / So if the votes are but equal, Orestes wins.' Aeschylus, *The Oresteia*, trans. David Grene and Wendy O'Flaherty (Chicago: University of Chicago Press, 1989), pp. 161–2.
42. Hegel, *Phenomenology of Spirit*, p. 288.

13 We Are Not Sublime: Love and Sacrifice, Abraham and Ourselves

Sylviane Agacinski*

When I started re-reading *Fear and Trembling*, a few years after I had written *Aparté*,[1] I found myself fascinated once again by what Johannes de Silentio calls the *sublimity* of Abraham's sacrifice, and my reflections here still bear the mark of that fascination.[2] The 'here I am' with which Abraham replied to the God who was demanding the death of his son was always, for me, a paradigm of faith, of utter devotion, of the absolute risk of religious love. It seemed to offer a glimpse of a mysterious heroism that surpassed not only our understanding, but that of the religious poet too, or rather the poet of the religious.[3] But now, returning to *Fear and Trembling* after a long absence, I am more suspicious of this exaltation of greatness, immensity and the absolute, and I have suspicions about the idea of the formless and the faceless too. The sublime and the sentiment of the sublime presuppose some absolute greatness in comparison with which, as Kant says, 'all else is small'.[4] However much they may differ amongst themselves, all thoughts of the sublime, all eulogies to it, necessarily proceed by reference to some conception of sacrifice, a conception for which the idea of sacrificing a tiny remnant, the little one, will always be possible or conceivable.

For me, the question raised by the theme of the sublime affects any way of thinking which either takes itself to be somehow capable of infinity, or else suffers as a result of its incapacity for it.[5] The sublime call or demand that issues from the infinite or the absolute involves a condemnation of finitude, a condemnation which is present in all forms of nostalgia for the incommensurable.

* Sylviane Agacinski, 'We Are Not Sublime: Love and Sacrifice, Abraham and Ourselves', from Jonathan Rée and Jane Chamberlain (eds.), *Kierkegaard: A Critical Reader* (Oxford: Blackwell, 1998), 129–51. First published in this version in Sylviane Agacinski, *Critique de l'égocentrisme* (Paris: Galilée, 1996). Translation © Jonathan Rée. Reprinted by kind permission of Jonathan Rée, Philosophy Department, Middlesex University.

In this respect the legacy of Kierkegaard is at the very least twofold. As a thinker of existence, he recalls existing individuals to their finitude, blocking off all access to the point of view of the absolute, and forcing us back to our first responsibility, our primary task: namely, to have our being in the mode of existence. He confronts existing individuals with the unappeasable responsibility which requires that an arch-decision be made: the decision to exist as a singularity in time.

But on the other hand, to the extent that existence is derived and created, it also reveals itself as difference. The other—in the shape of the father or God—will always have gone before it and marked it in advance. Existence is always infinitely indebted to this absolute antecedence, this inconceivable origin. In order to take up the burden of this originary debt, the existing individual must take up the passion and panic of thought itself (of intelligence), and learn to vindicate or even love the fact that, in relation to God, it is always *in the wrong*. Thus Kierkegaard not only calls on us to think from within finite existence; he also insists on the absolute wrongness of finitude.

It is the same as Antigone: the existing individual is primarily an inheritor, that is to say a child; but the choice of existence may also be that of sacrifice, of a sacrificed existence. The child wants to remain 'hidden within its father'.

Let me also comment on the first word of my title: *We* are not sublime. It could be the *we* of a single epoch or it could be the *we* of several: Kierkegaard's and our own, for example. Or it could be the *we* of those who are simply *bewildered* by Abraham's faith—those who, regretfully or not, have (so to speak) lost their capacity for the sublime: for instance, those who can no longer sustain any relationship with the absolute, the great and the eternal; or perhaps those who no longer need to sustain it, because they have moved beyond the contradiction between the finite and the infinite (a Hegelian *we*, as it might be).

Or it might be a *we* by which I speak to someone indirectly, as Søren spoke to Regine in so many of his writings. It might, for example, be a way of saying 'we ought to be able to love each other eternally following our loss—if only we were sublime. . . . '. Or again, to say to another: 'We know we lack eternity, but this knowledge means that we do not lack it after all. We have time; but we have nothing else. We are not sublime.' Which would imply: above all let us avoid being sublime, for everything that exists is *finite*.

Fear and Trembling is all about the question of trembling in the face of sacrifice. Did Abraham tremble? And who is it in us that fears

Abraham and trembles before him? It is about silence as well. Abraham stayed silent: after all what could he have said? And it is also about reason—the kind of rationality that seeks to ward off the ever-present threat of criminality, by setting up laws and the universality of law in the hope of eliminating the risk that the individual will be led astray by faith, led into an aside [*aparté*] with God. So was Abraham sublime? Can the question make any sense for us? Surely not: we have no way of getting the gods to speak. There is nothing for us to listen for. But Abraham was the man who listened to God.

Johannes de Silentio was a poet, a poet of the religious. And Johannes tells us: 'Look at Abraham, he is sublime.' But he also says, in effect: 'I myself am incapable of faith, I am only the poet of the Knight of Faith.'[6] Thus we are already within the field of aesthetics.

So can the sublime be understood other than as an aesthetic category? If we described Abraham's religious faith by means of the category of 'sublimity', would this not signal a forgetting of religiosity? But perhaps Johannes never speaks of anything else except this irrevocable forgetting.

Abraham's duty was both secret and scandalous. He was the man who would not allow himself to be tempted by moral duty, his duty as a father—a duty that anyone could understand, whereas no one could share in the unique unreason of his obedience. His madness, the madness of faith, lies in this absolute singularity: Abraham's relationship with God is that of one absolute to another. It cannot be confined to the moral order or the universality of law: morality has to be 'teleologically suspended'. There is no language to express the uniqueness of this relationship. So Abraham cannot speak, and he cannot be understood: otherwise he would inhabit 'generality'—alongside Agamemnon, the tragic hero who could still be understood by Iphigenia. But why speak on Abraham's behalf? Perhaps only in order to say: 'I am not sublime.' If Kierkegaard can be said to have spoken to Regine in the voice of Johannes, surely it was simply to tell her: 'I am not sublime.' And also, perhaps: 'What a shame that we are not sublime, you and I, that unlike Abraham we cannot resign ourselves infinitely to loss—without weakness, without suffering, and without uncertainty—and then continue to believe that nothing is impossible and we will be restored to each other.'

Faith is not necessarily madness, but it always *might* be. In this respect, Kant and Kierkegaard were in agreement: where reason gives out, madness may always take over. Hence the terror that Abraham strikes into us, and our trembling before his crime. The crime must be faced unflinchingly, and that is what Johannes forces himself to do by means of the stories he tells and retells four times over: the preparations, the journey to Mount Moriah, the Knife: 'Silently he arranged the firewood and bound Isaac; silently he drew the knife.'[7]

He did not have time to use the knife. But still he bound Isaac. The name of this episode—the *akedah*—is derived from this binding and these bonds: it is the story of a son being *bound*. The son was bound hand and foot by his father; and Sarah might have died merely to hear tell of it. Oedipus too was bound at the feet.

Genesis does not give Abraham a moment for hesitation. God told him: 'Take now thy son, thine only son Isaac, whom thou lovest, and get thee into the land of Moriah; and offer him there for a burnt offering upon one of the mountains which I will tell thee of.

'And Abraham rose up early in the morning, and saddled his ass. . . .'[8]

THE NIGHT OF ABRAHAM

Abraham's ability to respond immediately and without hesitation makes his action all the more bewildering. But the idea that he did not really hesitate is itself an interpretation, projected on to Abraham's silence, in the text of Genesis, in the period between hearing God's command and setting off for Moriah.

What can that night have been like? We have no way of knowing. Did Abraham manage to get any sleep? Are we to imagine him calm, steady and fearless? Are we to suppose that he made up his mind immediately? No doubt Abraham responded to God's call without delay. But what happened during that night? And if Abraham had doubts then, can we be sure he was not assailed by further doubts when the final moment came? How does one embark on a crime? Where is the 'beginning' when it comes to inflicting or giving death [*donner la mort*]?

God allowed Abraham to tie up his son on the altar. He did not provide the lamb for the sacrifice except *in extremis*. The four tales told by Johannes—'it was early in the morning'—have the appearance of repetitions or repeats, different versions of a single scene. You take a step back, and then start over again, in slow motion. The purpose is to *represent* the incident to oneself, rather than simply to 'think' it, since thought is always hastening towards an ending: we know it was only a test, and that Isaac will be spared *in the end.* But knowing the ending would efface the entire trial.

And if Isaac really was spared (but could he really be spared, after having seen his father raise the knife above him?), then did Abraham ever really embark on his crime? If you are engaged in a criminal act, at what point does it become impossible to turn back? If Abraham made all the preparations but then stayed his hand, if he hesitated at the final second, the last moment, then surely he would remain, for himself, completely guilty of the crime?

But as we know, the angel intervened: 'Abraham stretched forth his hand, and took the knife to slay his son.' But the angel of the Lord called to him out of heaven, and said, 'Abraham, Abraham.'[9]

How much time remained before the slaughter itself, before Isaac would actually have died? A second would be enough, or even less, for Abraham to cast aside the knife.

I like to think that Abraham might not have gone through with the sacrifice anyway, but that he did not know it. He had made all the preparations, organized everything meticulously, and resigned himself to the death of his son—the son who was a gift from God himself. Mourning had already entered his heart. That is what Johannes describes as the movement of 'infinite resignation'.

The interminable moment began with Abraham's preparations, and it lasted till the very end of his journey. Throughout this time—three whole days—Abraham was forced to contemplate the imminent death of Isaac, the death which was already on its way, and already present to Abraham: for it was Abraham who was going to inflict it, and who must therefore have 'willed' and accepted it. But the 'courage' of Abraham need not, I think, be seen as expressing a straightforward 'decision', based on a faith untouched by doubt. Nevertheless Johannes writes: 'But he did not doubt, he did not look in anguish to the left and to the right.'[10]

But one might also imagine a trembling, agitated Abraham, filled with uncertainty and anguish: for one thing—though this only touches the surface—because Abraham's 'will' and 'resolution' can never be known, given the intervention of the angel. Or rather, it may be a mistake to see it in terms of resolution or an 'act of will' at all—unless will is understood, following Hobbes, in the sense of a 'will and testament'. When death arrives, calling an absolute halt to any alterations of our arrangements, inclinations and desires, then the last inclination and arrangement are regarded as the 'will of the deceased'.

It is always the '*last* appetite' or the '*last* fear' which, in retrospect, acquires the status of our 'will', with all the assurance and mastery of execution that this term implies. But in reality, the will is more commanded than commanding; an event has interposed itself and put an end to the succession of our desires and fears, a succession which continues, according to Hobbes, 'till the action be either done, or some accident come between, to make it impossible.'[11]

On the other hand, Abraham's exemplary obedience presupposes a classical conception of resolution, decision, and execution: the act of resolution must be independent of all external forces. It would appear that Abraham showed no sign of hesitation, nothing that might suggest the slightest doubt. The time he spent on the preparations testifies to the nature of his obedience to God. But the intervention of the angel was going to *halt* the sacrifice all the same, in several senses. The incident which was going to occur would mean that Abraham's hand would be stayed as it lifted the knife, halted in a kind of freeze-frame. God would have exacted the pledge he required; the sacrifice would have taken place in that the death sentence had been pronounced. But at the same time, God will have stopped the sacrifice, substituting a lamb for Isaac, and the sacrifice will actually not have taken place. A death sentence [*arrêt de mort*] in a different sense of the word.

The intervention of the angel of Jehovah was an astonishing marvel; but somehow Abraham seemed to have been expecting it all along: 'My son, God will provide himself a lamb for a burnt offering.'[12]

But Abraham's reply to Isaac suggests, I suspect, that as well as Abraham being tested by God, God was being put to the test by Abraham. 'Just how far will you let me go? Behold: I do as I am commanded, but are you really going to let me slaughter my son?' Johannes tries to demonstrate Abraham's faith by saying that he 'believed that God would not demand Isaac of him'. But the point could also be expressed negatively: Abraham did *not* believe that God would demand the sacrifice of Isaac. And this formulation can itself be read in two different ways: either 'he did not *believe* that God would demand Isaac' or 'he did not believe that *God* would demand Isaac'. In other words, did Abraham really believe in a God who would have required Isaac to be sacrificed?

Did he put God to the test? This interpretation would imply, paradoxically perhaps, that the relationship between Abraham and God was marked by a certain sense of humour: 'So you want my son? Sure. But I bet you don't really want me to go through with it.' In that sense, Abraham's faith would reside not in blind obedience, but in scepticism. 'Let's see if God is really asking me to sacrifice Isaac. But I don't believe it. . . .'

UTTER DEVOTION

And Abraham would have been right: God did not want Isaac slaughtered. But if Abraham was putting God to the test, it is not clear what he would have done if the angel had not intervened. Admittedly the supposition that Abraham was testing God takes us a long way from what Johannes calls Abraham's madness. It means crediting Abraham with a kind of free relationship to God, and imagining that one can sit in judgement on divine justice while remaining within the limits of reason alone. And the supposition that Abraham did *not* believe that *God* was really asking him to give up his son certainly takes Abraham a long distance from the text of the Bible (which of course Johannes did as well, thought in a different way). Abraham himself does not seem to have considered any such questions, at least not in Genesis: he was in the hands of God, and belonged to him utterly. He could not assume that God was going to return Isaac to him 'on the basis of the absurd' since if God then appeared to break his promise, it would not be for Abraham to judge him. To Johannes, the faith of Abraham was comparable to that of Job.

Abraham accepted immediately what Job slowly came to acknowledge. For Job finally realized that there was an absurd pride in wanting to be in the right against God, or even in merely wanting to understand God's reasons, or demanding that God be 'fair'. God's response to Job did not consist in giving him arguments or 'reasons', but in presenting a sublime vision of his power, so that no one could ever again hope to grasp anything of this power or greatness. Faced with the incommensurable and the absolute, Job realized that his protestations were ridiculous. In the end he fell silent. One is never in the right against God. No one is ever in the right against the Creator.

To fear God is to accept this absolute failure in advance. God alone can judge.

And perhaps what Kierkegaard added to this fearful humility, so powerfully present in the Old Testament, was an element of sheer joy.

There is a fearful happiness in being able to lose oneself immediately in the desire to *respond* by saying, simply and absolutely: 'Here I am.' And by saying it in silence. Passionate love always tends towards this kind of devotion, a cheerful accession, faithful and unguarded, to the desire of the other.

If there is such a thing as love, can it refuse to take this absolute risk? Could there be a love that was not sublime?

But it seems to me that philosophy—the claim of reason and the claim to reason, the need to be in the right and always to judge for oneself—necessarily implies, in various ways, the end of this devotion. It implies the end of passion in general, the end of religion as well as love, the end of the sublime devotion which says to the other: 'Thy will be done.' The question would then be whether there can be a conception of love that does not depend on the sublime: could there be a love that owes nothing either to aesthetics, or ethics, or religion?

THE SUBLIME LAW

One thing that never varies in the uses of the word 'sublime', Kierkegaard's included, is its reference to something incommensurable and absolutely vast, something which could not be represented at all, except perhaps through what Kant called a 'negative representation'. The same definition also applies to Hegel's use of the term in his *Aesthetics.*[13]

When we speak of an 'end of the sublime', we mean something like the end of Abraham's faith, or the end of the conception of an omnipotent creator, or, more generally, the end of our fear of something absolutely *external* to us which might be capable of exciting either devotion or respect. But there is also a different kind of sublimity: the moral sublime, which came into existence with the interiorization of absolute immensity. That is why the *sentiment* or *feeling* of the sublime became, for Kant, 'a feeling of a supersensible faculty within us'.[14] In Kant, the fear was exorcized: the absolute was no longer external. It is as if it had been turned inward so that we need no longer bow down before anything external, but only before the moral law *within.*

Religion can thus be brought within the limits of 'reason alone'. If the Old Testament retained some archetypal value for Kant, it was only as an illustration of the idea that every representation necessarily falls short of absolute immensity, which meant that it was mere vanity to wish to represent the absolute, when this absolute had been dislodged, and the moral law had taken the place of divinity. As Kant wrote: 'the veiled Goddess before whom we kneel, is the moral law within us'. Or again: 'Perhaps there is no more sublime passage in the Jewish Law than the commandment: "Thou shalt not make unto thee any graven image, or any likeness of any thing that is in heaven above, or that is in the earth beneath, or that is in the water under the earth." . . . The very same holds good of our representation of the moral law and of our native capacity for morality.'[15]

When the law has been turned inwards, so that immensity becomes human and religion is reduced to morality, then only two things can still be sublime: the person who respects the moral law, and this respect itself. As Kant says: 'Even *freedom from affection* . . . in a mind that strenuously follows its unswerving principles is sublime.'[16]

But Abraham was not following any principles. And he was not sublime. From Kant's point of view, there was nothing in Abraham apart from his crime, his isolation, and his waywardness.

Hegel's *Aesthetics* retained the Kantian idea of the sublime as the attempt to represent the unrepresentable, but the reference to the sublime as the moral law was abandoned. The sacred art of the sublime was now seen as testifying that the absolute had been conceived inadequately, as an absolutely remote divinity, separate from its creatures and its creation. Hegel's thought implied the end of the sublime, in both its religious and its moral forms. Only the aesthetic category of sublimity remained.

That is why Hegel found sublimity in Hebrew poetry: 'God is the creator of the universe. This is the purest expression of the sublime itself.'[17] For the sublime is the affirmation that the works of spirit are absolutely external to it—God's works primarily, but human works as well. According to Hegel, the art of the sublime can be regarded as uniquely holy, and—since such an art would have to express the relationship between God and the world he had created, while avoiding 'representing' him or portraying any particular image of him—it could only take the form of poetry. The relationship between creation and creator then appears as one of absolute dependence and remoteness. The created world is not regarded as the 'true manifestation' of God, but remains *external* to him: a finite world, emptied of God, but testifying directly to his power and his glory. God's creatures can then experience nothing but their own finitude and the 'impassable gulf' that separates them from God.[18] Their unworthiness before God makes them 'tremble before God's wrath', but nevertheless leaves it open for the individual to adopt an affirmative relationship to God by obeying the divine law and attributing every misfortune to some violation of it. Thus the sublime could be said to refer both to the absolute otherness of God—the relationship without relationship to this absolute—and to the sacred art which attempts to express this 'relationship', or rather this separation.

For Hegel, a symbol always expresses the discrepancy between form and meaning, the inadequacy of the perceptible exterior to the interiority which it represents. And the relationship between created reality and its creator is marked by the same discrepancy: God transcends and exceeds the reality in which he is manifest. Thus the sublimity of God resides in his transcendence of works that testify to his glory without being able to contain it.

The sublimity of sacred art is meant to 'express' the sublimity of God, who remains the reference point of all creation, and its constant allusion, even though he is withdrawn from the world, invisible, and beyond representation. Sacred art can therefore do nothing but express an impossible 'relationship' to God, to a God removed from the world, and it can never display his essence.

It will be noted that the art which corresponds to a God who has withdrawn into lonely isolation is a sacred art in which the plastic or visual arts can have no place, since God can be given neither shape nor form. The only way to evoke the relationship between the visible and the invisible is through words. In Hegelian aesthetics, the sacred art of the sublime can only be the art of poetry.

And the same applies to pantheism: 'where pantheism is pure, there is no visual art for its representation.'[19] Any form of expression which would limit God to some permanent, precise and individual shape would be ruled out by the omnipresence (or immanence) of God just as effectively as it is by his separation from the world. For the visual arts present precise shapes: they 'bring to our vision only as existent and static the determinate and individual thing.' If, as pantheism asserts, substance is constantly passing from one determination to the next, 'abandoning it in order to proceed to another', controlling all contingencies but not confining itself within them, then God cannot possibly take on any one individual shape.[20] Either way (the absolute transcendence of God or his absolute immanence), all individual shapes have to be obliterated.

There is another example of sublimity, already mentioned by Longinus and taken over by Hegel, for which the word of God appears as a condition of his withdrawal from the world: 'God said, Let there be light: and there was light.'[21] Here is Hegel's commentary: 'The Lord, the one substance, does proceed to manifestation, but the manner of creation is the purest, even bodiless, ethereal manifestation; it is the word, the manifestation of thought as the ideal power, and with its command that the existent shall be, the existent is immediately and actually brought into being in silent obedience.'[22] The withdrawal and transcendence of God are possible only to the extent that creation is *spiritual*, that things are not brought forth by natural procreation from the breast of God. God's spiritual authority has the form of command over bodily creatures. The words of God are commands: the created world, finite and emptied of God, can have no relationship with God except by listening to his law, as the only true manifestation of his power.

The withdrawal of God from the world means that his creatures are left with only one form of relationship to him: that of *listening* or attentive obedience. Having removed himself from the world, God is present only through his law, his voice: listening to this voice is our only possible relationship to the Creator. If God's word of command is the condition of creation and hence of the world's relationship to God, then conversely the relationship of creatures to their Creator must consist in listening—and listening in silence.

But sacred poetry is not poetry for poetry's sake. Rather it is part of religion, and the concept of a sublime *art* could not arise unless 'we' had already lost our 'relationship' to the God of the Old Testament. The term *sublime* belongs to a philosophy which was seeking to locate Jewish religion within a theory of symbolism in general: the category of the sublime belongs to a form of thought which supposes that concrete spirituality has 'transcended' the abstract hebraic vision of infinity. To call the sublime by its name is to transcend it, and so to have lost it. More specifically, to call creation 'sublime' is to use an aesthetic concept in order to proclaim that a representation is inadequate to what it is supposed to represent or embody.

The Bible says: God is *not* his creation, and the distinctive character of Jewish thought lies in this discrepancy. It is a way of thinking which dwells on the non-correspondence between Spirit and the world which it has created. But according to Hegel this conception of God does not measure up to the real and concrete divine substance. Such sublimity falls short of God. The conception of God as removed from the world is inadequate, and therefore *merely* symbolic. Poetry, mere poetry.

Religion and poetry merge into each other here, and distance themselves from any conceptual grasp of Spirit in and for itself. It is only 'for us' that such a conception can be 'sublime', or such poetry symbolic: by reference to 'our' concept of symbolism and the Kantian concept of the sublime in the *Critique of Judgement*, that is to say to the theme of the non-correspondence or *inadequacy* of representation to an infinite which it nevertheless strives to represent. Hegel's use of the category of the sublime presupposed that he had *already* succeeded in transcending, overcoming and transforming the *inadequate* conception of God as creator, and thus reducing religion to a mere representation (an *inadequate* representation) of the truth. 'We'—we dialecticians—have negated the idea of God as the negation of the phenomenal world. And this negation of the negation enables us to conceive of the reconciliation of the spiritual and the sensible, the subjective and the objective. Sublimity is born in this reconciliation, but dies in it too, in the retrospective naming of the unrepresentable.

Those who sustained a relationship with the absolute in the form of the moral law could still be sublime. But we dialecticians have no wish to be sublime, so we are able to make the claim: 'we are not sublime'. Religious sublimity, dialectically transcended, mutates into aesthetic sublimity.

If Abraham's sacrifice, or his devotion, can be described as aesthetically sublime, then they are no more than the transcended shapes of a transcended form of religious thinking: 'consciousness of an impassable gulf between the being of God and the being of men', as Hegel said of Judaism in 'The Spirit of Christianity and its Fate.'[23] But if philosophical aesthetics always associates the sublime with an 'impassable gulf', it can only do so *after* the gulf has supposedly been bridged. Religiosity as such can never think of itself as *sublime*, any more than sacred art can think of itself as *art*.

And Abraham's faith could only be 'sublime' to those for whom it had been transcended or lost for ever. That is why Johannes's poetic meditations on Abraham's sacrifice will never constitute a religious text, or imply a genuine return of faith: perhaps they are only representations of its obliteration. And it is not only God that is hidden: the image of a man who believed in God is concealed from us too. Hegel denied the withdrawal of God from the world, in a dialectical negation of the *negative* God of creation. For the poet of the sublime, however, there could only be a forgetting of this divine withdrawal: a withdrawal of the withdrawal, perhaps.

But if Hegel's philosophy transcends the sublimity of Hebrew religion and poetry, that of Kant denies the sublimity of Abraham altogether. Why should that be?

THE MADNESS OF ABRAHAM

For Kant, nothing can be absolutely immense except the voice of Reason. Only the law of Reason can impose absolute and universal obligations on *humanity*, and nothing else could be truly sublime. This turning inward of the religious toward the moral, which we have already mentioned above, was achieved by means of the Kantian conception of *rational faith* as providing the only criterion for judging religious observances and beliefs; and it completely destroyed the religious value and greatness of Abraham's obedience. Abraham could not possibly be sublime; moreover Judaism itself could not even be a genuine religion if it permitted such a clash between religion and morality.

But Abraham had to choose between religion and morality, or at least he thought he had to: on this point at least, the author of *Religion Within the Limits of Reason Alone* is in complete agreement with the author of *Fear and Trembling.*

Johannes observes that the temptation which Abraham was called upon to resist was no ordinary one. It was not a temptation to fail in his moral duty. On the contrary: moral duty is precisely what tempted Abraham to disobey God's command. Hence the religious trial of Abraham entailed the 'teleological suspension' of the ethical. It required the individual whom God was putting to the test to place himself above the universal. That is the paradox. And Kant and Johannes both used the same words to describe Abraham's 'choice': it makes you tremble, and it fills you with horror. The whole of *Religion within the Limits of Reason Alone* was designed to denounce Abraham and banish such acts of reason-blind faith from the sphere of religion. This exclusion was needed in order to avoid any possibility of error concerning what is 'truly agreeable to God', and to preclude any relationship to a God whose law was not simply the moral law, and capable of being comprehended by Reason. Any religious language that involved vision, revelation, imagination, or feeling was contaminated with empiricity, and was merely the expression of singularities: it was neither instructive nor edifying. It could always err and mislead: 'It is at least possible that in this instance a mistake has prevailed.' It was precisely the *possibility* of this false and misleading voice that Kant invoked in connection with the command that Abraham should 'slaughter his own son like a lamb'. To Kant this command was not only monstrous but absurd, in view of God's promise concerning

Abraham's descendants. To obey such a commandment, such a 'terrible injunction', would necessarily be to act without conscience, or unconscientiously. 'This is the case with respect to all historical and visionary faith; that is, the *possibility* ever remains that an error may be discovered in it. Hence it is unconscientious to follow such a faith with the possibility that perhaps what it commands or permits may be wrong, i.e. with the danger of disobedience to a human duty which is certain in and of itself.'[24]

Johannes knew it too. He knew that Abraham must be 'either a murderer or a man of faith', and that is why he wrote that 'one approaches him with a *horror religiosus*, as Israel approached Mount Sinai'.[25]

But the Kantian identification of religion with rational faith and a purely ethical religion raises a problem: for it is not clear that Christianity—which for Kant was the only religion—really is a purely ethical religion.

When Kant wrote that 'steadfast diligence in morally good life-conduct is all that God requires of men, to be subjects in His kingdom and well-pleasing to him',[26] he deliberately ignored the problems of faith, of belief in the incarnation, the demand for love addressed to all of us by Christ, and the irreducibility of this love—or any other love—to reason. Love is an individual response to a unique call: a call addressed directly to me. Anyone who answers this call by saying 'Here I am' is acting like Abraham and overstepping the limits of reason alone.

Kant's 'pure rational faith' may well be genuinely pure; but in that case it can no longer be faith. By reducing Christianity to a purely ethical religion, Kant was abstracting from faith in Jesus Christ, and from the mystery of the trinity and the incarnation, and hence from the absolute risk which inheres in the belief that God was *this particular man*, an empirical and historical reality. He abstracted from love for the God-become-man who gave the infinite such a specific face. And yet Abraham was a man of faith only to the extent that his faithfulness—his 'answer' to God's call: 'here I am'—was a leap into danger. (Can it really be *God* who is asking this of me; can *this* really be what he wants?) And faith in Christ is another absolute risk: could this particular man really be the son of God? Thus *Religion Within the Limits of Reason Alone* cannot comprehend either the faith of Abraham or that of the apostles: neither obedience to the God who hides his face, nor love for the God incarnate.

The philosopher of 'reason alone' was not addressing himself to a singularity: he was concerned with humankind in general, universal humanity. The Kantian conception of religion is inseparable from a discourse in which 'humanity' has already been defined.

The preface to the second edition of *Religion Within the Limits of Reason Alone* specifies that its author speaks as 'a teacher of pure reason'.[27] For Kant, education was 'perverted' as soon as it became priestly, mystagogical, or aristocratic. This kind of teaching drew on the authority of mysterious voices and visions, secrets handed down through obscure traditions, and poetical, cryptic language. . . .

Anything that could not be said unequivocally by the voice of reason belonged to empirical singularity, to the private sphere, and had nothing to do with genuine education. The reason why the teachable coincided with the rational lay in the very nature of education, whose only possible goal was the improvement and general good of *humanity* as such. The teachable was confined to the universalizable, and reason—as the faculty for knowledge of the unconditioned absolute—was the only true master. Outside it there was no education. Religion *unsettles* us by abandoning us all to our singularity; but philosophy reassures us by identifying the true with the universal. Kantian humanity has a horror of going mad, and it would never risk sharing the madness of Abraham.

The only way religion could become universal, therefore, was by being incorporated into philosophy. If all of us must, in virtue of our humanity, be capable of honouring God, then God's laws must be purely moral, and accessible to all of us solely in virtue of our own reason: '*Pure religious faith* alone can found a universal church; for only rational faith can be believed in and shared by everyone.'[28]

It was not impossible for an 'ecclesiastical faith'—a historical faith based merely on facts—to coincide with the true rational faith, but it would be a pure coincidence, or the grace of a benevolent providence. Hence there was only one religion, one teaching, one voice, and one language (a language which should, if possible, be spoken without a hint of artifice or style).

Abraham, however, exalted individuality into an absolute. He put an absolute human singularity into a direct relationship with the absolute of his God: a necessarily secret relationship. Abraham could not even understand himself, since to do so would be to stray into the sphere of universality. And this lack of mediation cut him off from any use of language that might *constrain* his singularity. He responded to the voice that said 'Come', by saying 'Here I am.' But he did not answer it. At least that is how Johannes saw it.

'Here I am' is not exactly an answer. Nor is it an indication of servile obedience. To say 'Here I am' is to speak protectively, like a mother:— 'I'm here.' As if to say, 'don't worry, you're not alone'. The figure of a maternal Abraham. . . . Maybe God wanted to make sure that he could take the place of the child? A jealous God.

THE WITHDRAWAL OF ABRAHAM

The words 'Here I am' could never be spoken out of duty, and they could not possibly be addressed to 'humanity in general'. Nevertheless they speak of something absolute: whatever happens, whatever you wish, here I am. It is an unconditional *yes*, and it is neither moral nor fair. The experience of this *yes* does not arise from any kind of knowledge. It is not even an experience: those who give themselves up to their *yes* are not the kind of classical subjects in relation to whom empirical knowledge is defined, but neither are they the subjects of a mystical experience that presupposes some direct communion with the absolute.

Faith cannot be taught, and neither can love (perhaps they are the same). And that is why Johannes was neither a philosopher nor a believer, but a poet. He did not speak the language of philosophy, and neither was he able to say 'yes'. He simply said he could not understand Abraham—that was the point he wanted to emphasize. Of course he referred to the 'Here I am'—but only as an *impossibility* for him, and no doubt for us too. For us, Abraham has disappeared into the night, into his night, and for us it remains as dark as ever. We have no knowledge to shine upon his shadowed face.

'I can only admire him', says Johannes. It is as if we were left with absolutely nothing, except perhaps our admiration for Abraham as a man of faith. And if we can still see him as sublime, it is only because we cannot understand either his God or his devotion: his obedience and his *yes* are now beyond our measure.

Johannes's text bears witness to a gap between religious poetry and the poetry of the religious.[29] The sublimity of the creator and his creation have been replaced by the sublimity of Abraham's ability to enter into a relationship with God, and it is this figure of Abraham that is now unrepresentable, erased, withdrawn. To say that Abraham is sublime is to say that he has become a stranger to us. We tremble before the man of faith just as he trembled before his God. Abraham encountered the mystery of God, but we only encounter the mystery of Abraham.

HUMAN LOVES

Religious devotion may be closely connected with erotic love, but Kierkegaard never equated the two. Adoration and unconditional obedience belong to our love for God, not for each other.

> Erotic love is still not the eternal; it is the beautiful dizziness of infinity; its highest expression is the foolhardiness of riddles. This explains its attempting an even dizzier expression, 'to love a person more than God.'[30]

Erotic love is all too human, it is love by predilection—love according to preference and choice. It is quite unlike the adoration and obedience that God inspires, and also unlike the love of our neighbour that God requires of us in the Gospels: 'Thou shalt love thy neighbour as thyself.'

The second chapter of *Works of Love* is called 'Thou *shalt* love.' Writing now under his own name, Kierkegaard insists on the need to give up the immediacy of human love—the precariousness and danger, the jealousy and anguish—in favour of eternal love, which owes nothing to either luck or chance. The love that binds us to each other cannot achieve peace, eternity, or truth, unless it can detach itself from the contingencies of individual tenderness and subject itself to the medium of law. Freed from the whims of inclination, our love for our neighbour comes to resemble a Kantian sublime respect for principles. But love cannot be 'reunited' with the principle of law unless it breaks away from the singularity of its object and occasion. It achieves eternal certainty by becoming a duty. 'Thou shalt love. *Only when it is a duty to love, only then is love eternally secured against every change, eternally made free in blessed independence, eternally and happily secured against despair.*'[31]

This 'thou shalt' serves to shelter love from change. And the unconditional 'duty to love' grants love both peace and independence: 'that love has the law for its existence in the relation of love itself to the eternal'.[32]

If the one I love tells me: 'I cannot love you any longer', my pride would probably make me say: 'Then it's all over between us'—which shows that my love was not independent. But if I replied 'I must still love you all the same' then my love would be eternally free and independent—a love '*sheltered by despair*'.[33] In this way, the law of love can be said to reintroduce the safety net of a universal imperative.

Kierkegaard knew that love, even when it is happy, loves with '*the power of despair*'. He knew that despair never takes us by surprise in our unhappiness but simply reveals that we were in despair already.[34] What hands us over to despair is not unhappiness, but our lack of the eternal—a lack which marks all human loves.

The power of love is surely the same as the power of despair. But if this despair really is inextricably linked with our lack of the eternal, it can also be understood, I suspect, as a means of freeing ourselves from vain optimism and foolish notions about eternity and immortality. Without this essential lack, and our acceptance of it, we would never be able to form any conception of giving, or conceive of love as a gift. What more can I give than my time—that is to say not my life or death, but my essential mortality. Lovers dream of dying in each other's arms, dying for each other, and watching each other die, like Romeo and Juliet, as if they wanted to make a gift to each other of their own mortality.

For Kierkegaard, however, the command to love draws its sustenance from eternity, responding to the primordial duty *not to despair.*

> When it is made impossible to possess the beloved in time, eternity says, 'Thou shalt love'—that is, eternity saves love from despair by making it eternal.[35]

It saves it from despair by preserving it: 'Thou shalt preserve love and thou shalt preserve thyself and by and in preserving yourself preserve love.'[36]

No doubt it is necessary to have dwelt in absolute despair in order to understand the force of the commandment which strikes it down and says: 'You must not despair.' One might say: preserve yourself from despair, preserve yourself by preserving your love, your own love, unconditionally and for all eternity. Do not die to your own love, do not die to yourself: preserve yourself. But if lovers take such precautions, then surely they are simply seeking their *own* survival. And this passion for eternal preservation through dutiful love is precisely what separates us from the other as such, what separates us from the *event* of the other, of time, of randomness, of luck, of finitude—and of love. Or at least, of love in its essential precariousness, the love which is directed towards an empirical mortal individual, on whom it knowingly depends; and lovers surrender themselves to such individualities only because giving oneself away is always dangerous, or rather because one is bound to lose every time. How could we ever make a gift, if we did not know that we are destined to grow old and die, if we were not giving something that can be reckoned up, something that we know will *pass away*? Of course the eternal does not rush past us, but it does not come up to meet us either. How could eternity ever belong to what happens, to events? And how should we conceive of love, except as an event that comes upon our mortal existence and takes it by surprise—entrusting everything we thought we were, everything we thought we possessed, to the unsafe keeping of another mortal, and taking the other into our own keeping as well.

No doubt the injunction to preserve love in order to preserve oneself could make me independent of the other, if not indifferent: I would no longer be prey to either anguish or jealousy, even if I ceased to be loved, even if I were abandoned. I would love for eternity. Thus Søren could say to Regine: 'I have abandoned you, but I shall love you for ever, and that is the standard by which my love should be measured. What more could you ask for?' But we may have our doubts about the humility of those who make it their duty to love for all eternity: they abase themselves before the 'thou shalt', but not before the other. That is how they are able to be 'independent'.

For what is left of love, after the madness of religious devotion, and after the ethical injunction to love eternally? Surely the humblest love is what occurs when one individuality simply attends to another, finitude inclined toward finitude. In a case of ethical respect or dutiful loving, my relationship flows from a requirement which is indifferent to the individuality of the other, and what I owe to the other is inextricable from what I owe to myself: keeping myself, keeping myself free, and keeping myself free of despair. Love as a duty will always be egocentric. But what distinguishes love at its humblest from devotion is that it does not treat the finite individuality to which it attends as if it were an absolute; it sustains and affirms its finitude through a tenderness which is as singular—as random and unfair—as existence itself.

This kind of tenderness is therefore *neither* ethical *nor* religious, and it has no interest in freedom as classically conceived, or in law. It is an attachment, the link which makes one existence necessary for another, and which allows existences to depend upon and suffer through each other. If love is a duty, however, then it can free itself from its object and adhere only to the law. Without law, as Kierkegaard writes, there can be absolutely no freedom.[37] And the theme of freedom as autonomy crops up just when you would least expect it: in love, but in love understood as a commandment: 'Thou shalt love.' This is a paradoxical love, to be sure: the love that frees me from its object: it frees me from the object by freeing me from the risk of losing it, the risk of mourning. 'Such a love neither stands nor falls with the contingency of its object.'[38] What Kierkegaard referred to as the courage of loving in eternity is in fact the 'courage' of giving up in advance whatever might be taken away from us—in the hope of getting it back again. But surely there is another kind of courage: the courage of accepting the event of loss, and enduring it without anticipation. Why should we *not* have to suffer? By what right? As Freud put it in his essay 'On Transience': 'What is painful may none the less be true.'[39]

Losing in order to win: it would seem that this is the law of the spirit as well as the spirit of the law, of the law of detachment: losing the finite in order to keep it, and anticipating the loss. A tactic of sacrifice. Making a sacrifice of the instant, the ephemeral, the unique, and the immediate. That is also the law of memory, of memorial interiorization, of recollection. Mourning everywhere, and the anticipation of mourning. Merely by thinking, the existing individual strains to avoid suffering. And Kierkegaard was not exempt from this law.

Law always requires the same thing, whatever its source and however it may be defined (divine law, moral duty, unconditional love for our neighbour); it requires a dissolution of ties—of the ties that attach us to finite individualities, the ties that bind individual bodily existences together. How did God refer to Isaac? He called him: *thy son, thine only son, whom thou lovest.* Isaac was to be sacrificed so that the most natural of physical bonds should be broken. Otherwise there could be no access to spirituality, or law, or freedom.

To love in eternity, in conformity with the religious movement of the infinite, would be to fulfil the requirements of law in a sublime sacrifice of the finite. But existing can also mean being able to love the finite, and being capable of finitude, of saying yes to finitude, that is to say, to time. To subject oneself to the ephemeral, to suffer it, to suffer loss without suffering it in *advance*, to accept the time of the wound and the wound of time; and to accept the event of the other.

Notes

1. Sylviane Agacinski, *Aparté: Conceptions et morts de Sören Kierkegaard* (Aubier Montaigne, Paris, 1977), translated by Kevin Newmark as *Aparté: Conceptions and Deaths of Soren Kierkegaard* (Florida State University Press, Gainesville, 1988.

2. Johannes de Silentio—the pseudonym in whose name *Fear and Trembling* was published—remarks for example that 'to change the leap into life into walking, absolutely to express the sublime in the pedestrian—only that knight can do it, and this is the one and only marvel.' See *Fear and Trembling, Repetition*, translated by Howard V. Hong and Edna H. Hong (Princeton University Press, Princeton, 1983), p. 41.
3. Cf. *The Sickness Unto Death*, translated by Howard V. Hong and Edna H. Hong (Princeton University Press, Princeton, 1980), p. 78: 'He becomes a poet of the religious in the same way as one who became a poet through an unhappy love affair and blissfully celebrates the happiness of erotic love.' See also n. 29 below, p. 149, and n. 7 to Ricoeur, p. 24 above.
4. Immanuel Kant, *Critique of Judgement*, translated by James Creed Meredith (Oxford University Press, Oxford, 1952), Part One, Section One, Book Two, §25, p. 97.
5. Nevertheless I feel quite close to an essay by Jean-Luc Nancy which strikingly argues that a 'sublime sacrifice' can never provide the 'sovereign satisfaction of a spirit capable of infinity'. The sublime does not lie *beyond* the limit; rather it is the emotion of a subject *at the limit.* But his highly original approach to the sublime and to freedom (a freedom which is both sacrificing and sacrificed) is not the one I shall be adopting here. [See Jean-Luc Nancy, 'L'offrande sublime' in *Du Sublime* (Belin, Paris, 1986).]
6. Cf. two statements from Problema III of *Fear and Trembling*: 'no poet can find his way to Abraham', and 'I am not a poet, and I go at things only dialectically.' See *Fear and Trembling, Repetition*, pp. 118, 90.
7. Cf. the section of *Fear and Trembling* entitled 'Stemning' ('Attunement' or 'Exordium'). See *Fear and Trembling, Repetition*, translated by Howard V. Hong and Edna H. Hong (Princeton University Press, Princeton, 1983), pp. 9–14, p. 12.
8. Genesis 22: 2–3.
9. Genesis 22: 11.
10. 'Eulogy on Abraham', *Fear and Trembling*, p. 22.
11. Thomas Hobbes, *Humane Nature: Or, the Fundamental Elements of Policie* (1650), in William Molesworth, *The English Works of Thomas Hobbes* (11 vols, London, 1839–45), vol. IV, p. 68. Hobbes continues as follows: 'In deliberation, the last appetite, as also the last fear, is called *will*, viz. the last appetite, will to do, or will to omit. It is all one therefore to say *will* or *last will*; for, though a man express his present inclination and appetite concerning the disposition of his goods, by words or writings; yet shall it not be counted his will, because he hath still liberty to dispose of them otherways; but when death taketh away that liberty, then it is his will.'
12. Genesis 22: 8.
13. See G. W. F. Hegel, *Aesthetics: Lectures on Fine Art*, translated by T. M. Knox (2 vols, Oxford University Press, Oxford, 1975), vol. 1, p. 363.
14. *Critique of Judgement*, Part One, Section One, Book Two, §25, p. 97.
15. *Critique of Judgement*, Part One, Section One, Book Two, §29, p. 127; see also Exodus 20: 4.
16. *Critique of Judgement*, Part One, Section One, Book Two, §29, p. 124.
17. 'The Art of the Sublime' in G. W. F. Hegel, *Aesthetics: Lectures on Fine Art*, vol. 1, p. 373.

18. See 'The Spirit of Christianity and its Fate' in G. W. F. Hegel, *Early Theological Writings*, translated by T. M. Knox and Richard Kroner (University of Chicago Press, Chicago, 1948), p. 265.
19. Hegel, *Aesthetics*, p. 366.
20. Hegel, *Aesthetics*, p. 366.
21. See Genesis 1: 3, and Longinus, *On the Sublime*, ix 10.
22. Hegel, *Aesthetics*, pp. 373–4.
23. Hegel, *Early Theological Writings*, p. 265.
24. Immanuel Kant, *Religion Within the Limits of Reason Alone* (1793), translated by Theodore M. Greene and Hoyt H. Hudson (Harper and Row, New York, 1960), p. 175.
25. 'Problema I', *Fear and Trembling*, pp. 57, 61; cf. Exodus 19: 24.
26. *Religion Within the Limits of Reason Alone*, p. 94.
27. *Religion Within the Limits of Reason Alone*, p. 11.
28. *Religion Within the Limits of Reason Alone*, p. 94.
29. 'The reason a religious poet is a dubious category in relation to the paradoxical-religious is that, esthetically, possibility is higher than actuality, and the poetic consists in the ideality of imaginative intuition. This is why we not infrequently see hymns that, although stirring and childlike and poetic through a tinge of imagination verging on the fantastic, are not, viewed categorically, Christian.' See *Concluding Unscientific Postscript*, translated by Howard V. Hong and Edna H. Hong (2 vols, Princeton University Press, Princeton, 1992), p. 580; see also pp. 351, 357. See also n. 3 above and n. 7 to Ricoeur, p. 24 above.
30. *Works of Love*, translated by Howard V. Hong and Edna H. Hong (Princeton University Press, Princeton, 1995), p. 19.
31. *Works of Love*, p. 29. This and other translations have been amended to read 'thou shalt' for 'you shall' in order to accord with Matthew 22: 39 in the Authorized Version.
32. *Works of Love*, p. 38.
33. Agacinski here paraphrases Kierkegaard. 'If when another person says, "I cannot love you any longer," one proudly answers, "Then I can stop loving you"—is this independence? Alas, it is dependence, because whether he will continue to love or not depends upon whether the other will love. But the person who answers, "In that case I *shall* still continue to love you"—that person's love is made eternally free in blessed independence. He does not say it proudly—dependent on his pride—no, he says it humbly, humbling himself under eternity's "Thou shalt"; and for that very reason he is independent./ *Only when it is duty to love, only then is love eternally and happily secured against despair.*' *Works of Love*, pp. 39–40.
34. 'When spontaneous love despairs over misfortune, it only becomes manifest that it was in despair, that in its happiness it had also been in despair.' *Works of Love*, p. 40.
35. *Works of Love*, p. 41.
36. *Works of Love*, p. 43.
37. 'Without law, freedom does not exist at all, and it is law that gives freedom.' *Works of Love*, pp. 38–9.
38. 'en saadan Kjerlighed staaer og falder ikke med sin Gjenstands

Tilfældighed'—a passage mistranslated by Hong and Hong (*Works of Love*, p. 39) as 'love stands and does not fall'.

39. 'Auch das schmerzliche kann wahr sein.' Sigmund Freud, 'Vergänglichkeit' (1915), translated by James Strachey as 'On Transience' in Albert Dickson, ed., *Art and Literature* (Pelican Freud Library, vol. 1, Penguin, Harmondsworth, 1985), pp. 267–90.

14 'Is it not remarkable that Nietzsche . . . should have hated Rousseau?'

Woman, femininity: distancing Nietzsche from Rousseau

Penelope Deutscher*

Sarah Kofman, Jacques Derrida and Paul de Man have all suggested curious similarities between the work of Rousseau and Nietzsche.[1] This chapter uses that circumstance as a springboard from which to argue that the Rousseauist and Nietzschean conceptions of femininity, while apparently similar, are radically opposed when assessed by Nietzschean criteria.

I deliberately slant the comparison such that Nietzsche's conception starts to be distanced from Rousseau's misogyny, and thus the discussion ends with Nietzsche as the more appealing of the pair, an unmasker of an arch-Rousseauist 'idealism' of women and an apologist for '*proud women*'. Of course, the fact that Nietzsche's account of women can be distinguished from Rousseau's does not preclude its being otherwise misogynist. Nevertheless, through setting them against extremely like passages in Rousseau, I reinterpret many of those Nietzschean passages which have been most disturbing to various feminist readings, so that the comparison between Rousseau and Nietzsche offers an opportunity to reconsider our understanding of a Nietzschean sexual difference, sexual distance and sexual antagonism.

APPARENT SIMILARITIES BETWEEN ROUSSEAU AND NIETZSCHE

Nietzsche despised Rousseau, jeering that he was a 'moral tarantula' and an 'abortion' (Nietzsche 1982: 3), 'sick with unbridled vanity and

* Penelope Deutscher, 'Is it not remarkable that Nietzsche . . . should have hated Rousseau? Woman, Femininity: Distancing Nietzsche from Rousseau', from Paul Patton (ed.), *Nietzsche: Feminist and Political Theory* (Sydney: Allen and Unwin, 1993), 162–88. Reprinted by permission.

unbridled self-contempt' (Nietzsche 1968a: 101). But Jacques Derrida has commented that he finds Nietzsche's antipathy for Rousseau most surprising. He reminds us of Rousseau's account of sexual difference whereby a man should be strong and active; and a woman weak and passive. Then he interrupts, 'Is it not remarkable that Nietzsche, sharing this conception of femininity, of the degradation of culture and of the genealogy of morals as servitude to the slave should have hated Rousseau? (Derrida 1976: 342, trans. modified).

Certainly, there is a strong resemblance between the Rousseauist and Nietzschean conceptions of women: both denounce the equality of the sexes, both recommend that men keep their distance from women, both argue for a certain 'resistance' between the sexes. So, can we distinguish these conceptions?

One thing to note is that superficial resemblances between Rousseau and Nietzsche often prove the 'marker' of a deeper conceptual antipathy between the two. For example, where—as Derrida suggests—both philosophers praise the vigorous ancient Greek and Roman epochs and denounce their degradation into a modern, softened culture, and both discuss this degradation in terms of a genealogy of morality, in fact for Rousseau the cultural degradation is the degeneration of virtue and pity whereas for Nietzsche the genesis of morality and pity is the cultural degradation. Nietzsche himself is very precise that it is on the basis of this kind of difference that he is 'contra Rousseau': 'You have', he says, 'the choice of concluding with Rousseau that "this pitiable civilisation is to blame for our bad morality", or against Rousseau that "our good morality is to blame for this pitiableness of our civilisation"' (Nietzsche 1982: 100).

Furthermore, when Nietzsche declares that he, 'like' Rousseau, speaks of a 'return to nature', he tells us how to interpret the kind of superficial resemblances one encounters between the two philosophers. Where he describes Rousseau's return as a 'going-back', he calls his own return a 'going-*up*' (Nietzsche 1968a: 101). He describes Rousseau's nature as 'idealistic', as 'idyll and opera' (Nietzsche 1968b: 72), his own as 'frightful' although 'high and free'. Where Emile might be an example of Rousseau's 'return to nature', Nietzsche cited *Napoleon* as a piece of 'return to nature' as he understood it.

For Nietzsche it is important to ask what sense each philosopher gives to the terms 'nature' and 'return', and to *sniff*[2] the instincts each expressed. Rousseau's return to nature, he affirms, reeks of reactivity, self-loathing and *ressentiment* against the aristocratic culture (Nietzsche 1968b: 61–2). So, in the case of an apparent similarity,

Nietzsche particularly recommended that in order to distinguish the two philosophers, we should listen more carefully to the details, ask whether each had given the same meaning to a term both employed, and listen to the instincts each seemed to express—active or reactive? We can apply these criteria to the proposal that the Rousseauist and Nietzschean conceptions of femininity are akin.

FORESHORTENED AND TYPOLOGICAL NIETZSCHEAN READINGS

If we must examine the meanings each philosopher gives to his terms, we should certainly bear in mind Nietzsche's very particular style of interpretation. For example, Nietzsche's attention is directed to the instincts Rousseau manifests, rather than to the details of his argument, about which he is particularly vague, as we see when he denounces Rousseau as a personification of the subsequent French Revolution (Nietzsche 1968a: 102) and speaks of a Rousseauist 'return to nature' despite Rousseau's insistence that one could not 'return' to the mythological state of nature (Rousseau 1987a: 34). However, if we juxtapose Nietzsche's understanding of the term 'Rousseau' with his understanding of the term 'feminism' we begin to understand the roughness of detail as part of a sustained interpretative mode. Again, Nietzsche sketches with very broad strokes—vaguely claiming that emancipists idealize women, preach chastity, and imitate men (Nietzsche 1969a: 267; 1966: 163–4). It could even be said that when Nietzsche denounces what he terms 'feminism', there is little difference between the sense that Nietzsche has given to the term 'feminism' and the sense that Nietzsche has given to the term 'Rousseau'. Antithetical when represented in terms of their precise content, they nevertheless take on almost the same meaning in Nietzsche's texts: reactivity, idealism and egalitarianism.

Thus, Nietzsche's terms are often so radically '*foreshortened*'[3] that what is foregrounded and relevant is *only* the presence of reactivity, idealism, egalitarianism. No sense can be made of his denunciation of 'Rousseau' or 'feminism' unless the foreshortened meaning of these terms is read with the denunciation. In other words, when Nietzsche denounces 'Rousseau', and when he denounces 'feminism', what he is denouncing *is* reactivity, *ressentiment*, idealism, egalitarianism.

We can further demonstrate the need to read Nietzsche in terms of the meaning of a term at the point of its denunciation if we examine two passages. First, in the opening to *Daybreak*, Nietzsche denounces God, virtue, truth, justice, all the ancient ideals, every kind of faith, as, 'the whole of European feminism,[4] (or idealism if you prefer that word)' (Nietzsche 1982: 4).

The passage is comprehensible only if read as a foreshortening of the terms 'idealism' and 'feminism' to the point of their being interchangeable for Nietzsche. This can be read with a second passage, a posthumous fragment where Nietzsche aligns 'Rousseau' with 'feminism'. One might presume that this occurs because 'idealism' and 'feminism' are again interchangeable terms—but no. In this passage, 'feminism' signifies femininity, described as 'rule of feeling, sovereignty of the senses', and Rousseau is being seen to express that feminine sensibility (Nietzsche 1968b: 59). Again, the shifting between these terms, and the fact that when mobilized they may mean no more than 'sensibility', 'reactivity' or 'idealism', is such that it is essential to read a Nietzschean comment *with* the foreshortened sense of such terms.

Lastly, we see the same problem when, although Nietzsche seems to condemn feminism on the grounds that it contravenes the eternal feminine (Diprose 1989: 32) he *also* denounces feminism for invoking an idealized 'eternal feminine', a 'woman-in-herself' inherently capable of rational pursuits if immersed in different social practices. This is apparent when Nietzsche mocks women who idealize the notion of a 'woman-in-herself' (*Weib an sich*)[5] in their fight for the emancipation of women (Nietzsche 1969a: 267):

> Woman wants to become self-reliant: and for that reason she is beginning to enlighten man about 'woman-in-herself' [*Weib an sich*].
>
> (Nietzsche 1966: 162, trans. modified)

> woman adduces Madame Roland, or Madame de Staël or Monsieur [*sic*] George Sand . . . as if they proved anything in favour of 'woman-in-herself' [*Weib an sich*].
>
> (Nietzsche 1966: 164, trans. modified)

We can set against this the grounds on which Rousseau denounces sexual equality. Rousseau considers that the confusion of sexual difference which occurs when women take to literature and public speaking is a corruption of their *essential nature* as man's complement—the soothing, pleasing, domestic helpmeet. While Nietzsche seems to resemble Rousseau in denouncing sexual equality, the very terms of Nietzsche's denunciation would rather *apply* to Rousseau. Indeed, he is just as scathing of men who, he says, are all-too-ready to believe in this, 'malignant idealism', the 'eternal feminine' (Nietzsche 1969a: 267), which he describes as an 'entirely imaginary value'[6] (1972: 271) which manages to idealize women's servility[7] (Nietzsche 1974a: 18). So, in Nietzschean terms, feminism and Rousseau can also be equated in so far as they both, on his reading, idealize an eternal feminine.[8]

WOMEN AS WEAK, WOMEN'S PITY FOR THE OTHER

It follows that when we discover that both Rousseau and Nietzsche associated women with weakness, and with a sensibility to pity, we must first ask what each philosopher means by 'pity' in order to unravel the apparent resemblance. We need also to remember the device of foreshortening through which Nietzsche makes his references to women as representatives of a weak type, and that this device distinguishes the structure of his own comments about women from those of Rousseau.

First, we should note that while both philosophers associate women with pity, pity has a very different connotation for each. Rousseau elevates pity as a natural virtue awoken in man in the mythical state of nature by his imagination, which allows him to identify with the other's weakness and suffering (Rousseau 1966: 32). This facilitates a sensibility to the other which is responsible for all the social virtues: generosity, mercy, benevolence and friendship, all these being, as Rousseau explains, 'the products of a constant pity' (Rousseau 1987a: 54). Now Nietzsche agrees that pity is a basis for all the social 'virtues'—see, for example, his comments on the 'morality of pity' (Nietzsche 1969a: 19)—and he agrees that it is a particular 'sensibility' to the other's demand. However, on this basis Nietzsche does not elevate but rather denounces pity, precisely because he associates that sensibility to the other with weakness, with the weak type. Rousseau makes the weakness and sensibility to the other which pity involves a virtue—but Nietzsche *unmasks* that virtue. He denounces pity on at least two grounds. First, it is a 'self-ishness',[9] an appropriation[10] of the other to the ends of our own satisfaction with ourself, 'dressed-up' as a 'self*less*ness' (Nietzsche 1982: 83–5). Second, it is a weakness when it derives from our own inability to withstand the 'appeal' from the weak[11] (Nietzsche 1969a: 228).

If we ask what Rousseau and Nietzsche each mean by associating women with a particular propensity for pity, we find that where

Rousseau is elevating women for their weak susceptibility,[12] Nietzsche is denouncing women on these same grounds (Nietzsche 1982: 89; 1969a: 232). We must then remember our supplementary problem, of what Nietzsche means when he says *in this context*, 'woman'. As has often been pointed out (Derrida 1979: 97; Kofman 1986: 228; Diprose 1989: 27), there are multiple versions of women in the Nietzschean texts. Rather than denouncing women for their propensity to pity, Nietzsche seems rather to use women in this instance as a device through which to denounce pity. For, although he does (in *Ecce Homo*) use women to represent the weak type, he does also (elsewhere) use women to represent an ideal strong type. He also uses so much—indeed *all* of a contemporary culture to represent the weak type, that it does seem that Nietzsche's attack is directed more consistently at weakness and pity, than consistently at women, and that women are attacked only where Nietzsche has foreshortened 'women' so extremely that their connotation is the pity and reactivity that he attacks.

WOMEN AT A DISTANCE

The question of Nietzsche's desire to keep a certain distance from the weak, who are sometimes represented by women, leads us to the similarity that both Nietzsche and Rousseau recommend that a certain distance be kept from women. It is particularly in relation to their recommendation that man 'respect' a sexual distance, phrased in terms of a respect for women's 'modesty' that Sarah Kofman has argued that the texts of Rousseau and Nietzsche are 'joined' (*se communiquent*) (Kofman 1988: 201). In *Nietzsche et la scène philosophique*, Kofman argues that Nietzsche's idea of respect for women's distance or 'veil' expresses a fear of women, a castration anxiety. Woman's modesty, she interprets, 'permits the male to desire a woman without being petrified (*médusé*); it is a veil . . . , a spontaneous defense' (Kofman 1988: 191). While her assertion of the similarity between this account in Nietzsche and Rousseau is confined to a brief remark in a footnote, Kofman does indeed, in her *Le Respect des femmes*, present us with an analogous interpretation of the Rousseauist investment in a 'respect' for woman's '*pudeur*'. In working through the different senses of the Rousseauist and Nietzschean notions of 'sexual distance' we shall also have an opportunity to clarify the question of the similarity asserted by Kofman.

Now, for both Rousseau and Nietzsche, the notion of keeping women at a distance has both a positive and a negative sense. For Rousseau, the need for a distance between the sexes refers both to the sexual division between the public and private spheres, and it also refers to a certain threat of contamination that women pose to men. He explains this in his 'Letter to M. D'Alembert', where he states that man's sexual identity is jeopardized by excessive contact with women, for man is rendered effeminate by such contact, thus: 'The two sexes ought to come together sometimes; and to live separated ordinarily . . . by a commerce that is too intimate . . . the women make us into women' (Rousseau 1960: 100). Thus, in so far as Rousseau sometimes presents women as elevated objects to be idolized at a respectful distance, Sarah Kofman argues in *Le Respect des femmes* that this is a kind of Rousseauist ruse which protects men from contamination by women under the guise of a respectful admiration (Kofman 1982: 66).

Certainly, Nietzsche sometimes recommends that the strong keep their distance from the weak, so as not to become overly contaminated by their rancour and *ressentiment.* In so far as he sometimes represents women as weak and rancorous, we could say that this is the pejorative sense in which Nietzsche seems to be like Rousseau in recommending that a distance be kept from women because of the threat of contamination. We see this when Nietzsche exclaims:

> Finally women! One half of mankind is weak, typically sick, changeable, inconstant—woman needs strength in order to cleave to it; she needs a religion of weakness that glorifies being weak . . . or better, she makes the strong the weak – she rules when she succeeds in overcoming the strong!
>
> (Nietzsche 1968a: 460)

Before we see the two philosophers as akin in their account of woman as weak and contagious, we need to ask what each considers is in danger of being contaminated. For Rousseau, the threat is to sexual identity, to masculinity. He confesses, in fact, indirectly, to the instability and fragility of masculinity, to its dependence on a distance from women. Rousseau also indirectly confesses to the fragility of man's position as 'natural master' of woman, quite apart from his overt and sustained view that nature also intends domestic woman to be the private 'manager' of man. This latter view is not meant to preclude the account of man as the 'natural master', for, claims Rousseau, 'There is quite a difference between arrogating to oneself the right to command and governing him who commands' (Rousseau 1991: 408). Yet

Rousseau nevertheless seems to consider that man's commanding position is very easily jeopardized. Man, we find, can be subjugated by woman by excessive mingling with her, and also by desiring her, or loving a particular woman, or by marrying a woman of a higher social class. Man must constantly be on his guard against this threat—if not, 'then the woman, pretending to authority, acts as a tyrant toward the head of the house, and the master becomes a slave and finds himself the most ridiculous of creatures' (Rousseau 1991: 408).

For Nietzsche, the threat posed is not to man's sexual identity,[13] but rather to what he terms active forces and the 'Great Health' of the strong (Nietzsche 1974b: 346). He asserts, rather than indirectly confessing to, the fragility of active healthy forces in a contemporary, reactive society. This means that he is not obliged to resort to covert means in order to maintain an account of the superiority of the strong. In other words, he does not claim that the strong are 'really' the natural masters, and yet suggests that they had better not let the weak claim authority for a moment, neither love the weak too particularly, nor spend too much time in their proximity, or they'll find out that the weak have metamorphosed into the strong! True, the weak represent a danger to, may tyrannize or even jeopardize the health of the healthy. But while the weak type may tyrannize the strong type (Kofman 1988: 179), the threat they pose is never that they might thereby metamorphose into a strong type (Nietzsche 1969a: 121–5). Thus, the strong are not driven to dress up the weak in *moral* lofty colours, to elevate them on to a pedestal such that one would not approach the weak too closely while speaking 'most respectfully' of them. When Nietzsche recommends a 'pathos of [guarding a] distance' from the weak, and thus sometimes from women, this is not a covert attempt to uphold a most fragile masquerade in the distribution of values. For the threat posed is not that the weak may become, or are really the strong, but rather that they may weaken the strong. It is for this reason that Nietzsche sometimes advises the strong to distance themselves from them.

There is, furthermore, the second, positive Nietzschean understanding of a necessary distance between the sexes. Here he affirms women's art 'of grace, of play, of chasing away worries, of lightening burdens and taking things lightly—and her subtle aptitude for agreeable desires!' (Nietzsche 1966: 163). This tallies, of course, with the particular version of woman seen passing at some distance, where Nietzsche speaks of woman's 'action at a distance', her most magical and powerful effect. In the well-known metaphor, he likens women to mysterious sailing ships seen gliding by. 'In these quiet regions', he says, 'even the loudest surf turns to quiet and life itself into a dream about life' (Nietzsche 1974b: 123–4).

But despite the fact that Nietzsche is like Rousseau in emphasizing women's gaiety, their laughter and delightful, soothing and charming effect on men (Rousseau 1991: 358, 363), Nietzsche makes it clear that in order for women to have this effect, women must be at a necessary distance from men. While if Rousseau approaches too closely to women, he will find his masculinity jeopardized, if Nietzsche approaches too closely, he will find that woman takes on a different perspective. Approaching closely to women, man may find a jangling hubbub. 'Yet! Yet!', he reminds, 'Noble enthusiast, even on the most beautiful sailboat there is a lot of noise and unfortunately, much small and petty noise' (Nietzsche 1974b: 124).

Here, it seems that Nietzsche's irony is directed not so much at the effect of women's 'action at a distance' (he seems to agree that this effect is magical, rather than ridiculing it as 'illusory') but rather at the 'noble enthusiast' who might be overly carried away with his beautiful sailing vision. For Nietzsche reminds us that man *longs* for the 'happiness and seclusion' that women seem to offer, that he is 'apt' to think—in other words, that he has a certain investment in thinking—that nearer to women the tumult would cease and that there abides his 'better self'.

Now, what these comments suggest is that while both Rousseau and Nietzsche speak of the pleasing effect of woman, where woman is constructed as man's 'better self', nevertheless each philosopher accounts rather differently for the masculine investment in elevating woman such that she has this delightful effect. I want to make several points here.

First, although Nietzsche criticizes Rousseau on a number of points, he does not specifically refer to his conception of woman. Nevertheless, he offers a critique of a masculine investment in women's 'action at a distance' which strikes us as particularly applicable to the Rousseauist construction. Where Nietzsche reminds us that man longs for the happiness and seclusion which he seems to see faraway in women, that man is *apt* to think that alongside women abides his better self, we think irresistibly of Rousseau's version of a harmonious, peaceful complementarity between the sexes, and the Rousseauist vision of woman as the distanced, gentle companion. Nietzsche suggests that men like to conceive of women as ideals and celestial objects. Thus Nietzsche speaks of 'man's belief that a fundamentally different ideal is wrapped up in women' (Nietzsche 1966: 148), saying

> Men have hitherto treated women like birds which have strayed down to them from the heights.
>
> (Nietzsche 1966: 147)

> Man created woman—but out of what? Out of a rib of his God, of his 'ideal'.
>
> (Nietzsche 1968a: 23)

Here, we can't but think of the relationship that Sarah Kofman has pointed out (Kofman 1982: 68–9): the striking resemblance between Rousseau's conception of man's stance before woman and his stance before God. When Rousseau is before Mme de Warens, when Saint-Preux is before Julie and when Emile is before Sophie, man's relationship is that of respectful adoration, a humble abasement of man before an object that one would not profane by attempting to approach too closely. When Rousseau describes the appropriate relation to God, we see the same economy of respectful distance and humble self-abasement:

> Seized with respect, [man] halts and does not touch the veil, content with the knowledge that the immense Being is beneath it.
>
> (Rousseau 1969: 1,137)

Some difference between Rousseau and Nietzsche's conception of women delighting men at a distance seems to be implied by Nietzsche's wariness of man's desire to excessively elevate and idealize woman. Pursuing this, we might say, second, that there seems to be significant difference between Rousseau and Nietzsche in terms of what they take to be behind what they both term the 'veil'—the 'veil' referring to the impediment of voluntary distance erected between man and woman, or between man and God, or between man and truth or indeed between man and nature's secrets.

Rousseau's respect is for an ideal which he believes lies *behind* the veil. Nietzsche says that the charming and tranquil effect of women is produced by their distance. It is the veil itself, rather than the ideal one believes is behind the veil, which produces the charming effect. Yet although Nietzsche is rather mocking of the noble enthusiast who wants to believe in the ideal behind the veil, we should nevertheless note that he does not denounce the effect itself as an *illusion*. Because, for Nietzsche, as again has frequently been pointed out by Kofman among others, there is no last truth lying behind a veil that a philosopher might hope to uncover:

> We no longer believe that truth remains truth when the veils are withdrawn.... Today we consider it a matter of decency not to wish to see

everything naked, or to be present at everything, or to understand and 'know' everything.

(Nietzsche 1974b: 38)

What this means is that the magical effect which women have on the noble enthusiast is not an illusion—rather the only illusion is his confusion of that powerful effect of the veil with a 'behind' of the veil. In other words, denying the last truth behind the veil, Nietzsche denies the truth of woman. Introducing his passages on women, Diprose reminds us that Nietzsche '*qualifies*',[14] 'These are after all only—*my* truths' (Nietzsche 1966: 162)—and it is entirely compatible with this that his metaphor for truth is woman. 'Supposing truth is a woman', he writes, dogmatic philosophers have been so inexpert with woman, so awkward and improper, as to approach her with 'gruesome seriousness and clumsy obtrusiveness' (Nietzsche 1966: 2). But, he comments elsewhere, 'perhaps truth is a woman who has reasons for not letting us see her reasons' (Nietzsche 1974b: 38).

So we see here the slippage between the question of whether there is a truth of woman (I would say that Rousseau thinks so, while Nietzsche does not) and whether there is truth itself behind the veil for which woman is a metaphor (again I would say that Rousseau thinks so, and Nietzsche doesn't). In other words, the slippage between the status of 'truth itself' and that of the 'truth of woman' occurs in both Rousseau and Nietzsche's texts. The slippage occurs because both philosophers give a feminine connotation to both nature and truth. We have already seen the feminine connotation that Nietzsche gives to truth—supposing truth is a woman, he says, we should respect her modesty, we should not, as scientists, attempt to unveil her, because her modesty is necessary. Instead of woman being the 'Emperor' wearing no clothes, rather there is nothing *behind* her clothes, her veil. We see again, the slippage between Rousseau's notion of respect for women, and his notion of respect for 'nature's secrets', or the 'eternal wisdom' for whom his metaphor is a woman, in the following passages from his 'Discourse on the sciences and the arts':

This is how luxury, dissolution and slavery have at all times been the punishment for the arrogant attempts that we have made to leave the happy ignorance where eternal wisdom had placed us. The heavy veil with which she covered all her operations, seemed to give us sufficient warning that she had not destined us for vain enquiries. . . . Peoples, know then once and for all that nature wanted to protect you from science, just as a mother wrests a dangerous weapon from the hands of her child; that all the secrets she hides from you are so many evils from which she is protecting you.

(Rousseau 1987b: 10)

But while the slippage between the 'truth' of woman and woman as a metaphor for truth is common to Rousseau and Nietzsche, the reasons *why* one must respect feminine modesty, whether of woman, or of truth, are entirely opposed. This is where we can interrogate Kofman's interpretation that the texts of Rousseau and Nietzsche are 'joined' on this point. I want to suggest that we should be sensitive to the differences in the Rousseauist and Nietzschean investment in a distance between the sexes, and the difference in their conceptions of the 'veil'. For, whereas the Nietzschean respect is for the truth that there is no ultimate truth behind the veil, the Rousseauist respect is precisely for the truth behind the veil.

So let's return to the suggestion from Kofman and Derrida that Nietzsche's economy of 'respect' for the distance of woman stems from an economy of *fear* of (castrating) woman, and thus Kofman's suggestion about the alliance between Rousseau and thus Nietzsche on this point. We note first that in the case of Derrida's *Spurs*, man's fearful wariness of what's (not) behind woman's veil is only one aspect of a three-part version of woman. Derrida's triad of Nietzschean women is a triad of masculine versions of woman, in which woman is either denounced as dissimulator by credulous man in the name of truth, or else denounced for manipulating effects of truth (here the abyss of non-truth behind the masquerade is terrifying) or affirmed as dissimulator, in the name of the absence of truth. In the latter, non-truth remains an 'abyss', but is *affirmed* as such (Derrida 1979: 97). Nietzsche's various masks include his interpretation of women in all these different terms, at various times. So we could interpret Kofman's suggestion about the alliance between Nietzsche and Rousseau in terms of the fact that at least *one* of Nietzsche's masculine versions of women is a 'Rousseauist' version. This is the version in which women's distance must be 'respected' in order to avert the threat posed by women. We might say that Nietzsche's temporary face here is the Rousseauist man—a man elevating women to a distanced, charming ideal in order to stave off the threat she poses to him.

But while both Rousseau—and one of the Nietzschean masks—defer with 'respect' the threat posed by women, the threat is still very differently understood. Rousseau staves off the threat posed by women in the name of the truth identified by Derrida in the first of the three Nietzschean 'propositions' about women. Rousseau is the credulous man of the first proposition. We see his belief in truth expressed in his fear that woman may be deceiving man, his disapproval of all things artificial and deceptive, his refusal to approach nature's secrets in the name of the truth behind the veil. While Nietzsche *identifies* the 'credulous' man threatened by the perversion of truth, he also articulates a second threat: that of non-truth, the abyss, and the manipulation by woman of non-truth in her seductive truth-effect, and he *also* manages to go beyond the perspective of woman as threatening.

And this is why it is important to acknowledge, as Kofman does, that Derrida insists on the 'enigmatic but necessary congruence between [Nietzsche's] "feminist" and "anti-feminist" claims' (Kofman 1988: 201). For a necessary congruence suggests that we read Nietzsche's occupation of a credulous [Rousseauist] mask *with* his identification of non-truth as potentially threatening, and yet also with the affirmative mask that ridicules both the credulity in truth and the fear of non-truth. Put bluntly, Rousseau proposes no such critique of his own credulity or his own fears about women.

Finally, we have seen that for Rousseau, man should respect the veil over truth because he should be content to live in a 'happy ignorance'. When affirmative, Nietzsche's 'respect' is no fearful humility. It is not a recommendation to men that they live in a happy ignorance but rather the *opposite*—that they be *courageous* enough to face the absence of ultimate truths, and for that reason, not attempt to unveil all. It is in this context that we must read the apparent proximity of the following affirmations.

Rousseau:

> one would say that nature had taken precautions to conceal this fatal secret from us.
>
> (Rousseau 1987b: 66)

> Peoples, know then once and for all that nature wanted to protect you from science.
>
> (Rousseau 1987a: 10)

Nietzsche:

> One should have more respect for the bashfulness with which nature has hidden behind riddles and iridescent uncertainties. Perhaps truth is a woman who has reasons for not letting us see her reasons?
>
> (Nietzsche 1974b: 38)

Again, it is Nietzsche's own proposal for how to interpret more carefully the apparent similarities between himself and Rousseau which is instructive here. His proposal suggests that we pay attention, not only, as we have done, to the question of what each philosopher means by the 'veil', but also that we pay attention to the instincts each expresses in recommending that we not approach it too closely. We might say that Rousseau's 'respect' is a voluntary self-abasement, a stunting of forces, a desire for contented ignorance, for a benevolent protectionism (as Nietzsche once described the Rousseauist nature), a stance of 'humility' before his ideal. Nietzsche was not wrong to denounce Rousseau precisely for his idealism and his self-abasement. It may be that one of the Nietzschean masks expresses a *ressentiment* toward women, and this would be the elevation of women into a glorious ideal where this expresses a fear of the non-truth of women and an aversion to close and dangerous proximity to her.[15] However, it is most important that we sniff no 'humility', no self-abasement in the *affirmative* pleasure Nietzsche does describe in the enjoyment of woman at a 'magical' distance (if that perspective is affirmed *as* a perspective) given that such a humility could only be, in Nietzsche's terms, a stunting and abasement of his own forces and the expression of a weak and reactive type.

THE RESISTANCE BETWEEN THE SEXES

So, I want to use this question of what instincts are expressed and whether forces are stunted or strengthened, to assess the ways in which Rousseau and Nietzsche affirm the need for a 'resistance' between the sexes. We have seen that for Nietzsche, woman's soothing, delightful effect is sustained only by her distance from men. So, what does man find when he approaches more closely to women? Certainly, he does not find the truth of woman, for as we know, there is no truth of woman. Nevertheless, he finds another, different effect, or we could say, another, different perspective. Now, we have already encountered one of these different women, and this is the woman who represents rancour, *ressentiment*, reactivity and feminism as Nietzsche understands it. While we also know that there is at the very least a 'third' woman, the third woman I wish to discuss here is the woman of turbulence and resistance. This is the woman of 'antagonism between the sexes', as Nietzsche puts it, and in fact, this is one of the various accounts in which Nietzsche speaks 'positively' about women.

Nietzsche describes this antagonism separating man and woman as 'most abysmal', as the necessity of an eternally hostile tension (Nietzsche 1966: 147), as, 'harsh, terrible, enigmatic and immoral (Nietzsche 1974b: 319). He describes procreation as depending on the duality of the sexes and involving perpetual strife, with only periodically intervening reconciliation (Nietzsche 1967: 33), where 'something new is born from two enemy principles'[16] (Nietzsche 1978: 187). Nietzsche's comments about the relations between the sexes being a case of 'love thy enemy' (Nietzsche 1972: 377) are not as sarcastic as they sometimes sound, because of his revaluation of the notion of 'enemy relations'.[17]

Now I want, of course, to juxtapose this account with the ideal of a harmonious complementarity between the sexes as envisaged by Rousseau.

First, we know that both Rousseau and Nietzsche oppose egalitarianism of the sexes in the name of what each calls '*natural*' relations between the sexes. Thus, both Rousseau and Nietzsche defend their versions of sexual difference against denunciations of the 'contra-nature', for example Rousseau condemns Plato's 'civil promiscuity which throughout confounds the two sexes in the same employments and in the same labours', as a subversion of nature (Rousseau 1991: 363). Nietzsche condemns the emancipation of women as a 'malignant idealism' and a 'contra-nature', aiming to poison 'the good conscience, what is natural in sexual love' (Nietzsche 1969a: 267–8).

But Nietzsche has already warned us to ask 'What is this nature Rousseau speaks of?' and cautioned us about the difference between Rousseau's 'good', 'benevolent' nature, and his own terrible nature; we need to apply this distinction to their respective reliance on conceptions of 'natural' relations between the sexes. While Rousseau's 'natural' relations offer an ideal alternative to the contemporary state of degraded relations between the sexes in which Rousseau thinks that man develops a *fear* of women, in Nietzsche's version of a 'natural' relation between the sexes it is precisely fear that man should bear woman. While fear between the sexes is for Rousseau a contra-nature, for Nietzsche, fearful relations are affirmed in his 'terrible' nature. Nietzsche explains that the terrible man will accord woman her 'due tribute of contempt and fear'[18] (Nietzsche 1968b: 526).

What does Nietzsche understand by sexual antagonism? In *Beyond Good and Evil* it is described as the man of 'depth' being 'obliged' to think of woman in something described as the 'oriental way' thus: 'he must conceive of woman as a possession, as property that can be locked, as something predestined for service' (Nietzsche 1966: 167). Nietzsche's 'sexual antagonism' is always described as a matter of how man likes to, or is obliged to, or 'must' see woman—as tantalizing savage creatures to capture and enclose. However, we are told that woman resists man's idea of her, she combats these affronts and is dangerous (Nietzsche 1966: 169–70, 87, 88), and it may be for this reason that when Zarathustra holds forth to the Old Woman on the subject of women, that she cautions him not to go near them without his whip (Nietzsche 1969b: 93).

In reading Nietzsche's account of how men 'must' see woman—as a potentially servile object—we must remember that Nietzsche exposes the man who elevates woman to a divine ideal as a means of rendering her *servile.* While Nietzsche argues that man pursues woman as an object, 'pre-destined for service', he also seems to incorporate into that notion woman's resistance to this attempt to ensnare her. This resistance seems to play a part in the notion of antagonism between the sexes as enemy principles.

Furthermore, it is to be remarked that this 'man of depth' is described as having 'that depth of benevolence [*Wohlwollens*] which is capable of severity and hardness and easily mistaken for them' (Nietzsche 1966: 167). For benevolence has a particular, revalued sense for Nietzsche. In *Ecce Homo* he explains that attacking one's enemy is a kind of 'benevolence' [again, '*Wohlwollens*'][19] and of 'gratitude': it is a mark of 'respect', of 'distinction' and 'recognition' of the other as a 'worthy' and 'equal'[20] enemy (Nietzsche 1969a: 231–3). So Nietzsche's conception of enemy relations should be read as insisting on the recognition and distinction of the other as the enemy which he considers is involved. It is a recognition that he would not think Rousseau accords the other, precisely because Rousseau conceives of the other in terms of pity, and for Nietzsche pity is among other things an appropriation of rather than a recognition of the other.

However, in *The Gay Science*, Nietzsche again describes 'sexual antagonism'. Here he describes the difference of the sexes in love. This, he says, is a relationship where woman gives herself to man in a complete gift, in a 'total abandon' [*vollkommene Hingabe*] 'and not mere surrender', of soul and body, without reserve, to man—and where man's forces thereby accumulate (Nietzsche 1974b: 319). What is difficult to reconcile with the notion of enemy, antagonistic relations between the sexes is Nietzsche's presentation of what seems to be an extreme *docility* on the part of women. It is hard to see—if man desires that woman give herself completely[21] and if woman does indeed make herself over to him as an 'absolute gift'—why Nietzsche should describe these relations as '*terrible* and enigmatic': indeed, we seem to be brought back to a harmonious complementarity, to a Rousseauist sexual difference.

In this regard, perhaps we should note first, that curiously, in the Rousseauist account, woman does *not* give herself over to man as a perfect gift. For Nietzsche, when woman gives herself, she does so without restriction and without reserve. But Rousseau's woman 'properly' resists man. The resistance is a strategic and temporary reserve followed by a modest consent.[22] For Nietzsche, there is no modesty, no chaste self-governing in the sexual antagonism and the unrestrained gift of the woman. Perhaps he would argue that both men's and women's forces are weakened in the Rousseauist relations between the sexes, since man abases himself before woman, and since women modestly inhibit their own desires in their resistance to man, and then 'let themselves be vanquished' (Rousseau 1960: 86). Again, that the point is always the instincts expressed by the account of woman, rather than the 'details' of that account, is particularly apparent in the fact that Nietzsche disparages 'misogynists'.[23] Since Nietzsche, conceiving man and woman as natural enemies, gives a positive value to that relationship, we should distinguish it from a kind of hatred for women that he does denounce:

> Misogynists—'Woman is our enemy'—out of the man who says that to other men there speaks an immoderate drive which hates not only itself but its means of satisfaction as well.
>
> (Nietzsche 1982: 165)

What distinguishes the Nietzschean and 'misogynist' versions of 'enemy relations' between the sexes is activity as opposed to reactivity. For Nietzsche asserts that where the misogynist takes women as his enemy, he expresses instincts of self-hatred, indeed those same instincts which Rousseau is said to express in his lofty idealism and thus in his elevating women to a lofty ideal.

Rather than Nietzsche's ideal man abasing himself before woman in love, he is said to be rendered 'richer in "himself"' (Nietzsche 1974b: 319), and his forces increase when woman gives herself to him in an unreserved and unrestrained gift. So, Nietzsche's account would need to be assessed in terms of whether or not the protagonists' forces increase through their encounter—Nietzsche certainly considers that those of men would, in ideal relations between the sexes. But this will occur only if woman is the worthy, strong opponent, so that while man *covets* her as a servile object, she must *resist* that man, or that version of herself. When she does give herself over to man, this must not be in the spirit of surrender in so far as this implies a weakening of forces, but in a complete, affirmative gift of herself.

So we might well ask about woman's forces, which Nietzsche does not mention often. There are times when Nietzsche does not restrict the growth of forces that is produced by sexual antagonism to men alone, when he speaks generally of 'the increase of forces, for example, in the dance between the sexes'[24] (Nietzsche 1972: 328) and elsewhere again he speaks specifically of woman's forces which increase from the dance between the sexes, in the 'drunkenness called love' (Nietzsche 1968b: 425). Since Zarathustra tells women that their greatest hope should be to bear the overman (Nietzsche 1969: 92), Nietzsche is sometimes taken to exclude the concept of the noble woman. Yet there is an account in *Daybreak* of ideal relations between 'complete men' and 'complete women' which suggests otherwise:

> *Different kinds of pride*—Women grow pale at the thought that their beloved may not be worthy of them, men pale at the idea that they may not be worthy of their beloved. I am speaking of whole women, whole men.
>
> (Nietzsche 1982: 174)

Here, Nietzsche goes on to explain that, 'Such men, as men who are *customarily* confident and full of the feeling of power, acquire in a state of passion a sense of shame and doubt', and the women, who, says Nietzsche, 'normally feel themselves the weak and *surrendering* sex' (trans. modified, my emphasis: '*solche Frauen aber fühlen sich sonst immer als die Schwachen, zur Hingebung Bereiten*')[25] now, in a Nietzschean ideal of relations between the sexes:

> acquire in the exceptional state of passion their pride and their feeling of power—which asks: who is worthy of me?

So we could read Nietzsche's account of the 'perfect' woman (*ein vollkommeneres Weib*) in *The Gay Science* who devotes herself entirely to man so that his own forces grow (Nietzsche 1974b: 319), *with* the account of the 'whole' woman (*von ganzen Frauen*) in *Daybreak* whose forces grow such that they proudly ask who merit them. The repetition between these passages of the idea of 'wholeness' or 'perfection' as opposed to the idea of 'surrender' is important here. First, although the 'devoted' woman in *The Gay Science* is described as thereby becoming what Nietzsche terms 'perfect', this seems less like the rhetoric for the perfect housewife (the complete, devoted woman) given that Nietzsche *also* describes the 'proud' woman who goes *beyond surrender and docility* as a 'complete' woman. Second, the 'devoted' woman of *The Gay Science* is like the 'proud woman' in that she is defined *against* (in opposition to) a weak and '*surrendering*' woman [*vollkommene Hingabe* (*nicht nur Hingebung*)]—in both cases, there is a going-beyond of a certain kind of women's surrender to man. Although the version of the 'proud' woman emphasizes more strongly an increase in women's forces than does the account of the 'devoted' woman, I think that in both cases the point may be the kind of women both proud and devoted women are set against—weak, or restrained women of surrender.

Certainly, in both cases, the point is the 'why'—*why* does Nietzsche emphasize a notion of a 'complete' woman? In both cases, antagonistic sexual relations are conceived entirely in terms of producing an increase in the forces of the protagonists. The point, even of the 'devoted' woman, is that she does not give herself half-heartedly, but unreservedly, affirmatively. Perhaps Nietzsche's immoderate devoted woman is a re-evaluation of the traditional ideal of the devoted woman, who like Rousseau's Sophie, resists man modestly and temporarily, and subdues her own passions so as to manipulate those of Emile.

Nietzsche's account of the devoted woman does focus on the maximization of *men's* forces, but it is not that the non-maximization of women's forces is the necessary condition of the maximization of men's forces. This is the importance of the opposition to 'women of surrender'. The woman's unrestrained gift of herself is, in Nietzsche's view, affirmative—but so is the woman of pride who asks who is worthy of her—and so is the woman who is dangerous, who is to be feared, resisting man's ideals of woman, in the most obvious account of the resistance between the sexes.

In resisting Emile, it is important that Sophie is deliberately complicit with Emile's 'version' of her, as elevated, superior object towards whom he must strain, and that the tutor indirectly advises Sophie that her role must be to sustain this version of woman. In comparison, we must ask if Nietzsche requires of women that they cut the cloth of themselves according to the image demanded of them. Certainly, he acknowledges that woman often does form herself such that she is complicit with a masculine version of herself (Nietzsche 1974b: 126). But he also presents an ideal of woman as a dangerous opponent who resists rather than abets man's version of her, and must in fact do so if the kind of sexual antagonism which might sharpen the wits and forces of each is to be sustained. We might add that it is perhaps congruent with such an account that such a woman may sometimes give herself over in a passionate, perfect gift.[26]

Nietzsche's critique is not aimed at the fact that there will always be a masculine investment in the production of certain interpretations of women. He seems to suggest that this is inevitable, just as it is inevitable that he has his own interpretations, his own truths of women (Nietzsche 1966: 162). Therefore, a Nietzschean critique of the Rousseauist conception of woman would not denounce this as being 'merely' Rousseau's conception of woman, for the status of this 'mere' is lost at the point of the exclusion of ultimate truths about women, Nietzsche's facetious comment about his own 'mere' truths about women notwithstanding. A Nietzschean critique of the Rousseauist conception of women would not be aimed at the fact that Rousseau's interpretation of woman was mediated by a certain desire to produce a certain interpretation of woman. The Nietzschean critique would not be directed at the terms and notions of woman deployed by Rousseau (difference, distance, no touching at the veil, abhorring the contra-nature) for these are terms deployed by Nietzsche himself. But a Nietzschean critique would nevertheless devastate the Rousseauist conception of woman, because of the instincts the Rousseauist conception of woman expresses. The Rousseauist fear of woman is not love of antagonism, but fear of contamination. The Rousseauist fear of contamination is not distancing from the weak, but a rendering weak of oneself. The Rousseauist idealization of woman is not a vision of a woman of maximized forces, but a lowering of forces in self-abasement. The Rousseauist notion of the contra-nature is not a 'contra', the stunting of our own forces, but an abasement before a transcendental directive. The question, for Nietzsche, is not whether man is 'overly' invested in producing 'his' woman, but rather, the nature of the instincts which are manifest in the interpretation.

Acknowledgements

This material formed part of a longer work submitted as a DEA in History of Philosophy, Université de Paris I, 1991. Sarah Kofman's 1990–91 *Ecce Homo* seminar was a constant influence. Thanks also to Jean-Philippe Mihière, Sarah Kofman, Richard Peres, Florence Laborir, Paul Patton and Paul Redding for critical comments and assistance with language difficulties.

Notes

1. It so happens that each of these three is associated with deconstruction, and that each asserts a series of very surprising resemblances between Rousseau and Nietzsche in a string of footnotes and asides in their work. Paul de Man suggests similarities between their conceptions of a will to power or a 'power to will' (de Man 1979: 140), between their critiques of organized, politicized Christianity (de Man 1979: 223), between their conceptions of metaphor as the origin of 'literal' meaning (de Man 1979: 122–3, 154), between their conceptions of the specifically human mode of the promise (de Man 1979: 273), between their conceptions of physiological foundations to our notions of good and evil (de Man 1979: 244) and in the fact that they are both what he calls 'rhetorically self-conscious' philosophers (de Man 1979: 226). Sarah Kofman also argues that the Rousseauist and Nietzschean accounts of metaphor as the origin of 'literal' language are akin; however, she argues that both the early Nietzsche and Rousseau conserve a 'logocentric' hierarchy of original over tributary meaning (Kofman 1983: 18, 57, 153). Kofman also suggests that Rousseau's texts accord with the Nietzschean version of woman's modesty as her highest virtue (Kofman 1986: 246). This last is a point that I return to later in the chapter.
2. Here, I am thinking of Nietzsche's account of a 'healthy' instinct: 'My instinct for cleanliness is characterized by a perfectly uncanny sensitivity so that the proximity or—what am I saying?—the inmost parts, the "entrails" of every soul are physiologically perceived by me—smelled' (Nietzsche 1969a: 233).
3. The suggestion is that the account of Nietzsche's perspectivism in terms of artistic metaphors such that (as this is expressed by Nehamas), in any representation, certain elements are foregrounded at the expense of others and the subject matter thereby 'created' by the artist (Nehamas 1985: 55), applies here to Nietzsche's account of Rousseau and feminism. Here, Nietzsche's 'foregrounding' is an extreme 'foreshortening', in which it is the presence of *ressentiment*, idealism and egalitarianism only which are dramatically at the fore, and the precise detail and content of 'Rousseau' or 'feminism' dramatically obscure. This is a different account of Nietzsche's 'foreshortening' than that to be found in Kofman (1988: 186). Here, Kofman uses the term to describe Nietzsche's account of the flattening, 'frog perspective' in which the weak defer before and interpret the world in terms of elevated 'high' concepts (God, truth, reality) such that their perspective of evaluation is 'bottom' to 'top'.
4. '*Dem ganzen europäischen Femininismus (oder Idealismus, wenn man's lieber hört)*'.
5. It seems '*Weib an sich*' is not so much 'woman *as such*' as translated by R. J. Hollingdale but 'woman in herself' as Kaufmann does here (though not consistently) translate it. This strengthens the suggestion that in these passages Nietzsche attacks feminists not for their contravention of the eternal feminine, but for their deployment of a notion of the eternal feminine, a conception that he rejects. Or, we might say that any notion of the eternal feminine that Nietzsche does invoke to denounce the idealist notion of an eternal feminine is a re-valued 'eternal feminine' and not the 'same', idealist eternal feminine he denounces. Thus, an alternative to seeing Nietzsche as *ambivalent* on this point would be the idea of the 're-evaluation of old nouns'. Kofman

insists on the constant reading of Nietzsche in these terms (Kofman 1988: 178)—here, the 'eternal feminine' would be the re-valued 'old noun'.

6. (*Das Weib, das ewig Weibliche: ein bloß imaginärer Werth, an den allein des Mann glaubt.*) Here, Nietzsche tells us that only men believe in the 'entirely imaginary' values, 'woman' and the 'eternal feminine'. Elsewhere, as we see, he tells us of the propensity of certain women to believe in these 'imaginary values', also the emancipists, for example.
7. '*Die absolute Hingebung (in der Religion) als Reflex der sklavischen Hingebung oder der weiblichen (—das Ewig-Weibliche ist der idealisirte Sklavensinn)*'.
8. One could pursue Diprose's question of whether Nietzsche does invoke the notion of the eternal feminine that he denounces (Diprose 1989: 32). For one thing, the phrasing of 'the emancipated are anarchists in the world of the eternally feminine' is ambiguous (*Im Grunde sind die Emancipirten die Anarchisten in der Welt des 'Ewig-Weiblichen'*). Is Nietzsche attacking emancipists because they undermine the eternal feminine, or because they invoke it? There is an element of mockery in the phrase '*der Welt des "Ewig-Weiblichen"*' which suggests the latter. For another thing, the preceding passage: 'Perhaps I am the first psychologist of the eternal feminine. They all love me', etc., seems rather tongue-in-cheek given that it immediately precedes Nietzsche's mockery of such a notion. Even if Nietzsche does deploy an 'eternal feminine', this must certainly be read *with* his own sarcasm about such a conception, and can't be simply seen as 'self-contradiction' without raising the question of how to read Nietzsche's constant 'self-contradictions'—sometimes as his masks, sometimes as his re-valuation of old terms and so on. Diprose does not assert that Nietzsche has simply contradicted himself. For, on her reading, the 'essential self' that Nietzsche rejects is not *the same* as the eternal feminine that she considers he does insist on. The difference, she says, is that Nietzsche admits that he is interpreting an image of himself when he acknowledges his dependence on the 'eternal feminine'. We could add—the emancipist who believes in the eternal feminine would be like Rousseau, and unlike Nietzsche, in believing in the 'truth of woman'.
9. Its aim is to generate or reinforce a version of the self: it is not aimed at, or open to the other. Thus it is an expression of the will to power masquerading as a superior moral virtue.
10. For his employment of this term, see also Nietzsche (1974b: 176).
11. It should be noted that apart from other scathing accounts of the psychology of pity which Nietzsche gives, he also sometimes refers to his own 'pity' for humanity. Here, pity has taken on a re-valued sense for Nietzsche, so that this is not, of course, incoherent with his denunciation of pity. See, for example, Nietzsche's description of what he calls 'my kind of pity' (Nietzsche 1968b: 198).
12. Derrida has pointed out (Derrida 1976: 173) that Rousseau particularly uses mothers and their maternal love for their child in his examples of the expression of pity for the weak. There is also the fact that Julie finally capitulates to Saint-Preux and to her own desire because of her pity for him, and Rousseau's references to slaves and women being the only people 'weak' (susceptible) enough to try to prevent brawlers about to tear each other's throats out (Rousseau 1987a: 55).
13. It seems to me that this interpretation can be sustained despite the occurrence

of an association by Nietzsche of strength and active forces with 'virility', see for example the use of the term 'emasculation' to describe the weak rendering the strong weak (Nietzsche 1969a: 124). Although this might seem to reinforce the notion of 'surprising similarities' between Rousseau and Nietzsche, the distinction between these two accounts of the fragility of 'virility' would still have to be traced in terms of the difference between their accounts of the fragility of the strong, as suggested above.

14. Of course, we have to tread a little carefully with this qualification, for Nietzsche does not mean that these are only 'his' truths as opposed to some truths that might be the eternal and final truths. Given that he rejects the possibility of the latter, the status of the 'qualification' '*only*' becomes ambiguous and interesting.
15. However, it is important that this would not be the mask of Nietzsche's 'anti-feminism'. Nietzsche's 'anti-feminism' entirely expresses his notion of a 'healthy' distance from the reactive. He does not consider the weak the 'worthy enemy' but rather the threat to pure air. He does consider that the strong may be repelled by and desire distance from the weak without this being the equivalent of their own weakness or *ressentiment.* Strangely, it is not Nietzsche's denunciation of women but rather a certain mode of his *elevation* of women that we might identify as reactive, in so far as it is a conversion into a lofty vision of women of what is in fact a fear of the abyss. Here, interpretations of women as castrating might be reactive—while the affirmation of the abyss would be active.
16. Draft for *The Birth of Tragedy*, Notebook fragment, 1870–71 cross-referenced by Colli and Montinari for section no. 1, *The Birth of Tragedy* (Roughly: 'The fact that nature tied the birth of tragedy to these two fundamental instincts, the Apollonian and the Dionysian might appear as much of a fissure of reason as an arrangement by that same nature which tied the propagation of the species to the duality of the sexes, something which grand Kant always found surprising. For the common secret is the fact that from two enemy principles something new can be born such that these two divided instincts appear to be a unity: in this sense, reproduction is just like a work of tragic art in that its worth can be like the pledge of the rebirth of Dionysus, like a beam of hope on the eternally mourning aspect of Demeter.') The themes raised by Ainley (1988) about procreation, generation and childbirth as affirmative in Nietzschean terms and as giving Nietzsche a metaphor for an affirmative, creative principle are interesting here. Kofman has also pointed out that where childbirth and woman give rise to a general, Nietzschean metaphor, that Nietzsche has already mediated that exploitation of the metaphor of woman as a generating, life-giving force with his interpretation of woman as affirmative in these terms.
17. These comments give another complexion to the passage in *Zarathustra*: 'Woman is not yet capable of friendship' [which is to say enemy relations, since the best friend is, of course, the best enemy]. In any case, Nietzsche immediately continues there: 'But tell me, you men, who among you is capable of friendship?' (Nietzsche 1978: 57). Nietzsche, while sometimes dubious about woman's capacity for enemy relations with man, seems to consider at least that this is their ideal relationship, and is dubious that men are ready for such relations. In *Zarathustra*, we are told that woman is *not yet* capable of

being man's friend—and this is the same passage in which we are told that the best friend is the best enemy, in which enemy relations and the notion of the 'worthy' enemy are affirmed. Thus, 'You should honour even the enemy in your friend. . . . In your friend you should possess your best enemy. Your heart should feel closest to him when you oppose him.' And, 'Are you a tyrant? If so, you cannot be a friend. Are you a slave? If so, you cannot have friends. In woman, a slave and a tyrant have all too long been concealed. For that reason, woman is not yet capable of friendship: she knows only love' (Nietzsche 1969b: 83).

18. This ideal relation needs to be distinguished from Nietzsche's account of all-too-human women, 'typed' as weak, reactive, rancorous, prone to 'the cult of pity' (1968b: 460) for whom Nietzsche bears an antipathy which is not the ideal antagonism he speaks of—although there is often blurring between these accounts. This point about needing to distinguish different conceptions that are nevertheless blurred in Nietzsche is tangly. It might involve distinguishing on the one hand his contempt for the [weak, reactive] woman 'mastering' man (Nietzsche 1968b: 460) from a 'fear' of women expressed in an affirmative 'antagonism between the sexes'.

    In general, obviously Nietzsche's antipathy for the weak needs to be distinguished from the kind of antagonism that is valorized in ideal enemy relations. In one kind of antagonism, Nietzsche recommends distance *from* the weak (distancing the strong from the weak), in another kind of antagonism, he considers that [antagonistic] enemy relations imply a *respect* and acknowledgement of the enemy. While Nietzsche values an engagement with the enemy, this does not preclude his also valuing distance between enemies, certainly in so far as one should not attempt to know the enemy 'too well', and in so far as one does not learn the 'truth' of the enemy through engaging with her/him. Perhaps this is best articulated as the difference between distancing oneself *from* [the weak], and the distance *between* [the strong and the strong].

19. '*Wohlwollens*' is the term employed both in *Ecce Homo* (Nietzsche 1969b: 232) and *Beyond Good and Evil* (Nietzsche 1966: 167), although the repetition is less evident where the latter has been translated as benevolence, but the former has been translated as 'goodwill'.

20. Again, here there has to be a distinction between the notion of equality as loss of individualism, or inability to encounter the individual, and here, a re-valued notion of equality—finding the worthy equal—a worthy enemy: 'Equality before the enemy: the first presupposition of an honest duel' (Nietzsche 1969a: 232).

21. 'Man, when he loves a woman, wants precisely this love from her' (Nietzsche 1974b: 319).

22. This resistance is woman's strategem since, as Emile's tutor instructs Sophie, it allows her to govern her husband. Woman's modesty is also nature's strategem, since the modesty with which woman is endowed restrains both women and men from the excess of sexual relations which would lead to their own destruction.

23. Colli and Montinari suggest that Nietzsche's reference here is to Schopenhauer (Nietzsche 1970: 317), which is particularly interesting in the light of Nietzsche's comments in *On the Genealogy of Morals* about Schopenhauer's *need* for enemies, including women (Nietzsche 1969b: 106). At one point then,

Nietzsche would seem to read Schopenhauer's misogyny as reactive, at another as active.

24. '*Das Mehr von Kraft z. B. beim Tanz der Geschlechter*'.
25. In a footnote to his translation of *The Gay Science*, p. 363 (Nietzsche 1974b: 319), Kaufmann emphasizes his translation of '*nicht nur Hingebung*' as 'not mere surrender' rather than 'not mere devotion'. However, in *Daybreak*, the fact that 'complete women' again are said to go beyond their 'usual' state of weakness and surrender is obscured by the fact that the repetition of 'Hingebung' is suppressed, here by Hollingdale. In my text, however, I do want to focus on the repetition of the idea of 'surrender' as that which women go beyond either in 'pride' or in the 'complete gift'.
26. In the French translations of Nietzsche established by Colli and Montinari, the 'total abandon' and not 'mere surrender' that woman is said to understand by 'love' is translated as a 'perfect gift', thus: '*Ce que la femme entend par amour est assez clair: parfait don (non pas seulement abandon) du corps et du l'âme sans restriction et sans réserve*' (Nietzsche 1989: 270).

    If 'perfect gift' is appropriate in this context, might we suspect here after all a fantasy of an 'unveiled', 'authentic woman'—finally a woman who would *not* be 'giving herself' (acting, holding in reserve) even as she 'gave herself'? (In that case, would Nietzsche's mask here be other than that whereby he affirms woman as dissimulation, who might thereby be considered an 'imperfect' gift in the fantasy of the total presence of woman?)

Bibliography

Ainley, A. (1988) '"Ideal selfishness"—Nietzsche's metaphor of maternity', in D. F. Krell and D. Wood (eds) *Exceedingly Nietzsche*, London: Routledge.

de Man, P. (1979) *Allegories of Reading*, New Haven, Conn. and London: Yale University Press.

Derrida, J. (1976) *Of Grammatology*, trans. G. C. Spivak, Baltimore, Md.: Johns Hopkins University Press.

—— (1979) *Spurs/Eperons*, trans. B. Harlow, Chicago and London: University of Chicago Press.

Diprose, R. (1989) 'Nietzsche, ethics and sexual difference', *Radical Philosophy* 52: 27–33.

Kofman, S. (1982) *Le Respect des femmes*, Paris: Editions Galilée.

—— (1983) *Nietzsche et la métaphore*, Paris: Editions Galilée.

—— (1986) *Nietzsche et al scène philosophique*, Paris: Editions Galilée.

—— (1988) 'Baubô: theological perversion and fetishism',* trans. T. Strong, in M. A. Gillespie and T. B. Strong (eds) *Nietzsche's New Seas*, Chicago and London: University of Chicago Press (*translation of excerpt from S. Kofman, *Nietzsche et la scène philosophique*).

Nehamas, A. (1985) *Nietzsche—Life as Literature*, Cambridge, Mass. and London: Harvard University Press.

Nietzsche, F. (1966) *Beyond Good and Evil*, trans. W. Kaufmann, New York: Vintage.

—— (1967) *The Birth of Tragedy and The Case of Wagner*, trans. W. Kaufmann, New York: Vintage.
—— (1968a) *Twilight of the Idols*, trans. R. J. Hollingdale, Harmondsworth: Penguin.
—— (1968b) *The Will to Power*, trans. R. J. Hollingdale and W. Kaufmann, New York: Vintage.
—— (1969a) *On the Genealogy of Morals and Ecce Homo*, trans. W. Kaufmann, New York: Vintage.
—— (1969b) *Thus Spoke Zarathustra*, trans. R. J. Hollingdale, Harmondsworth: Penguin.
—— (1970) *Aurore*, trans. J. Hervier, Paris: Gallimard (Folio).
—— (1972) *Nachgelassene Fragmente, Anfang 1888 bis Anfang Januar 1889*, Berlin and New York: Walter de Gruyter.
—— (1974a) *Nachgelassene Fragmente Herbst 1885 bis Herbst 1887*, Berlin and New York: Walter de Gruyter.
—— (1974b) *The Gay Science*, trans. W. Kaufmann, New York: Vintage.
—— (1978) *Nachgelassene Fragmente Herbst 1869 bis Herbst 1872*, Berlin and New York: Walter de Gruyter.
—— (1982) *Daybreak*, trans. R. J. Hollingdale, Harmondsworth: Penguin.
—— (1989) *Le Gai savoir*, trans. P. Klossowski, Paris: Gallimard (Folio).
Rousseau, J.J. (1960) 'Letter to M. D'Alembert on the theatre', in *Politics and the Arts*, trans. A. Bloom, Glencoe, III.: Free Press of Glencoe.
—— (1966) 'Essay on the origin of languages', in J. J. Rousseau and H. Herder, *Two Essays on the Origin of Languages*, trans. J. H. Moran and A. Gode, Chicago and London: University of Chicago Press.
—— (1969) 'Lettre à M. Franquières', in *Oeuvres Complètes*, tome IV, Paris: Bibliothèque de la Pléiade, Editions Gallimard.
—— (1987a) 'Discourse on the origin of inequality', in *The Basic Political Writings*, trans. D. A. Cress, Indianapolis, Ind. and Cambridge: Hackett.
—— (1987b) 'Discourse on the sciences and the arts', in *The Basic Political Writings*, trans. D. A. Cress, Indianapolis, Ind. and Cambridge: Hackett.
—— (1991) *Emile*, trans. A. Bloom, Harmondsworth: Penguin.

Further Reading

AGACINSKI, SYLVIANE, *Aparte: Conceptions and Deaths of Soren Kierkegaard*, trans. Kevin Newmark (Tallahassee: Florida State University Press, 1988).

AINLEY, ALISON, '"Ideal Selfishness": Nietzsche's Metaphor of Maternity', in David Farrell-Krell and David Wood (eds.), *Exceedingly Nietzsche* (London: Routledge, 1988), 116–30.

ALLANEN, LILLI, 'Descartes's Dualism and the Philosophy of Mind', *Revue de Metaphysique et de Morale*, 3 (1989), 391–413.

—— 'Reconsidering Descartes' Notion of the Mind–Body Union', *Synthese*, 106 (1996), 3–20.

ALLEN, PRUDENCE, *The Concept of Woman: The Aristotelian Revolution 750 BC–AD 1250* (London: Eden Press, 1985).

ANNAS, JULIA, 'Plato's Republic and Feminism', *Philosophy*, 51 (1976), 307–21.

—— 'Plato and Aristotle on Friendship and Altruism', *Mind*, 86 (1977), 532–44.

—— *An Introduction to Plato's Republic* (Oxford: Clarendon Press, 1981).

ATHERTON, MARGARET, 'Cartesian Reason and Gendered Reason', in Louise Antony and Charlotte Witt (eds.), *A Mind of One's Own: Feminist Essays on Reason and Objectivity* (Boulder, Colo.: Westview Press, 1993), 19–34.

—— 'Doing the History of Philosophy as a Feminist', in Louise Antony and Diana Meyers (eds.), *American Philosophical Association Newsletter on Feminism and Philosophy*, 1993.

—— (ed.), *Women Philosophers of the Early Modern Period* (Indianapolis: Hackett, 1994).

BAIER, ANNETTE, 'Cartesian Persons', in her *Postures of the Mind: Essays on Mind and Morals* (Minneapolis: University of Minnesota Press, 1985), 74–92.

—— 'Trust and Anti-trust', *Ethics*, 96 (1986), 231–60.

—— *A Progress of Sentiments: Reflections on Hume's Treatise* (Cambridge, Mass.: Harvard University Press, 1991).

—— 'Hume: The Reflective Women's Epistemologist?', in Louise Antony and Charlotte Witt (eds.), *A Mind of One's Own* (Boulder, Colo.: Westview Press, 1993), 35–49.

—— 'David Hume, Spinozist', *Hume Studies*, 19 (1993), 237–52.

—— 'What do Women Want in a Moral Theory?', in her *Moral Prejudices: Essays on Ethics* (Cambridge, Mass.: Harvard University Press, 1994), 1–17.

BAR AN, BAT-AMI, 'Could there be a Humean Sex-Neutral General Idea of Man?', *Philosophy Research Archives*, 13 (1987–8), 366–77.

—— *Engendering Origins: Critical Feminist Readings in Plato and Aristotle* (Albany: State University of New York Press, 1994).

Baron, Marcia, 'Impartiality and Friendship', *Ethics*, 101 (1991), 836–57.

—— 'Kant on Ethics and Claims of Detachment', in Robin Schott (ed.), *Feminist Interpretations of Immanuel Kant* (University Park: Pennsylvania State University Press, 1997), 145–70.

Battersby, Christine, 'An Inquiry Concerning the Humean Woman', *Philosophy*, 56 (1981), 303–12.

—— *The Phenomenal Woman: Feminist Metaphysics and the Patterns of Identity* (Cambridge: Polity Press, 1998).

—— 'Stages on Kant's Way: Aesthetics, Morality and the Gendered Sublime', in Peggy Z. Brand and Carolyn Korsmeyer (eds.), *Feminism and Tradition in Aesthetics* (University Park: Pennsylvania State University Press, 1995), 88–114.

Benhabib, Seyla, *Situating the Self: Gender, Community and Postmodernism in Contemporary Ethics* (New York: Routledge, 1993).

Blum, Lawrence A., 'Kant's and Hegel's Moral Rationalism: A Feminist Perspective', *Canadian Journal of Philosophy*, 12 (1982), 287–302.

Bordo, Susan, 'The Cartesian Masculinisation of Thought', *Signs, Journal of Women in Culture and Society*, 11 (1986), 439–56.

—— *The Flight to Objectivity: Essays on Cartesianism and Culture* (Albany: State University of New York Press, 1987).

—— *Feminist Interpretations of René Descartes* (University Park: Pennsylvania State University Press, 1999).

Bowery, Anne-Marie, 'Diotima Tells Socrates a Story: A Narrative Analysis of Plato's *Symposium*', in Julie Ward (ed.), *Feminism and Ancient Philosophy* (London: Routledge, 1996), 155–74.

Derrida, Jacques, 'Plato's Pharmacy', in *Dissemination*, trans. B. Johnson (Chicago: University of Chicago Press, 1981), 61–171.

—— 'White Mythology: Metaphor in the Text of Philosophy', in *Margins of Philosophy*, trans. A. Bass (Brighton: Harvester Press, 1982), 207–72.

—— 'Whom to Give to (Knowing Not to Know)', chapter 3 of *The Gift of Death*, trans. David Wills (Chicago: University of Chicago Press, 1995); repr. in Jonathan Rée and Jane Chamberlain (eds.), *Kierkegaard: A Critical Reader* (Oxford: Blackwell, 1998), 151–74.

Deutscher, Max (ed.), *Michèle Le Dœuff: Operative Philosophy and Imaginary Practice* (New York: Humanity Books, 2000).

Deutscher, Penelope, *Yielding Gender: Feminism, Deconstruction and the History of Philosophy* (London: Routledge, 1997).

—— 'Disappropriations: Sarah Kofman and Luce Irigaray', in Dorothea Olkowski (ed.), *Resistance, Flight, Creation: Feminist Enactments of French Philosophy* (Ithaca, NY: Cornell University Press 2000).

—— '"Imperfect Discretion": Interventions into the History of Philosophy by Twentieth Century French Women Philosophers', *Hypatia*, 15 2 (2000), 160–80.

DEUTSCHER, PENELOPE, and OLIVER, KELLY (eds.), *Enigmas: Essays on Sarah Kofman* (Ithaca, NY: Cornell University Press, 1999).

DIPROSE, ROSALYN: 'Nietzsche, Ethics and Sexual Difference', *Radical Philosophy*, 52 (1989), 27–33.

—— 'In Excess: The Body and the Habit of Sexual Difference', 6 (1991), 156–71 [A critique of Hegel on the Antigone story].

—— 'Nietzsche and the Pathos of Distance', in Paul Patton (ed.), *Nietzsche, Feminism & Political Theory* (London: Routledge, 1993), 1–26.

EASTON, SUSAN, 'Functionalism and Feminism in Hegel's Political Thought', *Radical Philosophy*, 38 (1984), 2–8.

—— 'Hegel and Feminism', in David Lamb (ed.), *Hegel and Modern Philosophy* (London: Croom Helm, 1987).

FERRELL, ROBYN, 'Rival Reading: Deleuze on Hume', *Australasian Journal of Philosophy*, 73 (1995), 585–93.

FREELAND, CYNTHIA (ed.), *Feminist Interpretations of Aristotle* (University Park: Pennsylvania State University Press, 1998).

FRICKER, MIRANDA, and HORNSBY, JENNIFER (eds.), *The Cambridge Companion to Feminism in Philosophy* (Cambridge: Cambridge University Press, 2000).

GATENS, MOIRA, 'Rousseau and Wollstonecraft: Nature vs Reason', *Australasian Journal of Philosophy*, 64, supplement (1991), 1–15.

—— 'Spinoza, Love and Responsibility', in *Imaginary Bodies: Ethics, Power and Corporeality*' (London: Routledge, 1996), 109–24.

—— with LLOYD, GENEVIEVE, *Collective Imaginings: Spinoza, Past and Present* (London: Routledge, 1999).

GILLIGAN, CAROL, *In a Different Voice: Psychological Theory and Women's Development* (Cambridge, Mass.: Harvard University Press, 1982).

HALPERIN, DAVID, 'Why is Diotima a Woman?', in David Halperin (ed.), *One Hundred Years of Homosexuality and Other Essays on Greek Love* (New York: Routledge, 1990), 113–51.

—— 'Plato and the Erotics of Narrativity', in Julia Annas (ed.), *Oxford Studies in Ancient Philosophy* (Oxford: Oxford University Press, 1992), 93–129.

HAWTHORNE, SUSAN, 'Diotima Speaks through the Body', in Bat-Ami Bar-On (ed.), *Engendering Origins* (Albany: State University of New York Press, 1994), 83–96.

HEINAMAA, SARA, 'Wonder and (Sexual) Difference: Cartesian Radicalism in Phenomenological Thinking', in Tuomo Aho and Mikko Yronsuuri (eds.), *Norms and Modes of Thinking in Descartes*, Acta Philosophica Fennica 64 (Helsinki, 1999).

HERMAN, BARBARA, 'Could it be Worth Thinking about Kant on Sex and Marriage?', in Louise Antony and Charlotte Witt (eds.), *A Mind of One's Own* (Boulder, Colo.: Westview Press, 1993), 49–67.

Hodge, Joanna, 'Women and the Hegelian State', in E. Kennedy and S. Mendus (eds.), *Women in Western Political Philosophy* (Brighton: Wheatsheaf Books, 1987), 127–58.

Homiak, Marcia, 'Virtue and Self-Love in Aristotle's Ethics', *Canadian Journal of Philosophy*, 11 4 (1981), 532–54.

—— 'The Pleasure of Virtue in Aristotle's Moral Theory', *Pacific Philosophical Quarterly*, 66 (1985), 1–2: 93–110.

—— 'Politics as Soul Making: Aristotle on Becoming Good', *Philosophia*, 20 1–2 (1990), 167–93.

Irigaray, Luce, *The Speculum of the Other Woman* (Ithaca, NY: Cornell University Press, 1985), trans. G. Gill from *Speculum de l'autre femme* (Paris: Minuit, 1974).

—— *An Ethics of Sexual Difference*, trans. C. Burke and G. Gill (Ithaca, NY: Cornell University Press, 1993).

—— 'The Eternal Irony of the Community', trans. Gillian C. Gill, in Patricia Mills (ed.), *Feminist Interpretations of G. W. F. Hegel* (University Park: Pennsylvania State University Press, 1996), 45–58.

—— 'Wonder: A Reading of Descartes in *The Passions of the Soul*', trans. Carolyn Burke and Gillian C. Gill, in Susan Bordo. (ed.), *Feminist Interpretations of René Descartes* (University Park: Pennsylvania State University Press, 1999), 105–14.

Jacobson, Anne Jaap, *Feminist Interpretations of David Hume* (University Park: Pennsylvania State University Press, 2000).

James, Susan, 'Spinoza the Stoic', in T. Sorell (ed.), *Rise of Modern Philosophy* (Oxford: Oxford University Press, 1993), 289–316.

—— 'Ethics as the Control of the Passions', in Michael Ayers and Dan Garber (eds.), *The Cambridge History of Seventeenth Century Philosophy* (Cambridge: Cambridge University Press, 1997), vii. 5.

—— 'Power and Difference: Spinoza's Conception of Freedom', *Journal of Political Philosophy*, 4 (1996), 207–28.

—— 'Susan James talks to Genevieve Lloyd and Moira Gatens: The Power of Spinoza: Feminist Conjunctions', *Hypatia*, 15 (2000), 40–58.

Kittay, Eva Feder, 'Woman as Metaphor', *Hypatia*, 3(2) (1988), 63–86.

Kofman, Sarah, *Nietzsche et la métaphore* (Paris: Payot, 1972).

—— *Nietzsche et la scène philosophique* (Paris: U G E, 1979).

—— 'Rousseau's Phallocratic Ends', *Hypatia*, 3 (1989), 123–36.

—— 'The Economy of Respect: Kant and Respect for Women', trans. Nicola Fisher, in Robin Schott (ed.), *Feminist Interpretations of Immanuel Kant* (University Park: Pennsylvania State University Press, 1997), 355–72.

Kotzin, Rhoda Hadassah, 'Aristotle's Views on Women', in *American Philosophical Association Newsletter on Philosophy and Feminism*, 88 (1989), 21–25.

—— 'Ancient Greek Philosophy', entry in Alison M. Jaggar and Iris Marion

Young (eds.), *A Companion to Feminist Philosophy* (Oxford: Blackwell, 1998), 9–20.

Kuykendall, Eleanor H., 'Introduction to Sorcerer Love, by Luce Irigiray', *Hypatia*, 3 (1989), 28–31.

Le Dœuff, Michèle, 'Women and Philosophy', trans. Debbie Pope, *Radical Philosophy*, 17 (1977), 2–11; also published as 'Long Hair, Short Ideas', in *The Philosophical Imaginary* (London: Athlone Press, 1989), 100–28.

—— *L'Étude et le rouet* (Paris: Éditions du Seuil, 1989); trans. Trista Selous as *Hipparchia's Choice: An Essay Concerning Women, Philosophy, Etc.* (Oxford: Blackwell, 1991).

—— *Recherches sur l'imaginaire philosophique* (Paris: Payot, 1980); trans. Colin Gordon as *The Philosophical Imaginary* (London: Athlone Press, 1989).

Leon, Celene, and Walsh, Sylvia (eds.), *Feminist Interpretations of Soren Kierkegaard* (University Park: Pennsylvania State University Press, 1997).

Lloyd, Genevieve, *The Man of Reason: 'Male' and 'Female' in Western Philosophy* (London: Methuen, 1984; 2nd edn. London: Routledge, 1993).

—— 'Rousseau on Reason, Nature and Woman', *Metaphilosophy*, 14 (1983), 308–26.

—— *Part of Nature: Self-Knowledge in Spinoza's Ethics* (Ithaca, NY: Cornell University Press, 1993).

—— 'Maleness, Metaphor and the "Crisis of Reason"', in Louise M. Antony and Charlotte Witt (eds.), A Mind of One's Own: Feminist Essays on Reason and Objectivity (Boulder: Westview Press, 1993), 69–84.

—— 'Hume on the Passion for Truth', in Anne Jaap Jacobson (ed.), *Feminist Interpretations of David Hume* (University Park: Pennsylvania State University Press, 2000), 39–59.

—— 'Feminism in History of Philosophy: Appropriating the Past', in M. Fricker and J. Hornsby (eds.), *The Cambridge Companion to Feminism in Philosophy* (Cambridge: Cambridge University Press, 2000), 245–63.

—— with Gatens, Moira, *Collective Imaginings: Spinoza, Past and Present* (London: Routledge, 1999).

Lopez-McAlister, Linda (ed.), *Hypatia's Daughters: Fifteen Hundred Years of Women Philosophers* (Bloomington: Indiana University Press, 1996).

Lovibond, Sabina, 'Feminism in Ancient Philosophy: The Feminist Stake in Greek Rationalism', in Miranda Fricker and Jennifer Hornsby (eds.), *The Cambridge Companion to Feminism in Philosophy* (Cambridge: Cambridge University Press, 2000), 10–28.

Menage, Gilles, *The History of Women Philosophers* (1690), trans. Beatrice H. Zedler (Lantham, Md.: University Press of America, 1984).

Mills, Patricia Jagentowicz (ed.), *Feminist Interpretations of G. W. F. Hegel* (University Park: Pennsylvania State University Press, 1996).

Morris, Meaghan, 'Operative Reasoning: Michèle Le Dœuff, Philosophy and Feminism', *Ideology and Consciousness*, 9 (1981–2).

NAGL-DOCEKAI, H., 'Feminist Ethics: How it could Benefit from Kant's Moral Philosophy', trans. Stephanie Morgenstern, in R. Schott (ed.), *Feminist Interpretations of Immanuel Kant* (University Park: Pennsylvania State University Press, 1997), 101–24.

NUSSBAUM, MARTHA, 'The Speech of Alcibiades: A Reading of the *Symposium*', chapter 6 in *The Fragility of Goodness: Luck and Ethics in Greek Tragedy and Philosophy* (Cambridge: Cambridge University Press, 1986), 165–95.

—— 'Therapeutic Arguments: Epicurus and Aristotle', in Malcolm Schofield and Gisela Striker (eds.), *The Norms of Nature: Studies on Hellenistic Ethics*, (Cambridge: Cambridge University Press, 1986), 31–74.

—— *Love's Knowledge: Essays on Philosophy and Literature* (Oxford: Oxford University Press, 1990).

—— (ed.), 'The Poetics of Therapy: Hellenistic Ethics in its Rhetorical and Literary Context', *Apeiron* (special edn.) 23(4) (1990).

—— 'Non-Relative Virtues: An Aristotelian Approach', in M. C. Nussbaum and A. Sen (eds.), *The Quality of Life* (Oxford: Clarendon Press, 1993), 242–69.

—— 'Tragedy and Self-Sufficiency: Plato and Aristotle on Fear and Pity', *Oxford Studies in Ancient Philosophy* 10 (1992), 107–59.

—— *Therapy of Desire* (Princeton: Princeton University Press, 1994).

—— 'Poetry and the Passions: Two Stoic Views', in J. L. Brunschwig and M. Nussbaum (eds.), *Passions and Perceptions: The 5th Symposium Hellenisticum* (Cambridge: Cambridge University Press, 1993), 97–149.

NYE, ANDREA, 'The Hidden Host: Irigaray and Diotima at Plato's Symposium', *Hypatia*, 3 (1989), 45–61.

—— *The Princess and the Philosopher: Letters of Elisabeth of Palatine to René Descartes* (Lanham, Md.: Rowman and Littlefield, 1999).

OKIN, SUSAN MOLLER, 'Philosopher Queens and Private Wives: Plato on Women and the Family', *Philosophy and Public Affairs*, 6 (1977), 345–69.

OLIVER, KELLY, *Womanising Nietzsche: Philosophy's Relation to* 'The Feminine' (New York: Routledge, 1995).

—— and PEARSALL, MARILYN (eds.), *Feminist Interpretations of Friedrich Nietzsche* (University Park: Pennsylvania State University Press, 1998).

O'NEILL, EILEEN, *Women Philosophers of the Seventeenth and Eighteenth Centuries: A Collection of Primary Sources* (Oxford: Oxford University Press, 1998).

—— 'Women Cartesians, "Feminine Philosophy" and Historical Exclusion', in Susan Bordo (ed.), *Feminist Interpretations of René Descartes* (University Park: Pennsylvania State University Press, 1999), 232–60.

PATTON, PAUL (ed.), *Nietzsche, Feminism and Political Theory* (London: Routledge, 1993).

RAVVEN, HEIDI, 'Has Hegel Anything to Say to Feminists?', *Owl of Minerva*,

19 (1988), 149–68; also in Robin Schott (ed.), *Feminist Interpretations of Immanuel Kant* (University Park: Pennsylvania State University Press, 1997), 225–52.

RAVVEN, HEIDI, 'Spinoza's Materialist Ethics: The Education of Desire', *International Studies in Philosophy*, 22 (1990), 59–78.

REUTER, MARTINA, 'Questions of the Body, Sexual Difference and Equality in Cartesian Philosophy', Academic Dissertation, Department of Philosophy, University of Helsinki, 2000.

ROONEY, P. 'Gendered Reason: Sex, Metaphor, and Conceptions of Reason', *Hypatia*, 6 (1991), 77–103.

—— 'Recent Work in Feminist Discussions of Reason', *American Philosophical Quarterly*, 31 (1994), 1–16.

RORTY, AMÉLIE (ed.), *Explaining Emotions* (Berkeley and Los Angeles: University of California Press, 1980).

—— 'From Passions to Emotions and Sentiments', *Philosophy*, 57 (1982), 159–72.

—— *Essays on Descartes's Meditations* (Berkeley and Los Angeles: University of California Press, 1986).

—— 'Cartesian Passions and the Union of Mind and Body', in Amélie Rorty (ed)., *Essays on Descartes's Meditations* (Berkeley and Los Angeles: University of California Press, 1986), 513–34.

—— 'The Two Faces of Spinoza', *Review of Metaphysics*, 41 (1987), 299–316.

—— *Mind in Action: Essays in the Philosophy of Mind* (Boston: Beacon Press, 1988).

—— 'Descartes on Thinking with the Body', in John Cottingham (ed.), *The Cambridge Companion to Descartes* (Cambridge: Cambridge University Press, 1992), 371–92.

—— 'Descartes and Spinoza on Epistemological Egalitarianism', *History of Philosophy Quarterly*, 13 (1996), 35–53.

SAXONHOUSE, ARLENE W., 'Eros and the Female in Greek Political Thought: An Interpretation of Plato's Symposium', *Political Theory*, 12 (1984), 5–27.

SCHOTT, ROBIN, *Cognition and Eros: A Critique of the Kantian Paradigm* (Boston: Beacon Press, 1988).

—— 'The Gender of Enlightenment', in James Schmidt (ed.), *What is Enlightenment?* (Berkeley and Los Angeles: University of California Press, 1996), 471–87.

—— (ed.), *Feminist Interpretations of Immanuel Kant* (University Park: Pennsylvania State University Press, 1997).

SEDGWICK, SALLY, 'Can Kant's Ethics Survive the Feminist Critique?', *Pacific Philosophical Quarterly*, 71 (1990), 60–79; also in Robin Schott (ed.), *Feminist Interpretations of Immanuel Kant* (University Park: Pennsylvania State University Press, 1997), 77–100.

SHAPIRO, LISA, 'Élisabeth et Descartes: la maladie, le remède et la nature féminine', in Elisabeth Beranger, Ginette Castro, and Marie-Lise Paoli (eds.), *Femme et nature* (Bordeaux: Maison des Sciences de l'Homme d'Aquitaine, 1997).

Spelman, Elizabeth, 'Woman as Body: Ancient and Contemporary Views', *Feminist Studies*, 8 (1982), 109–31.

—— 'Aristotle and the Politicization of the Soul', in S. Harding and M. Hintikka (eds.), *Discovering Reality: Feminist Perspectives on Epistemology, Metaphysics, Methodology, and Philosophy of Science* (Dordrecht: D. Reidel Publishing Co., 1983), 17–30.

—— 'Anger and Insubordination', in Ann Garry and Marilyn Pearsall (eds.), *Women, Knowledge and Reality: Explorations in Feminist Philosophy* (Boston: Unwin Hyman, 1989), 263–74.

Tuana, Nancy (ed.), *Woman and the History of Philosophy* (New York: Paragon House, 1992).

—— *The Less Noble Sex: Scientific, Religious and Philosophical Conception of Women's Nature* (Bloomington: Indiana University Press, 1993).

—— (ed.), *Feminist Interpretations of Plato* (University Park: Pennsylvania State University Press, 1994).

Waithe, Mary Ellen (ed.), *A History of Women Philosophers* (Boston: Martinus Nihjoff, 1987).

—— 'On Not Teaching the History of Philosophy', *Hypatia*, 4 (1989), 132–8.

Ward, Julie (ed.), *Feminism and Ancient Philosophy* (London: Routledge, 1996).

Wartenberg, Thomas E., 'Descartes's Mood: The Question of Feminism in the Correspondence with Elisabeth', in Susan Bordo (ed.), *Feminist Interpretations of René Descartes* (University Park: Pennsylvania State University Press, 1999), 190–212.

Whitford, Margaret, 'Luce Irigaray's Critique of Rationality', in M. Griffiths and Margaret Whitford (eds.), *Feminist Perspectives in Philosophy* (Bloomington: Indiana University Press, 1983), 109–30.

—— *Luce Irigaray: Philosophy in the Feminine* (New York: Routledge, 1991).

Wider, Kathleen, 'Women Philosophers in the Ancient Greek World: Donning the Mantle', *Hypatia*, 1 (1986), 21–62.

Index